Top-Down Network Design

Priscilla Oppenheimer

Macmillan Technical Publishing
201 West 103rd Street
Indianapolis, Indiana 46290

Top-Down Network Design

Priscilla Oppenheimer

Copyright © 1999 Macmillan Technical Publishing

Cisco Press logo is a trademark of Cisco Systems, Inc.

Published by:
Macmillan Technical Publishing
201 West 103rd Street
Indianapolis, IN 46290 USA

Printed in the United States of America 1 2 3 4 5 6 7 8 9 0

Library of Congress Cataloging-in-Publication Number 98-84274

ISBN: 1-57870-069-8

Warning and Disclaimer

This book is designed to provide information about **top-down network design**. Every effort has been made to make this book as complete and as accurate as possible, but no warranty or fitness is implied.

The information is provided on an "as is" basis. The author, Macmillan Technical Publishing, and Cisco Systems, Inc., shall have neither liability nor responsibility to any person or entity with respect to any loss or damages arising from the information contained in this book or from the use of the discs or programs that may accompany it.

The opinions expressed in this book belong to the author and are not necessarily those of Cisco Systems, Inc.

Feedback Information

At Cisco Press, our goal is to create in-depth technical books of the highest quality and value. Each book is crafted with care and precision, undergoing rigorous development that involves the unique expertise of members from the professional technical community.

Readers' feedback is a natural continuation of this process. If you have any comments regarding how we could improve the quality of this book, or otherwise alter it to better suit your needs, you can contact us at ciscopress@mcp.com. Please make sure to include the book title and ISBN in your message.

We greatly appreciate your assistance.

Associate Publisher	Jim LeValley
Executive Editor	Alicia Buckley
Cisco Systems Program Manager	H. Kim Lew
Managing Editor	Caroline Roop
Acquisitions Editor	Tracy Hughes
Development Editor	Lisa M. Thibault
Project Editor	Theresa Mathias
Technical Reviewers	Alexander B. Cannara
	Dave Jansson
	Hank Mauldin
Team Coordinator	Amy Lewis
Book Designer	Argosy
Cover Designer	Karen Ruggles
Indexer	Kevin Fulcher

Trademark Acknowledgments

About the Author

Priscilla Oppenheimer has been developing data communications and networking systems since 1980 when she earned her master's degree in information science from the University of Michigan. After many years as a software developer, she became a technical instructor and training developer and taught more than 2,000 network engineers from most of the Fortune 500 companies. Her employment at such companies as Apple Computer, Network General, and Cisco Systems gave her a chance to troubleshoot real-world network design problems and the opportunity to develop a practical methodology for enterprise network design.

About the Technical Reviewers

These reviewers contributed their considerable practical, hands-on expertise to the entire development process for *Top-Down Network Design*. As the book was being written, these folks reviewed all the material for technical content, organization, and flow. Their feedback was critical to ensuring that *Top-Down Network Design* fits our reader's need for the highest quality technical information.

Alexander B. Cannara is an electrical engineer, software and networking consultant, and educator. He has 16 years experience in the computer-networking field, including 11 years in managing, developing, and delivering technical training. Alex has 11 years experience in consulting, including seven years helping hundreds of organizations with network problems and design issues—he founded the Network General Languru™ Consulting Service. Alex received his BSEE degree from Lehigh University, and received MSEE, DEE, and MS Statistics degrees from Stanford. At Stanford, he performed research and published reports in plasma physics. In business, he designed analog and digital instrumentation for four years, applying for a patent on one design. He returned to Stanford to study computer systems and their educational application, receiving a PhD in Mathematical Methods in Educational Research.

Subsequently, Alex performed statistical research on government contract under USOE Title I, and codeveloped a computer-assisted instruction system for handicapped children under a U.S. Department of Education sponsorship. Since that time, he has been involved with the semiconductor, software, and networking industries, both in technical management and consulting. He has worked at Ballantine Laboratories, RMC Research, Zilog, Gibbons & Associates, Mitsubishi Semiconductor, AMD, 3Com, and Network General. Outside those industries, he has taught courses in engineering, programming, and networking at Stanford, University of San Francisco, and International Technological University. Alex is experienced in many computer languages and network protocols. He is a member of IEEE, the Computer Society, and the AAAS.

Alex lives with his wife and son in Menlo Park, California; his two older daughters have completed or will soon complete college. The Cannaras' interests include travel and all the normal family things.

Dave Jansson is Senior Technical Instructor at Cisco Systems, Inc., and a Certified Cisco Systems Instructor with more than 26 years technical training experience, both in development and delivery. Prior to Cisco he held positions at Apple Computer as a Senior Network Support Engineer and Senior Technical Support Engineer. Before joining Apple in 1982, he was with ROLM Systems in its Technical Training department. Dave has been in the development and rollout of several major products and technologies for many Cisco, Apple, and ROLM network and communications products. Prior to these positions, Dave served in the United States Navy and has received several commendations for pioneering work in applied communications systems technology. He has co-authored several engineering publications along with writing course material and technical books, as well as consulting and teaching for the past 18 years.

Dave lives in the Cupertino, California, area and is an active presenter with Operation Lifesaver, an organization dedicated to teaching railroad crossing safety, as well as a member of other technical societies. A single dad, he enjoys camping, exploring, and sharing adventures with his nine-year-old son.

Hank Mauldin is a consulting engineer for Cisco Systems, Inc., working for the Office of the CTO. He has worked with Cisco for more than five years evaluating and designing data networks. Areas of expertise include IP routing protocols, quality of service, and security, in general. Hank has recently written an internal IPSec design guide and done extensive testing with IPSec. Prior to Cisco, he worked for several different system integrators, and has more than 10 years of data networking experience. Hank holds a master's degree in information system technology from George Washington University.

Dedications

To my parents, Dr. Stephen T. Worland, Ph.D., and Mrs. Roberta Worland, M.S. They gave me an appreciation for knowledge, logic, and analysis, and taught me that "where there's a will, there's a way."

Acknowledgments

Most of all I would like to thank my technical reviewers, Hank Mauldin, David Jansson, and Dr. Alex Cannara, for their thorough reviews and insightful comments. I believe the reader will also be grateful that I was able to incorporate some of the knowledge and wisdom they have gained in their many years in the computer-networking industry. Cumulatively, they have more than 60 years experience designing and engineering computer systems.

I also wish to acknowledge my "virtual mentor," Dr. Peter Welcher. Although I have never met Peter outside cyberspace, we have shared numerous e-mail discussions on network design. I tried to incorporate some of his real-world examples of the typical problems network designers face.

I am very grateful to my development editor, Lisa Thibault. She put in numerous hours to help me realize my vision for this book and provided many sensible suggestions regarding the text. I would also like to thank Tracy Hughes and Julie Fairweather for their encouragement and project-management skills.

I wish to acknowledge Dr. Bjorn Frogner of NetPredict, Inc., who helped with the network-modeling and testing example in Chapter 9. His years of experience with modeling and simulation techniques were a valuable contribution to the book.

Special thanks go to my husband, Alan, who acted as a great sounding board and participated in many hours of technical discussions, and didn't complain too much when I yelled at my computer. (He thought I should have used a Macintosh.)

Priscilla Oppenheimer

Contents at a Glance

Contents

Preface

New business practices are driving changes in enterprise networks. The transition from an industrial to an information economy has changed how employees do their jobs, and the emergence of a global economy of unprecedented competitiveness has accelerated the speed at which companies must adapt to technological and financial changes.

To reduce the time to develop and market products, companies are empowering employees to make strategic decisions that require access to sales, marketing, financial, and engineering data. Employees at corporate headquarters and in worldwide field offices, as well as telecommuters in home offices, need immediate access to data, regardless of whether the data is on centralized or departmental servers.

To sell and distribute products into foreign markets, businesses are relying on global alliances, partnerships, and virtual corporations. To improve communication with partners, employees, and customers, enterprises are implementing such new applications as electronic commerce, videoconferencing, Internet telephony, push-based information dissemination, and distance learning. Businesses are merging their voice and data networks into global enterprise networks that are critical to the organization's business success.

To accommodate increasing requirements for bandwidth, scalability, and reliability, vendors and standards bodies introduce new protocols and technologies at a rapid rate. Network designers are challenged to develop state-of-the-art networks even though the state of the art changes on a monthly, if not weekly or daily, basis.

Whether you are a novice network designer or a seasoned network architect, you probably have concerns about how to design a network that can keep pace with the accelerating changes in the internetworking industry. The goal of this book is to give you a systematic design methodology that can help you meet an organization's requirements, regardless of the newness or complexity of applications and technologies.

THE TOP-DOWN NETWORK DESIGN PROCESS

Top-down network design is a systematic network design process that focuses on a customer's applications, technical objectives, and business goals. It is a methodology that helps you design a logical view of a network, including a traffic-flow description and architectural topology, before developing a physical view. With top-down network design, the emphasis is put on planning before implementation.

Top-down network design is also iterative. Top-down design helps you analyze overall goals and then adapt your proposed design as you gather more details on specific requirements.

Top-down network design is a discipline that grew out of the success of structured software programming and structured system design. When structured programming techniques were introduced in the late 1970s, they revolutionized the way software and data processing systems were developed.

According to Trish Sarson and Chris Gane, in their book *Structured Systems Analysis: Tools and Techniques*, the output of a design project should be a model of a complete system. Instead of focusing on physical components, for example, hard disk space or random-access memory, a designer should build a logical (non-physical) model first. A logical model of the system allows users, designers, and implementers to see how the whole system works and how the parts fit together. A model provides a common reference to use when discussing the logical functions of the system.

The principles in Sarson and Gane's book apply to network design as well as software design. Their book was one of the first books written on structured design (1979). Despite some of the anachronisms in the book, such as talking about CRT screens as state-of-the-art technology, the techniques described are still relevant today.

OBJECTIVES

The purpose of *Top-Down Network Design* is to help you design networks that meet a customer's business and technical goals. Whether your customer is another department within your own company or an external client, this book provides you with tested processes and tools to help you understand traffic flow, protocol behavior, and internetworking technologies. After completing this book, you will be equipped to design enterprise networks that meet a customer's requirements for functionality, capacity, performance, availability, scalability, affordability, security, and manageability.

AUDIENCE

This book is for you if you are an internetworking professional responsible for designing and maintaining medium- to large-sized enterprise networks. If you are a network engineer, architect, or technician who has a working knowledge of network protocols and technologies, this book will provide you with practical advice on applying your knowledge to internetwork design.

This book also includes useful information for consultants, systems engineers, and sales engineers who design corporate networks for clients. In the fast-paced pre-sales environment of many systems engineers, it often is difficult to slow down and insist on a top-down, structured systems analysis approach. Wherever possible, this book includes shortcuts and assumptions that can be made to speed up the network design process.

ORGANIZATION

This book is built around the steps for top-down network design. It is organized into four parts that correspond to the major phases of network design.

Part I: Identifying Your Customer's Needs and Goals

Part I covers the requirements analysis phase. This phase starts with identifying business goals and technical requirements. The task of characterizing the existing network, including the physical structure and the performance of major network segments and routers, follows. The last step in this phase is to analyze network traffic, including traffic flow and load, protocol behavior, and quality of service (QoS) requirements.

Part II: Logical Network Design

During the logical network design phase, the network designer develops a network topology. Depending on the size of the network and traffic characteristics, the topology can be flat or hierarchical. The network designer also devises a network-layer addressing model, and selects bridging, switching, and routing protocols. Logical design also includes security and network management design.

Part III: Physical Network Design

The physical network design phase starts with selecting technologies and devices for campus networks, including Ethernet, Token Ring, Fiber Distributed Data Interface (FDDI), and Asynchronous Transfer Mode (ATM) technologies; and routers, switches, hubs, and cabling to implement the technologies. Selecting technologies and devices for the enterprise network follows. Enterprise technologies include Frame Relay, ATM, Integrated Services Digital Network (ISDN), Digital Subscriber Line (DSL), and dial-up technologies. Enterprise devices include enterprise routers, wide area network (WAN) switches, and remote-access servers.

Part IV: Testing, Optimizing, and Documenting Your Network Design

The final steps in top-down network design are to write and implement a test plan, build a prototype or pilot, optimize the network design, and document your work with a network design proposal. If your test results indicate any performance problems, then during this phase you should update your design to include such optimization features as traffic shaping and advanced router queuing and switching mechanisms.

Appendix A characterizes network traffic when network stations boot. It provides information for IP, AppleTalk, NetWare, NetBIOS, and SNA sessions.

PART I

Identifying Your Customer's Needs and Goals

CHAPTER 1

Analyzing Business Goals and Constraints

This chapter serves as an introduction to the rest of the book by describing top-down network design. The first section explains how to use a systematic, top-down process when designing computer networks for your customers. Depending on your job, your customers might be other departments within your company, those to whom you are trying to sell products, or clients of your consulting business.

After describing the methodology, this chapter focuses on the first step in top-down network design: analyzing your customer's business goals. Business goals include the capability to run network applications to meet corporate business objectives, and the need to work within business constraints, such as budgets, limited networking personnel, and tight timeframes.

This chapter also covers what some people call the eighth layer of the Open Systems Interconnection (OSI) reference model: workplace politics. To ensure the success of your network design project, you should gain an understanding of any corporate politics and policies at your customer's site that could affect your project.

The chapter concludes with a checklist to help you determine if you have addressed the business issues in a network design project.

USING A TOP-DOWN NETWORK DESIGN METHODOLOGY

According to Albert Einstein:

> The world we've made as a result of the level of thinking we have done thus far creates problems that we cannot solve at the same level at which we created them.

To paraphrase Einstein, network engineers and users have the ability to create network design problems that cannot be solved at the same level at which they were created. This predicament can result in networks that are hard to understand and troubleshoot. It can also result in networks that don't perform as well as expected, don't scale as the need for growth arises (as it almost always does), and don't match a customer's requirements. A solution to this problem is to use a systematic, top-down network design methodology that focuses on a customer's requirements, constraints, and goals.

Many network design tools and methodologies in use today resemble the "connect-the-dots" game that some of us played as children. These tools let you place internetworking devices on a palette and connect them with LAN or WAN media. The problem with this methodology is that it skips the steps of analyzing a customer's requirements and selecting devices and media based on those requirements.

Good network design must recognize that a customer's requirements embody many business and technical goals, including requirements for availability, scalability, affordability, security, and manageability. Many customers also want to specify a required level of network performance, often called a *service level*. Difficult network design choices and tradeoffs must be made when designing the logical network before any physical devices or media are selected.

When a customer expects a quick response to a network design request, a bottom-up (connect-the-dots) network design methodology can be used, if the customer's applications and goals are well known. However, network designers often think they understand a customer's applications and requirements only to discover, after a network is installed, that they did not capture the customer's most important needs. Unexpected scalability and performance problems appear as the number of network users increases. These problems can be avoided if the network designer uses top-down methods that perform requirements analysis before technology selection.

Top-down network design is a methodology for designing networks that begins at the upper layers of the OSI reference model before moving to the lower layers. It focuses on applications, sessions, and data transport before the selection of routers, switches, and media that operate at the lower layers.

The top-down network design process includes exploring divisional and group structures to find the people for whom the network will provide services and from whom you should get valuable information to make the design succeed.

Top-down network design also is iterative. To avoid getting bogged down in details too quickly, it is important to first get an overall view of a customer's requirements. Later, more detail can be gathered on protocol behavior, scalability requirements, technology preferences, and so on. Top-down network design recognizes that the logical model and the physical design may change as more information is gathered.

Because top-down methodology is iterative, some topics are covered more than once in this book. For example, this chapter discusses network applications. Network applications are discussed again in Chapter 4, "Characterizing Network Traffic," which covers network traffic caused by application- and protocol-usage patterns. A top-down approach lets a network designer get "the big picture" first and then spiral downward into detailed technical requirements and specifications.

ANALYZING BUSINESS GOALS

Understanding your customer's business goals and constraints is a critical aspect of network design. Armed with a thorough analysis of your customer's business objectives, you can propose a network design that will meet with your customer's approval.

It is tempting to overlook the step of analyzing business goals, because analyzing such technical goals as capacity, performance, security, and so on is more interesting to many network engineers. Analyzing technical goals is covered in the next chapter. In this chapter, you will learn the importance of analyzing business goals, and you will pick up some techniques for matching a network design proposal to a customer's business objectives.

Working with Your Client

Before meeting with your customer to discuss business goals for the network design project, it is a good idea to research your client's business. Find out what industry the client is in. Learn something about the client's market, suppliers, products, services, and competitive advantages. With the knowledge of your customer's business and its external relations, you can position technologies and products to help strengthen the customer's status in the customer's own industry.

In your first meeting with your customers, ask them to explain the organizational structure of the company. Your final internetwork design will probably reflect the corporate structure, so it is a good idea to gain an understanding of how the company is structured in departments, lines of business, vendors, partners, and field or remote offices. Understanding the corporate structure will help you locate major user communities and characterize traffic flow. Characterizing traffic flow is covered in Chapter 4, "Characterizing Network Traffic."

NOTES

Understanding the corporate structure will also help you recognize the management hierarchy. One of your primary goals in the early stages of a network design project should be to determine who the decision-makers are. Who will have the authority to accept or reject your network design proposal? Sometimes, this can be a rather complicated issue, as discussed in the section, "Politics and Policies," later in this chapter.

Ask your customer to state an overall goal of the network design project. Explain that you want a short, business-oriented statement that highlights the business purpose of the new network. Why is the customer embarking on this new network design project? For what will the new network be used? How will the new network help the customer be more successful in the customer's business?

After discussing the overall business goals of the network design project, ask your customer to help you understand the customer's criteria for success. What goals must be met for the customer to be satisfied? Sometimes success is based on operational savings because the new network allows employees to be more productive. Sometimes success is based on the ability to increase revenue or build partnerships with other companies. Make sure you know up front how "success" is defined by executives, managers, end users, network engineers, and any other stakeholders. Also, determine whether the customer's definition of success will change as yearly fiscal goals change.

In addition to determining the criteria for success, you should ascertain the consequences of failure:

- What will happen if the network design project fails or if the network, once installed, does not perform to specification?

- How visible is the project to upper-level management?

- Will the success (or possible failure) of the project be visible to executives?

- To what extent could unforeseen behavior of the new network disrupt business operations?

In general, gather enough information to feel comfortable that you understand the extent and visibility of the network design project.

You should try to get an overall view of whether the new network is critical to the business's mission. Investigate the ramifications of the network failing or experiencing problems. Chapter 2, "Analyzing Technical Goals and Constraints," discusses the details of performance and reliability analysis, but at this point in the design process, you should start addressing these issues. (Remember that top-down network design is iterative. Many network design requirements are addressed more than once.)

Changes in Enterprise Networks

Enterprise networks at many corporations have been undergoing major changes. The value of making vast amounts of corporate data available to employees, customers, and business partners has been recognized. Corporate employees, field employees, and telecommuters need access to sales, marketing, engineering, and financial data, regardless of whether the data is stored on centralized or distributed servers or mainframes. Suppliers and customers need access to inventory and ordering information.

Network applications have become mission critical. Despite this trend, large budgets for networking and telecommunications operations have been reduced at some companies. Many companies have gone through difficult reengineering projects to reduce operational costs, and are still looking for ways to manage networks with fewer people, reduce the recurring costs of WAN circuits, and use technology to increase worker productivity.

Until recently, telecommunications and voice networks were separate. Telecommunications engineers knew little about data networks, and networking engineers did not know the difference between a Time Division Multiplexer (TDM) and a Tandem Switching System (TSS). In today's environment, voice, data, and video networks are merging.

In traditional voice and data terminal/mainframe networks, data flow and throughput were predictable. Closed communications systems were the norm, and data sources were well known. In today's networks, Internet surfing is ubiquitous. It is hard to predict data flow and the timing of bursts of data when users are jumping from one Web site to another, possibly downloading videos or animation files.

In addition to Web surfing, increased outsourcing, alliances, partnerships, and virtual corporations have an affect on network data flow. Many companies are moving to a global network-business model, where the network is used to reach partners, vendors, resellers, sales prospects, and customers.

Another trend is *Virtual Private Networking* (VPN), where private networks make use of public service networks to get to remote locations or possibly other organizations. Customers getting involved in VPN projects have concerns about reliable and predictable performance, as well as data throughput requirements. VPN is covered in Chapter 5, "Designing a Network Topology."

Customers who still have a lot of old telecommunications and data-processing services are embarking on large network design projects. For example, geographically dispersed enterprises with large TDM-based WAN networks are migrating to Frame-Relay routed networks and ATM switched networks. Enterprises that depend on Systems Network Architecture (SNA) or other transaction-oriented protocols are migrating to Internet Protocol (IP) networks. These customers have concerns about security, speed, delay, and delay variation.

Other companies are embarking on network design projects to improve corporate communications, using such new applications as videoconferencing, LAN telephony, and distance learning. Corporations are also updating computer-aided design (CAD) and computer-aided manufacturing (CAM) applications with the goal of improving productivity and shortening product-development cycles.

Many companies are enhancing their networks so they can offer better customer support and new services. Some companies recognize the opportunity to resell WAN bandwidth once a network has been optimized to reduce wasted bandwidth.

Another typical business goal is to buy, or merge with, another company, or establish partnerships with other companies. This goal is often linked to the goal of expanding to new countries and continents. Scalability often is a concern for global businesses trying to keep up with worldwide market expansion and the increasing need for partnerships with remote resellers and suppliers.

Typical Network Design Business Goals

If you keep in mind the changes in business strategies and enterprise networking discussed in the previous section, it becomes possible to list some typical network design business goals:

- Increase revenue and profit

- Improve corporate communications

- Shorten product-development cycles and increase employee productivity

- Build partnerships with other companies

- Expand into worldwide markets

- Move to a global-network business model

- Modernize out-dated technologies

- Reduce telecommunications and network costs, including overhead associated with separate networks for voice, data, and video

- Expand the data readily available to all employees and field offices so they make better business decisions

- Improve security and reliability of mission-critical applications and data

- Offer better customer support

- Offer new customer services

Identifying the Scope of a Network Design Project

One of the first steps in starting a network design project is to determine its scope. Ask your customer if the design is for a new network or a modification to an existing one. Also ask your customer to help you understand if the design is for a single network segment, a set of LANs, a set of WAN or remote-access networks, or the whole enterprise network.

NOTES

Designers rarely get a chance to design a network from scratch. Usually a network design project involves an upgrade to an existing network. However, this is not always the case. Some senior network designers have developed completely new next-generation networks to replace old networks. Other designers have designed networks for a new building or new campus. Even in these cases, however, the new network usually has to fit into an existing infrastructure, for example, a new campus network that has to communicate with an existing WAN.

When analyzing the scope of a network design, you can refer to the seven layers of the OSI reference model to specify the types of functionality the new network design must address. Figure 1–1 shows the OSI reference model.

Figure 1–1
The Open Systems Interconnection (OSI) reference model.

Layer 7	Application
Layer 6	Presentation
Layer 5	Session
Layer 4	Transport
Layer 3	Network
Layer 2	Data Link
Layer 1	Physical

In addition to using the OSI reference model, this book also uses the following terms to define the scope of a network and the scope of a network design project:

- **Segment**. A single network based on a particular Layer-2 protocol. May include hubs, repeaters, and multistation-access units (MAUs).

- **LAN**. A set of bridged or switched segments, usually based on a particular Layer-2 protocol (although mixed LANs are possible). May have one or more Layer-3 protocols associated with it.

- **Building network**. Multiple LANs within a building, usually connected to a building-backbone network.

- **Campus network**. Multiple buildings within a local geographical area (within a few miles), usually connected to a campus-backbone network.

- **Remote access**. Dial-in or dial-out solutions, either analog or digital.

- **WAN**. A geographically dispersed network including point-to-point, Frame Relay, ATM, and other long-distance connections.

- **Enterprise network**. A large and diverse network, consisting of campuses, remote access services, and one or more WANs. An enterprise network is also called an *internetwork*.

Explain to your customer any concerns you have about the scope of the project, including technical and business concerns. Subsequent sections in this chapter discuss politics and scheduling, which are tightly linked to the scope of a network design project. (Many network designers have learned the hard way what happens when you don't help your customers match the schedules of their projects to the scope.)

Identifying a Customer's Network Applications

At this point in the design process you have identified your customer's business goals and the scope of the project. It is now time to focus on the real reason networks exist: applications. The identification of your customer's applications should include both current applications and new applications. Ask your customer to help you fill out a chart, such as the one in Table 1–1.

NOTES

This chart identifies network applications. In Chapters 2 and 4, the Network Applications chart will be enhanced to include technical requirements and network-traffic characteristics. At this point, your goal is simply to identify network applications.

Table 1–1   Network Applications

Name of Application	Type of Application	New Application? (Yes or No)	Criticality	Comments

For "Name of Application," simply use a name that your customer gives you. This could be an industry-standard name, such as Lotus Notes, or it could be an application name that only means something to the customer, (especially for a home-grown application). For new applications, the name might be a code name for a software-development project.

For "Type of Application," you can use any appropriate text that describes the type of application, or you can classify the application as one of the following standard network applications:

- Electronic mail
- File sharing/access
- Groupware
- Web browsing
- Network game
- Remote terminal

- File transfer
- Database access/update
- Desktop publishing
- Push-based information dissemination
- Electronic whiteboard
- Terminal emulation

- Calendar
- Online directory (phone book)
- Medical imaging
- Distance learning
- Videoconferencing
- Internet or intranet voice
- Internet or intranet fax
- Point of sales (retail store)
- Sales order entry
- Electronic commerce
- Management reporting
- Financial modeling
- Sales tracking
- Human resources management
- Computer-aided design
- Computer-aided manufacturing
- Inventory control and shipping
- Process control and factory floor
- Telemetry

The preceding list includes user applications. The Network Applications chart should also include *system* applications (or, if you prefer, you can do a separate chart for system applications). System applications include the following types of network services:

- User authentication and authorization
- Host naming
- Remote booting
- Remote configuration download
- Directory services
- Network backup
- Network management
- Software distribution

In the "Criticality" column of the Network Applications chart, you can give each application a ranking from 1 to 3 with the following meanings:

> 1 - extremely critical
>
> 2 - somewhat critical
>
> 3 - not critical

Later, you can gather more specific information on mission-criticality, including precisely how much downtime is acceptable (if the customer can quantify availability requirements).

In the "Comments" column, add any observations relevant to the network design. For example, include any information you have about corporate directions, such as plans to stop using an application in the future, or specific rollout schedules and regional-use plans.

ANALYZING BUSINESS CONSTRAINTS

In addition to analyzing business goals and determining your customer's need to support new applications, it is important to analyze any business constraints that will affect your network design.

Politics and Policies

It has been said that there are two things not to talk about with friends—politics and religion. It would be nice if you could escape discussing office politics and technological religion (technology preferences) with a network design customer, but avoiding these topics puts your project at risk.

In the case of office politics, your best bet is to listen rather than talk. Your goal is to learn about any hidden agendas, turf wars, biases, group relations, or history behind the project that could cause it to fail. In some cases, a similar project was already tried and didn't work. You should determine if this has happened in your case and, if it has, the reasons why the project failed or never had a chance to come to fruition.

Pay attention to personnel issues that could affect the project. Which manager or managers started the project and how much do they have at stake? Are there any managers, network engineers, or users who want the project to fail for any reason?

Find out who your advocates and opponents are. In some cases, no matter how technically sound your network design is, there will be people who have a negative reaction to it.

Be sure to find out if your project will cause any jobs to be eliminated. Some network design projects involve automating tasks that were once done by highly paid workers. These workers will obviously have reasons to want the project to fail.

While working with a client, you will gain a feeling for the client's business style. One aspect of style that is important to understand is tolerance to risk. Is risk-taking rewarded in the company, or are most people afraid of change? Knowing the employment history of the decision-makers will help you select appropriate technologies. The employment history of the decision-makers affects their tolerance to risk and their biases toward certain technologies. Understanding these issues will help you determine if your network design should be conservative or if it can include new, state-of-the art technologies and processes.

It is important that you discuss with your customer any policies (religion) regarding protocols, standards, and vendors. Find out if the company has standardized on any transport, routing, desktop, or other protocols. Determine if there is any doctrine regarding open versus proprietary solutions. Find out if there are any policies on approved vendors or platforms. In many cases, a company has already chosen technologies and products for the new network and your design must fit into the plans.

Finally, ask your customer if there are any policies regarding distributed authority for network design and implementation. For example, are there departments that control their own internetworking purchases? Find out if departments and end users are involved in choosing their own applications. Make sure you know who the decision-makers are for your network design project.

In the rush to get to technical requirements, network designers sometimes ignore non-technical issues, which is a mistake. Many brilliant network designs have been rejected by a customer because the designer focused on the lower layers of the OSI reference model, and forgot about company politics and technical religion.

Budgetary and Staffing Constraints

Your network design must fit the customer's budget. The budget should include allocations for equipment purchases, software licenses, maintenance and support agreements, testing, training, and staffing. The budget might also include consulting fees (including your fees) and outsourcing expenses.

Throughout the project, work with your customer to identify requirements for new personnel, such as additional network managers. Point out the need for personnel training, which will affect the budget for the project.

In general, it is a good idea to analyze the abilities of the networking staff. How much in-house expertise is there? Should you recommend any training or outsourcing for network operations and management? The technologies and protocols that you recommend will depend on the abilities of internal staff. It is not a good idea to recommend a complex routing protocol, such as Open Shortest Path First (OSPF), for example, if the engineering staff is just starting to learn internetworking concepts (unless you also recommend a comprehensive training plan).

To ensure the success of your project, determine who controls the network budget—the information systems (IS) department, network managers, or users' departments? How much control do users and groups have over network expenditures? Are there any departmental charge-back schemes?

Regardless of who controls the budget, one common network design goal is to contain costs. Chapter 2, "Analyzing Technical Goals and Constraints," discusses typical tradeoffs that must be made to meet the goal of affordability while achieving good performance and reliability.

If possible, work with your customer to develop a return on investment (ROI) analysis for the network design. Make a business case to the customer that explains how quickly the new network will pay for itself, due to reduced operational costs, improved employee productivity, or the enabling of higher revenue potential and market expansion.

Scheduling

An additional business-oriented topic that you should review with your customer is the timeframe for the network design project. When is the final due date and what are the major milestones? In most cases, management of the project schedule is the customer's obligation, not yours, but you should ask the customer to give you a copy of the schedule and to keep you informed about any slips in the schedule.

Many tools exist for developing a schedule that includes milestones, resource assignments, critical-path analysis, and so on. Take a look at these aspects of the schedule and voice your view on whether the schedule is practical, considering what you have learned about the scope of the project. During the technical-analysis stage and the logical- and physical-design phases of the project, be sure to keep the schedule in mind. As you iteratively develop a concrete understanding of the technical scope of the network design project, point out any concerns you have about the schedule.

BUSINESS GOALS CHECKLIST

You can use the following checklist to determine if you have addressed your client's business-oriented objectives and concerns:

- ☐ I have researched the customer's industry and competition.

- ☐ I understand the customer's corporate structure.

- ☐ I have compiled a list of the customer's business goals, starting with one overall business goal that explains the primary purpose of the network design project.

- ☐ The customer has identified any mission-critical operations.

- ☐ I understand the customer's criteria for success and the ramifications of failure.

- ☐ I understand the scope of the network design project.

- ☐ I have identified the customer's network applications (using the Network Applications chart).

- ☐ The customer has explained policies regarding approved vendors, protocols, or platforms.

- ☐ The customer has explained any policies regarding open versus proprietary solutions.

- ☐ The customer has explained any policies regarding distributed authority for network design and implementation.

☐ I know the budget for this project.

☐ I know the schedule for this project, including the final due date and major milestones, and I believe it is practical.

☐ I have a good understanding of the technical expertise of my clients and any relevant internal or external staff.

☐ I have discussed a staff-education plan with the customer.

☐ I am aware of any office politics that might affect the network design.

SUMMARY

This chapter covered typical network design business goals and constraints. It also talked about the top-down process for gathering information on goals, and the importance of using systematic methods for network design. Using systematic methods will help you keep pace with changing technologies and customer requirements. The next chapter covers analyzing technical goals and constraints.

This chapter also talked about the importance of analyzing your customer's business style, tolerance to risk, biases, and technical expertise. You should also work with your customer to understand the budget and schedule for the network design project to make sure the deadlines and milestones are practical.

Finally, it is important to start gaining an understanding of your client's corporate structure. Understanding the corporate structure will help you analyze data flow and develop a network topology, which usually parallels the corporate structure. It will also help you identify the managers who will have the authority to accept or reject your network design, which will help you prepare and present your network design appropriately.

CHAPTER 2

Analyzing Technical Goals and Constraints

This chapter provides techniques for analyzing a customer's technical goals for an enterprise network design. Analyzing your customer's technical goals can help you confidently recommend technologies that will perform to your customer's expectations.

Typical technical goals include scalability, availability, performance, security, manageability, usability, adaptability, and affordability. Of course, there are tradeoffs associated with these goals. For example, meeting strict requirements for performance can make it hard to meet a goal of affordability. The section, "Making Network Design Tradeoffs," later in this chapter discusses tradeoffs in more detail.

One of the objectives of this chapter is to give you terminology that will help you discuss technical goals with your customer. Network designers and users have many terms for technical goals, and, unfortunately, many different meanings for the terms. This chapter can help you use the same terms as your customer and mean the same things by the terms.

This chapter concludes with a checklist to help you determine whether you have addressed all of your customer's technical goals and constraints.

SCALABILITY

Scalability refers to how much growth a network design must support. For many enterprise network design customers, scalability is a primary goal. Large companies are adding users, applications, additional sites, and external network connections at a rapid rate. The network design you propose to a customer should be able to adapt to increases in network usage and scope.

Planning for Expansion

Your customer should be able to help you understand how much the network will expand in the next year and in the next two years. (Ask your customer to analyze goals for growth in the next five years also, but be aware that not many companies have a clear five-year vision.) You can use the following list of questions to analyze your customer's short-term goals for expansion:

- How many more sites will be added in the next year? The next two years?

- How extensive will the networks be at each new site?

- How many more users will access the corporate internetwork in the next year? The next two years?

- How many more servers (or hosts) will be added to the internetwork in the next year? The next two years?

Expanding the Data Available to Users

Chapter 1, "Analyzing Business Goals and Constraints," talked about a common business goal of expanding the data available to employees who use enterprise networks. Managers are empowering employees to make strategic decisions that require access to sales, marketing, engineering, and financial data. Traditionally this data was stored on departmental LANs. Today this data is often stored on centralized servers.

For years, networking books and training classes taught the 80/20 rule for capacity planning: 80 percent of traffic stays local in departmental LANs and 20 percent of traffic is destined for other departments or external networks. This rule is no longer universal and is rapidly moving to the other side of the scale. Many companies have centralized servers residing on server farms located on building or campus backbone networks. In addition, corporations are increasingly implementing intranets that enable employees to access centralized World Wide Web servers using Internet Protocol (IP) technologies.

At some companies, employees can access intranet Web servers to arrange business travel, search online phone directories, order equipment, and attend distance-learning training classes. The Web servers are centrally located, which breaks the classic 80/20 rule.

In the 1990s, there has also been a trend of companies connecting internetworks with other companies to collaborate with partners, resellers, suppliers, and strategic customers. The term *extranet* is gaining popularity to describe an internal internetwork that is accessible by outside parties. If your customer has plans to implement an extranet, you should document this in your list of technical goals so you can design a topology and provision bandwidth appropriately.

In the 1980s, mainframes running Systems Network Architecture (SNA) protocols stored most of a company's financial and sales data. In the 1990s and beyond, the value of making this data available to more than just financial analysts has been recognized. The business goal of making data available to more departments often results in a technical goal of merging an SNA network with an enterprise IP network. Chapter 7, "Selecting Bridging, Switching, and Routing Protocols," provides more detail on how to migrate SNA data to an IP network.

In summary, the business goal of making more data available to users results in the following technical goals for scaling and upgrading corporate enterprise networks:

- Connect separated departmental LANs into the corporate internetwork

- Solve LAN/WAN bottleneck problems caused by large increases in internetwork traffic

- Provide centralized servers that reside on server farms or an intranet

- Merge an independent SNA network with the enterprise IP network

- Add new sites to support field offices and telecommuters

- Add new sites to support communication with customers, suppliers, resellers, and other business partners

Constraints on Scalability

When analyzing a customer's scalability goals, it is important to keep in mind that there are impediments to scalability inherent in networking technologies. Selecting technologies that can meet a customer's scalability goals is a complex process with significant ramifications if not done correctly. For example, selecting a flat network topology with Layer 2 switches can cause problems as the number of users scales, especially if the users' applications or network protocols send numerous broadcast frames. (Switches forward broadcast frames to all connected segments.)

Subsequent chapters in this book consider scalability again. Chapter 4, "Characterizing Network Traffic," discusses the fact that network traffic—for example, broadcast traffic—affects the scalability of a network. Part 2, "Logical Network Design," provides details on the scalability of routing and bridging protocols. Part 3, "Physical Network Design," provides information on the scalability of LAN and WAN technologies and internetworking devices. Remember that top-down network design is an iterative process. Scalability goals and solutions are revisited during many phases of the network design process.

AVAILABILITY

Availability refers to the amount of time a network is available to users and is often a critical goal for network design customers. Availability can be expressed as a percent uptime per year, month, week, day, or hour, compared to the total time in that period. For example, in a network that offers 24-hour, seven-days-a-week service, if the network is up 165 hours in the 168-hour week, availability is 98.21 percent.

Network design customers don't use the word *availability* in everyday English and have a tendency to think it means more than it does. In general, availability means how much time the network is operational. Availability is linked to redundancy, but redundancy is not a network goal. Redundancy is a solution to the goal of availability. Redundancy means adding duplicate links or devices to a network to avoid downtime.

Availability is also linked to reliability, but has a more specific meaning (percent uptime) than reliability. Reliability refers to a variety of issues, including accuracy, error rates, stability, and the amount of time between failures. Some network users use the term *recoverability* to specify how easily and in what timeframe a network can recover from problems. Recoverability is an ingredient of availability.

Availability is also associated with *resiliency*, which is a word that is becoming more popular in networking magazines. Resiliency means how much stress a network can handle and how quickly the network can rebound from problems. A network that has good resiliency usually has good availability.

NOTES

Sometimes network engineers classify *capacity* as part of availability. The thinking is that even if a network is available at Layer 1 (the physical layer), it is not available from a user's point of view if there is not enough capacity to send the user's traffic.

For example, Asynchronous Transfer Mode (ATM) has a connection admission control (CAC) function that regulates the number of cells allowed into an ATM network. If the capacity and quality of service requested for a connection are not available, cells for the connection are not allowed to enter the network. This problem could be considered an availability issue. However, this book classifies capacity with performance goals. Availability is considered simply a goal for percent uptime.

One other aspect of availability is disaster recovery. Most large institutions have a plan for recovering from natural disasters, such as floods, fires, hurricanes, and earthquakes. Also, some large enterprises (especially service providers) must plan how to recover from satellite outages. Satellite outages can be caused by meteorite storms, collisions with space debris, solar flares, or system failures. Unfortunately, some institutions have also found the need to specify a recovery plan for man-made disasters, such as bombs or hostage situations. A disaster recovery plan includes a process for keeping data backed up in a place that is unlikely to be hit by disaster, as well as a process for switching to backup technologies if the main technologies are affected by a disaster. The details of disaster-recovery planning are outside the scope of this book.

Specifying Availability Requirements

You should encourage your customers to specify availability requirements with precision. Consider the difference between an uptime of 99.70 percent and an uptime of 99.95 percent. An uptime of 99.70 percent means the network is down 30 minutes per week, which is not acceptable to many customers. An uptime of 99.95 percent means the network is down five minutes per week, which probably is acceptable. Availability requirements should be specified with at least two digits following the decimal point.

It is also important to specify a timeframe with percent uptime requirements. Go back to the example of 99.70 percent uptime, which equated to 30 minutes of downtime per week. A downtime of 30 minutes in the middle of a working day is probably not acceptable. But a downtime of 30 minutes every Saturday evening for regularly scheduled maintenance might be fine.

Not only should your customers specify a timeframe with percent uptime requirements, but they should also specify a time unit. Availability requirements should be specified as uptime per year, month, week, day, or hour. Consider an uptime of 99.70 percent again. This uptime means 30 minutes of downtime during a week. The downtime could be all at once, which would be a problem, or it could be spread out over the week. An uptime of 99.70 percent could mean that approximately every hour the network is down for 10.70 seconds. Will users notice a downtime of 10.70 seconds? Perhaps. For many applications, however, a downtime of 10.70 seconds every hour is tolerable.

Try doing the math yourself for a network goal of 99.80 percent uptime. How much downtime is permitted in hours per week? How much downtime is permitted in minutes per day and seconds per hour? Which values are acceptable?

The Cost of Downtime

In general, a customer's goal for availability is to keep mission-critical applications running smoothly, with little or no downtime. A method to help both you and your customer understand availability requirements is to specify a cost of downtime. For each critical application, document how much money the company loses per hour of downtime. (For some applications, such as order processing, specifying money lost per minute might have more impact.) If network operations will be outsourced to a third-party network management firm, explaining the cost of downtime can help the firm understand the criticality of applications to a business's mission.

Specifying the cost of downtime can also help clarify whether in-service upgrades must be supported. In-service upgrades refer to mechanisms for upgrading network equipment and services without disrupting operations. Most internetworking vendors sell high-end internetworking devices that include hot-swappable components for in-service upgrading.

Mean Time Between Failure and Mean Time to Repair

In addition to expressing availability as a percent uptime, you can define availability as a mean time between failure (MTBF) and mean time to repair (MTTR). You can use MTBF and MTTR to calculate availability goals when the customer wants to specify explicit periods of uptime and downtime, rather than a simple percent uptime value.

MTBF is a term that comes from the computer industry and is best suited to specifying how long a computer or computer component will last before it fails. When specifying availability requirements in the networking field, MTBF is sometimes designated with the more cumbersome phrase *mean time between service outage* (MTBSO), to account for the fact that a network is a service, not a component. Similarly, MTTR can be replaced with the phrase *mean time to service repair* (MTTSR). This book uses the simpler and better-known terms MTBF and MTTR.

A typical MTBF goal for a network that is highly relied upon is 4,000 hours. In other words, the network should not fail more often than once every 4,000 hours or 166.67 days. A typical MTTR goal is one hour. In other words, the network failure should be fixed within one hour. In this case, the mean availability goal is

4,000 / 4,001 = 99.98 percent

A goal of 99.98 percent is typical for mission-critical operations.

TIPS

When specifying availability using MTBF and MTTR, the equation to use is as follows:
Availability = MTBF / (MTBF + MTTR)
Using this availability equation allows a customer to clearly state the acceptable frequency and length of network outages.

Remember that what is calculated is the mean. The variation in failure and repair times can be high and must be considered as well. It is not enough to just consider mean rates, especially if you depend on external service agents (vendors or contractors) who are not under your tight control. Also, be aware that customers might need to specify different MTBF and MTTR goals for different parts of a network. For example, the goals for the core of the enterprise network are probably much more stringent than the goals for a switch port that only affects one user.

Although not all customers can specify detailed application requirements, it is a good idea to identify availability goals for specific applications, in addition to the network as a whole. Application availability goals can vary widely depending on the cost of downtime. For each application that has a high cost of downtime, you should document the acceptable MTBF and MTTR.

For MTBF values for specific networking components, you can generally use data supplied by the vendor of the component. Most router, switch, and hub manufacturers can provide MTBF and MTTR figures for their products. You should also investigate other sources of information, such as trade publications, to avoid any credibility problems with figures published by manufacturers. Search for variability figures as well as mean figures. Also, try to get written commitments for MTBF, MTTR, and variability values from the providers of equipment and services.

NETWORK PERFORMANCE

When analyzing technical requirements for a network design, you should isolate your customer's criteria for accepting the performance of a network, including throughput, accuracy, efficiency, delay, and response time.

Many mathematical treatises have been written on network performance. This book approaches network performance in a practical and mostly non-mathematical way, avoiding the daunting equations that appear in mathematical treatments of performance. Although the equations are much simpler than they seem, they are usually not necessary for understanding a customer's goals. The objective of this section is to offer an uncomplicated view of network performance, including real-world conclusions you can draw when there is no time to do a mathematical analysis.

Analyzing a customer's network performance goals is tightly tied to analyzing the existing network, which is covered in Chapter 3. Analyzing the existing network will help you determine what changes need to be made to meet performance goals. Network performance goals are also tightly linked to scalability goals. You should gain an understanding of plans for network growth before analyzing performance goals.

Network Performance Definitions

Many network design customers cannot quantify their performance goals beyond, "It has to work with no complaints from users." If this is the case, you can make assumptions regarding throughput, response time, and so on. On the other hand, some customers have specific performance requirements, based on a service level that has been agreed upon with network users. The following list provides definitions for network performance goals that you can use when analyzing precise requirements:

- **Capacity (bandwidth)**. The data-carrying capability of a circuit or network, usually measured in bits per second (bps)

- **Utilization**. The percent of total available capacity in use

- **Optimum utilization**. Maximum average utilization before the network is considered saturated

- **Throughput**. Quantity of error-free data successfully transferred between nodes per unit of time, usually seconds

- **Offered load**. Sum of all the data all network nodes have ready to send at a particular time

- **Accuracy**. The amount of useful traffic that is correctly transmitted, relative to total traffic

- **Efficiency**. A measurement of how much effort is required to produce a certain amount of data throughput

- **Delay (latency)**. Time between a frame being ready for transmission from a node and delivery of the frame elsewhere in the network

- **Delay variation**. The amount of time average delay varies

- **Response time**. The amount of time between a request for some network service and a response to the request

Optimum Network Utilization

Network utilization is a measurement of how much bandwidth is used during a specific time period. Utilization is commonly specified as a percentage of capacity. For example, a network-monitoring tool might state that network utilization on an Ethernet segment is 30 percent, meaning that 30 percent of the capacity is in use.

Network analysis tools use varying methods for measuring bandwidth usage and averaging the usage over elapsed time. Usage can be averaged every millisecond, every second, every minute, every hour, and so on. Some tools use a weighted average whereby more recent values are weighted more prominently than older values. Chapter 3, "Characterizing the Existing Internetwork," discusses measuring network utilization in more depth.

Your customer might have a network design goal for the maximum average network utilization allowed on shared segments. Actually, this is a design constraint more than a design goal. The design constraint states that if utilization on a segment is more than a pre-defined threshold, then that segment must be divided into multiple shared or switched segments.

A typical "rule" for shared Ethernet is that average utilization should not exceed 37 percent, because beyond this limit, the collision rate allegedly becomes excessive. This is not a hard-and-fast rule. The 37 percent limit comes from studies done by the Institute of Electrical and Electronics Engineers (IEEE) comparing carrier sense multiple access collision detection (CSMA/CD) to token passing.

Token passing makes a node wait for a token before sending. At modest loads, this wait means that token passing causes more delay (latency) than Ethernet. If more stations are added to a token ring, then the latency is even worse because the token must pass through each station.

However, at around 37 percent utilization on a medium shared by 50 stations, Ethernet frames experience more delay than token ring frames, because the rate of Ethernet collisions becomes significant. (The study used 128-byte frames and compared 10-Mbps Ethernet to 10-Mbps token passing. The results are only slightly different if 4-Mbps or 16-Mbps token ring is used.)

The key point of the IEEE study was that token passing extracts a higher toll for each station added. For 100 stations, Ethernet frames start experiencing more delay than token ring frames at 49 percent load, instead of the 37 percent load for 50 stations. Armed with this knowledge about the IEEE study, you can help your customer understand which, if any, maximum network-utilization goals are appropriate.

Consider the case of an Ethernet segment that is shared by only two stations: a client that sends requests and a server that responds after receiving requests. In this case, is it a problem if network utilization exceeds 37 percent? There are no collisions because the server and client never try to send at the same time, so the 37 percent rule, which is concerned with collisions, does not apply. The load should be almost 100 percent unless the client or server are slow.

In the case of token passing technologies, such as Token Ring and Fiber Distributed Data Interface (FDDI), a typical goal for optimum average network utilization is 70 percent. Collisions are not a factor for token ring networks, but a goal of 100 percent average utilization is unrealistic. A 70 percent threshold for average utilization means that peaks in network traffic can probably be handled without obvious performance degradation. (The variability of typical loads would need to be studied to determine the exact behavior of peaks.)

If customers have a goal of reducing network utilization to free up capacity for new applications, you can work with them to select technologies that curtail bandwidth usage. For example, in a LAN environment, Novell NetWare users should upgrade to client software that takes advantage of Novell's burst-mode and Sequenced Packet Exchange version II (SPX II) technologies.

For wide area networks (WANs), optimum average network utilization is about the same as for token ring networks—70 percent. A network utilization of 70 percent should support peaks in network traffic caused by unexpected downloads from remote sites. Most WANs have less capacity than LANs, so more care is needed in selecting bandwidth that can cover actual, reasonable variations. Customers have many options for technologies that can reduce bandwidth utilization on WANs, including advanced routing-protocol features, compression, repetitive pattern suppression (RPS), and voice activity detection (VAD). Optimizing bandwidth utilization is covered in more detail in Chapter 12, "Optimizing Your Network Design."

NOTES

RPS, also called *data frame multiplexing (DFM)* or *run-length encoding*, is an option for WAN data circuits that replaces repeating strings of data by a single occurrence of the string and a code that indicates to the far end how many repetitions of the string were in the original data.

VAD is a technology that compresses voice traffic by not sending packets in the absence of speech. Other types of traffic can use the extra bandwidth saved.

Throughput

Throughput is defined as the quantity of error-free data that is transmitted per unit of time. Throughput is often defined for a specific connection or session, but in some cases the total throughput of a network is specified. Ideally, throughput should be the same as capacity. However, this is not the case on real networks.

Capacity depends on the physical-layer technologies in use. The capacity of a network should be adequate to handle the offered load, even when there are peaks in network traffic. (Offered load is the data that all nodes have to send at a particular moment in time.) Theoretically, throughput should increase as offered load increases, up to a maximum of the full capacity of the network. However, network throughput depends on the access method (for example, token passing or collision detection), the load on the network, and the error rate.

Figure 2–1 shows the ideal situation, where throughput increases linearly with the offered load, and the real world, where throughput tapers off as the offered load reaches a certain maximum.

Figure 2–1
*Offered
load and
throughput.*

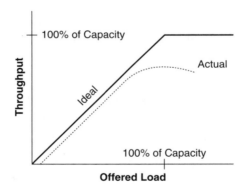

Throughput of Internetworking Devices

Some customers specify throughput goals in terms of the number of packets per second (PPS) an internetworking device must process. (In the case of an ATM device, the goal is cells per second, or CPS.) The throughput for an internetworking device is the maximum rate at which the device can forward packets without dropping any packets.

Most internetworking vendors publish PPS ratings for their products, based on their own tests and independent tests. To test an internetworking device, engineers place the device between traffic generators and a traffic checker. The traffic generators send packets ranging in size from 64 bytes to 1,518 bytes for Ethernet. By running multiple generators, the investigation can test devices with multiple ports.

The generators send bursts of traffic through the device at an initial rate that is half of what is theoretically possible for test conditions. If all packets are received, the rate is increased. If all packets are not received, the rate is decreased. This process is repeated until the highest rate at which packets can be forwarded without loss is determined. PPS values for small frames are much higher than PPS values for large frames, so be sure you understand which value you are looking at when reading vendor test results for an internetworking device.

Many internetworking devices can forward packets at the theoretical maximum, which is also called wire speed. The theoretical maximum is calculated by dividing bandwidth by packet size, including any headers, preambles, and inter-frame gaps. Table 2–1 shows the theoretical maximum PPS for one Ethernet stream, based on frame size.

Table 2–1   Maximum Packets Per Second (PPS)

Frame Size (in bytes)	10-Mbps Ethernet Maximum PPS
64	14,880
128	8,445
256	4,528
512	2,349
768	1,586
1,024	1,197
1,280	961
1,518	812

To understand the PPS value for a multiport device, testers send multiple streams of data and compare the results to the theoretical maximum. For example, a Cisco Catalyst 5000 switch can forward to 30 ports the theoretical maximum throughput of 30 Ethernet streams of 64-byte packets, which is

$$14,880 \times 30 = 446,400 \text{ PPS}$$

It can also forward to 30 ports the theoretical maximum for 1,518-byte packets, which is

$$812 \times 30 = 24,360 \text{ PPS}$$

Application-Layer Throughput

Most end users are concerned about the throughput rate for applications. Marketing materials from some networking vendors refer to application-layer throughput as *goodput*. Calling it goodput sheds light on the fact that it is a measurement of good and relevant application-layer data transmitted per unit of time.

It is possible to improve throughput such that more data per second is transmitted, but not increase goodput, because the extra data transmitted is overhead or retransmissions. It is also possible to increase throughput by not using compression. More data is transmitted per unit of time, but the user sees worse performance.

A simple goal for throughput based on data-per-second rates between stations does not identify the requirements for specific applications. When specifying throughput goals for applications, make it clear that the goal specifies good (error-free) application-layer data per unit of time. Application-layer throughput is usually measured in kilobytes or megabytes per second.

Work with your customer to identify throughput requirements for all applications that can benefit from maximized application-layer throughput, such as file transfer and database applications. (Throughput is not important for all applications, for example, some interactive character-based applications that don't need large screen updates.) Explain to your customer the factors that constrain application-layer throughput, which include the following:

- End-to-end error rates

- Protocol functions, such as handshaking, windows, and acknowledgments

- Protocol parameters, such as frame size and retransmission timers

- The PPS or CPS rate of internetworking devices

- Lost packets or cells at internetworking devices

- Workstation and server performance factors:

    —Disk-access speed

    —Disk-caching size

    —Device driver performance

    —Computer bus performance (capacity and arbitration methods)

    —Processor (CPU) performance

    —Memory performance (access time for real and virtual memory)

    —Operating-system inefficiencies

    —Application inefficiencies or bugs

If necessary, work with your customer to identify application throughput problems caused by errors or inefficiencies in protocols, operating systems, and applications. Protocol analyzers are important tools for this. Chapter 3, "Characterizing the Existing Internetwork," discusses isolating performance problems in more detail.

Accuracy

The overall goal for accuracy is that the data received at the destination must be the same as the data sent by the source. Typical causes of data errors include power surges or spikes, impedance mismatch problems, poor physical connections, failing devices, and noise caused by electrical machinery. Sometimes software bugs can cause data errors also, though software problems are a less common cause of errors than physical-layer problems. Frames that have an error must be retransmitted, which has a negative effect on throughput. In the case of IP networks, the Transmission Control Protocol (TCP) provides retransmission of data.

For WAN links, accuracy goals can be specified as a bit error rate (BER) threshold. If the error rate goes above the specified BER, then the accuracy is considered unacceptable. Analog links have a typical BER threshold of about 1 in 10^5. Digital circuits have a much lower error rate than analog circuits, especially if fiber-optic cable is used. Fiber-optic links have an error rate of about 1 in 10^{11}. Copper links have an error rate of about 1 in 10^6.

For LANs, a BER is not usually specified, mainly because measuring tools, such as protocol analyzers, focus on frames, not bits. But you can approximate a BER by comparing the number of frames with errors in them to the total number of bytes seen by the measuring tool. A good threshold to use is that there should not be more than one bad frame per 10^6 bytes of data.

On shared Ethernet, errors are often the result of collisions. Two stations try to send a frame at the same time and the resulting collision damages the frames, causing Cyclic Redundancy Check (CRC) errors. Depending on the size of the Ethernet network, many of these collisions happen in the 8-byte preamble of the frames and are not registered by troubleshooting tools. If the collision happens past the preamble and somewhere in the first 64 bytes of the data frame, then this is registered as a legal collision and the frame is called a runt frame. A general goal for Ethernet collisions is that less than 0.1 percent of the frames should be affected by a legal collision (not counting the collisions that happen in the preamble).

A collision that happens beyond the first 64 bytes of a frame is a late collision. Late collisions are illegal and should never happen. Ethernet networks that are too large experience late collisions because stations sending minimum-sized frames cannot hear other stations within the allowed timeframe. The extra propagation delay caused by the excessive size of the network causes late collisions between the most widely-separated nodes. Faulty repeaters and network interface cards can also cause late collisions.

In the case of Token Ring networks, accuracy goals sometimes include goals for minimizing media-access control (MAC) error reports. Token Ring includes a rich MAC-layer protocol for reporting problems. MAC error-reporting frames are the result of physical-layer problems or the result of the normal insertion and de-insertion of ring stations. Any goals for reducing MAC error-reporting frames must take into account that one or two errors are normal when a station enters or leaves the ring.

NOTES

It is also normal to see a ring purge frame from the Token Ring active monitor when a station enters or leaves the ring. A *ring purge frame* reinitializes the network. The active monitor sends a ring purge frame when the token gets lost. If the ring purge

frame returns to the active monitor, then the active monitor knows that the ring is operational. The active monitor then initiates a ring poll and, if the poll succeeds, releases
a token that can be captured for data transmission. Two seconds after sending the ring
purge frame, the active monitor sends an error report, notifying the ring error monitor
that the token was lost.

Efficiency

Efficiency is a term borrowed from engineering and scientific fields. It is a measurement of how effective an operation is in comparison to the cost in effort, energy, time,
or money. Efficiency specifies how much overhead is required to produce a required
outcome. For example, you could measure the efficiency of a method for boiling
water. Does most of the energy go to actually boiling the water or does a lot of the
energy get wasted heating the electrical wiring, the pot the water is in, and the air
around it? How much overhead is required to produce the desired outcome?

Efficiency also provides a useful way to talk about network performance. For example, shared Ethernet, as we have discussed, is inefficient when the collision rate is
high. (The amount of effort to successfully send a frame becomes considerable
because so many frames experience collisions.) Network efficiency specifies how
much overhead is required to send traffic, whether that overhead is caused by collisions, token-passing, error-reporting, rerouting, acknowledgments, large frame headers, and so on.

Large frame headers are an obvious cause for inefficiency. A good network performance goal is that applications should minimize the amount of bandwidth used by
headers by using the largest possible frame the MAC layer allows. Using a large frame
maximizes the amount of useful application data compared to header data, and
improves application-layer throughput.

Figure 2–2 shows a bandwidth pipe used by small frames and the same pipe used by
large frames. The header of each frame is shaded. Note that there is an inter-frame
gap between each frame in addition to the headers. From the graphic, you can see that
large frames use bandwidth more efficiently than small frames.

Figure 2–2
Bandwidth uti-
lization effi-
ciency for
small versus
large frames.

Figure 2–2
Bandwidth uti-
lization effi-
ciency for
small versus
large frames.

The maximum frame size is a tradeoff with the BER discussed in the previous section. Bigger frames have more bits and hence are more likely to be hit by an error. If there were no errors, an infinitely big frame would be the most efficient (although not the most fair to other senders!). If a frame is hit by an error, then it must be retransmitted, which wastes time and effort and reduces efficiency. The bigger the frame, the more bandwidth is wasted retransmitting. So, because networks experience errors, frame sizes are limited to maximize efficiency (and provide fairness), as shown in Table 2–2.

Table 2-2   Maximum Frame Sizes

Technology	Maximum Valid Frame
10- and 100-Mbps Ethernet	1,518 bytes (including the header and CRC)
4-Mbps Token Ring	4,500 bytes
16-Mbps Token Ring	18,000 bytes
FDDI	4,500 bytes
ATM with ATM Adaptation Layer 5 (AAL5)	65,535 bytes (AAL5 payload size)
ISDN Basic Rate Interface (BRI) and Primary Rate Interface (PRI) using the Point-to-Point Protocol (PPP)	1,500 bytes
T1	Not specified but 4,500 bytes generally used

Delay and Delay Variation

Users of interactive applications expect minimal delay in receiving feedback from the network. In addition, users of multimedia applications require a minimal variation in the amount of delay that packets experience. Delay must be constant for voice and video applications. Variations in delay, called *jitter*, cause disruptions in voice quality and jumpiness in video streams.

Older applications, such as SNA-based applications, are also sensitive to delay. In traditional SNA environments, delay could be carefully planned and measured. When SNA is migrated to a multiprotocol network, however, it is harder to predict delay. Unexpected delays can occur because of bursty LAN traffic and routers taking a long time to converge after a link outage. Long delays cause SNA sessions to timeout.

NOTES

In a multiprotocol internetwork, SNA runs above the connection-oriented (Type 2) Logical Link Control protocol, also known as *LLC2*. With LLC2, when a station sends a frame, it expects a response within a timeframe defined by the T1 timer. If the station does not receive a response, it resends the frame. The number of times to resend is set by the retries counter. The default settings are two seconds for T1 and six for the number of retries.

In complex multiprotocol networks, you might have to increase the T1 timer or retries counter to guarantee that delay does not exceed

T1 + (T1 × retries)

You can also avoid timeouts by configuring a local router to respond to LLC2 frames. (Chapter 7, "Selecting Bridging, Switching, and Routing Protocols," covers these issues in more detail.)

Applications that use the Telnet protocol are also sensitive to delay because the user expects quick feedback when typing characters. With the Telnet remote echo option, the character typed by a user doesn't appear on the screen until it has been acknowledged and echoed by the far end, and the near end has sent an acknowledgment for the echo. You should determine if your customer plans to run any applications based on delay-sensitive protocols, such as Telnet or SNA. Digital Equipment Corporation's Local Area Transport (LAT) protocol is also sensitive to delay and supports few adjustments for improving its behavior on networks with high delay.

Causes of Delay

Any goals regarding delay must take into account fundamental physics. Despite science fiction, any signal experiences a propagation delay resulting from the finite speed of light, which is about 300,000 kilometers per second (or 186,000 miles per second for metric-challenged readers in the United States). Network designers can also remember 1 nanosecond per foot. These values are for light traveling in a vacuum. A signal in a cable or optical fiber travels approximately 2/3 the speed of light in a vacuum.

Delay is relevant for all data transmission technologies, but especially for satellite links and long terrestrial cables. Geostationary satellites are in orbit above the earth at a height of about 36,000 kilometers, or 24,000 miles. This long distance leads to a delay of about 270 milliseconds (ms) for an intercontinental satellite hop. In the case of terrestrial cable connections, delay is about 1 ms for every 200 kilometers (120 miles).

Another fundamental cause for delay is the time to put digital data onto a transmission line, which depends on the data volume and the speed of the line. For example, to transmit a 1,024-byte packet on a 1.544-Mbps T1 line takes about 5 ms.

An additional fundamental delay is packet-switching delay. *Packet-switching delay* refers to the latency accrued when bridges, switches, and routers forward data. The latency depends on the speed of the internal circuitry and CPU, and the switching architecture of the internetworking device. The delay can be quite small. Scott Bradner of the Network Device Testing Laboratory at Harvard University periodically conducts latency tests on submitted network equipment. Bradner has tested Layer-2 and Layer-3 switches with latencies in the 10 to 50 microsecond range for 64-byte Ethernet IP packets. Routers have higher latencies than switches, but router vendors continually make progress on reducing latency.

When a packet comes into a router, the router checks its routing table, decides which interface should send the packet, and encapsulates the packet with the correct header and trailer. Routing vendors, such as Cisco Systems, have advanced caching mechanisms so that a frame destined for a known destination can receive its new encapsulation very quickly without requiring the CPU to do any table lookup or other processing. These mechanisms minimize packet-switching delay.

Packet-switching delay can also include *queuing delay*. The number of packets in a queue on a packet-switching device increases exponentially as utilization increases, as you can see from Figure 2–3. If utilization is 50 percent, the average queue depth is 1 packet. If utilization is 90 percent, the average queue depth is 9 packets. Without going into mathematical queuing theory, the general rule of thumb for queue depth is:

queue depth = utilization/(1 – utilization)

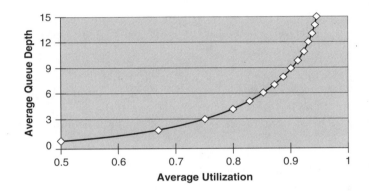

Figure 2–3
Queue depth and bandwidth utilization.

Consider the following example. A packet switch has five users, each offering packets at a rate of 10 packets per second. The average length of the packets is 1,024 bits. The packet switch needs to transmit this data over a 56-Kbps WAN circuit.

Load = 5 × 10 × 1,024 = 51,200 bps
Utilization = 51,200/56,000 = 91.4 percent
Average number of packets in the queue = (0.914)/(1 – 0.914) = 10.63 packets

By increasing bandwidth on a WAN circuit you can decrease queue depth and hence decrease delay. Alternately, to improve performance, you can use an advanced queuing algorithm that outputs certain types of packets first—for example, voice or video packets. Advanced router queuing techniques are discussed in more detail in Chapter 12, "Optimizing Your Network Design."

Delay Variation

As customers implement new digital voice and video applications, they are becoming concerned about delay and delay variation. Additionally, customers are becoming more aware of the issues associated with supporting bursty LAN traffic on the same network that carries delay-sensitive traffic. If bursts in LAN traffic cause jitter, audio and video streams experience problems that disrupt communications.

Desktop audio/video applications can minimize jitter by providing a buffer that the network puts data into. Display software or hardware pulls data from the buffer. The insulating buffer reduces the effect of jitter because variations on the input side are smaller than the total buffer size and therefore not obvious on the output side. The data is smoothed on the output, and the user experiences no ill effects from the input jitter.

If possible, you should gather exact requirements for delay variation from a customer. For customers who cannot provide exact goals, a good rule of thumb is that the variation should be less than one or two percent of the delay. For example, for a goal of an average delay of 40 ms, the variation should not be more than 400 or 800 microseconds.

Short fixed-length cells, for example ATM 53-byte cells, are inherently better than frames for meeting delay and delay-variance goals. To help understand this concept, consider the analogy of people trying to get onto an escalator. The escalator is like a bandwidth pipe. At first, each person gets onto the escalator in an orderly fashion and the delay is predictable. Then a school class arrives and the children are all holding hands, expecting to get onto the escalator all at once! What happens to your delay if you happen to be behind the children?

A gaggle of school children holding hands is analogous to a large frame causing extra delay for small frames. Consider the case of a user starting a file transfer using 1,518-byte frames. This user's data affects bandwidth usage and queuing mechanisms at internetworking devices, causing unexpected delay for other traffic. Good throughput for one application causes delay problems for another application.

Cell-relay technologies—for example, ATM—were designed to support traffic that is sensitive to delay and jitter. Depending on the class of service, ATM lets a session specify a maximum cell transfer delay (MCTD) and cell delay variation (MCDV). Chapter 4, "Characterizing Network Traffic," describes ATM service classes in more detail.

Response Time

Response time is the network performance goal that users care about most. Users don't know about propagation delay and jitter. They don't understand throughput in packets per second or in megabytes per second. They aren't concerned about bit-error rates, although perhaps they should be! Users recognize the amount of time to receive a response from the network system. They also recognize small changes in the expected response time and become frustrated when the response time is long.

Users begin to get frustrated when response time is more than about 100 ms or 1/10th of a second. Beyond 100 ms, users notice they are waiting for the network to display a Web page, echo a typed character, start downloading e-mail, and so on. If the response happens within 100 ms, most users do not notice any delay.

The 100-ms threshold is often used as a timer value for protocols that offer reliable transport of data. For example, many TCP implementations retransmit unacknowledged data after 100 ms by default. (Good TCP implementations also adjust the retransmit timer based on network conditions. TCP should keep track of the average amount of time to receive a response and dynamically adjust the retransmit timer based on the expected delay.)

The 100-ms response time threshold applies to interactive applications. For bulk applications, such as transferring large files or graphical Web pages, users are willing to wait at least 10 to 20 seconds. Technically savvy users expect to wait even longer if they know the file is large and the transmission medium is slow. If your network users are not technically savvy, you should provide some guidelines on how long to wait, depending on the size of files and the technologies in use (modems, high-speed digital networks, geostationary satellites, and so on).

SECURITY

Security design is one of the most important aspects of enterprise network design, especially as more companies add Internet and extranet connections to their internetworks. An overall goal that most companies have is that security problems should not disrupt the company's ability to conduct business. Network design customers need assurances that a design offers some protection against business data and other resources getting lost or damaged. Every company has trade secrets, business operations, and equipment to protect.

The first task in security design is planning. Planning involves analyzing risks and developing requirements. This chapter briefly discusses security planning. Chapter 8, "Developing Network Security and Network Management Strategies," covers planning for secure networks in more detail.

As is the case with most technical design requirements, achieving security goals means making tradeoffs. Security implementations can add to the cost of deploying and operating a network. Strict security policies can also affect the productivity of users, especially if some ease-of-use must be sacrificed to protect resources and data. Poor security implementations can annoy users, causing them to think of ways to get around security policies. Security can also affect the redundancy of a network design if all traffic must pass through encryption devices.

Security Risks

Ask your customer to help you understand the risks associated with not implementing a secure network. How sensitive is the customer's data? What would be the financial cost of someone accessing the data and stealing trade secrets? What would be the financial cost of someone changing the data?

As companies attach to the Internet they need to consider the additional risks of outsiders getting into the corporate network and doing damage. Customers who access remote sites across a Virtual Private Network (VPN) need to analyze the security features offered by the VPN service provider.

Some customers worry about hackers putting protocol analyzers on the Internet or VPN and sniffing packets to see passwords, credit-cards numbers, or other private data. This is not as big a risk as it appears. Credit-card numbers are almost always sent encrypted, using technologies such as the Secure Sockets Layer (SSL) protocol. Even when passwords or credit cards are not encrypted, it is extremely difficult to find these minute pieces of data in the midst of millions of packets.

On the other hand, hackers do have the ability to access and change sensitive data on enterprise networks. Consider the possibility of a hacker damaging an enterprise's image by changing the enterprise's public Web pages. You may have read about some of the cases of hackers changing U.S. government Web pages. These security breaches affected the government's image in two ways: the changed Web pages had silly graphics and text, and the government lost credibility because it appeared that it was easy to hack into government networks.

In general, hackers have the ability to attack computer networks in the following ways:

- Use resources they are not authorized to use

- Keep authorized users from accessing resources (also called denial-of-service attacks)

- Change, steal, or damage resources

- Take advantage of well-known security holes in operating systems and application software

- Take advantage of holes created while systems, configurations, and software releases are being upgraded

In addition to considering outside hackers as a security risk, companies should heed problems caused by inept or malicious internal network users. According to security surveys that Ernst and Young conducts every year, the biggest security problem facing companies today is software viruses that spread when users download software from untrusted sites. Companies reported that following viruses, the next most significant cause of problems was inadvertent user errors. This was followed by malicious acts by internal users. These problems were more common than malicious acts from the outside or industrial espionage.

Security Requirements

A customer's primary security requirement is to protect resources from being incapacitated, stolen, altered, or harmed. Resources can include network hosts, servers, user systems, internetworking devices, system and application data, and a company's image.

Other more specific requirements could include one or more of the following goals:

- Let outsiders (customers, vendors, suppliers) access data on public Web or FTP servers but not access internal data

- Authorize and authenticate branch-office users, mobile users, and telecommuters

- Detect intruders and isolate the amount of damage they do

- Authenticate routing-table updates received from internal or external routers

- Protect data transmitted to remote sites across a VPN

- Physically secure hosts and internetworking devices (for example, keep devices in a locked room)

- Logically secure hosts and internetworking devices with user accounts and access rights for directories and files

- Protect applications and data from software viruses

- Train network users and network managers on security risks and how to avoid security problems

- Implement copyright or other legal methods of protecting products and intellectual property

MANAGEABILITY

Every customer has different objectives regarding the manageability of a network. Some customers have precise goals, such as a plan to use the Simple Network Management Protocol (SNMP) to record the number of bytes each router receives and sends. Other clients have less specific goals. If your client has definite plans, be sure to document them, because you will need to refer to the plans when selecting equipment. In some cases, equipment has to be ruled out because it does not support the management functions a customer requires.

To help customers who don't have specific goals, you can use International Organization for Standardization (ISO) terminology to define network management functions:

- **Performance management.** Analyzing traffic and application behavior to optimize a network, meet service-level agreements, and plan for expansion

- **Fault management.** Detecting, isolating, and correcting problems; reporting problems to end users and managers; tracking trends related to problems

- **Configuration management.** Controlling, operating, identifying, and collecting data from managed devices

- **Security management.** Monitoring and testing security and protection policies, maintaining and distributing passwords and other authentication and authorization information, managing encryption keys, auditing adherence to security policies

- **Accounting management.** Accounting of network usage to allocate costs to network users and/or plan for changes in capacity requirements

Almost all customers have a need for fault and configuration management. Many customers also need performance and security management. Some customers need accounting management. Network management is discussed in more detail in Chapter 8, "Developing Network Security and Network Management Strategies."

USABILITY

A goal that is related to manageability, but is not exactly the same as manageability, is usability. Usability refers to the ease-of-use with which network users can access the network and services. Whereas manageability focuses on making network managers' jobs easier, usability focuses on making network users' jobs easier.

It is important to gain an understanding of how important usability is to your network design customer, because some network design components can have a negative affect on usability. For example, strict security policies can have a negative affect on usability (which is a tradeoff that most customers are willing to make, but not all customers). You can plan to maximize usability by deploying user-friendly host-naming schemes and easy-to-use configuration methods that make use of dynamic protocols, such as the Dynamic Host Configuration Protocol (DHCP).

ADAPTABILITY

When designing a network, you should try to avoid incorporating any elements that would make it hard to implement new technologies in the future. A good network design can adapt to new technologies and changes. Changes can come in the form of new protocols, new business practices, new fiscal goals, new legislation, and a myriad of other possibilities. For example, some states have enacted environmental laws that require a reduction in the number of employees driving to work. To meet the legal requirement to reduce automobile emissions, companies need their remote-access designs to be flexible enough to adapt to increasing numbers of employees working at home.

The adaptability of a network affects its availability. For example, consider the need for a network to adapt to environmental changes. Some networks must operate in environments that change drastically from day to night or from winter to summer. Extreme changes in temperature can affect the behavior of electronic components of a network. A network that cannot adapt cannot offer good availability.

A flexible network design is also able to adapt to changing traffic patterns and quality of service (QoS) requirements. For some customers, the selected WAN or LAN technology must adapt to new users randomly joining the network to use applications that require a constant-bit-rate service. Chapter 4, "Characterizing Network Traffic," discusses QoS requirements in more detail.

One other aspect of adaptability is how quickly internetworking devices must adapt to problems and to upgrades. For example, how quickly do switches and bridges adapt to another switch failing, causing a change in the spanning-tree topology? How quickly do routers adapt to new networks joining the topology? How quickly do routing protocols adapt to link failures? These issues are discussed in more detail in Chapter 7, "Selecting Bridging, Switching, and Routing Protocols."

AFFORDABILITY

The final technical goal this chapter covers is *affordability*. Affordability is sometimes called *cost-effectiveness*. Most customers have a goal for affordability, though sometimes other goals such as performance and availability are more important. Affordability is partly a business goal, and, in fact, was discussed in Chapter 1, "Analyzing Business Goals and Constraints." It is covered again in this chapter because of the technical issues.

The primary goal of affordability is to carry the maximum amount of traffic for a given financial cost. Financial costs include non-recurring equipment costs and recurring network operation costs.

In campus networks, low cost is often a primary goal. Customers expect to be able to purchase affordable switches that have numerous ports and a low cost per port. They expect cabling costs to be minimal and service-provider charges to be minimal or non-existent. They also expect network interface cards (NICs) for end systems and servers to be inexpensive. Depending on the applications running on end systems, low cost is often more important than availability and performance in campus network designs.

For enterprise networks, availability is usually more important than low cost. Nonetheless, customers are looking for ways to contain costs for enterprise networks. Recurring monthly charges for WAN circuits are the most expensive aspect of running a large network. To reduce the cost of operating a WAN, customers often have one or more of the following technical goals for affordability:

- Use a routing protocol that minimizes WAN traffic

- Use a routing protocol that selects minimum-tariff routes

- Consolidate parallel leased lines carrying voice and data into fewer WAN trunks

- Select technologies that dynamically allocate WAN bandwidth, for example, ATM rather than time-division multiplexing (TDM)

- Improve efficiency on WAN circuits by using such features as compression, voice activity detection (VAD), and repetitive pattern suppression (RPS)

- Eliminate underutilized trunks from the internetwork and save money by eliminating both circuit costs and trunk hardware

- Use technologies that support oversubscription

With old-style TDM networks, the core backbone capacity had to be at least the sum of the speeds of the incoming access networks. With cell and frame switching, oversubscription is common. Because of the bursty nature of frame-based traffic, access-port speeds can add up to more than the speed of a backbone network, within reason. Enterprise network managers who have a goal of reducing operational costs are especially interested in solutions that will let them oversubscribe their trunks, while still maintaining service guarantees they have offered their users.

The second most expensive aspect of running a network, following the cost of WAN circuits, is the cost of hiring, training, and maintaining personnel to operate and manage the network. To reduce this aspect of operational costs, customers have the following goals:

- Select internetworking equipment that is easy to configure, operate, maintain, and manage

- Select a network design that is easy to understand and troubleshoot

- Maintain good network documentation to reduce troubleshooting time

- Select network applications and protocols that are easy to use so that users can support themselves to some extent

Making Network Design Tradeoffs

When analyzing a customer's goals for affordability, it is important to gain an understanding of how important affordability is compared to other goals. Despite what politicians tell us about federal budgets during an election year, in the real world, meeting goals requires making tradeoffs. This section describes some typical network design tradeoffs.

To meet high expectations for availability, redundant components are often necessary, which raises the cost of a network implementation. To meet rigorous performance requirements, high-cost circuits and equipment are required. To enforce strict security policies, expensive monitoring might be required and users must forgo some ease-of-use. To implement a scalable network, availability might suffer, because a scalable network is always in flux as new users and sites are added. To implement good throughput for one application might cause delay problems for another application.

To implement affordability might mean availability must suffer. One cause of network problems can be inadequate staffing and reduced training due to overzealous cost-cutting. These mistakes have hurt many sizeable organizations and are hard to recover from. Once the network staff is gone, outsourcing becomes a necessity, which may end up being more costly.

To help you analyze tradeoffs, ask your customer to identify a single driving network design goal. This goal can be the same overall business goal for the network design project that was identified in Chapter 1, or it can be a rephrasing of that goal to include technical issues. In addition, ask your customer to prioritize the rest of the goals. Prioritizing will help the customer get through the process of making tradeoffs.

One analogy that helps with prioritizing goals is the "kid in the candy store with a dollar bill" analogy. Using the dollar-bill analogy, explain to the customer that he or she is like a child in a candy store that has exactly one dollar to spend. The dollar can be spent on different types of candy: chocolates, licorice, jelly beans, and so on. But each time more money is spent on one type of candy, less money is available to spend on other types. Ask customers to add up how much they want to spend on scalability, availability, network performance, security, manageability, usability, adaptability, and affordability. For example, a customer could make the following selections:

Scalability	20
Availability	30
Network performance	15
Security	5
Manageability	5
Usability	5
Adaptability	5
Affordability	15
Total (must add up to 100)	**100**

Keep in mind that sometimes making tradeoffs is more complex than what has been described because goals can differ for various parts of an internetwork. One group of users might value availability more than affordability. Another group might deploy state-of-the-art applications and value performance more than availability. In addition, sometimes a particular group's goals are different than the overall goals for the internetwork as a whole. If this is the case, document individual group goals as well as goals for the network as a whole. Later when selecting network technologies, you might see some opportunities to meet both types of goals—for example choosing LAN technologies that meet individual group goals, and WAN technologies that meet overall goals.

TECHNICAL GOALS CHECKLIST

You can use the following checklist to determine if you have addressed all your client's technical objectives and concerns:

☐ I have documented the customer's plans for expanding the number of sites, users, and servers/hosts for the next year and next two years.

☐ The customer has told me about any plans to migrate departmental servers to server farms or intranets.

☐ The customer has told me about any plans to migrate an SNA network to the multiprotocol internetwork.

☐ The customer has told me about any plans to implement an extranet to communicate with partners or other companies.

☐ I have documented a goal for network availability in percent uptime and/or MTBF and MTTR.

☐ I have documented any goals for maximum average network utilization on shared segments.

☐ I have documented goals for network throughput.

Table 2-3   Network Applications Technical Requirements

Name of Application	Type of Application	New Application? (Yes or No)	Criticality	Cost of Downtime	Acceptable MTBF

☐ I have documented goals for PPS throughput of internetworking devices.

☐ I have documented goals for accuracy and acceptable BERs.

☐ I have discussed with the customer the importance of using large frame sizes to maximize efficiency.

☐ I have identified any applications that have a more restrictive response-time requirement than the industry standard of less than 100 ms.

☐ I have discussed network security risks and requirements with the customer.

☐ I have gathered manageability requirements, including goals for performance, fault, configuration, security, and accounting management.

☐ Working with my customer, I have developed a list of network design goals, including both business and technical goals. The list starts with one overall goal and includes the rest of the goals in priority order. Critical goals are marked as such.

☐ I have updated the Network Applications chart to include the technical application goals shown in Table 2–3.

Chapter 1, "Analyzing Business Goals and Constraints," provided a Network Applications chart. At this point in the design process, you can expand the chart to include technical application requirements, such as MTBF, MTTR, and throughput and delay goals, as shown in Table 2–3.

Acceptable MTTR	Throughput Goal	Delay must be less than:	Delay variation must be less than:	Comments

SUMMARY

This chapter covered technical requirements for a network design, including scalability, availability, network performance, security, manageability, usability, adaptability, and affordability. It also covered typical tradeoffs that must be made to meet these goals.

Analyzing your customer's technical and business goals prepares you to carry out the next steps in the top-down network design process, including making decisions regarding network technologies to recommend to a customer. Researchers who study decision models say that one of the most important aspects of making a sound decision is having a good list of goals. At this point in the network design process, you have gathered both business and technical goals. You should make a list of your customer's most important technical goals and merge this list with the list of business goals you made in Chapter 1.

You should put the goals in the list in priority order, starting with the overall most important business and technical goal, and following with critical goals and then less critical goals. Later, you can make a list of options and correlate options with goals. Any options that do not meet critical goals can be eliminated. Other options can be ranked by how well they meet a goal. This process can help you select network components that meet a customer's requirements.

CHAPTER 3

Characterizing the Existing Internetwork

According to Abraham Lincoln:

> If we could first know where we are and whither we are tending, we could better judge what to do and how to do it.

An important step in top-down network design is to examine a customer's existing network to better judge how to meet expectations for network scalability, performance, and availability. Examining the existing network includes learning about the topology and physical structure, and assessing the network's performance.

By developing an understanding of the existing network's structure, uses, and behavior, you can determine whether a customer's design goals are realistic. You can document any bottlenecks or network-performance problems, and identify internetworking devices and links that will need to be replaced because the number of ports or capacity is insufficient for the new design. Identifying performance problems can help you select solutions to solve problems as well as develop a baseline for future measurements of performance.

Most network designers do not design networks from scratch. Instead, they design enhancements to existing networks. Being able to develop a successful network design requires that you develop skills in characterizing an incumbent network to ensure interoperability between the existing and anticipated networks. This chapter describes techniques and tools to help you develop those skills. This chapter concludes with a Network Health Checklist that documents typical thresholds for diagnosing a network as "healthy."

CHARACTERIZING THE NETWORK INFRASTRUCTURE

Characterizing the infrastructure of a network means developing a network map and learning the location of major internetworking devices and network segments. It also includes documenting the names and addresses of major devices and segments, and identifying any standard methods for addressing and naming. Documenting the types and lengths of physical cabling, and investigating architectural and environmental constraints, are also important aspects of characterizing the network infrastructure.

Developing a Network Map

Learning the location of major hosts, interconnection devices, and network segments is a good way to start developing an understanding of traffic flow. Coupled with data on the performance characteristics of network segments, location information gives you insight into where users are concentrated and the level of traffic a network design must support.

At this point in the network design process, your goal is to obtain a map of the already-implemented network. Some design customers may have maps for the new network design as well. If that is the case, then you may be one step ahead, but be careful of any assumptions that are not based on your detailed analysis of business and technical requirements.

Tools for Developing Network Maps

Not all customers can provide a detailed and up-to-date map of the existing network. In many cases, you need to develop the map yourself. Companies that are constantly working in "fire-fighting" mode do not have time to proactively document the existing network.

To develop a network drawing, you should invest in a good network-diagramming tool. Visio Corporation's Visio Professional is one of the premiere tools for diagramming networks. Visio Professional ships with templates for typical LANs and WANs, icons for common network and telecommunications devices, and the ability to draw WANs on top of a geographical map and LANs on top of a building or floor plan.

To create more detailed network diagrams, you can use the Visio Network Equipment product, an add-on library of 10,000 manufacturer-specific shapes with port-level detail. If a customer has equipment documented in a spreadsheet or database, you can use the Visio Network Diagram Wizard to draw a diagram based on the network-equipment spreadsheet or database.

Some companies offer diagramming and network documentation tools that automatically discover the existing network. Pinpoint Software's ClickNet Professional is one such tool. ClickNet Professional uses various network-management protocols and other mechanisms to automatically learn and document the infrastructure of a customer's network. The tool automatically learns about internetworking devices and workstations, including CPU type, software versions, amount of memory, and the number of ports and network-interface cards. The tool includes the ability to customize a network map with backgrounds, floor plans, icons, and text. It also supports "what-if" analysis to determine the impact of projected network design changes.

NetSuite Development is another company that specializes in network-discovery and design tools. NetSuite Professional Audit is similar to ClickNet in its support for automatic discovery. The information gathered in a discovery session can be linked to the NetSuite Advanced Professional Design application to populate a design schematic. NetSuite Advanced Professional Design helps you design complex multi-layer networks. The application provides access to a library of network devices and includes a validation engine to let you test some aspects of a network design.

What Should a Network Map Include?

Regardless of the tools you use to develop a network map, your goal should be to develop (or obtain from your customer) a map (or set up maps) that includes the following:

- Geographical information, such as countries, states or provinces, cities, and campuses

- WAN connections between countries, states, and cities

- Buildings and floors, and possibly rooms or cubicles

- WAN and LAN connections between buildings and between campuses

- An indication of the data-link layer technology for WANs and LANs (Frame Relay, ISDN, 10-Mbps or 100-Mbps Ethernet, Token Ring, and so on)

- The name of the service provider for WANs

- The location of routers and switches, though not necessarily hubs

- The location and reach of any Virtual Private Networks (VPNs) that connect corporate sites via a service provider's WAN

- The location of major servers or server farms

- The location of mainframes

- The location of major network-management stations

- The location and reach of any virtual LANs (VLANs). (If the drawing is in color, you can draw all devices and segments within a particular VLAN in a specific color.)

- The topology of any firewall security systems

- The location of any dial-in and dial-out systems

- Some indication of where workstations reside, though not necessarily the explicit location of each workstation

- A depiction of the logical topology or architecture of the network

---

NOTES

While documenting the network infrastructure, take a step back from the diagrams you develop and try to characterize the logical topology of the network as well as the physical components. The logical topology illustrates the architecture of the network, which can be hierarchical or flat, structured or unstructured, layered or not, and other possibilities. The logical topology also describes methods for connecting devices in a geometric shape, for example, a star, ring, bus, hub and spoke, or mesh.

The logical topology can affect your ability to upgrade a network. For example, a flat topology does not scale as well as a hierarchical topology. A typical hierarchical topology that does scale is a core layer of high-end routers and switches that are optimized for availability and performance, a distribution layer of routers and switches that implement policies, and an access layer that connects users via hubs, switches, and other devices. Logical topologies are discussed in more detail in Chapter 5, "Designing a Network Topology."

Figure 3–1 shows a typical high-level network diagram for an electronics manufacturing company. The drawing shows a physical topology, but it is not hard to step back and visualize that the logical topology is a hub-and-spoke shape with three layers. The core layer of the network is a 16-Mbps Token Ring network. The distribution layer includes routers and bridges, and Frame Relay and T1 links. The access layer comprises 4-Mbps and 16-Mbps Token Ring networks. An Ethernet network hosts the company's World Wide Web server. As you can see from the figure, the network included some rather old equipment. The company required design consultation to select new technologies to eliminate performance problems caused by Token-Ring bridges dropping frames.

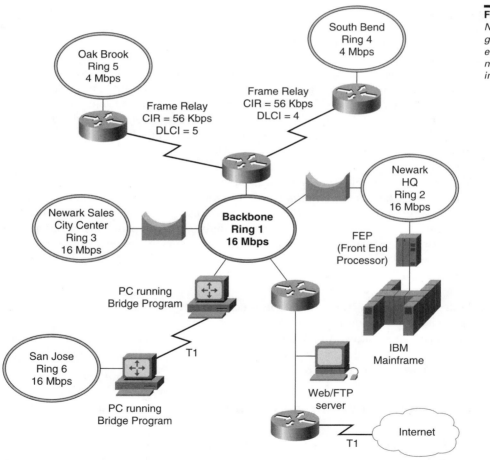

Figure 3–1
Network diagram for an electronics manufacturing company.

Characterizing Network Addressing and Naming

Characterizing the logical infrastructure of a network involves documenting any strategies your customer has for network addressing and naming. Addressing and naming are discussed in greater detail in Part II of this book, "Logical Network Design."

When drawing detailed network maps, include the names of major sites, routers, network segments, and servers. Also document any standard strategies your customer uses for naming network elements. For example, some customers name sites using airport codes. (San Francisco = SFO, Oakland = OAK, and so on.) You may find that a customer suffixes names with an alias that describes the type of device, for example, *rtr* for router. Some customers use a standard naming system, such as the Domain Name System (DNS), for IP networks.

You should also investigate the network-layer addresses your customer uses. Your customer's addressing scheme (or lack of any scheme) can influence your ability to adapt the network to new design goals. For example, your customer might use illegal IP addresses that will need to be changed or translated before connecting to the Internet. As another example, current IP subnet masking might limit the number of nodes in a LAN or VLAN.

Your customer might have a goal of using route summarization, which is also called *route aggregation* or *supernetting*. *Route summarization* reduces routes in a routing table, routing-table update traffic, and overall router overhead. Route summarization also improves network stability and availability, because problems in one part of a network are less likely to affect the whole internetwork. Summarization is most effective when address prefixes have been assigned in a consistent and contiguous manner, which is often not the case.

Your customer's existing addressing scheme might affect the routing protocols you can select. Some routing protocols do not support classless addressing, variable-length subnet masking (VLSM), or discontiguous subnets. A *discontiguous subnet* is a subnet that is divided, as shown in Figure 3–2. Subnet 108 of network 10 is divided into two areas that are separated by network 192.168.49.0.

Characterizing Wiring and Media

To help you meet scalability and availability goals for your new network design, it is important to understand the cabling design and wiring of the existing network. Doc-

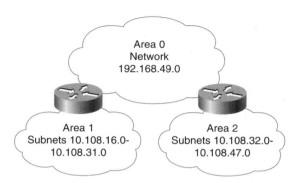

Figure 3–2
An example of a discontiguous subnet.

umenting the existing cabling design can help you plan for enhancements and identify any potential problems. If possible, you should document the types of cabling in use as well as cable distances. Distance information is useful when selecting data-link-layer technologies based on distance restrictions.

While exploring the cabling design, assess how well equipment and cables are labeled in the current network. The extent and accuracy of labeling will affect your ability to implement and test enhancements to the network.

Your network diagram should document the connections between buildings. The diagram should include information on the number of pairs of wires and the type of wiring (or wireless technology) in use. The diagram should also indicate how far buildings are from one another. Distance information can help you select new cabling. For example, if you plan to upgrade from copper to fiber cabling, the distance between buildings can be much longer. (Selecting cabling is discussed in more detail in Chapters 9 and 10.)

Probably the wiring (or wireless technology) between buildings is one of the following:

- Single-mode fiber

- Multi-mode fiber

- Shielded twisted pair (STP) copper

- Category-5 unshielded-twisted-pair (UTP) copper

- Coaxial cable

- Microwave

- Laser

- Radio

- Infra-red

Within buildings, try to locate telecommunications wiring closets, cross-connect rooms, and any laboratories or computer rooms. If possible, determine the type of cabling that is installed between telecommunications closets and in work areas. (Some technologies, for example, 100Base-TX Ethernet, require Category-5 cabling.) Gather information about both vertical and horizontal wiring. As shown in Figure 3–3, *vertical wiring* runs between floors. *Horizontal wiring* runs from telecommunications closets to wallplates in cubicles or offices. *Work-area wiring* runs from the wallplate to a workstation in a cubicle or office.

Figure 3–3
An example of campus network wiring.

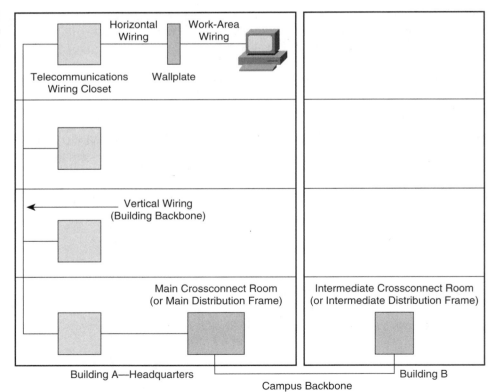

In most buildings, the cabling from a telecommunications closet to a workstation is approximately 100 meters, including the work-area wiring which is usually just a few meters. If you have any indication that the cabling might be longer than 100 meters, you should use a *time-domain reflectometer (TDR)* to verify your suspicions. (TDR functionality is included in most cable testers.) Many network designs are based on the assumption that workstations are no more than 100 meters from the telecommunications closet.

For each building, you can fill out the chart shown in Table 3–1. The data that you fill in depends on how much time you have to gather information and how important you think cabling details will be to your network design. If you do not have a lot of information, than just put an **X** for each type of cabling present and document any assumptions (for example an assumption that workstations are no more than 100 meters from the telecommunications closet). If you have time to gather more details, then include information on the length and number of pairs of cables. If you prefer, you can document building wiring information in a network diagram instead of in a table.

Table 3-1 Building Wiring

Building Name:			
Location of telecommunications closets:			
Location of cross-connect rooms and demarcations to external networks:			
Logical wiring topology (structured, star, bus, ring, centralized, distributed, mesh, tree, or whatever fits):			

Vertical Wiring:						
	Coaxial	**Fiber**	**STP**	**Category 3 UTP**	**Category 5 UTP**	**Other**
Vertical Shaft 1						
Vertical Shaft 2						
Vertical Shaft *n*						

Table 3-1   Building Wiring, Continued

	Coaxial	Fiber	STP	Category 3 UTP	Category 5 UTP	Other
Horizontal Wiring:						
Floor 1						
Floor 2						
Floor 3						
Floor *n*						
Work-Area Wiring:						
	Coaxial	Fiber	STP	Category 3 UTP	Category 5 UTP	Other
Floor 1						
Floor 2						
Floor 3						
Floor *n*						

Checking Architectural and Environmental Constraints

When investigating cabling, pay attention to such environmental issues as the possibility that cabling will run near creeks that could flood, railroad tracks or highways where traffic could jostle cables, or construction or manufacturing areas where heavy equipment or digging could break cables.

Be sure to determine if there are any legal right-of-way issues that must be dealt with before cabling can be put into place. For example, will cabling need to cross a public street? Will it be necessary to run cables through property owned by other companies? Finally, for some wireless technologies, such as laser or infra-red, make sure there aren't any obstacles blocking the line of sight.

Within buildings, pay attention to architectural issues that could affect the feasibility of implementing your network design. Make sure the following architectural elements are sufficient to support your design:

- Air conditioning

- Heating

- Ventilation

- Power

- Protection from electromagnetic interference

- Clear paths for wireless transmission and an absence of confusing reflecting surfaces

- Doors that can lock

- Space for:

  —Cabling (conduits)

  —Patch panels

  —Equipment racks

  —Work areas for technicians installing and troubleshooting equipment

CHECKING THE HEALTH OF THE EXISTING INTERNETWORK

Studying the performance of the existing internetwork gives you a baseline measurement from which to measure new network performance. Armed with measurements of the present internetwork, you can demonstrate to your customer how much better the new internetwork performs once your design is implemented.

Many of the network-performance goals discussed in Chapter 2, "Analyzing Technical Goals and Constraints," are overall goals for an internetwork. Since the performance of existing network segments will affect overall performance, it is important that you study the performance of existing segments to determine how to meet overall network performance goals.

If an internetwork is too large to study all segments, then you should analyze the segments that will interoperate the most with the new network design. Pay particular attention to backbone networks and networks that connect old and new areas.

In some cases, a customer's goals might be at odds with improving network performance. The customer might want to reduce costs, for example, and not worry about performance. In this case, you will be glad that you documented the original performance so that you can prove that the network was not optimized to start with and your new design has not made performance worse.

By analyzing existing networks, you can also recognize legacy systems that must be incorporated into the new design. Sometimes customers are not aware that older protocols are still running on their internetworks. By capturing network traffic with a protocol analyzer as part of your baseline analysis, you can identify which protocols are really running on the network and not rely on customers' beliefs.

The Challenges of Developing a Baseline of Network Performance

Developing an accurate baseline of a network's performance is not an easy task. One challenging aspect is selecting a time to do the analysis. It is important that you allocate a lot of time (multiple days) if you want the baseline to be accurate. If measurements are made over too short a timeframe, temporary errors appear more significant than they are.

In addition to allocating sufficient time for a baseline analysis, it is also important to find a typical time period to do the analysis. A baseline of normal performance should not include non-typical problems caused by exceptionally large traffic loads. For example, at some companies, end-of-the quarter sales processing puts an abnormal load on the network. In a retail environment, network traffic can increase five times around Christmas time. Network traffic to a Web server can unexpectedly increase as much as 10 times if the Web site gets linked to other popular sites or listed in search engines.

In general, errors, packet/cell loss, and latency increase with load. To get a meaningful measurement of typical accuracy and delay, try to do your baseline analysis during periods of normal traffic load. (On the other hand, if your customer's main goal is to improve performance during peak load, then be sure to study performance during peak load. The decision whether to measure normal performance, performance during peak load, or both, depends on the goals of the network design.)

Some customers do not recognize the value of studying the existing network before designing and implementing enhancements. Your customer's expectations for a speedy design proposal might make it difficult for you to take a step back and insist on time to develop a baseline of performance on the existing network. Also, your other job tasks and goals, especially if you are a sales engineer, might make it impractical to spend days developing a precise baseline.

The work you do before the baseline step in the top-down network design methodology can increase your efficiency in developing a baseline. A good understanding of your customer's technical and business goals can help you decide how thorough to make your study. Your discussions with your customer on business goals can help you identify segments that are important to study because they carry critical and/or backbone traffic. You can also ask your customer to help you identify typical segments from which you can extrapolate conclusions about other segments.

Analyzing Network Availability

To document availability characteristics of the existing network, gather any statistics that the customer has on the mean time between failure (MTBF) and mean time to repair (MTTR) for the internetwork as a whole as well as major network segments. Compare these statistics with information you have gathered on MTBF and MTTR goals, as discussed in Chapter 2, "Analyzing Technical Goals and Constraints." Does the customer expect your new design to increase MTBF and decrease MTTR? Are the customer's goals realistic considering the current state of the network?

Talk to the network engineers and technicians about the causes of the most recent and most disruptive periods of downtime. Acting like a forensic investigator, try to get many sides to the story. Sometimes myths develop about what caused a network outage. (You can usually get a more accurate view of problem causes from engineers and technicians than from users and managers.)

You can use Table 3–2 to document availability characteristics of the current network.

Table 3-2   Availability Characteristics of the Current Network

	MTBF	MTTR	Date and Duration of Last Major Downtime	Cause of Last Major Downtime
Enterprise (as a whole)				
Segment 1				
Segment 2				
Segment 3				
Segment n				

Analyzing Network Utilization

Network utilization is a measurement of how much bandwidth is in use during a specific time interval. Utilization is commonly specified as a percentage of capacity. If a network monitoring tool says that network utilization on an FDDI segment is 70 percent, for example, this means that 70 percent of the 100-Mbps capacity is in use, averaged over a specified timeframe or window.

Different tools use different averaging windows for computing network utilization. Some tools let the user change the window. Using a long interval can be useful for reducing the amount of statistical data that must be analyzed, but granularity is sacrificed. As Figure 3–4 shows, it can be informative (though tedious), to look at a chart that shows network utilization averaged every minute.

Figure 3–4
Network utilization in minute intervals.

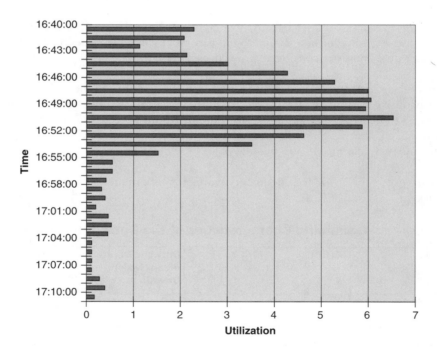

Figure 3–5 shows the same data averaged over hour intervals. Note that the network was not very busy so neither chart goes above seven percent utilization. Note also that changing to a long interval can be misleading because peaks in traffic get averaged out

(the detail is lost). In Figure 3–4, you can see that the network was relatively busy around 4:50 PM. You cannot see this in Figure 3–5, when the data was averaged every hour.

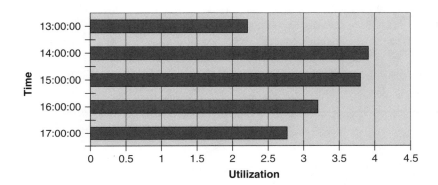

Figure 3–5
*Network utili-
zation in hour
intervals.*

As it turns out, 4:50 PM was the time of day that many of the network users turned their machines off and went home for the day. Each station leaving the Token-Ring network caused an error frame to be sent to the ring error monitor and a configuration frame to be sent to the configuration server, causing the peak in network utilization. So the peak in network traffic wasn't really interesting in this case, unless you were spying on the workers to make sure they didn't go home before 5 PM! Usually peaks in network utilization are something you want to know about when conducting a baseline analysis. In general, you should record network utilization with sufficient granularity in time to see short-term peaks in network traffic so that you can accurately assess the capacity requirements of devices and segments.

Changing the interval to a very small amount of time, say a fraction of a second, can be misleading also, however. Be wary of switch vendors who measure utilization on your network in millisecond increments and recommend that you update from a shared medium to a switched technology because short-term network utilization is dangerously high. To understand the concern, consider a very small time interval. In a packet-sized window, at a time when a station is sending traffic, the utilization is 100 percent, which is what is desired.

TIPS

The size of the averaging window for network utilization measurements depends on your goals. When troubleshooting network problems, keep the interval very small, either minutes or seconds. A small interval helps you recognize peaks caused by problems such as broadcast storms or stations retransmitting very quickly due to a misconfigured timer. For performance analysis and baselining purposes, use an interval of 1 to 5 minutes. For long-term load analysis, to determine peak hours, days, or months, set the interval to 10 minutes.

When developing a baseline, it is usually a good idea to err on the side of gathering too much data. You can always summarize the data later. When characterizing network utilization, use protocol analyzers or other monitoring tools to measure utilization in 1 to 5 minute intervals on each major network segment. If practical, leave the monitoring tools running for at least one or two typical days. If the customer's goals include improving performance during peak times, measure utilization during peak times and typical times. To determine if the measured utilization is healthy, use the Network Health Checklist that appears at the end of this chapter.

Bandwidth Utilization by Protocol

Developing a baseline of network performance should also include measuring utilization from broadcast traffic versus unicast traffic, and by each major protocol. As discussed in Chapter 4, "Characterizing Network Traffic," some protocols send excessive broadcast traffic, which can seriously degrade performance, especially on switched networks.

To measure bandwidth utilization by protocol, place a protocol analyzer on each major network segment and fill out a chart such as the one shown in Table 3–3. If the analyzer supports relative and absolute percentages, specify the bandwidth used by protocols as relative and absolute. *Relative usage* specifies how much bandwidth is used by the protocol in comparison to the total bandwidth currently in use on the segment. *Absolute usage* specifies how much bandwidth is used by the protocol in comparison to the total capacity of the segment (for example, in comparison to 10 Mbps on Ethernet).

Table 3-3   Bandwidth Utilization by Protocol

	Relative Network Utilization	Absolute Network Utilization	Broadcast/Multicast Rate
IP			
IPX			
AppleTalk			
DECnet			
Banyan			
NetBIOS			
SNA			
Other			

Analyzing Network Accuracy

The previous chapter talked about specifying network accuracy as a bit error rate (BER). You can use a BER tester (also called a *BERT*) on serial lines to test the number of damaged bits compared to total bits.

With packet-switched networks, it makes more sense to measure frame (packet) errors because a whole frame is considered bad if a single bit is changed or dropped. In packet-switched networks, a sending station calculates a cyclic redundancy check (CRC) based on the bits in a frame. The sending station places the value of the CRC in the frame. A receiving station determines if a bit has been changed or dropped by calculating the CRC again and comparing the result to the CRC in the frame. A frame with a bad CRC is dropped and must be retransmitted by the sender. Usually an upper-layer protocol has the job of retransmitting frames that do not get acknowledged.

A protocol analyzer can check the CRC on received frames. As part of your baseline analysis, you should track the number of frames received with a bad CRC every hour for one or two days. Because it is normal for errors to increase with utilization, document errors as a function of the number of bytes seen by the monitoring tool. A good rule-of-thumb threshold for considering errors unhealthy is that a network should not have more than one bad frame per megabyte of data. (Calculating errors this way lets you simulate a serial BERT. Simply calculating a percentage of bad frames compared to good frames does not account for the size of frames and hence does not give a good indication of how many bits are actually getting damaged.)

Some network monitors let you print a report of the top 10 stations sending frames with CRC errors. Token-Ring monitors let you print a report of the top 10 stations sending error reports to the ring error monitor. You should correlate the information on stations sending the most errors with information you gathered on network topology to identify any areas of a network that are prone to errors, possibly due to electrical noise or cabling problems.

TIPS

Network problems are usually not caused by the stations sending bad frames or error reports. The stations reporting problems are usually the "victims" not the "perpetrators." In the case of Token Ring, the problem is usually caused by a station or cabling problem upstream from the station reporting the problem. In the case of Ethernet, it is more difficult to pinpoint the cause of problems. With a thorough investigation, however, you usually can isolate a problematic area of the network where frames are damaged by a bad repeater, electrical problem, cabling fault, or misbehaving network interface card.

In addition to tracking data-link layer errors, such as CRC errors, a baseline analysis should include information on upper-layer problems. A protocol analyzer that includes an expert system, such as Network Associate's Sniffer network analyzer, speeds the identification of upper-layer problems by automatically generating diagnoses and symptoms for network conversations and applications.

Accuracy should also include a measurement of lost packets. You can measure lost packets while measuring response time, which is covered later in this chapter in the "Analyzing Delay and Response Time" section. When sending packets to measure how long it takes to receive a response, document any packets that do not receive a response, presumably because either the request or the response got lost. Correlate the information about lost packets with other performance measurements to determine if the lost packets indicate a need to increase bandwidth, decrease CRC errors, or upgrade internetworking devices. You can also measure lost packets by looking at statistics kept by routers on the number of packets dropped from input or output queues.

Analyzing ATM Errors

The ATM Forum specifies ATM accuracy in terms of a cell error ratio (CER), cell loss ratio (CLR), cell misinsertion rate (CMR), and severely errored cell block ratio (SECBR).

The CER is the number of errored cells divided by the total number of successfully transferred cells plus errored cells. The CLR is the number of lost cells divided by the total number of transmitted cells.

CMR on a connection is caused by an undetected error in the header of a cell being transmitted on a different connection. SECBR occurs when more than a certain number of errored cells, lost cells, or misinserted cells are observed in a received cell block. A *cell block* is a sequence of cells transmitted consecutively on a given connection.

If you do not have tools that can measure cell errors, you can still check the performance of an ATM network by analyzing the level of frame errors and upper-layer problems. With ATM, if a cell is lost or damaged, all cells comprising a complete LAN/WAN frame must be retransmitted. A good protocol analyzer can measure frame errors and upper-layer problems to help you characterize performance on an internetwork that includes ATM segments.

Analyzing Network Efficiency

The previous chapter talked about the importance of using maximum frame sizes to increase network efficiency. Bandwidth utilization is optimized for efficiency when applications and protocols are configured to send large amounts of data per frame, thus minimizing the number of frames and round-trip delays required for a transaction. The number of frames per transaction can also be minimized if the receiver is configured with a large receive window allowing it to accept multiple frames before it must send an acknowledgment. The goal is to maximize the number of data bytes compared to the number of bytes in headers and in acknowledgement packets sent by the other end of a conversation. Changing transmit and receive packet-buffer sizes at clients and servers can result in optimized frame sizes and receive windows.

To determine if your customer's goals for network efficiency are realistic, you should use a protocol analyzer to examine the current frame sizes on the network. Many protocol analyzers let you output a chart such as the one in Figure 3–6 that documents how many frames fall into standard categories for frame sizes.

Figure 3–6
*Bar graph of
frame sizes on
a Token Ring
network.*

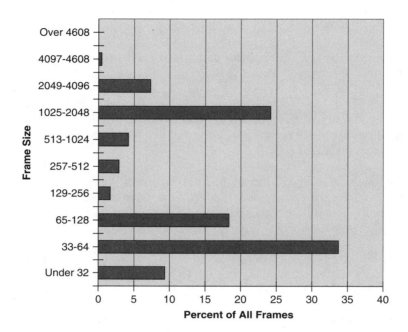

A simple way to determine an *average* frame size is to divide the total number of megabytes seen on a segment by the total number of frames in a specified timeframe. Unfortunately, this is a case where a simple statistical technique does not result in useful data. The average frame size is not a very meaningful piece of information. On most networks, there are many small frames, many large frames, but very few average-sized frames. Small frames consist of acknowledgments and control information. Data frames fall into the large frame-size categories (if the network has been optimized). A line graph of frame sizes, such as the graph in Figure 3–7, helps demonstrate this point.

Frame sizes typically fall into what is called a *bimodal distribution*, also known as a *camel-back distribution*. There is a "hump" on either side of the average but not many values near the average.

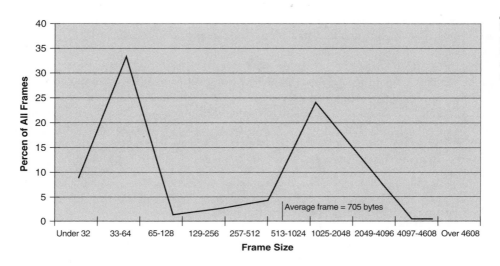

Figure 3–7
Line graph of frame sizes on a Token Ring network.

TIPS

Network performance data is /often bimodal, multi-modal, or skewed from the mean. (*Mean* is another word for average.) Frame size is usually bimodal. Response time from a server can also be bimodal, if sometimes the data is quickly available from random-access memory (RAM) cache and sometimes the data is retrieved from a slow mechanical disk drive.

When network-performance data is bimodal, multi-modal, or skewed from the mean, you should document a standard deviation with any measurements of the mean. *Standard deviation* is a measurement of how widely data disperses from the mean. If you do not have time to calculate standard deviation, a graph of the data can illustrate the deviation, as shown in Figure 3–7. Figure 3–7 shows that very few data points fall at the mean and many data points fall in two "humps" away from the mean.

Analyzing frame sizes can help you understand the health of a network, not just the efficiency. For example, an excessive number of Ethernet runt frames (less than 64 bytes) can indicate too many collisions. It is normal for collisions to increase with utilization that results from access contention. If collisions increase even when utilization does not increase or even when only a few nodes are transmitting, there could be a component problem, such as a bad repeater or network interface card.

On Token-Ring networks, frames that are less than 32 bytes are probably media-access control (MAC) frames. Network stations use MAC frames to identify themselves during the ring-poll process and to report changes and errors. Too many MAC frames can indicate a problem. (Knowing how many is "too many" requires a previous baseline.) If the number of MAC frames seems suspicious, view the contents of the frames on a protocol analyzer. Check for excessive error reports and beacon frames. *Beacon frames* indicate a serious problem on both Token Ring and FDDI networks.

Analyzing Delay and Response Time

To verify that performance of a new network design meets a customer's requirements, it is important to measure response time between significant network devices before and after a new network design is implemented. Response time can be measured many ways. Using a protocol analyzer, you can look at the amount of time between frames and get a rough estimate of response time at the data-link layer, transport layer, and application layer. (This is a rough estimate because packet arrival times on an analyzer can only approximate packet arrival times on end stations.)

A more common way to measure response time is to send ping packets and measure the round trip time (RTT) to send a request and receive a response. While measuring RTT, you can also measure an RTT variance. *Variance measurements* are important for applications that cannot tolerate much jitter, for example, voice and video applications. You can also document any loss of packets.

NOTES

In an IP environment, a *ping packet* is an Internet Control Message Protocol (ICMP) echo packet. To measure response time on AppleTalk networks, use the AppleTalk Echo Protocol (AEP). For Novell NetWare networks, you can use the Internetwork Packet Exchange (IPX) ping packet. When testing with an IPX ping, be careful to use the right ping version. There is a Cisco Systems, Inc., proprietary IPX ping to which only Cisco routers respond, and a different IPX ping packet specified by Novell. Novell servers and Cisco routers respond to the Novell IPX ping (as long as the Cisco routers are running a recent version of the Cisco Internetwork Operating System [IOS] software).

You can use Table 3–4 to document response time measurements. The table uses the term *node* to mean *router, server, client,* or *mainframe.*

Table 3-4   Response-Time Measurements

	Node A	Node B	Node C	Node D
Node A	X			
Node B		X		
Node C			X	
Node D				X

Depending on the amount of time you have for your analysis and depending on your customer's network design goals, you should also measure response time from a user's point of view. On a typical workstation, run some representative applications and measure how long it takes to get a response for typical operations, such as checking e-mail, sending a file to a server, downloading a Web page, updating a sales order, printing a report, and so on. Measure how much time a workstation takes to boot.

Sometimes applications or protocol implementations are notoriously slow or poorly written. Some peripherals are known to cause extra delay because of incompatibilities with operating systems or hardware. By joining mailing lists and newsgroups and reading information in journals and on the World Wide Web, you can learn about causes of response-time problems. Be sure to do some testing on your own also, though, since every environment is different.

In addition to testing user applications, test the response time for system protocols, for example Domain Name System (DNS) queries, Dynamic Host Configuration Protocol (DHCP) requests for an IP address, requests for a list of zones on an AppleTalk network, and so on. Chapter 4, "Characterizing Network Traffic," covers protocol issues in more detail.

Although your customer might not give you permission to simulate network problems, it also makes sense to do some testing of response times when the network is experiencing problems or change. For example, if possible, measure response times while routing protocols are converging after a link has gone down. Measure response time during convergence again, after your new design is implemented, to see if the results have improved. As covered in Chapter 11, "Testing Your Network Design," you can test network problems on a pilot implementation.

Checking the Status of Major Routers on the Internetwork

The final step in characterizing the existing internetwork is to check the behavior of the major routers on the internetwork. This includes routers that connect layers of a hierarchical topology, backbone routers, and routers that will have the most significant roles in your new network design.

Checking the behavior and health of a router includes determining how busy the router is (CPU utilization), how many packets the router has processed, how many packets the router has dropped, and the status of buffers and queues. Your method for assessing the health of a router depends on the router vendor and architecture. In the case of Cisco routers, you can use the following Cisco IOS commands:

- **show interfaces.** Displays statistics for network interface cards, including the input and output rate of packets, a count of packets dropped from input and output queues, the size and usage of queues, a count of packets ignored due to lack of I/O buffer space on a card, and how often interfaces have restarted.

- **show processes.** Displays CPU utilization for the last five seconds, one minute, and five minutes, and the percentage of CPU used by various processes, including routing protocols, buffer management, and user-interface processes.

- **show buffers.** Displays information on buffer sizes, buffer creation and deletion, buffer usage, and a count of successful and unsuccessful attempts to get buffers when needed.

You can also use the Simple Network Management Protocol (SNMP) to check the health of a router. Following is a list of useful router performance variables in Cisco's private extension to the Internet standard Management Information Base II (MIB II):

- **BusyPer.** CPU busy percentage in the last five-second period.

- **AvgBusy1.** One-minute exponentially-decayed moving average of the CPU busy percentage.

- **AvgBusy5.** Five-minute exponentially-decayed moving average of the CPU busy percentage.

- **LocIfInputQueueDrops.** The number of packets dropped because the input queue was full.

- **LocIfOutputQueueDrops.** The number of packets dropped because the output queue was full.

- **LocIfInIgnored.** The number of input packets ignored by the interface.

- **BufferElMiss.** The number of buffer-element misses. (You can also check misses for small, medium, big, large, and huge buffer pools.)

- **BufferFail.** The number of buffer allocation failures.

To analyze router health, you need to check the variables listed above on a regular basis over a few days. To get a precise and complete portrayal of router performance, a long-term study (lasting a few weeks or months) should be done, using some of the tools mentioned in the next section and in Chapter 8, "Developing Network Security and Network Management Strategies." (As a network designer it is probably not your job to do the long-term study. You should encourage your customer to assign network engineers or consultants to the job of proactively studying long-term router performance.)

TOOLS FOR CHARACTERIZING THE EXISTING INTERNETWORK

This chapter has already mentioned some tools for characterizing an existing network, including network-discovery tools, protocol analyzers, SNMP tools, and Cisco IOS commands. To help you select tools, this section provides more information on tools.

Protocol Analyzers

A *protocol analyzer* is a fault-and-performance-management tool that captures network traffic, decodes the protocols in the captured packets, and provides statistics to characterize load, errors, and response time. Some analyzers include an expert system that automatically identifies network problems.

One of the best known protocol analyzers is the Sniffer Network Analyzer from Network Associates, Inc. (Network Associates purchased Network General, the original manufacturer of the Sniffer Network Analyzer, in 1997). The Sniffer network analyzer decodes hundreds of protocols and applies expert analysis to diagnose problems and recommend corrective action. Because the Sniffer network analyzer has been on the market longer than most other analyzers, it has the most sophisticated protocol decoding and expert system.

Another noteworthy protocol analyzer is EtherPeek from the AG Group. The AG Group has versions of EtherPeek for the Macintosh operating system, Windows 95, and Windows NT. Because the AG Group developed EtherPeek for the Macintosh first, it is very easy to use and install. EtherPeek decodes all major protocols and includes a nice feature for displaying in real time a tree structure of protocols within protocols. EtherPeek includes plug-in modules for expert analysis.

Remote Monitoring Tools

The Internet Engineering Task Force (IETF) developed the Remote Monitoring (RMON) MIB in the early 1990s to address shortcomings in the standard SNMP MIBs for gathering statistics on data-link and physical-layer parameters. The IETF developed the RMON MIB to enable network managers to collect traffic statistics, analyze Ethernet problems, plan network upgrades, and tune network performance. In 1994, Token-Ring statistics were added. Other types of statistics, for example, application-layer and WAN statistics, are under development.

RMON facilitates gathering statistics on the following data-link-layer performance factors:

- CRC errors

- Ethernet collisions

- Token-Ring soft errors

- Frame sizes

- The number of packets in and out of a device

- The rate of broadcast packets

The RMON MIB alarm group lets a network manager set thresholds for network parameters and automatically deliver alerts to management consoles. RMON also supports capturing packets and sending the captured packets to a network-management station for protocol decoding. RMON is discussed in more detail in Chapter 8, "Developing Network Security and Network Management Strategies."

Cisco Tools for Characterizing an Existing Internetwork

Cisco has a complete range of tools for characterizing an existing internetwork, ranging from the Cisco Discovery Protocol to sophisticated Netsys tools.

Cisco Discovery Protocol

The Cisco Discovery Protocol (CDP) specifies a method for Cisco routers and switches to send configuration information to each other on a regular basis. Analyzing CDP data can help you characterize the topology of an existing network (although you should use more sophisticated tools for large networks). If you enable CDP on a router and neighboring routers, you can use the show cdp neighbors detail command to display the following information about neighboring routers:

- Which protocols are enabled

- Network addresses for enabled protocols

- The number and types of interfaces

- The type of platform and its capabilities

- The version of Cisco IOS software

Enterprise Accounting for NetFlow

Cisco Enterprise Accounting for NetFlow can help you understand bandwidth usage and allocation, quality of service (QoS) levels, router usage, and router port usage. NetFlow accounting recognizes network flows and characterizes network and router usage by user (IP address), application, and department.

Netsys Service-Level Management Suite

The Cisco Netsys Service-Level Management Suite enables defining, monitoring, and assessing network connectivity, security, and performance. The Cisco Netsys Performance Service Manager is particularly useful for characterizing an existing network as part of a network design proposal.

CiscoWorks

CiscoWorks is a series of SNMP-based internetwork management software applications to allow device monitoring, configuration maintenance, and troubleshooting of Cisco devices. Health Monitor is a CiscoWorks application that lets you view information about the status of a device, including buffer usage, CPU load, available memory, and protocols and interfaces being used. Threshold Manager allows you to set RMON alarm thresholds and retrieve RMON event information. You can set thresholds for network devices using Cisco-provided default or customized policies.

CiscoWorks Blue Internetwork Performance Monitor (IPM) provides mechanisms to isolate performance problems, diagnose latency, perform trend analysis, and determine the possible paths between two devices and display the performance characteristics of each path. Performance measurement capability is supported for both IP and Systems Network Architecture (SNA) session paths.

Other Tools for Characterizing an Existing Internetwork

You can search the Web to learn more about the following tools that have become industry standards for monitoring network and router performance.

The Proactive Management family of products from Network Associates consists of the RouterPM tool for monitoring Cisco routers, RouterPM Blue for SNA networks, SwitchPM for Cisco switches, and FrameRelayPM for multi-vendor frame relay devices. The Proactive Management tools let you use a Web browser to view statistics and reports about router and network usage, and identify and resolve enterprise-wide performance and capacity-planning problems.

In April 1996, the Internet community awarded Merit Network, Inc., a grant to develop a freeware, turn-key network statistics package for managers of Internet sites. Merit Network, Inc., gained a reputation for expertise in network management because of its successful management of the NSFNET backbone of the Internet. The Network Statistics Collection and Reporting Facility (NetSCARF) team at Merit developed the *Scion software package*, which collects network-management information from network routers and makes the information available in HTML (Web) format.

The Multi Router Traffic Grapher (MRTG) is a tool for monitoring network traffic load and other performance characteristics of a routed network. MRTG generates HTML pages containing GIF images that provide a live (real-time) graphical representation of network traffic. MRTG is based on the Perl scripting language and C programming language and runs on the UNIX and Windows NT operating systems. Many sites around the world use MRTG to proactively manage network traffic, monitor QoS commitments, and bill customers based on network usage. MRTG is available under a GNU public license. The only thing that author Tobias Oetiker asks users to do is send him a picture postcard. (The author lives in Zurich, Switzerland. A search on the Web can find his most recent address.)

The Cooperative Association for Internet Data Analysis (CAIDA) maintains a taxonomy of network measurement tools. The group's focus is research and network design tools, rather than operational network management, so the taxonomy is quite relevant to the discussions in this chapter. For more information on the CAIDA taxonomy, go to the Web site www.caida.org/Tools/taxonomy.html.

Also, several mailing lists discuss traffic measurement and analysis tools, including the Internet Statistics Measurement and Analysis (ISMA) mailing list and the IETF Internet Protocol Performance Metrics (IPPM) working group mailing list. To subscribe to the ISMA mailing list, send mail to isma-request@nlanr.net. For more information on the IPPM working group, see the group's Web site at: io.advanced.org/IPPM/.

NETWORK HEALTH CHECKLIST

You can use the following Network Health Checklist to assist you in verifying the health of an existing internetwork. The network health checklist is generic in nature and documents a best-case scenario. The thresholds might not apply to all networks.

☐ The network topology and physical infrastructure are well documented.

☐ Network addresses and names are assigned in a structured manner and are well documented.

☐ Network wiring is installed in a structured manner and is well labeled.

☐ Network wiring between telecommunications closets and end stations is generally no more than 100 meters.

☐ Network availability meets current customer goals.

☐ Network security meets current customer goals.

□ No shared Ethernet segments are becoming saturated. (50 percent average network utilization in a 10-minute window.)

□ No shared Token Ring segments are becoming saturated. (70 percent average network utilization in a 10-minute window.)

□ No shared FDDI segments are becoming saturated. (70 percent average network utilization in a 10-minute window.)

□ No WAN links are becoming saturated. (70 percent average network utilization in a 10-minute window.)

□ No segments have more than one CRC error per million bytes of data.

□ On Ethernet segments, less than 0.1 percent of packets are collisions. There are no late collisions.

□ On Token Ring segments, less than 0.1 percent of packets are soft errors not related to ring insertion. There are no beacon frames.

□ Broadcast traffic is less than 20 percent of all traffic on each network segment. (Some networks are more sensitive to broadcast traffic and should use a 10 percent threshold.)

□ Wherever possible, frame sizes have been optimized to be as large as possible for the data-link layer in use.

□ No routers are overutilized. (Five-minute CPU utilization is under 75 percent.)

□ On an average, routers are not dropping more than 1 percent of packets. (For networks that are intentionally oversubscribed to keep costs low, a higher threshold can be used.)

□ The response time between clients and hosts is generally less than 100 milliseconds (1/10 of a second).

SUMMARY

This chapter covered techniques and tools for characterizing a network before designing enhancements to the network. Characterizing an existing network is an important step in top-down network design because it helps you verify that a customer's technical-design goals are realistic. It also helps you understand the current topology and locate existing network segments and equipment, which will be useful information when the time comes to install new equipment. As part of the task of characterizing the existing network, you should develop a baseline of current performance. Baseline performance measurements can be compared to new measurements once your design is implemented to demonstrate to your customer that your new design (hopefully) improves performance.

CHAPTER 4

Characterizing Network Traffic

This chapter describes techniques for characterizing traffic flow, traffic volume, and protocol behavior. The techniques include recognizing traffic sources and data stores, documenting application and protocol usage, and evaluating network traffic caused by common protocols. Upon completion of this chapter, you will be able to analyze network traffic patterns to help you select appropriate logical and physical network design solutions to meet a customer's goals.

The previous chapter talked about characterizing the existing network. Because analyzing the existing situation is an important step in a systems analysis approach to design, this chapter discusses characterizing traffic flow on the existing network. The chapter also covers new network design requirements, building on the first two chapters that covered business and technical design goals. This chapter refocuses on design requirements and describes requirements in terms of traffic flow, traffic load, protocol behavior, and quality of service (QoS) requirements.

CHARACTERIZING TRAFFIC FLOW

Characterizing traffic flow involves identifying sources and destinations of network traffic and analyzing the direction and symmetry of data traveling between sources and destinations. In some applications, the flow is bidirectional and symmetric. (Both ends of the flow send traffic at about the same rate.) In other applications, the flow is bidirectional and asymmetric. Client stations send small queries and servers send large streams of data. In a broadcast application, the flow is unidirectional and asymmetric.

This section talks about characterizing the direction and symmetry of traffic flow on an existing network and analyzing flow for new network applications.

Identifying Major Traffic Sources and Stores

To understand network traffic flow, you should first identify user communities and data stores for existing and new applications.

NOTES

Chapter 3, "Characterizing the Existing Network," talked about locating major hosts, interconnect devices, and network segments on a customer's network. The tasks discussed in Chapter 3 facilitate the tasks discussed in this chapter of identifying major user communities and data stores.

A *user community* is a set of workers who use a particular application or set of applications. A user community can be a corporate department or set of departments. However, in many environments, application usage crosses departmental boundaries. As more corporations use matrix management and form virtual teams to complete ad-hoc projects, it becomes more necessary to characterize user communities by application and protocol usage rather than by departmental boundary.

To document user communities, ask your customer to help you fill out the User Communities chart shown in Table 4–1. For the location column in Table 4–1, use location names that you already documented on a network map. For applications, use application names that you already documented in the Network Applications charts in Chapters 1 and 2. An example of a filled-in chart is included in the case study in Chapter 9, "Selecting Technologies and Devices for Campus Networks."

Table 4–1   User Communities

User Community Name	Size of Community (Number of Users)	Location(s) of Community	Application(s) Used by Community

In addition to documenting user communities, characterizing traffic flow also requires that you document major data stores. A *data store* (sometimes called a *data sink*) is an area in a network where application-layer data resides. A data store can be a server, a server farm, a mainframe, a tape backup unit, a digital video library, or any device or component of an internetwork where large quantities of data are stored. To help you document major data stores, ask your customer to help you fill out Table 4–2. For the location, application, and user-community columns, use names that you already documented on a network map and other charts.

Table 4–2   Data Stores

Data Store	Location	Application(s)	Used by User Community (or Communities)

Documenting Traffic Flow on the Existing Network

Documenting traffic flow involves identifying and characterizing individual traffic flows between traffic sources and stores. Traffic flows have recently become a hot topic for discussion in the Internet community. A lot of progress is being made on defining flows, measuring flow behavior, and allowing an end station to specify performance requirements for flows.

To understand traffic flow behavior better, you can read Request for Comments (RFC) 2063, "Traffic Flow Measurement: Architecture." RFC 2063 describes an architecture for the measurement and reporting of network traffic flows, and discusses how the architecture relates to an overall traffic flow architecture for intranets and the Internet.

Measuring traffic flow behavior can help a network designer determine which routers should be peers in routing protocols that use a peering system, such as the Border Gateway Protocol (BGP). Measuring traffic flow behavior can also help network designers do the following:

- Characterize the behavior of existing networks

- Plan for network development and expansion

- Quantify network performance

- Verify the quality of network service

- Ascribe network usage to users and applications

An *individual network traffic flow* can be defined as protocol and application information transmitted between communicating entities during a single session. A flow has attributes such as direction, symmetry, routing path and routing options, number of packets, number of bytes, and addresses for each end of the flow. A communicating entity can be an end system (host), a network, or an autonomous system.

The simplest method for characterizing the size of a flow is to measure the number of Mbytes per second between communicating entities. To characterize the size of a flow, use a protocol analyzer or network management system to record load between important sources and destinations and then fill out charts such as the one shown in Table 4–3. The objective is to document the Mbytes per second between pairs of autonomous systems, networks, hosts, and applications. To fill out the charts, place the monitoring device in the core of the network and let it collect data for one or two days. To fill out the Path column, you can turn on the record-route option in an IP network. In non-IP networks you can estimate the path by looking at routing tables and analyzing network traffic on multiple segments.

Table 4–3   Network Traffic Flow on the Existing Network

	Destination 1		Destination 2		Destination 3		Destination *n*	
	Mbytes per Second	Path	Mbytes per Second	Path	Mbytes per Second	Path	Mbytes per Second	Path
Source 1								
Source 2								
Source 3								
Source *n*								

Characterizing Types of Traffic Flow for New Network Applications

As mentioned before, a network flow can be characterized by its direction and symmetry. Direction specifies whether data travels in both directions or in just one direction. Direction also specifies the path that a flow takes as it travels from source to destination through an internetwork. Symmetry describes whether the flow tends to have higher performance or QoS requirements in one direction than the other direction. Many network applications have different requirements in each direction. Some new transmission technologies, such as Asymmetric Digital Subscriber Line (ADSL), take advantage of asymmetric requirements.

A good technique for characterizing network traffic flow is to classify applications as supporting one of a few well-known flow types:

- Terminal/host traffic flow

- Client/server traffic flow

- Peer-to-peer traffic flow

- Server/server traffic flow

- Distributed computing traffic flow

In his book, *Practical Computer Network Analysis and Design*, James D. McCabe does an excellent job of characterizing and distinguishing flow models. The following description of flow types is partially based on McCabe's work.

Terminal/Host Traffic Flow

Terminal/host traffic is usually asymmetric. The terminal sends a few characters and the host sends many characters. Telnet is an example of an application that generates terminal/host traffic. The default behavior for Telnet is that the terminal sends in a single packet each character a user types. The host returns multiple characters, depending on what the user typed. As an illustration, consider the beginning of a Telnet session that starts with the user typing a user name. Once the host receives each packet for the characters in the name, the host sends back a message (such as Password required) in one packet.

NOTES

Default Telnet behavior can be changed so that instead of sending one character at a time, the terminal sends characters after a timeout or after the user types a carriage return. This behavior uses network bandwidth more efficiently but can cause problems for some applications. For example, the *vi editor* on UNIX systems must see each character immediately to recognize whether the user has pressed a special character for moving up a line, down a line, to the end of a line, and so on.

With some full-screen terminal applications, such as some IBM 3270-based terminal applications, the terminal side sends characters typed by the user and the host side returns data to repaint the screen. The amount of data transferred from the host to the terminal equals the size of the screen plus commands and attribute bytes. *Attribute bytes* specify the color and highlighting of characters on the screen. The screen is usually 80 characters wide by 24 lines long, which equals 1,920 characters. The full transfer is a few thousand bytes once attribute bytes and commands are added. More modern terminal applications just send changes to the user's screen, thus reducing network traffic.

Client/Server Traffic Flow

Client/server traffic is the best known and most widely used flow type. Examples of client/server implementations include NetWare, AppleShare, Banyan, Network File System (NFS), and Windows NT. With client/server traffic, the flow is usually bidirectional and asymmetric. Requests from the client are usually less than 64 bytes, except when writing data to the server, in which case they are larger. Responses from the server range from 64 bytes to 1,500 bytes or more, depending on the maximum frame size allowed for the data-link layer in use.

In a TCP/IP environment, many applications are implemented in a client/server fashion, although the applications were invented before the client/server model was invented. For example, the File Transfer Protocol (FTP) has a client and server side. FTP clients use FTP applications to talk to FTP servers.

X Windows is an example of a server (the screen manager) that actually runs on the user's machine. This can lead to a great deal of traffic in both directions, such as when the user enables a blinking cursor or ticking clock that needs continual updating across the network, even when the user isn't present.

These days, Hypertext Transfer Protocol (HTTP) is probably the most widely used client/server protocol. Clients use a Web browser application, such as Netscape, to talk to Web servers. The flow is bidirectional and asymmetric. Each session often lasts just a few seconds because users tend to jump from one Web site to another.

The flow for HTTP traffic is not always between the Web browser and the Web server because of caching. When users access data that has been cached to their own systems, there is no network traffic. Another possibility is that a network administrator has set up a cache engine. A *cache engine* is software or hardware that saves WAN bandwidth by making recently-accessed Web pages available locally.

Two special cases of the client/server architecture are diskless stations and network computers. *Diskless stations* were more popular in the early 1990s when hard drives were very expensive. A diskless station uses a protocol such as BOOTP or Reverse Address Resolution Protocol (RARP) to get its IP address from a server. Once the station has an address, the station continues to access the server to store and retrieve data. The amount of traffic in a network with many diskless stations is generally more than a basic client/server environment.

Although diskless stations are less common than they once were, network computers have the potential to become quite common in business and educational environments. A *network computer* is similar to a diskless station. A network computer gets its IP address from a server, usually using the Dynamic Host Configuration Protocol (DHCP), and relies on the server to run applications and store data. The user at the network computer simply runs a Java-enabled Web browser. No other applications or data are stored on the network computer. This keeps the price of the network computer down to a few hundred dollars and increases desktop manageability and control.

The downside of network computing is that the amount of data flowing from the server to the network computers can be substantial, especially when many computers start up at the same time every day. Networks that include network computers should be carefully designed with sufficient capacity and an appropriate topology. Switched networking (rather than shared media) is recommended, and to avoid problems caused by too much broadcast traffic, each switched network should be limited to a few hundred network computers and their server(s). The switched networks can be connected via routers for communications between departments and accessing outside networks such as the Internet.

Peer-to-Peer Traffic Flow

With peer-to-peer traffic, the flow is usually bidirectional and symmetric. Communicating entities transmit approximately equal amounts of protocol and application information. There is no hierarchy. Each device is considered as important as each other device, and no device stores substantially more data than any other device. In small LAN environments, network administrators often set up PCs in a peer-to-peer configuration so that everyone can access each other's data and printers. There is no central file or print server. Another example of a peer-to-peer environment is a set of multi-user UNIX hosts where users set up FTP, Telnet, HTTP, and NFS sessions between hosts. Each host acts as both a client and server. There are many flows in both directions.

One other example of a peer-to-peer application is a meeting between business people at remote sites using videoconferencing equipment. In a meeting, every attendee can communicate as much data as needed at any time. All sites have the same QoS requirements. A meeting is different than a situation where videoconferencing is used to disseminate information. With information dissemination, such as a training class or a speech by a corporate president to employees, most of the data flows from the central site. A few questions are permitted from the remote sites. Information dissemination is usually implemented using a client/server model.

Server/Server Traffic Flow

Server/server traffic includes transmissions between servers and transmissions between servers and management applications. Servers talk to other servers to implement directory services, to cache heavily-used data, to mirror data for load balancing and redundancy, to back up data, and to broadcast service availability. Servers talk to management applications for some of the same reasons, but also to enforce security policies and to update network management data.

With server/server network traffic, the flow is generally bidirectional. The symmetry of the flow depends on the application. With most server/server applications, the flow is symmetrical, but in some cases there is a hierarchy of servers, with some servers sending and storing more data than others.

Distributed Computing Traffic Flow

Distributed computing refers to applications that require multiple computing nodes working together to complete a job. Some complex modeling and rendering tasks cannot be accomplished in a reasonable timeframe unless multiple computers process data and run algorithms simultaneously.

As an example, Digital Domain, a production studio in Venice, California, generated the visual effects for the movie "Titanic" using 160 433-MHz DEC Alpha systems in a distributed-computing environment. The systems were connected via 100-Mbps Ethernet and used NFS to share files. Most of the machines used the Linux operating system. Some of the machines ran Windows NT. The Alpha systems were used to add scene elements such as the ocean, people, birds, and smoke to the model of the Titanic to make the ship appear docked, sailing, or sunk in the ocean.

Distributed computing is also used in the semiconductor industry to serve the extreme computing needs of microchip design and verification, and in the defense industry to provide engineering simulations.

With distributed computing, data travels between a task manager and computing nodes and between computing nodes. In his book, *Practical Computer Network Analysis and Design*, McCabe distinguishes between tightly-coupled and loosely-coupled computing nodes. Nodes that are tightly coupled transfer information to each other frequently. Nodes that are loosely coupled transfer little or no information.

With some distributed computing applications, the task manager tells the computing nodes what to do on an infrequent basis, resulting in little traffic flow. With other applications, there is frequent communication between the task manager and the computing nodes. In some cases, the task manager allocates tasks based on resource availability, which makes predicting flow somewhat difficult.

Characterizing traffic flow for distributed-computing applications might require you to study the traffic with a protocol analyzer or model potential traffic with a network simulator.

Documenting Traffic Flow for Network Applications

To document traffic flow for new (and existing) network applications, characterize the flow type for each application and list the user communities and data stores that are associated with applications. You can use Table 4–4 to enhance the Network Applications charts already discussed in Chapters 1 and 2. When filling out Table 4–4, use the same application names you used in the other charts. (The protocols, approximate bandwidth requirement, and QoS requirements columns are described later in this chapter.)

Table 4–4   Network Applications Traffic Characteristics

Name of Application	Type of Traffic Flow	Protocol(s) Used by Application	User Communities That Use the Application	Data Stores (Servers, Hosts, and so on)	Approximate Bandwidth Requirement for the Application	QoS Requirements

When identifying the type of traffic flow for an application, select one of the well-known types:

- Terminal/host

- Client/server

- Peer-to-peer

- Server/server

- Distributed computing

If necessary, add a comment to qualify the type of flow. For example, if the type is terminal/host and full screen, make sure to say this, because in a full screen application, the host sends more data than in a so-called dumb terminal application. If the flow type is distributed computing, then add some text to specify whether the computing nodes are tightly or loosely coupled.

CHARACTERIZING TRAFFIC LOAD

To select appropriate topologies and technologies to meet a customer's goals, it is important to characterize traffic load with traffic flow. Characterizing traffic load can help you design networks with sufficient capacity for local usage and internetwork flows.

Because of the many factors involved in characterizing network traffic, traffic load estimates are unlikely to be precise. The goal is simply to avoid a design that has any critical bottlenecks. To avoid bottlenecks, you should research application usage patterns, idle times between packets and sessions, frame sizes, and other traffic behavioral patterns for application and system protocols.

Calculating Theoretical Traffic Load

As described in Chapter 2, *traffic load* (sometimes called *offered load*) is the sum of all the data network nodes have ready to send at a particular time. A general goal for most network designs is that the network capacity should be more than adequate to handle the traffic load. The challenge is to determine if the capacity proposed for a new network design is sufficient to handle the potential load.

In his book, *Local and Metropolitan Area Networks*, William Stallings provides some back-of-the-envelope computations for calculating traffic load. Stallings points out that you can make an elementary calculation based simply on the number of stations transmitting, how quickly each station generates messages, and the size of messages. For example, for a network with a proposed capacity of 1 Mbps, if 1,000 stations send 1,000-bit frames every second, then the offered load equals the capacity. Although Stallings was referring to the capacity of a shared LAN, *capacity* could refer to the capacity of a WAN link, an entire internetwork or parts of an internetwork, or the backplane of a switch or router.

In general, to calculate whether capacity is sufficient, only a few parameters are necessary:

- The number of stations

- The average time that a station is idle between sending frames

- The time required to transmit a message once medium access is gained

By studying idle times and frame sizes with a protocol analyzer, and estimating the number of stations, you can determine if the proposed capacity is sufficient.

If you research traffic flow types, as discussed earlier in this chapter, you can develop more precise estimates of load. Instead of assuming that all stations have similar load-generating qualities, you can assume that stations using a particular application have similar load-generating qualities. Assumptions can be made about frame size and idle time for an application once you have classified the type of flow and identified the protocols (discussed later in this chapter) used by the application.

For a client/server application, idle time for the server depends on the number of clients using the server, and the architecture and performance characteristics of the server (disk access speed, RAM access speed, caching mechanisms, and so on). By studying network traffic from servers with a protocol analyzer, you can estimate an average idle time.

Idle time on the client side depends partly on user action, which means it is impossible to precisely predict idle time. However you can make estimates of idle time by studying traffic with a protocol analyzer and using scripts to simulate worst-case user actions, or by using a network modeling tool. A good network modeling tool knows what assumptions to make about idle time, MAC-layer delays, the distribution of packet arrival at servers and internetworking devices, and queuing and buffering behavior at internetworking devices.

Once you have identified the approximate traffic load for an application flow, you can estimate total load for an application by multiplying the load for the flow by the number of devices that use the application. The research you do on the size of user communities and the number of data stores (servers) can help you calculate an approximate aggregated bandwidth requirement for each application and fill in the "Approximate Bandwidth Requirement for the Application" column in Table 4-4.

Documenting the location of user communities and data stores, which you did in Table 4-1 and 4-2, can help you understand the amount of traffic that will flow from one segment to another. This can aid in the selection of backbone technologies and internetworking devices.

When estimating traffic load, in addition to investigating idle times between packets, frames sizes, and flow behavior, you should also investigate application usage patterns and QoS requirements. Some applications are used infrequently, but require a large amount of bandwidth when they are used. For example, perhaps workers normally access an Ethernet LAN to read e-mail, store small files on servers, and print small documents on network printers. But once every three months, they use real-time multimedia software on their PCs to watch the corporate president's speech on quarterly sales figures. This means that once a quarter traffic characteristics and QoS requirements are very different than normal.

In general, to accurately characterize traffic load, you need to understand application usage patterns and QoS requirements in addition to idle times and frame sizes. Some applications expect the network to simply make a best effort to meet load (bandwidth) requirements. Other applications, such as video applications, have inflexible requirements for a constant amount of bandwidth.

The next section covers characterizing usage patterns in more detail. The section, "Characterizing Quality of Service Requirements," later in this chapter discusses characterizing QoS requirements.

Documenting Application Usage Patterns

The first step in documenting application usage patterns is to identify user communities, the number of users in the communities, and the applications the users employ. This step, which was already covered earlier in this chapter, can help you identify the total number of users for each application.

In addition to identifying the total number of users for each application, you should also document the following information:

- The frequency of application sessions (number of sessions per day, week, month or whatever time period is appropriate)

- The length of an average application session

- The number of *simultaneous* users of an application

Armed with information on the frequency and length of sessions, and the number of simultaneous sessions, you can more accurately predict the aggregate bandwidth requirement for all users of an application. If it is not practical to research these details, then you can make some assumptions:

- You can assume that the number of users of an application equals the number of simultaneous users.

- You can assume that all applications are used all the time so that your bandwidth calculation is a worst-case (peak) estimate.

- You can assume that each user opens just one session and that a session lasts all day until the user shuts down the application at the end of the day.

Refining Estimates of Traffic Load Caused by Applications

To refine your estimate of application bandwidth requirements, you need to research the size of data objects sent by applications, the overhead caused by protocol layers, and any additional load caused by application initialization. (Some applications send much more traffic during initialization than during steady-state operation.)

Because applications and users vary widely in behavior, it is hard to accurately estimate the average size of data objects that users transfer to each other and to servers. (The true engineering answer to most questions related to network traffic is "it depends.") Table 4–5 provides some estimates for object sizes that you can use when making back-of-the-envelope calculations of application traffic load, but remember that the table does not take the place of a thorough analysis of actual application behavior.

Table 4–5 is partially based on a graph in the book *ATM: Theory and Applications*, by David E. McDysan and Darren L. Spohn.

Table 4–5   Approximate Size of Objects that Applications Transfer Across Networks

Type of Object	Size in Kbytes
Terminal screen	4
E-mail message	10
Web page (including simple GIF and JPEG graphics)	50
Spreadsheet	100
Word-processing document	200
Graphical computer screen	500
Presentation document	2,000
High-resolution (print quality) image	50,000
Multimedia object	100,000
Database (backup)	1,000,000

Estimating Traffic Overhead for Various Protocols

The previous section talked about characterizing application traffic load by looking at the size of data objects that applications transfer across networks. To completely characterize application behavior, you should investigate which protocols an application uses. Once you know the protocols, you can calculate traffic load more precisely by adding the size of protocol headers to the size of data objects. Table 4–6 shows some typical protocol header sizes.

Table 4–6   Traffic Overhead for Various Protocols

Protocol	Overhead Details	Total Bytes
Ethernet Version II	Preamble = 8 bytes, header = 14 bytes, CRC = 4 bytes, inter-frame gap (IFG) = 12 bytes	38
802.3 with 802.2	Preamble = 8 bytes, header = 14 bytes, LLC = 3 or 4 bytes, SNAP (if present) = 5 bytes, CRC = 4 bytes, IFG = 12 bytes	46
802.5 with 802.2	Starting delimiter = 1 byte, header = 14 bytes, LLC = 3 or 4 bytes, SNAP (if present) = 5 bytes, CRC = 4 bytes, ending delimiter = 1 byte, frame status = 1 byte	29
FDDI with 802.2	Preamble = 8 bytes, starting delimiter = 1 byte, header = 13 bytes, LLC = 3 or 4 bytes, SNAP (if present) = 5 bytes, CRC = 4 bytes, ending delimiter and frame status = about 2 bytes	36
HDLC	Flags = 2 bytes, addresses = 2 bytes, control = 1 or 2 bytes, CRC = 4 bytes	10
IP	Header size with no options	20
TCP	Header size with no options	20
IPX	Header size	30
DDP	Phase 2 long ("extended") header size	13

Estimating Traffic Load Caused by Workstation and Session Initialization

Depending on the applications and protocols that a workstation uses, workstation initialization can cause a significant load on networks due to the number of packets and, in some cases, the number of broadcast packets.

Appendix A shows network traffic caused by workstations booting on a network and setting up an initial network session. The tables in Appendix A show typical workstation behavior for the following protocols:

- Novell NetWare

- AppleTalk

- TCP/IP

- TCP/IP with DHCP

- NetBIOS (NetBEUI)

- NetBIOS with a Windows Internet Name Service (WINS) server

- SNA

Estimating Traffic Load Caused by Routing Protocols

At this point in the network design process you might not have selected routing protocols for the new network design, but you should have identified routing protocols running on the existing network. To help you characterize network traffic caused by routing protocols, Table 4–7 shows the amount of bandwidth used by typical distance-vector routing protocols. The table includes Novell's Service Advertising Protocol (SAP), although technically SAP is not a routing protocol.

Estimating traffic load caused by routing protocols is especially important in a topology that includes many networks on one side of a slow WAN link. A router sending a large distance-vector routing table every minute, and possibly sending Novell services as well, can use a significant percentage of WAN bandwidth. Because routing protocols limit the number of routes per packet, on large networks, a router sends multiple packets to send the whole table.

Table 4–7   Bandwidth Used by Routing Protocols

Routing Protocol	Default Update Timer (Seconds)	Route Entry Size (Bytes)	Routes Per Packet	Network and Update Overhead (Bytes)	Size of Full Packet
IP RIP	30	20	25	32	532
IP IGRP	90	14	104	32	1,488
AppleTalk RTMP	10	6	97	17	599
IPX SAP	60	64	7 services	32	480
IPX RIP	60	8	50	32	432
DECnet IV	40	4	368	18	1,490
VINES VRTP	90	8	104	30	862
XNS	30	20	25	40	540

CHARACTERIZING TRAFFIC BEHAVIOR

To select appropriate network design solutions, you need to understand protocol and application behavior in addition to traffic flows and load. For example, to select appropriate LAN topologies, you need to investigate the level of broadcast traffic on the LANs. To provision adequate capacity for LANs and WANs, you need to check for extra bandwidth utilization caused by protocol inefficiencies and non-optimal frame sizes or retransmission timers.

Broadcast/Multicast Behavior

A *broadcast frame* is a frame that goes to all network stations on a LAN. At the data-link layer, the destination address of a broadcast frame is FF:FF:FF:FF:FF:FF (all ones in binary). A *multicast frame* is a frame that goes to a subset of stations. For example, a frame destined to 01:00:0C:CC:CC:CC goes to all Cisco routers that are running the Cisco Discovery Protocol (CDP) on a LAN.

Layer-2 internetworking devices, such as switches and bridges, forward broadcast and multicast frames out all ports. The forwarding of broadcast and multicast frames can be a scalability problem for large flat (switched or bridged) networks. A router does not forward broadcasts or multicasts. All devices on one side of a router are considered part of a single *broadcast domain*.

In addition to including routers in a network design to decrease broadcast forwarding, you can also limit the size of a broadcast domain by implementing virtual LANs (VLANs). VLAN technology, which Chapter 5 discusses in more detail, allows a network administrator to subdivide users into subnets by associating switch ports with one or more VLANs. Although a VLAN can span many switches, broadcast traffic within a VLAN is not transmitted outside the VLAN.

Too many broadcast frames can overwhelm end stations, switches, and routers. It is important that you research the level of broadcast traffic in your proposed design and limit the number of stations in a single broadcast domain. The term *broadcast radiation* is often used to describe the effect of broadcasts spreading from the sender to all other devices in a broadcast domain. Broadcast radiation can degrade performance at network stations.

The network interface card (NIC) in a network station passes broadcasts and relevant multicasts to the CPU of the station. Some NICs pass all multicasts to the CPU, even when the multicasts are not relevant, because the NICs do not have driver software that is more selective. Intelligent driver software can tell a NIC which multicasts to pass to the CPU. Unfortunately, not all drivers have this intelligence.

The CPUs on network stations become overwhelmed when processing high levels of broadcasts and multicasts. Studies have shown that CPU performance is measurably affected by as few as 100 broadcasts and multicasts per second on a Pentium PC or SunSparc5 workstation. Macintosh CPUs are affected by as few as 15 broadcasts per second, although Macintoshes are smarter than PCs in their recognition of which multicasts are relevant. If more than 20 percent of the network traffic is broadcasts or multicasts, than the network needs to be segmented using routers or VLANs.

Another possible cause of heavy broadcast traffic is intermittent broadcast storms caused by misconfigured or misbehaving network stations. For example, a misconfigured subnet mask can cause a station to send address resolution protocol (ARP) frames unnecessarily because the station does not correctly distinguish between station and broadcast addresses, causing it to send ARPs for broadcast addresses.

In general, however, broadcast traffic is necessary and unavoidable. Routing and bridging protocols use broadcasts and multicasts to share information about the internetwork topology. Servers send broadcasts and multicasts to advertise their services. Desktop protocols such as AppleTalk, NetWare, NetBIOS, and TCP/IP require broadcast and multicast frames to find services and check for uniqueness of addresses and names.

When designing a network topology, which Chapter 5 covers in more detail, be sure to take into consideration the broadcast behavior of desktop protocols. Table 4–8 shows recommendations for limiting the number of stations in a single broadcast domain based on the desktop protocol(s) in use.

Table 4–8   The Maximum Size of a Broadcast Domain

Protocol	Maximum Number of Workstations
IP	500*
NetWare	300
AppleTalk	200
NetBIOS	200
Mixed	200

* If the IP users are running multimedia applications with high-bandwidth and low-delay requirements, and/or a high level of broadcast or multicast packets, the maximum number of workstations should be reduced to 200.

Network Efficiency

Characterizing network traffic behavior requires gaining an understanding of the efficiency of new network applications. *Efficiency* refers to whether applications and protocols use bandwidth effectively. Efficiency is affected by frame size, the interaction of protocols used by an application, windowing and flow control, and error-recovery mechanisms.

Frame Size

As already discussed in this book, using a frame size that is the maximum supported for the medium in use has a positive impact on network performance. For file transfer applications, in particular, you should use the largest possible maximum transmission unit (MTU). Depending on the protocol stacks that your customer will use in the new network design, the MTU can be configured for some applications.

In an IP environment, you should avoid increasing the MTU to larger than the maximum supported for the media traversed by the frames, in order to avoid fragmentation and reassembly of frames. When devices such as end nodes or routers need to fragment and reassemble frames, performance degrades.

If possible, use a protocol stack that supports MTU discovery. With MTU discovery, the software can dynamically discover and use the largest frame size that will traverse the network without requiring fragmentation. (If your customers use IP implementations that support MTU discovery, make sure it is enabled. Some implementations default to a configuration with MTU discovery disabled.)

To help you predict frame sizes on a network to better characterize traffic load, you can use Table 4–9, which shows typical default frame sizes for common protocols.

Table 4–9   Typical Approximate Frame Sizes for Popular Protocols (Not Including Data-Link Headers)

Protocol	Frame Size
Novell NetWare 3.x	600 bytes
Novell NetWare 4.x	1,500 bytes on Ethernet, 4,096 bytes on Token Ring and FDDI
AppleTalk	599 bytes
Telnet	60 bytes (counting the PAD)
FTP	1,500 bytes on Ethernet, 4,096 bytes on Token Ring and FDDI
HTTP	1,500 bytes
NFS	8,192 bytes divided into IP fragments

With some protocols, you cannot support very large frame sizes. AppleTalk, for example, does not support more than 599 bytes of user data. (This is because AppleTalk does not have a fragmentation and reassembly mechanism, and LocalTalk requires a small frame size, although Ethernet and Token Ring do not.)

In the case of NetWare, Novell originally supported only a small frame size because many of their customers used ARCNET which requires a small frame size, and Net-

Ware does not have a fragmentation and reassembly mechanism. With NetWare Version 4.0, Novell started supporting larger frame sizes for networks other than ARCNET, such as Ethernet and Token Ring. If your customer is not yet using version 4.0 or later, you can still use large frame sizes with older versions if you install the Large IPX (LIPX) enhancement.

In some environments, you should check to see if data-link layer parameters can affect frame size. In the case of FDDI, for example, stations agree on an *operational target token rotation timer* that specifies how quickly each station must see a free token. If the token rotation timer is too short, then no station can hold the token long enough to send large frames.

In Token-Ring networks, bridges can be configured with a maximum frame-size parameter that specifies the largest frame that the bridge can forward. Because bridges were often implemented in PCs in the early 1990s, many network administrators set the maximum frame size quite small to avoid using too much memory on the PC. End stations can learn the maximum frame size and adjust the size of frames they send. To maximize efficiency, make sure the maximum frame size on bridges is optimized. In an SNA environment, you should also check the maximum Request/Response Unit (RU) size on controllers and internetworking devices.

Protocol Interaction

Inefficiency on networks isn't caused only by small frame sizes. Inefficiency is also caused by the interaction of protocols and the misconfiguration of acknowledgement timers and other parameters. To help illustrate this point, Table 4–10 shows a protocol analyzer trace from a Token Ring network that is used by PCs running Windows 95 and the SMB and NetBIOS protocols to store and retrieve files on a server.

Table 4–10   Inefficient Network Application Running on a Windows 95 PC

Frame	Delta Time	Relative Time	Size	Cumulative Bytes	Destination	Source	Summary of Protocol Layers
1		0.000	95	95	Server	Joe	DLC AC=10, FC=40, FS=00 LLC C D=F0 S=F0 I NR=25 NS=21 NETB D=85 S=0A Data, 55 bytes SMB C F=0CE4 Read 1,028
2	1.209	1.209	26	121	Joe	Server	DLC AC=18, FC=40, FS=CC LLC C D=F0 S=F0 RR NR=22 P

**Table 4–10   Inefficient Network Application Running on a
Windows 95 PC, Continued**

Frame	Delta Time	Relative Time	Size	Cumulative Bytes	Destination	Source	Summary of Protocol Layers
3	0.010	1.219	26	147	Server	Joe	DLC AC=10, FC=40, FS=00 LLC R D=F0 S=F0 RR NR=25 F
4	1.129	2.347	40	187	Joe	Server	DLC AC=18, FC=40, FS=CC LLC C D=F0 S=F0 I NR=22 NS=25 P NETB D=0A S=85 Data ACK
5	0.012	2.359	26	213	Server	Joe	DLC AC=10, FC=40, FS=00 LLC R D=F0 S=F0 RR NR=26 F
6	0.004	2.363	1,128	1,341	Joe	Server	DLC AC=18, FC=40, FS=CC LLC C D=F0 S=F0 I NR=22 NS=26 NETB D=0A S=85 Data, 1,088 bytes SMB R OK
7	0.025	2.389	26	1,367	Server	Joe	DLC AC=10, FC=40, FS=00 LLC R D=F0 S=F0 RR NR=27
8	0.004	2.393	40	1,407	Server	Joe	DLC AC=10, FC=40, FS=00 LLC C D=F0 S=F0 I NR=27 NS=22 NETB D=85 S=0A Data ACK

The example shows reliability implemented at so many layers that efficiency is negatively affected. In frame 1, the user Joe reads 1,028 bytes of data from a file with the file handle 0CE4. The file server does not return the data until frame 6. Frames 2 through 5 demonstrate bandwidth wasted by lower-layer protocols sending acknowledgements too quickly.

In frame 2, the server acknowledges that it received Logical Link Control (LLC) message 21 and is now ready (NR) to receive message 22. The server also sets the poll bit (P) meaning that the server requires a response. Joe's station sends the response in frame 3.

In frame 4, the NetBIOS layer on the server acknowledges receiving the request in frame 1. The LLC layer sets the poll bit again, so Joe's station responds in frame 5. Finally, in frame 6, the server sends the 1,028 bytes of data (plus header information) that the client requested in frame 1. Frame 7 is an LLC acknowledgement, and frame 8 is a NetBIOS acknowledgement.

Reliability features such as timeouts, acknowledgements, and polling are implemented in three layers: LLC, NetBIOS, and SMB. (Token Ring also sets the address recognized and frame copied bits in the Frame Status (FS) field, so it could be argued that reliability is implemented in four layers.) Due to overhead and acknowledgements, 1,407 bytes were required to transfer 1,028 bytes of user data (counting the final LLC and NetBIOS acknowledgements from Joe's station). Approximately 27 percent of network traffic is overhead.

To improve efficiency on this network, the LLC and NetBIOS timers should be increased. If the timers are increased, LLC and NetBIOS can include their acknowledgements in the SMB response. Also, if possible, the network administrators should determine why the server sets the poll bit at the LLC layer and why the server took so long to return the SMB data. Perhaps the server's hard disk is slow or perhaps the application is slow. It is not known what the application was; perhaps it was a database application that has not been optimized.

Windowing and Flow Control

To really understand network traffic, you need to understand windowing and flow control. A TCP/IP device, for example, sends segments (packets) of data in quick sequence, without waiting for an acknowledgment, until its *send window* has been exhausted. A station's send window is based on the recipient's *receive window*. The recipient states in every TCP packet how much data it is ready to receive. This total can vary from a few bytes up to 65,535 bytes. The recipient's receive window is based on how much memory the receiver has and how quickly it can process received data. You can optimize network efficiency by increasing memory and CPU power on end stations, which can result in a larger receive window.

NOTES

Theoretically, the optimal window size is the bandwidth of a link multiplied by delay on the link. To maximize throughput and use bandwidth efficiently, the send window should be large enough for the sender to completely fill the bandwidth pipe with data before stopping transmission and waiting for an acknowledgement.

RFC 1323 illustrates the need for a larger window than the standard TCP window size of 65,535 bytes. The product of bandwidth times delay is larger than 65,535 bytes on links of very high speeds but long delay, such as high-capacity satellite channels and terrestrial fiber-optic links that go a long distance (for example, across the United

States). RFC 1323 refers to a path operating in this region as a *long, fat pipe*, and a network containing this path as an *LFN* (pronounced "elephant"). If your customer's network includes any LFNs, you should recommend implementations of TCP that are based on RFC 1323.

Some TCP/IP applications run on top of UDP, not TCP. In this case there is either no flow control or the flow control is handled at the session or application layer. The following list shows which protocols are based on TCP and which protocols are based on UDP.

- File Transfer Protocol (FTP): TCP port 20 (data) and TCP port 21 (control)

- Telnet: TCP port 23

- Simple Mail Transfer Protocol (SMTP): TCP port 25

- Hypertext Transfer Protocol (HTTP): TCP port 80

- Simple Network Management Protocol (SNMP): UDP port 161

- Domain Name System (DNS): UDP port 53

- Trivial File Transfer Protocol (TFTP): UDP port 69

- DHCP server: UDP port 67

- DHCP client: UDP port 68

- Remote Procedure Call (RPC): UDP port 111

Protocols that run on UNIX systems, such as NFS and Network Information Services (NIS), use RPC.

In a Novell NetWare environment, if the customer has upgraded to NetWare 4.0 or later, then the NetWare Core Protocol (NCP) at the application layer uses the *burst-mode protocol*. This is a sliding window protocol that behaves like TCP. If the customer is still using NetWare 3.x, the Packet-Burst Network Loadable Module (NLM) can be loaded. Without the burst-mode protocol, the client sends requests and the server responds to every request with either a short acknowledgment or error packet, or a longer packet with application-layer data.

Protocols that send a reply to each request are often called *ping-pong protocols*. Ping-pong protocols do not use bandwidth efficiently.

Error-Recovery Mechanisms

Poorly designed error recovery mechanisms can waste bandwidth. For example, if a protocol retransmits data very quickly without waiting a long enough time to receive an acknowledgment, this can cause performance degradation for the rest of the network due to the bandwidth used.

Connectionless protocols usually do not implement error recovery. Most data-link layer and network-layer protocols are connectionless. Some transport-layer protocols, such as UDP, are connectionless.

Error-recovery mechanisms for connection-oriented protocols vary. A good TCP implementation, for example, should implement an adaptive retransmission algorithm, which means that the rate of retransmissions slows when the network is congested. Using a protocol analyzer, you can determine if your customer's protocols implement effective error recovery or not. In some cases you can configure retransmission and timeout timers or upgrade to a better protocol implementation.

CHARACTERIZING QUALITY OF SERVICE REQUIREMENTS

Analyzing network traffic requirements isn't quite as simple as identifying flows, measuring the load for flows, and characterizing traffic behavior such as broadcast and error-recovery behavior. You need to also characterize the QoS requirements for applications.

Just knowing the load (bandwidth) requirement for an application is not sufficient. You also need to know if the requirement is flexible or inflexible. Some applications continue to work (although slowly) when bandwidth is not sufficient. Other applications, such as voice and video applications, are rendered useless if a certain level of bandwidth is not available. In addition, if you have a mix of flexible and inflexible applications on a network, you need to determine if it is practical to borrow bandwidth from the flexible application to keep the inflexible application working.

Simply estimating the average idle time between packets for applications is unfortunately not sufficient either. You need to know if the idle time is consistent or variable. Does the application require access to the medium at regularly scheduled times? Will the application continue to work even if there is unexpected delay in getting access to the medium?

The following section covers analyzing QoS requirements using ATM techniques and techniques that are being developed by the Internet Engineering Task Force (IETF) Integrated Services Working Group.

ATM Quality of Service Specifications

In their document, "Traffic Management Specification Version 4.0," the ATM Forum does an excellent job of categorizing the types of service that a network can offer to support different sorts of applications. Even if your customer has no plans to use Asynchronous Transfer Mode (ATM) technology, the ATM Forum terminology is still helpful because it identifies the parameters that different sorts of applications must specify to request a certain type of network service. These parameters include delay and delay variation, data-burst sizes, data loss, and peak, sustainable, and minimum traffic rates. Although you might have to replace the word "cell" with "packet" in some cases, the ATM Forum definitions can help you classify applications on any network, even non-ATM networks.

The ATM Forum defines five service categories, each of which is described in more detail later in this section:

- Constant bit rate (CBR)

- Realtime variable bit rate (rt-VBR)

- Non-realtime variable bit rate (nrt-VBR)

- Unspecified bit rate (UBR)

- Available bit rate (ABR)

For each service category, the ATM Forum specifies a set of parameters to describe both the traffic presented to the network and the QoS required of the network. The ATM Forum also defines traffic control mechanisms that the network can use to meet QoS objectives. The network can implement such mechanisms as connection admission control (CAC) and resource allocation differently for each service category.

Service categories are distinguished as being either realtime or non-realtime. CBR and rt-VBR are realtime service categories. Realtime applications, such as voice and video applications, require tightly constrained delay and delay variation. Non-realtime applications, such as client/server and terminal/host data applications, do not require tightly constrained delay and delay variation. Nrt-VBR, UBR, and ABR are non-realtime service categories.

It is important to work with your customer to correctly map applications and protocols to the correct service category in order to meet network performance objectives. A brief overview of ATM service categories is provided here. You can learn more about ATM service categories and traffic management by reading the document, "Traffic Management Specification Version 4.0."

Constant Bit Rate Service Category

When CBR is used, a source end system reserves network resources in advance and asks for a guarantee that the negotiated QoS be assured to all cells as long as the cells conform to the relevant conformance tests. The source can emit cells at the peak cell rate (PCR) at any time and for any duration and the QoS commitments should pertain. CBR is used by applications that need the capability to request a static amount of bandwidth to be continuously available during a connection lifetime. The amount of bandwidth that a connection requires is specified by the PCR value.

CBR service is intended to support realtime applications requiring tightly constrained delay variation (for example, voice, video, and circuit emulation), but is not restricted to these applications. The source may emit cells at or below the negotiated PCR or be silent for periods of time. Cells that are delayed beyond the value specified by the maximum cell transfer delay (maxCTD) parameter are assumed to be of significantly reduced value to the application.

Realtime Variable Bit Rate Service Category

rt-VBR connections are characterized in terms of a PCR, Sustainable Cell Rate (SCR), and Maximum Burst Size (MBS). Sources are expected to transmit in a bursty fashion, at a rate that varies with time. Cells that are delayed beyond the value specified by maxCTD are assumed to be of significantly reduced value to the application. rt-VBR service may support statistical multiplexing of realtime data sources.

Non-Realtime Variable Bit Rate Service Category

The nrt-VBR service category is intended for non-realtime applications that have bursty traffic characteristics. No delay bounds are associated with this service category. The service is characterized in terms of a PCR, SCR, and MBS. For cells that are transferred within the traffic contract, the application expects a low cell loss ratio (CLR). nrt-VBR service may support statistical multiplexing of connections.

Unspecified Bit Rate Service Category

UBR service does not specify any traffic-related service guarantees. No numerical commitments are made regarding the cell loss ratio or cell transfer delay (CTD) experienced by a UBR connection. A network may or may not apply PCR to the connection admission control (CAC) and usage parameter control (UPC) functions. (UPC is defined as the set of actions taken by the network to monitor and control traffic at the end-system access point.)

In the case where the network does not enforce PCR, the value of PCR is informational only. (It is still useful to negotiate PCR to allow the source to discover the smallest bandwidth limitation along the path of the connection.)

The UBR service category is intended for non-realtime applications including traditional computer communications applications such as file transfer and e-mail. With UBR, congestion control can be performed at a higher layer on an end-to-end basis.

Available Bit Rate Service Category

With ABR, the transfer characteristics provided by the network can change subsequent to connection establishment. A flow-control mechanism offers several types of feedback to control the source rate in response to changing ATM-layer conditions.

This feedback is conveyed to the source through control cells called *resource management cells*, or *RM-cells*. An end system that adapts its traffic in accordance with the feedback should experience a low CLR and obtain a fair share of the available bandwidth according to a network-specific allocation policy. The ABR service does not require bounding the delay or the delay variation experienced by a given connection. ABR service is not intended to support realtime applications.

On the establishment of an ABR connection, an end system specifies to the network both a maximum required bandwidth and a minimum usable bandwidth. These are designated as the peak cell rate (PCR) and the minimum cell rate (MCR). The MCR can be specified as zero. The bandwidth available from the network can vary, but not become less than MCR.

Integrated Services Working Group Quality of Service Specifications

In an IP environment, you can use the work that the Integrated Services Working Group is doing on QoS requirements. In RFC 2205, the working group describes the *Resource Reservation Protocol (RSVP)*. In RFC 2208, the working group provides information on the applicability of RSVP and some guidelines for deploying it. RFCs 2209-2216 are also related to supporting QoS on the Internet and intranets.

RSVP is a setup protocol used by a host to request specific qualities of service from the network for particular application flows. RSVP is also used by routers to deliver QoS requests to other routers (or other types of nodes) along the path(s) of a flow. RSVP requests generally result in resources being reserved in each node along the path.

RSVP implements QoS for a particular data flow using mechanisms collectively called *traffic control*. These mechanisms include the following:

- A *packet classifier* that determines the QoS class (and perhaps the route) for each packet

- An *admission control function* that determines whether the node has sufficient available resources to supply the requested QoS

- A *packet scheduler* that determines when particular packets are forwarded to meet QoS requirements of a flow

RSVP works in conjunction with mechanisms at end systems to request services. To ensure that QoS conditions are met, RSVP clients provide the intermediate network nodes an estimate of the data traffic they will generate. This is done with a *traffic specification (TSpec)* and a *service-request specification (RSpec)*, as described in RFC 2216.

NOTES

A TSpec is a description of the traffic pattern for which service is being requested. The TSpec forms one side of a "contract" between the data flow and the service "provider." Once a service request is accepted, the service provider agrees to provide a specific QoS as long as the flow's traffic continues to conform to the TSpec.

An RSpec is a specification of the quality of service a flow wishes to request from a network element. The contents of an RSpec are specific to a particular service. The RSpec might contain information about bandwidth required for the flow, maximum delay, or packet-loss rates.

The RSVP protocol provides a general facility for reserving resources. RSVP does not define the different types of services that applications can request. The Integrated Services Working Group describes services in RFCs 2210-2216. For a complete understanding of the working group's view of how integrated services should be handled on the Internet or an intranet, you should read the RFCs. The following description is an overview of the two major types of service: controlled-load service, and guaranteed service.

Controlled-Load Service

Controlled-load service is defined in RFC 2211 and provides a client data flow with a QoS closely approximating the QoS that same flow would receive on an unloaded network. Admission control is applied to requests to ensure that the requested service is received even when the network is overloaded.

The controlled-load service is intended for applications that are highly sensitive to overloaded conditions, such as real-time applications. These applications work well on unloaded networks, but degrade quickly on overloaded networks. A service, such as the controlled-load service, that mimics unloaded networks serves these types of applications well.

Assuming the network is functioning correctly, an application requesting controlled-load service can assume the following:

- A very high percentage of transmitted packets will be successfully delivered by the network to the receiving end nodes. (The percentage of packets not successfully delivered must closely approximate the basic packet-error rate of the transmission medium.)

- The transit delay experienced by a very high percentage of the delivered packets will not greatly exceed the minimum transmit delay experienced by any successfully delivered packet. (This minimum transit delay includes speed-of-light delay plus the fixed processing time in routers and other communications devices along the path.)

The controlled-load service does not accept or make use of specific target values for parameters such as delay or loss. Instead, acceptance of a request for controlled-load service implies a commitment by the network node to provide the requester with service closely equivalent to that provided to uncontrolled (best-effort) traffic under lightly loaded conditions.

A network node that accepts a request for controlled-load service must use admission-control functions to ensure that adequate resources are available to handle the requested level of traffic, as defined by the requestor's TSpec. Resources include link bandwidth, router or switch port-buffer space, and computational capacity of the packet-forwarding engine.

Guaranteed Service

RFC 2212 describes the network node behavior required to deliver a service called *guaranteed service* that guarantees both bandwidth and delay characteristics. Guaranteed service provides firm (mathematically provable) bounds on end-to-end packet-queuing delays. It does not attempt to minimize jitter and is not concerned about fixed delay, such as transmission delay. (Fixed delay is a property of the chosen path, which is determined by the setup mechanism, such as RSVP.)

Guaranteed service guarantees that packets will arrive within the guaranteed delivery time and will not be discarded due to queue overflows, provided the flow's traffic conforms to its TSpec. A series of network nodes that implement RFC 2212 assure a level of bandwidth that, when used by a regulated flow, produces a delay-bounded service with no queuing loss (assuming no failure of network components or changes in routing during the life of the flow).

Guaranteed service is intended for applications that need a guarantee that a packet will arrive no later than a certain time after it was transmitted by its source. For example, some audio and video playback applications are intolerant of a packet arriving after its expected playback time. Applications that have real-time requirements can also use guaranteed service.

In RFC 2212, a flow is described using a *token bucket*. A token bucket has a *bucket rate* and a *bucket size*. The rate specifies the continually sustainable data rate, and the size specifies the extent to which the data rate can exceed the sustainable level for short periods of time.

The rate is measured in bytes of IP datagrams per second, and can range from 1 byte per second to as large as 40 TB per second (the maximum theoretical bandwidth of a single strand of fiber). The bucket size can range from 1 byte to 250 GB. The range of values is intentionally large to allow for future bandwidths. The range is not intended to imply that a network node has to support the entire range.

The expectation of the Integrated Services Working Group is that a software developer can use the relevant RFCs to develop intelligent applications that can accurately set the bucket rate and size. An application usually can accurately estimate the expected queuing delay the guaranteed service will provide. If the delay is larger than expected, the application can modify its token bucket to achieve a lower delay.

As a network designer, you won't generally be called upon to estimate token-bucket rates and sizes. On the other hand, you should recognize which applications need guaranteed service and have some idea of their default behavior and whether a reconfiguration of the default behavior is possible. If an application can request terabytes-per-second bandwidth, you need to know this because of the negative effect it could have on other applications!

Documenting QoS Requirements

You should work with your customer to classify each network application in a service category. Once you have classified the application, then you should fill in the "QoS Requirements" column in Table 4–4, "Network Applications Traffic Characteristics."

If your customer has applications that can be characterized as needing controlled-load or guaranteed service, then you can use those terms when filling in the "QoS Requirements" column. If your customer plans to use ATM, then you can use the ATM Forum's terminology for service categories. Even if your customer does not plan to use ATM or IP, you can still use the ATM Forum or Integrated Services Working Group terminology. Another alternative is to simply use the terms *inflexible* and *flexible*. Inflexible is a generic word to describe any application that has specific requirements for constant bandwidth, delay, delay variation, accuracy, and throughput. Flexible, on the other hand, is a generic term for applications that simply expect the network to make a best effort to meet requirements. Many non-multimedia applications have flexible QoS requirements.

At this point in the network design process, you should also find out from your customer if any service-level agreements (SLAs) will be made with regards to applications. A *service-level agreement* is a contract between a network services provider and users that specifies precisely how well a network should perform. If your customer has any SLAs, refer to them in the "QoS Requirements" column of Table 4–4.

NETWORK TRAFFIC CHECKLIST

You can use the following checklist to determine if you have completed all the steps for characterizing network traffic:

- ☐ I have identified major traffic sources and stores on the existing network and documented traffic flow between them.

- ☐ I have categorized the traffic flow for each application as being terminal/host, client/server, peer-to-peer, server/server, or distributed computing.

- ☐ I have estimated the bandwidth requirements for each application.

- ☐ I have estimated bandwidth requirements for routing protocols.

- ☐ I have characterized network traffic in terms of broadcast/multicast rates, efficiency, frame sizes, windowing and flow control, and error-recovery mechanisms.

- ☐ I have categorized the QoS requirements of each application.

SUMMARY

This chapter provided techniques for analyzing network traffic caused by applications and protocols. The chapter discussed methods for identifying traffic sources and data stores, measuring traffic flow and load, documenting application and protocol usage, and evaluating quality of service (QoS) requirements.

SUMMARY FOR PART I

At this point in the network design process, you have identified a customer's network applications and the technical requirements for a network design that can support the applications. You should take another look at Table 4–4, "Network Applications Traffic Characteristics," and Table 2–3, "Network Applications Technical Requirements," to make sure you understand your customer's application requirements. If you want, you can merge these two tables so there is one row for each application.

A top-down methodology for network design focuses on applications. Chapter 1 covered identifying applications and business goals. Chapter 2 analyzed technical goals for applications and the network as a whole, such as availability, performance, and manageability. Chapter 3 concentrated on techniques for characterizing the existing network, and Chapter 4 refocused on technical requirements in terms of the network traffic characteristics of applications and protocols.

This summary wraps up Part I, "Identifying Your Customer's Needs and Goals." Part I presented the requirements-analysis phase of network design. The requirements analysis phase is the most important phase in top-down network design. Gaining a solid understanding of your customer's requirements helps you select technologies that meet a customer's criteria for success.

You should now be able to analyze a customer's business and technical goals and be ready to start developing a logical and physical network design. Part II, "Logical Network Design," covers designing a logical network topology, developing a network-layer addressing and naming model, selecting bridging and routing protocols, and planning a network security and management strategy.

PART II

Logical Network Design

CHAPTER 5

Designing a Network Topology

In this chapter, you will learn techniques for developing a network topology. A *topology* is a map of an internetwork that indicates network segments, interconnection points, and user communities. Although geographical sites can appear on the map, the purpose of the map is to show the geometry of the network, not the physical geography or technical implementation. The map is a high-level blueprint of the network, analogous to an architectural drawing that shows the location and size of rooms for a building, but not the construction materials for fabricating the rooms.

Designing a network topology is the first step in the logical design phase of the top-down network design methodology. To meet a customer's goals for scalability and adaptability, it is important to architect a logical topology before selecting physical products or technologies. During the topology design phase, you identify networks and interconnection points, the size and scope of networks, and the types of internetworking devices that will be required, but not the actual devices.

This chapter provides tips for both campus and enterprise network design, and focuses on hierarchical network design, which is a technique for designing scalable campus and enterprise networks using a layered, modular model. In addition to covering hierarchical network design, the chapter also covers redundant network design topologies and topologies that meet security goals. (Security is covered in more detail in Chapter 8, "Developing Network Security and Network Management Strategies.")

Upon completion of this chapter, you will be prepared to design a secure, redundant, and hierarchical topology for a network design customer that will meet the customer's business and technical goals. The topology will be a useful tool to help you and your customer begin the process of moving from a logical design to a physical implementation of the customer's internetwork.

HIERARCHICAL NETWORK DESIGN

To meet a customer's business and technical goals for a corporate network design, you might need to recommend a network topology consisting of many interrelated components. This task is made easier if you can "divide and conquer" the job and develop the design in layers.

Network design experts have developed the *hierarchical network design model* to help you develop a topology in discrete layers. Each layer can be focused on specific functions, allowing you to choose the right systems and features for the layer. For example, in Figure 5–1, high-speed WAN routers can carry traffic across the enterprise backbone, medium-speed routers can connect buildings at each campus, and switches and hubs can connect user devices and servers within buildings.

Figure 5–1
A hierarchical topology.

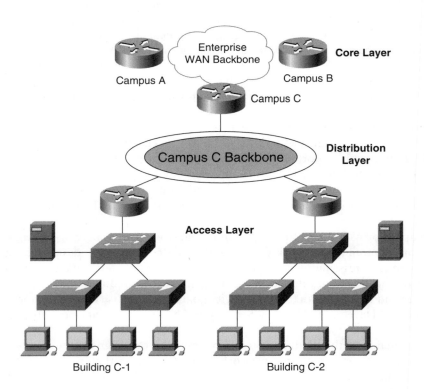

A typical hierarchical topology is:

- A core layer of high-end routers and switches that are optimized for availability and performance

- A distribution layer of routers and switches that implement policies

- An access layer that connects users via hubs, switches, and other devices

Why Use a Hierarchical Network Design Model?

Networks that grow unheeded without any plan in place tend to develop in an unstructured format. Dr. Peter Welcher, the author of network design and technology articles for *Cisco World* and other publications, refers to unplanned networks as *fur-ball networks*.

Welcher explains the disadvantages of a fur-ball topology by pointing out the problems that too many CPU adjacencies cause. When network devices communicate with many other devices, the workload required of the CPUs on the devices can be burdensome. For example, in a large flat (switched) network, broadcast packets are burdensome. A broadcast packet interrupts the CPU on each device within the broadcast domain, and demands processing time on every device for which a protocol understanding for that broadcast is installed. This includes routers, workstations, and servers.

Another potential problem with non-hierarchical networks, besides broadcast packets, is the CPU workload required for routers to communicate with many other routers and process numerous route advertisements. A hierarchical network design methodology lets you design a modular topology that limits the number of communicating routers.

Using a hierarchical model can help you minimize costs. You can purchase the appropriate internetworking devices for each layer of the hierarchy, thus avoiding spending money on unnecessary features for a layer. Also, the modular nature of the hierarchical design model enables accurate capacity planning within each layer of the hierarchy, thus reducing wasted bandwidth. Network management responsibility and network management systems can be distributed to the different layers of a modular network architecture to control management costs.

Modularity lets you keep each design element simple and easy to understand. Simplicity minimizes the need for extensive training for network operations personnel and expedites the implementation of a design. Testing a network design is made easy because there is clear functionality at each layer. Fault isolation is improved because network technicians can easily recognize the transition points in the network to help them isolate possible failure points.

Hierarchical design facilitates changes. As elements in a network require change, the cost of making an upgrade is contained to a small subset of the overall network. In large flat or meshed network architectures, changes tend to impact a large number of systems. Replacing one device can affect numerous networks because of the complex interconnections.

When scalability is a major goal, a hierarchical topology is recommended because modularity in a design enables creating design elements that can be replicated as the network grows. Because each instance of a module is consistent, expansion is easy to plan and implement. For example, planning a campus network for a new site might simply be a matter of replicating an existing campus network design.

Today's fast-converging routing protocols were designed for hierarchical topologies. Route summarization, which Chapter 6, "Designing Models for Addressing and Naming," covers in more detail, is facilitated by hierarchical network design. To control routing CPU overhead and bandwidth consumption, modular hierarchical topologies should be used with such protocols as Open Shortest Path First (OSPF), Intermediate System-to-Intermediate System (IS-IS), Border Gateway Protocol (BGP), and Enhanced Interior Gateway Routing Protocol (Enhanced IGRP).

Flat Versus Hierarchical Topologies

A flat network topology is adequate for very small networks. With a flat network design, there is no hierarchy. Each internetworking device has essentially the same job, and the network is not divided into layers or modules. A flat network topology is easy to design and implement, and it is easy to maintain, as long as the network stays small.

Flat WAN Topologies

A wide area network (WAN) for a small company can consist of a few sites connected in a loop. Each site has a WAN router that connects to two other adjacent sites via point-to-point links, as shown in Figure 5–2. As long as the WAN is small (a few sites), routing protocols can converge quickly, and communication with any other site can recover when a link fails. (As long as only one link fails, communication recovers. When more than one link fails, some sites are isolated from others.)

A flat loop topology is generally not recommended for networks with many sites, however. A loop topology can mean that there are many hops between routers on opposite sides of the loop, resulting in significant delay and a higher probability of failure. If your analysis of traffic flow indicates that routers on opposite sides of a loop topology exchange a lot of traffic, you should recommend a hierarchical topology instead of a loop. To avoid any single point of failure, redundant routers or switches can be placed at upper layers of the hierarchy, as shown in Figure 5–2.

The flat loop topology shown at the top of Figure 5–2 meets goals for low cost and reasonably good availability. The hierarchical redundant topology shown on the bottom of Figure 5–2 meets goals for scalability, high availability, and low delay.

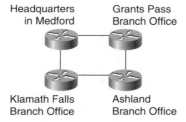

Flat Loop Topology

Figure 5–2
A flat loop topology (top) and a hierarchical redundant topology (bottom).

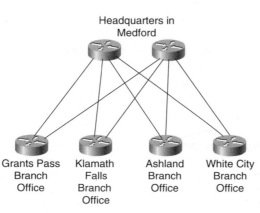

Hierarchical Redundant Topology

Flat LAN Topologies

A typical design for a small LAN is PCs and servers attached to one or more hubs in a flat topology. The PCs and servers implement a media-access control process, such as token passing or carrier-sense multiple access with collision detection (CSMA/CD) to control access to the shared bandwidth. The devices are all part of the same bandwidth domain and have the ability to negatively affect delay and throughput of other devices.

For networks with high bandwidth requirements, caused by numerous users and many traffic-intensive applications, network designers usually recommend attaching the PCs and servers to data-link-layer (Layer 2) switches instead of hubs. In this case, the network is segmented into small bandwidth domains so that a limited number of devices compete for bandwidth at any one time. (However, the devices do compete for service by the switching hardware and software, so it is important to understand the performance characteristics of candidate switches, as discussed in Chapter 9, "Selecting Technologies and Devices for Campus LANs.")

The number of nodes sharing one medium and the number of such media that are distinctly switched are design parameters to be determined carefully. Switching is more expensive than medium-sharing, so for some customers, hubs, or a combination of hubs and switches, are the best solution. For customers with high bandwidth and scalability requirements, switches can be used in place of hubs, dedicating each switch port to a single device. This provides dedicated bandwidth to each workstation, server, or other device.

As discussed in Chapter 4, devices connected in a switched or bridged network are part of the same broadcast domain. Switches forward broadcast frames out all ports. Routers, on the other hand, segment networks into separate broadcast domains. As documented in Table 4–8, a single broadcast domain should be limited to a few hundred devices so that devices are not overwhelmed by the task of processing broadcast traffic. By introducing hierarchy into a network design by adding routers, broadcast radiation is curtailed.

With a hierarchical design, internetworking devices can be deployed to do the job they do best. Routers can be added to a campus network design to isolate broadcast traffic. Switches can be deployed to maximize bandwidth for high-traffic applications, and hubs can be used when simple, inexpensive access is required. Maximizing overall performance by modularizing the tasks required of internetworking devices is one of the many benefits of using a hierarchical design model.

Mesh Versus Hierarchical-Mesh Topologies

Network designers often recommend a mesh topology to meet availability require-ments. In a *full-mesh topology*, every router or switch is connected to every other router or switch. A full-mesh network provides complete redundancy, and offers good performance because there is just a single-link delay between any two sites. A *partial-mesh network* has fewer connections. To reach another router or switch in a partial-mesh network might require traversing intermediate links, as shown in Figure 5–3.

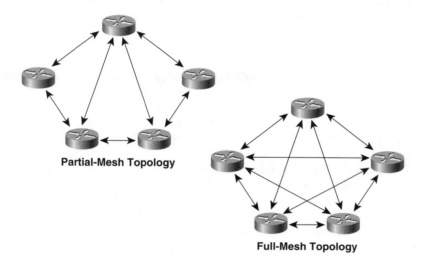

Partial-Mesh Topology

Full-Mesh Topology

Figure 5–3
A partial-mesh (left) and full-mesh (right) net-work topol-ogy.

NOTES

In a full-mesh topology, every router or switch is connected to every other router or switch. The number of links in a full-mesh topology is

$(N \times (N - 1))/2$

where N is the number of routers or switches. (Divide the result by 2 to avoid counting Router X-to-Router Y and Router Y-to-Router X as two different links.)

Although mesh networks feature good reliability, they have many disadvantages if they are not designed carefully. Mesh networks can be expensive to deploy and maintain. (A full-mesh network is especially expensive.) Mesh networks can also be hard to optimize, troubleshoot, and upgrade, unless they are designed using a simple, hierarchical model. In a non-hierarchical mesh topology, internetworking devices are not optimized for specific functions. Containing network problems is difficult because of the lack of modularity. Network upgrades are problematic because it is difficult to upgrade just one part of a network.

Mesh networks have scalability limits for groups of routers that broadcast routing updates or service advertisements. As the number of router CPU adjacencies increases, the amount of bandwidth and CPU resources devoted to processing updates increases.

A good rule of thumb is that you should keep broadcast traffic at less than 20 percent of the traffic on each link. This rule limits the number of adjacent routers that can exchange routing tables and service advertisements. This limitation is not a problem, however, if you follow guidelines for simple, hierarchical design. A hierarchical design, by its very nature, limits the number of router adjacencies.

Figure 5–4 shows a classic hierarchical and redundant enterprise design. The design uses a partial-mesh hierarchy rather than a full mesh. The figure shows an enterprise routed network, but the topology could be used for a switched campus network also.

Figure 5–4
A partial-mesh hierarchical design.

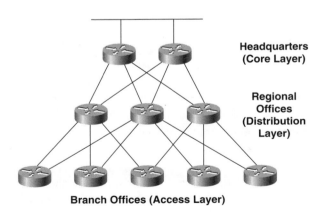

Headquarters (Core Layer)

Regional Offices (Distribution Layer)

Branch Offices (Access Layer)

For small and medium-sized companies, the hierarchical model is often implemented as a *hub-and-spoke topology* with little or no meshing. Corporate headquarters or a data center form the hub. Links to remote offices and telecommuter homes form the spokes as shown in Figure 5–5.

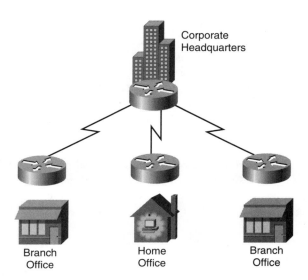

Figure 5–5
A hub-and-spoke hierarchical topology for a medium-sized business.

The Classic Three-Layer Hierarchical Model

Literature published by Cisco Systems, Inc., and other networking vendors talks about a classic three-layer hierarchical model for network design topologies. The three-layer model permits traffic aggregation and filtering at three successive routing or switching levels. This makes the three-layer hierarchical model scalable to large international internetworks. Although the model was developed at a time when routers delineated layers, the model can be used for switched or bridged networks as well as routed networks. Three-layer hierarchical topologies were shown in Figure 5–1 and Figure 5–4.

Each layer of the hierarchical model has a specific role. The core layer provides optimal transport between sites. The distribution layer connects network services to the access layer, and implements policies regarding security, traffic loading, and routing. In a WAN design, the access layer consists of the routers at the edge of the campus networks. In a campus network, the access layer provides switches or hubs for end-user access.

The Core Layer

The *core layer* of a three-layer hierarchical topology is the high-speed backbone of the internetwork. Because the core layer is critical for interconnectivity, you should design the core layer with redundant components. The core layer should be highly reliable and should adapt to changes quickly.

When configuring routers in the core layer, you should use routing features that optimize packet throughput. You should avoid using packet filters or other features that slow down the manipulation of packets. You should optimize the core for low latency and good manageability.

The core should have a limited and consistent diameter. Distribution-layer routers (or switches) and client LANs can be added to the model without increasing the diameter of the core. Limiting the diameter of the core provides predictable performance and ease of troubleshooting.

For customers who need to connect to other enterprises via an extranet or the Internet, the core topology should include one or more links to external networks. Corporate network administrators should discourage regional and branch-office administrators from planning their own extranets or connections to the Internet. Centralizing these functions in the core layer reduces complexity and the potential for routing problems, and is essential to minimizing security concerns.

The Distribution Layer

The *distribution layer* of the network is the demarcation point between the access and core layers of the network. The distribution layer has many roles, including controlling access to resources for security reasons, and controlling network traffic that traverses the core for performance reasons. The distribution layer is often the layer that delineates broadcast domains, (although this can be done at the access layer as well). If you plan to implement virtual LANs (VLANs), the distribution layer can be configured to route between VLANs.

The distribution layer allows the core layer to connect diverse sites while maintaining high performance. To maintain good performance in the core, the distribution layer can redistribute between bandwidth-intensive access-layer routing protocols and optimized core routing protocols. For example, the distribution layer can redistribute between AppleTalk's Routing Table Maintenance Protocol (RTMP) at the access layer and Enhanced IGRP for AppleTalk in the core layer.

To improve routing protocol performance, the distribution layer can summarize routes from the access layer. For some networks, the distribution layer offers a default route to access-layer routers and only runs dynamic routing protocols when communicating with core routers.

Another function that can occur at the distribution layer is address translation. With *address translation*, devices in the access layer can use private addresses. The address-translation function converts the private addresses to legitimate Internet addresses for packets that traverse the rest of the organization's internetwork or the Internet. Chapter 6, "Designing Models for Addressing and Naming," discusses address translation in more detail.

The Access Layer

The *access layer* provides users on local segments access to the internetwork. The access layer can include routers, switches, bridges, and shared-media hubs. As mentioned, switches are implemented at the access layer in campus networks to divide up bandwidth domains to meet the demands of applications that need a lot of bandwidth or cannot withstand the variable delay characterized by shared bandwidth.

For internetworks that include small branch offices and telecommuter home offices, the access layer can provide access into the corporate internetwork using wide-area technologies such as ISDN, Frame Relay, leased digital lines, and analog modem lines. You can implement routing features such as dial-on-demand (DDR) routing and static routing to control bandwidth utilization and minimize cost on access-layer remote links. (DDR keeps a link inactive except when specified traffic needs to be sent.)

Guidelines for Hierarchical Network Design

This section briefly describes some guidelines for hierarchical network design. Following these simple guidelines will help you design networks that take advantage of the benefits of hierarchical design.

The first guideline is that you should control the diameter of a hierarchical enterprise network topology. In most cases, three major layers are sufficient (as shown in Figure 5–4):

- The core layer

- The distribution layer

- The access layer

Controlling the network diameter provides low and predictable latency. It also helps you predict routing paths, traffic flows, and capacity requirements. A controlled network diameter also makes troubleshooting and network documentation easier.

Strict control of the network topology at the access layer should be maintained. The access layer is most susceptible to violations of hierarchical network design guidelines. Users at the access layer have a tendency to add networks to the internetwork inappropriately. For example, a network administrator at a branch office might connect the branch network to another branch, adding a fourth layer. This is a common network design mistake that is known as *adding a chain*. Figure 5–6 shows a chain.

In addition to avoiding chains, you should avoid backdoors. A *backdoor* is a connection between devices in the same layer, as shown in Figure 5–6. A backdoor can be an extra router, bridge, or switch added to connect two networks. Backdoors should be avoided because they cause unexpected routing problems and make network documentation and troubleshooting more difficult.

Figure 5–6
Backdoors and chains at the access layer.

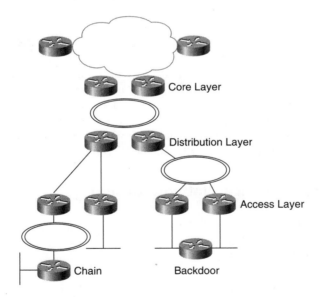

NOTES

Sometimes there are valid reasons for adding a chain or a backdoor. For example, an international network might require a chain to add another country. A backdoor is sometimes added to increase performance and redundancy between two parallel devices in a layer. But, in general, other design options can usually be found that let the design retain its hierarchical structure. To maximize the benefits of a hierarchical model, chains and backdoor should usually be avoided.

Finally, one other guideline for hierarchical network design is that you should design the access layer first, followed by the distribution layer, and then finally the core layer. By starting with the access layer, you can more accurately perform capacity planning for the distribution and core layers. You can also recognize the optimization techniques you will need for the distribution and core layers.

You should design each layer using modular and hierarchical techniques and then plan the interconnections between layers based on your analysis of traffic load, flow, and behavior. To better understand network traffic characteristics you can review the concepts covered in Chapter 4, "Characterizing Network Traffic." As you select technologies for each layer, as discussed in Part III of this book, you might need to go back and tweak the design for other layers. Remember that network design is an iterative process.

REDUNDANT NETWORK DESIGN TOPOLOGIES

Redundant network designs let you meet requirements for network availability by duplicating network links and interconnectivity devices. Redundancy eliminates the possibility of having a single point of failure on the network. The goal is to duplicate any required component whose failure could disable critical applications. The component could be a core router, a channel service unit (CSU), a power supply, a WAN trunk, a service provider's network, and so on.

Redundancy can be implemented in both campus and enterprise networks. Implementing redundancy on campus networks can help you meet availability goals for users accessing local services. Implementing enterprise-wide redundancy can help you meet overall availability and performance goals.

NOTES

    Because redundancy is expensive to deploy and maintain, you should implement redundant topologies with care. Be sure to select a level of redundancy that matches your customer's requirements for availability and affordability.

Before you select redundant design solutions, you should first analyze the business and technical goals of your customer, as Part I of this book discussed. Make sure you can identify critical applications, systems, internetworking devices, and links. Analyze your customer's tolerance for risk and the consequences of not implementing redundancy. Make sure to discuss with your customer the tradeoffs of redundancy versus low cost, and simplicity versus complexity. Redundancy adds complexity to the network topology and to network addressing and routing.

Backup Paths

To maintain interconnectivity even when one or more links are down, redundant network designs include a backup path for packets to travel when there are problems on the primary path. A *backup path* consists of routers and switches, and individual backup links between routers and switches, that duplicate devices and links on the primary path.

When estimating network performance for a redundant network design, you should take into consideration two aspects of the backup path:

- How much capacity does the backup path support?

- How quickly will the network begin to use the backup path?

You can use a network modeling tool to predict network performance when the backup path is in use. Sometimes the performance is worse than the primary path, but still acceptable.

It is quite common for a backup path to have less capacity then a primary path. Individual backup links within the backup path often use different technologies. For example, a leased line can be in parallel with a backup dial-up line or ISDN circuit.

Designing a backup path that has the same capacity as the primary path can be expensive and is only appropriate if the customer's business requirements dictate a backup path with the same performance characteristics as the primary path.

If switching to the backup path requires manual reconfiguration of any components, then users will notice disruption. For mission-critical applications, disruption is probably not acceptable. An automatic failover is necessary for mission-critical applications. By using redundant, partial-mesh network designs, you can speed automatic recovery time when a link fails.

One other important consideration with backup paths is that they must be tested. Sometimes network designers develop backup solutions that are never tested until a catastrophe happens. When the catastrophe occurs, the backup links do not work. In some network designs, the backup links are used for load balancing as well as redundancy. This has the advantage that the backup path is a tested solution that is regularly used and monitored as a part of day-to-day operations. Load balancing is discussed in more detail in the next section.

Load Balancing

The primary purpose of redundancy is to meet availability requirements. A secondary goal is to improve performance by supporting load balancing across parallel links.

Load balancing must be planned and in some cases configured. Some protocols do not support load balancing by default. For example, when running Novell's Routing Information Protocol (RIP), an Internetwork Packet Exchange (IPX) router can remember only one route to a remote network. You can change this behavior on a Cisco router by using the `ipx maximum-paths` command.

In ISDN environments, you can facilitate load balancing by configuring channel aggregation. *Channel aggregation* means that a router can automatically bring up multiple ISDN B channels as bandwidth requirements increase. The Multilink Point-to-Point Protocol (MPPP) is an Internet Engineering Task Force (IETF) standard for ISDN B-channel aggregation. MPPP ensures that packets arrive in sequence at the receiving router. To accomplish this, data is encapsulated within the Point-to-Point Protocol (PPP) and datagrams are given a sequence number. At the receiving router, PPP uses the sequence number to re-create the original data stream. Multiple channels appear as one logical link to upper-layer protocols.

Most vendor's implementations of IP routing protocols support load balancing across parallel links that have equal cost. (*Cost values* are used by routing protocols to determine the most favorable path to a destination. Depending on the routing protocol, cost can be based on hop count, bandwidth, delay, or other factors.) Cisco supports load balancing across six parallel paths. With the IGRP and Enhanced IGRP protocols, Cisco supports load balancing even when the paths do not have the same bandwidth (which is the main metric used for measuring cost for those protocols). Using a feature called *variance*, IGRP and Enhanced IGRP can load balance across paths that do not have precisely the same aggregate bandwidth. Cost, metrics, and variance are discussed in more detail in Chapter 7, "Selecting Bridging, Switching, and Routing Protocols."

Some routing protocols base cost on the number of hops to a particular destination. These routing protocols load balance over unequal bandwidth paths as long as the hop count is equal. Once a slow link becomes saturated, however, higher capacity links cannot be filled. This is called *pinhole congestion*. Pinhole congestion can be avoided by designing equal bandwidth links within one layer of the hierarchy, or by using a routing protocol that bases cost on bandwidth and has the variance feature.

Load balancing can be affected by advanced switching (forwarding) mechanisms implemented in routers. Advanced switching processes often cache the path to remote destinations to allow fast forwarding of subsequent packets to that destination. (The cache obviates the need for the router CPU to look in the routing table for a path.) The result of caching is that all packets destined to a particular destination take the same path. In this case, load balancing occurs across traffic flows to different destinations, but not on a packet-per-packet basis. Some newer technologies, such as Cisco Express Forwarding (CEF), can be configured to do packet-per-packet *or* destination-per-destination load balancing. Chapter 12, "Optimizing Your Network Design," covers CEF in more detail.

DESIGNING A CAMPUS NETWORK DESIGN TOPOLOGY

Campus network design topologies should meet a customer's goals for availability and performance by featuring small broadcast domains, redundant distribution-layer segments, mirrored servers, and multiple ways for a workstation to reach a router for off-net communications. Campus networks should be designed using a hierarchical model so that the network offers good performance, maintainability, and scalability.

Virtual LANs

A *virtual LAN (VLAN)* is an emulation of a standard LAN that allows data transfer to take place without the traditional physical restraints placed on a network. A network administrator can use management software to group users into a VLAN so they can communicate as if they were attached to the same wire, when in fact they are located on different physical LAN segments. Because VLANs are based on logical instead of physical connections, they are very flexible.

Companies that are growing quickly cannot guarantee that employees working on the same project will be located together. With VLANs, the physical location of a user does not matter. A network administrator can assign a user to a VLAN regardless of the user's location. In theory, VLAN assignment can be based on applications, protocols, performance requirements, security requirements, traffic-loading characteristics, or other factors.

VLANs allow a large flat network to be divided into subnets. This feature can be used to divide up broadcast domains. Instead of flooding all broadcasts out every port, a VLAN-enabled switch can flood a broadcast out only the ports that are part of the same subnet as the sending station.

In the past, some companies implemented large switched campus networks with few routers. The goals were to keep costs down by using switches instead of routers, and to provide good performance because presumably switches were faster than routers. Without the router capability of containing broadcast traffic, however, the companies needed VLANs. VLANs allow the large flat network to be divided into subnets. A router (or a routing module within a switch) was still needed for inter-subnet communication.

As routers become as fast as switches and Layer-3 functionality is added to switches, fewer companies will implement large, flat, switched networks, and there will be less of a need for VLANs.

VLAN-based networks can be hard to manage and optimize. Also, when a VLAN is dispersed across many physical networks, traffic must flow to each of those networks, which affects the performance of the networks and adds to the capacity requirements of trunk networks that connect VLANs.

Redundant LAN Segments

In campus LAN situations, it is common practice to design redundant links between LAN switches. Because most LAN switches implement the IEEE 802.1d spanning-tree algorithm, loops in network traffic can be avoided. The *spanning-tree algorithm* guarantees that there is one and only one active path between two network stations. The algorithm permits a redundant path that is automatically activated when the active path experiences problems.

The IEEE 802.1d standard is a good solution for redundancy, but not necessarily for load balancing, because only one path is active. Some switch vendors, such as Cisco Systems, let you implement one spanning tree per VLAN. If you use VLANs in a campus network design with Cisco switches, redundant links can offer load-balancing in addition to fault tolerance. Figure 5–7 shows a redundant campus LAN design that uses the spanning-tree algorithm and VLANs.

Figure 5–7
A campus hierarchical redundant topology.

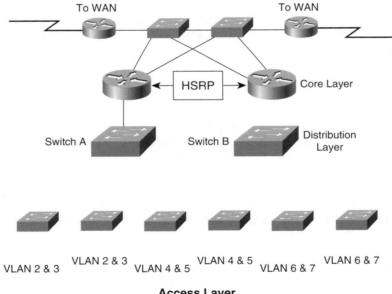

The IEEE 802.1d specification states that when multiple bridges (or switches) exist in a spanning tree, one bridge becomes the *root bridge*. Traffic always travels toward the root bridge. Only one path to the root bridge is active; other paths are disabled.

The design in Figure 5–7 takes advantage of the Cisco feature of one spanning tree per VLAN. Switch A acts as the root bridge for VLANs 2, 4, and 6. (Switch B can become the root bridge for those VLANs if Switch A fails.) Switch B acts as the root bridge for VLANs 3, 5, and 7. (Switch A can become the root bridge for those VLANs if Switch B fails.) The result is that both links from an access-layer switch carry traffic, and failover to a new root bridge happens automatically if one of the distribution-layer switches fails. Both load-balancing and fault tolerance are achieved.

The design in Figure 5–7 can scale to a very large campus network. The design has been tested on a network that has 8,000 users, 80 access-layer switches, 14 distribution-layer switches, and four core campus routers (not counting the routers going to the WAN).

You can install workgroup servers on each VLAN of the topology shown in Figure 5–7. You can also install redundant departmental and enterprise servers at the distribution and core layers, using 100-Mbps Ethernet full-duplex connections between the servers and switches. Full-duplex Ethernet is covered in more detail in Chapter 9, "Selecting Technologies and Devices for Campus Networks."

Server Redundancy

This section covers guidelines for server redundancy in a campus network design. File, Web, Dynamic Host Configuration Protocol (DHCP), name, database, configuration, and broadcast servers are all candidates for redundancy in a campus design, depending on a customer's requirements.

Once a LAN is migrated to using DHCP servers for the IP addressing of end systems, the DHCP servers become critical. Because of this, you usually should recommend redundant DHCP servers. The servers should hold redundant (mirrored) copies of the DHCP database of IP configuration information.

DHCP servers can be placed at either the access or distribution layer. In small networks, redundant DHCP servers are often placed at the distribution layer. For larger networks, redundant DHCP servers are usually placed in the access layer. This avoids excessive traffic between the access and distribution layers, and allows each DHCP server to serve a smaller percentage of the user population.

In large campus networks, the DHCP server is often placed on a different network segment than the end systems that use it. If the server is on the other side of a router, the router can be configured to forward DHCP broadcasts from end systems. The router forwards the broadcasts to a server address configured via the ip helper address command on a Cisco router. The router inserts the address of the interface that received the request into the giaddr field of the DHCP request. The server uses the giaddr field to determine which pool of addresses to choose an address from.

Name servers are less critical than DHCP servers because users can reach services by address instead of name if the name server fails, but because many users do not realize this, it is a good idea to plan for redundant name servers. *Name servers* implement the Internet Domain Name System (DNS), the Windows Internet Naming Service (WINS), and the NetBIOS Name Service (NBNS). Name servers can be placed at the access or distribution layer.

If ATM is used in a campus network design, it is a good idea to duplicate the ATM services used by clients running *ATM LAN emulation (LANE) software*. These services include the following:

- LAN Emulation Configuration Server (LECS)

- LAN Emulation Server (LES)

- Broadcast and Unknown Server (BUS)

LANE version 1.0 does not support redundant servers, but the ATM Forum is working on the LANE Network-to-Network Interface (LNNI) part of LANE version 2.0, which will support redundancy. Another option is to use the Cisco Simple Server Redundancy Protocol (SSRP). Campus ATM networks are covered in more detail in Chapter 9, "Selecting Technologies and Devices for Campus Networks."

In any application where the cost of downtime for file servers is a major concern, mirrored file servers should be recommended. For example, in a brokerage firm where traders access data in order to buy and sell stocks, the data can be replicated on two or more mirrored file servers. Mirrored file servers hold identical data. Updates to the data are synchronized across the servers. The servers should be on different networks and power supplies to maximize availability.

If complete server redundancy is not feasible due to cost considerations, mirroring or duplexing of the file server hard drives is a good idea. (*Duplexing* is the same as mirroring with the additional feature that the two hard drives are controlled by different disk controllers.)

Redundancy has both availability and performance advantages. With mirrored file servers, it is possible to share the workload between servers. Cisco Systems, Inc., has two products that enable workload balancing for TCP/IP services:

- LocalDirector

- DistributedDirector

These products provide workload balancing for Web, File Transfer Protocol (FTP), Telnet, and Simple Mail Transfer Protocol (SMTP) services.

LocalDirector distributes client requests across a cluster of local servers, for example servers in a server farm. DistributedDirector distributes TCP/IP services among globally-dispersed server sites. Because DistributedDirector understands routing protocols and network topologies, it can transparently redirect client requests to the closest responsive server. A network administrator can set up mirrored servers in geographically-dispersed sites and let users access the closest server. Benefits include reduced access time and lower transmissions costs.

NOTES

There is one caveat to keep in mind with mirrored file, DHCP, Web and other types of servers. Mirrored servers offer redundancy for the hardware, cabling, LAN connection, and power supply, but they do not offer software or data redundancy. Because mirrored servers hold replicated data, if the problem is in the data or the software's ability to access the data, then all the mirrored servers are affected.

Workstation-to-Router Redundancy

Workstations in a campus network must have access to a router to reach remote services. Because workstation-to-router communication is critical in most designs, you should consider implementing redundancy for this function.

A workstation has many possible ways to discover a router on its network, depending on the protocol it is running and also the implementation of the protocol. The next few sections describe methods for workstations to learn about routers, and redundancy features that guarantee a workstation can reach a router.

AppleTalk Workstation-to-Router Communication

An AppleTalk workstation remembers the address of the router that sent the most recent RTMP packet. Although the workstation does not participate in the routing protocol process, it does hear RTMP broadcast packets and copy into memory the address of the router that sent the broadcast. As long as there is at least one router on the workstation's network, the workstation can reach remote devices. If there are multiple routers on a workstation's network, the workstation very quickly learns a new way to reach remote stations when a router fails, because AppleTalk routers send RTMP packets every 10 seconds.

To minimize memory and processing requirements on an AppleTalk device, the AppleTalk specification states that a workstation remembers the address of only one router, (the router that most recently sent an RTMP packet). Recall that AppleTalk was designed to run on 128Kb-RAM Macintoshes and was optimized for simplicity. The result is that a workstation does not always use the most expedient method to reach a remote station. The workstation can select a path that includes an extra hop. Figure 5–8 shows the extra-hop problem.

Figure 5–8
The workstation-to-router extra-hop problem.

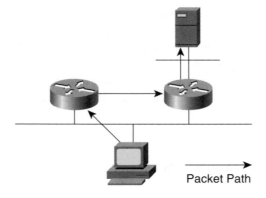

Packet Path

In 1989, Apple Computer, Inc., introduced AppleTalk Phase 2, which includes the *best router forwarding algorithm*. With the best router forwarding algorithm, a workstation can maintain a cache of the best routers to use to reach remote networks. If a destination network is in the cache, the workstation can avoid the extra-hop problem.

NOTES

The best router forwarding algorithm specifies that when a packet comes in to the network-layer datagram delivery protocol (DDP), if the source network number is not local, DDP copies into the cache the network number and the source data-link layer address in the packet. The data-link layer address is the address of the last router in the path from the remote station. Sending a packet to this router to get to the remote network should be the best route in terms of hops. The cache is aged every 40 seconds, so often the best router is not used for the initial packet in a session, but once a response is received, the workstation learns the best router to use.

Novell NetWare Workstation-to-Router Communication

Novell NetWare workstation-to-router communication is very simple. When a NetWare workstation determines that a packet is destined for a remote destination, the workstation broadcasts a *find-network-number request* to find a route to the destination. Routers on the workstation's network respond to the request. The workstation uses the first router that responds to send packets to the destination. If the workstation determines that it can no longer reach the destination, it automatically sends the find-network-number request again. If a router fails, as long as there is another router on the workstation's network, the workstation discovers the other router and the session continues.

IP Workstation-to-Router Communication

IP implementations vary in how they implement workstation-to-router communication. Some IP workstations send an address resolution protocol (ARP) frame to find a remote station. A router running *proxy ARP* can respond to the ARP request with the router's data-link-layer address. Cisco routers run proxy ARP by default.

The advantage of depending on proxy ARP to reach remote stations is that a workstation does not have to be manually configured with the address of a router. However, because proxy ARP has never been standardized, most network administrators do not depend on it. It is still very common for network administrators to manually configure an IP workstation with a default router. A *default router* is the address of a router on the local segment that a workstation uses to reach remote services. (The default router is sometimes called the *default gateway* for historical reasons.)

As was the case with AppleTalk, sometimes using the default router is not the most expedient path to the destination (see Figure 5–8). To get around the extra-hop problem and to add redundancy, some workstation IP implementations allow a network administrator to add static routes to a configuration file or to configure the workstation to run a routing protocol.

NOTES

In UNIX environments, workstations often run the RIP daemon to learn about routes. It is best if they run the RIP daemon in passive rather than active mode. In active mode, a workstation sends a RIP broadcast frame every 30 seconds. When many UNIX workstations run RIP in active mode, the amount of broadcast traffic significantly degrades network performance. In addition, there are security risks in allowing uncontrolled stations to run a routing protocol in active mode.

Another alternative for IP workstation-to-router communication is the *Router Discovery Protocol (RDP)*. Request for Comments (RFC) 1256 specifies the RDP extension to the Internet Control Message Protocol (ICMP). With RDP, each router periodically multicasts an ICMP *router advertisement packet* from each of its interfaces, announcing the IP address of that interface. Workstations discover the addresses of their local routers simply by listening for advertisements, in a similar fashion to the method AppleTalk workstations use to discover the address of a router. (The default advertising rate for RDP is once every 7 to 10 minutes, which is quite different than AppleTalk, which is once every 10 seconds).

When a workstation starts up, it can multicast an ICMP *router solicitation packet* to ask for immediate advertisements, rather than wait for the next periodic advertisement to arrive. RDP does not attempt to solve the extra-hop problem. Although most routers support RDP, few workstation IP implementations support it, so RDP is not widely used.

One reason that RDP has not become popular is that DHCP includes an option for a DHCP server to return the address of a default router to a client. As specified in RFC 2131, a server's response to a DHCP client's request for an IP address can include an options field in which the server can place one or more default router addresses. A preference level can be used to specify which default router is the best option. The server can also include a list of static routes in the options field.

The use of a statically configured default router is still quite popular, whether the configuration is done at each workstation or at a DHCP server that supports many workstations. Running routing protocols or router discovery protocols at workstations has proven to be a poor alternative because of traffic and processing overhead, security issues, and the lack of implementations for many platforms.

The problem with a static default router configuration is that it creates a single point of failure, particularly because many implementations keep track of only one default router. Loss of the default router results in workstations losing connections to remote sites and being unable to establish new connections.

Hot Standby Router Protocol

Cisco's *Hot Standby Router Protocol (HSRP)* provides a way for an IP workstation to keep communicating on an internetwork even if its default router becomes unavailable. The IETF is standardizing a similar protocol called the *Virtual Router Redundancy Protocol (VRRP)*. Routers in the core, distribution, or access layer can run HSRP. The campus design shown in Figure 5–7 features HSRP at the core layer.

HSRP works by creating a *phantom router*, as shown in Figure 5–9. The phantom router has its own IP and MAC addresses. Each workstation is configured to use the phantom as its default router. When a workstation broadcasts an ARP frame to find its default router, the active HSRP router responds with the phantom's MAC address. If the active router goes off line, a standby router takes over as active router, continuing the delivery of the workstation's packets. The change is transparent to the workstation.

HSRP routers on a LAN communicate among themselves to designate an active and standby router. The active router sends periodic hello messages. The other HSRP routers listen for the hello messages. If the active router fails, causing the other HSRP routers to stop receiving hello messages, the standby router takes over and becomes the active router. Because the new active router assumes both the IP and MAC addresses of the phantom, workstations see no change. They continue to send packets to the phantom's MAC address, and the new active router delivers those packets. The

Figure 5–9
*The Hot
Standby
Router Proto-
col (HSRP).*

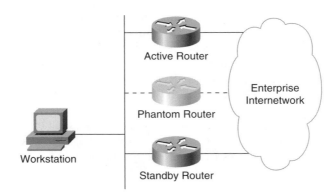

Active Router

Phantom Router

Standby Router

Workstation

Enterprise
Internetwork

hello timer should be configured to be short enough so that workstation applications and protocols do not drop connections before the standby router becomes active.

HSRP also works for proxy ARP. When an active HSRP router receives an ARP request for a station that is not on the local network, the router replies with the phantom's MAC address. If the router becomes unavailable, the new active router can still deliver the traffic.

DESIGNING AN ENTERPRISE NETWORK DESIGN TOPOLOGY

Enterprise network design topologies should meet a customer's goals for availability and performance by featuring redundant LAN and WAN segments in the intranet, and multiple paths to extranets and the Internet. For customers who lack the funds or technical expertise to develop their own WANs, Virtual Private Networking (VPN) can be used to connect private enterprise sites via a service provider's public network or the Internet. This section covers enterprise topologies that include redundant WAN segments and paths to the Internet, and VPN.

Redundant WAN Segments

Because WAN links can be critical pieces of an enterprise internetwork, redundant (backup) WAN links are often included in an enterprise network topology. A WAN network can be designed as a full mesh or a partial mesh. A full-mesh topology provides complete redundancy. It also provides good performance because there is just a single-link delay between any two sites. However, as already discussed in this chapter, a full mesh is costly to implement, maintain, upgrade, and troubleshoot. A hierarchical partial-mesh topology, as shown previously in Figure 5–4, is usually sufficient.

Circuit Diversity

When provisioning backup WAN links, you should learn as much as possible about the actual physical circuit routing. Different carriers sometimes use the same facilities, meaning that your backup path is susceptible to the same failures as your primary path. You should do some investigative work to ensure that your backup really is a backup. Network engineers use the term *circuit diversity* to refer to the optimum situation of circuits using different paths.

Because carriers lease capacity to each other and use third-party companies that provide capacity to multiple carriers, it is getting harder to guarantee circuit diversity. Also, carriers often merge with each other and mingle their circuits after the merge. As carriers increasingly use automated techniques for physical circuit re-routing, it becomes even more difficult to plan diversity because the re-routing is dynamic.

Nonetheless, you should work with the providers of your WAN links to gain an understanding of the level of circuit diversity in your network design. Carriers are usually willing to work with customers to provide information about physical circuit routing. (Be aware, however, that carriers sometimes provide inaccurate information, based on databases that are not kept current.) Try to write circuit-diversity commitments into contracts with your providers.

When analyzing circuit diversity, be sure to analyze your local cabling in addition to your carrier's services. Perhaps you have designed an ISDN link to back up a Frame Relay link. Do both of these links use the same cabling to get to the demarcation point in your building network? What cabling do the links use to get to your carrier? The cabling that goes from your building to the carrier is often the weakest link in a network. It can be affected by construction, flooding, ice storms, trucks hitting telephone poles, and other factors.

Multihoming the Internet Connection

The generic meaning of *multihoming* is to "provide more than one connection for a system to access and offer network services." The term *multihoming* is used in many specific ways also. A server, for example, is said to be multihomed if it has more than one network-layer address.

The term *multihoming* is increasingly being used to refer to the practice of providing an enterprise network more than one entry into the Internet. Redundant entries into the Internet provide fault tolerance for applications that require Internet access. An enterprise network can be multihomed to the Internet in many different ways, depending on a customer's goals. Figure 5–10 and Table 5–1 describe some methods for multihoming the Internet connection.

Figure 5–10
Options for multihoming the Internet connection.

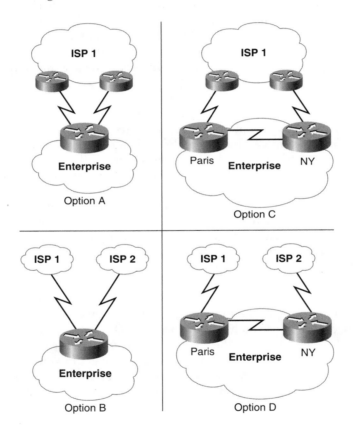

In the case of Options C and D, the goal might be to improve network performance by allowing European enterprise sites to access the Internet using the Paris router and North American sites to use the New York router. This can be accomplished by correctly configuring a default router on end stations and a default route on enterprise routers in Europe and North America. (A *default route* specifies where a packet should go if there is no explicit entry for the destination network in a router's routing table. Default route is also sometimes called *the gateway of last resort*.)

Table 4–16   Description of Options for Multihoming the Internet Connection

	Number of Routers at the Enterprise	Number of Connections to the Internet	Number of ISPs	Advantages	Disadvantages
Option A	1	2	1	WAN backup; low cost; working with one ISP can be easier than working with multiple ISPs	No ISP redundancy; router is a single point of failure; this solution assumes the ISP has two access points near the enterprise
Option B	1	2	2	WAN backup; low cost; ISP redundancy	Router is a single point of failure; it can be difficult to deal with policies and procedures of two different ISPs
Option C	2	2	1	WAN backup; especially good for geographically dispersed company; medium cost; working with one ISP can be easier than working with multiple ISPs	No ISP redundancy
Option D	2	2	2	WAN backup; especially good for geographically dispersed company; ISP redundancy	High cost; it can be difficult to deal with policies and procedures of two different ISPs

Your customer might have more complex goals than the simple goal in the previous paragraph. Perhaps your customer wants to guarantee that European enterprise sites access North American Internet sites via the New York router. A parallel goal is that North American enterprise sites access European Internet sites via the Paris router. This could be a reasonable goal when a constant, low latency is required for an application. The latency is more predictable if the first part of the path is across the enterprise intranet instead of the Internet. This goal is harder to meet than the first goal, however. It requires that the enterprise routers understand routes from the ISP and set preferences on those routes.

Another more complex goal is to guarantee that incoming traffic from the Internet destined for European enterprise sites uses the Paris router and incoming traffic for North American enterprise sites uses the New York router. This goal requires the enterprise routers to advertise to the Internet routes to enterprise sites. The routes must include metrics so that routers on the Internet know the preferred path to sites on the enterprise intranet.

One other caveat when an enterprise network is multihomed is the potential to become a *transit network* that provides interconnections for other networks. Looking at the pictures in Figure 5–10, consider that the enterprise router learns routes from the ISP. If the enterprise router advertises these learned routes, then it risks allowing the enterprise network to become a transit network and being loaded by unintended external traffic.

When an enterprise network becomes a transit network, routers on the Internet learn that they can reach other routers on the Internet via the enterprise network. To avoid this situation, enterprise routers should only advertise their own routes. (Alternatively they cannot run a routing protocol and depend on default and static routing).

In general, multihoming the Internet connection can be challenging if a customer's goals are complex. Encourage your customers to simplify their goals to ensure ease-of-implementation, scalability, stability, and affordability. You can point out that the Internet is continually being upgraded to higher-speed technologies, so it is becoming less necessary to reduce latency by guaranteeing that the first part of a path is across the intranet instead of the Internet. If your customer insists on complex multihoming goals, be sure to read the book *Internet Routing Architectures* by Bassam Halabi and published by Cisco Press/MTP to learn more about meeting complex multihoming goals.

Virtual Private Networking

Virtual private networks (VPNs) enable a customer to use a public network, such as the Internet, to provide a secure connection among sites on the organization's inter-network. Customers can also use VPNs to connect an enterprise intranet to an extranet to reach outside parties, such as partners, customers, resellers, and suppliers.

Traditionally, businesses have relied on private 56-Kbps or 1.544-Mbps T1 leased lines to link remote offices together. Leased lines are expensive to install and maintain. For many small companies, a leased line provides more bandwidth than is needed at too high a price. VPNs have emerged as a relatively inexpensive way for a company to connect geographically-dispersed offices via a service provider, as opposed to maintaining an expensive private WAN. The company's private data can be encrypted for routing through the service provider's network or the Internet.

A company can connect to the service provider's network using a variety of WAN technologies, including leased lines, Frame Relay, cable modems, digital subscriber lines (DSL), and so on. Virtual private networking does not require a permanent link. Dial-on-demand routing (DDR) can be used with analog modems or ISDN for those sites that wish to minimize costs by keeping the connection idle except when traffic is ready to send. Figure 5–11 shows a typical VPN for a medium-sized retail company.

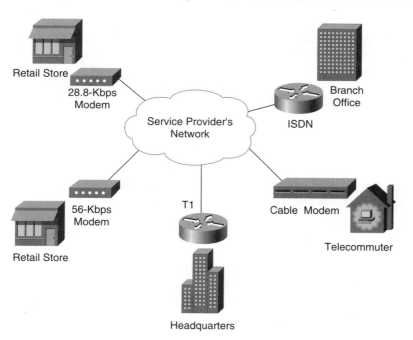

Figure 5–11
A virtual private network.

With VPN, security features such as firewalls and TCP/IP tunneling allow a customer to use a public network as a backbone for the enterprise network while protecting the privacy of enterprise data. Firewalls are discussed later in this chapter in the section "Secure Network Design Topologies."

The Layer 2 Tunneling Protocol (L2TP) is an emerging IETF standard for tunneling private data over public networks. Cisco and Microsoft are working with other industry leaders, such as 3Com and Ascend, to create the L2TP standard. Because the protocol is being developed as an IETF standard, different company's solutions should interoperate, which will give network designers flexibility when designing VPNs for customers.

SECURE NETWORK DESIGN TOPOLOGIES

This section discusses network security in relation to network topologies. Chapter 8, "Developing Network Security and Network Management Strategies," covers network security in more detail. The focus of this section is logical topologies, but physical security is also briefly mentioned.

Planning for Physical Security

When developing the logical topology of a network, you should begin to get an idea of where equipment will be installed. You should start working with your customer right away to make sure that critical equipment will be installed in computer rooms that have protection from unauthorized access, theft, vandalism, and natural disasters such as floods, fires, storms, and earthquakes. Physical security is not really an aspect of logical network design, but it is mentioned here because your logical topology might have an impact on it, and because the planning for physical security should start right away, in case there are lead times to build or install security mechanisms.

Meeting Security Goals with Firewall Topologies

According to the National Computer Security Association (NCSA), a *firewall* is "a system or combination of systems that enforces a boundary between two or more networks." A firewall can be a router with access control lists (ACLs), a dedicated hardware box, or software running on a PC or UNIX system. A firewall should be placed in the network topology so that all traffic from outside the protected network must pass through the firewall. A *security policy* specifies which traffic is authorized to pass through the firewall.

Firewalls are especially important at the boundary between the enterprise network and the Internet. A basic firewall topology is simply a router with a WAN connection to the Internet, a LAN connection to the enterprise network, and software that has security features. This elementary topology is appropriate if your customer has a simple security policy. Simple security policies can be implemented on the router with ACLs. The router can also use network address translation to hide internal addresses from Internet hackers.

For customers with the need to publish public data and protect private data, the firewall topology can include a public LAN that hosts Web, FTP, DNS, and SMTP servers. Security literature often refers to the public LAN as the *demilitarized* or *free-trade zone*. Security literature refers to a host on the free-trade zone as a *bastion host*, a secure system that supports a limited number of applications for use by outsiders. The bastion host holds data that outsiders can access, such as Web pages, but is strongly protected from outsiders using it for anything other than its limited purposes.

For larger customers, it is recommended that you use a dedicated firewall in addition to a router between the Internet and the enterprise network. To maximize security, you can run security features on the router and on the dedicated firewall. (To maximize performance, on the hand, you would not run security features on the router.) Figure 5–12 shows a free-trade zone secure topology.

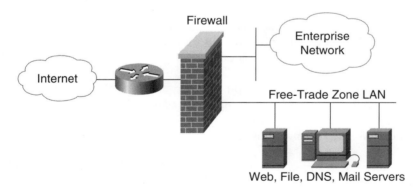

Figure 5–12
A free-trade zone topology.

An alternate topology is to use two routers as the firewall and place the free-trade zone between them, as shown in Figure 5–13. Security literature refers to this topology as the *three-part firewall topology*. The classic three-part firewall topology provides excellent protection. Its only disadvantage is that the configuration on the routers might be complex, consisting of many access control lists to control traffic in and out of the private network and the free-trade zone. Dedicated firewalls usually have a more graphical user interface (GUI) that lets you specify a security policy in an intuitive fashion.

Figure 5–13
A three-part firewall topology.

Web, File, DNS, Mail Servers

SUMMARY

This chapter focused on techniques for developing a topology for a network design. Designing a network topology is the first step in the logical design phase of the top-down network design methodology. By designing a logical topology before a physical implementation, you can increase the likelihood of meeting a customer's goals for scalability, adaptability, and performance.

This chapter discussed three models for network topologies: hierarchical, redundant, and secure models. All of these models can be applied to both campus and enterprise network design. The models are not mutually exclusive. Your goal should be to design hierarchical, redundant, and secure models based on your customer's goals.

Hierarchical network design lets you develop a network consisting of many interrelated components in a layered, modular fashion. Using a hierarchical model can help you maximize network performance, reduce the time to implement and troubleshoot a design, and minimize costs.

Redundant network designs let you meet requirements for network availability by duplicating network components. Redundancy eliminates single points of failure on the network. Redundancy also facilitates load balancing which increases network performance. Redundancy adds complexity and cost to the network, however, and should be designed with care.

Depending on your particular network design, you should plan a secure topology that protects core routers, demarcation points, cabling, modems, and so on. Adding one or more firewalls to your topology can help you protect enterprise networks from outside hackers.

After completing a logical topology for a customer, you should continue in the logical design phase by designing network addressing and naming models, selecting routing and bridging protocols, and developing network management and security strategies. These topics are covered in the next few chapters. Doing a thorough job in the logical design phase can ease your transition into the design of the physical implementation of the network. It can also prepare you for the job of selecting the right products and technologies for your customer.

CHAPTER 6

Designing Models for Addressing and Naming

This chapter provides guidelines for assigning addresses and names to internetwork components, including networks, subnets, routers, servers, and end systems. The chapter focuses on Internet Protocol (IP) addressing and naming, but includes tips for AppleTalk, Novell NetWare, and NetBIOS environments also. To benefit most from this chapter, you should already have a basic understanding of IP addressing, including address classes and subnet masks.

This chapter illustrates the importance of using a structured model for network-layer addressing and naming. Without structure, it is easy to run out of addresses, waste addresses, introduce duplicate addresses and names, and use addresses and names that are hard to manage. To meet a customer's goals for scalability, performance, and manageability, you should assign addresses and names systematically.

This chapter also demonstrates the importance of developing policies and procedures for addressing and naming. Policies often involve a plan for distributing authority for addressing and naming to avoid one department having to manage all addresses and names. A central authority can assign blocks of addresses and names in a hierarchical fashion to departments and branch offices.

Part I of this book recommends gaining an understanding of your customer's organizational structure, for example, departments, branch offices, business units and so on. This information is helpful when planning addresses and names. A topology map of the network is also useful, because it helps you see the hierarchy in the network and recognize where address boundaries exist. The addressing and naming step of the top-down network design process falls here in the methodology because it makes use of information you gathered in the previous phases of the network design process.

The addressing and naming step precedes selecting routing and bridging protocols, which is covered in the next chapter, because the addressing model you develop might dictate which routing protocols you can select. (For example, some routing protocols do not support variable-length subnet masking [VLSM]).

GUIDELINES FOR ASSIGNING NETWORK-LAYER ADDRESSES

Network-layer addresses should be planned, managed, and documented. Although an end system can learn its address dynamically, no mechanisms exist for assigning network or subnet numbers dynamically. These numbers must be planned and administered. Many vintage networks still exist where addressing was not planned or documented. These networks are hard to troubleshoot and do not scale.

The following list provides some simple rules for network-layer addressing that will help you architect scalability and manageability into a network design. These rules are described in more detail in later sections of this chapter.

- Design a structured model for addressing before assigning any addresses.

- Leave room for growth in the addressing model. If you do not plan for growth, you might later have to renumber many devices, which is labor-intensive.

- Assign blocks of addresses in a hierarchical fashion to foster good scalability and availability.

- Assign blocks of addresses based on the physical network, not on group membership, to avoid problems when groups or individuals move.

- Use meaningful numbers when assigning network addresses.

- If the level of network management expertise in regional and branch offices is high, you can delegate authority for addressing regional and branch-office networks, subnets, servers, and end systems.

- To maximize flexibility and minimize configuration, use dynamic addressing for end systems.

- To maximize security and adaptability, use private addresses with network address translation (NAT) in IP environments.

Using a Structured Model for Network-Layer Addressing

A *structured model for addressing* means that addresses are meaningful, hierarchical, and planned. AppleTalk addresses that include a building and floor number are structured. IP addresses that include a prefix and host part are structured. Assigning an IP network number to an enterprise network, and then subnetting the network number, and subnetting the subnets, is a structured (hierarchical) model for IP addressing.

A clearly documented structured model for addressing facilitates management and troubleshooting. Structure makes it easier to understand network maps, operate network management software, and recognize devices in protocol analyzer traces and reports. Structured addresses also facilitate network optimization and security because they make it easier to implement network filters on firewalls, routers, bridges, and switches.

A lot of companies have no model for addressing. When there is no model, and addresses are assigned in a haphazard way, the following problems can occur:

- Duplicate network and host addresses

- Illegal addresses that cannot be routed on the Internet

- Not enough addresses in total, or by group

- Addressees that cannot be used, and so are wasted

Using Meaningful Network Numbers

The rule that says you should use meaningful numbers when assigning network addresses is especially good advice for AppleTalk and Novell NetWare networks. In an AppleTalk network, a network administrator assigns a *cable range* to each network segment. The cable range value can be a single network number or a contiguous sequence of network numbers, for example, 2000–2010. Because AppleTalk network administrators are most familiar with "plug-and-play" systems, they have a tendency to use unstructured, undocumented, and ambiguous cable-range numbers. This makes the network hard to maintain and enhance. Instead, network administrators should use meaningful numbers.

For example, an administrator can encode a campus, building, or floor number in the cable range, as shown in Figure 6–1. In Figure 6–1, each cable range number has a building number (2 or 3) for its first digit, and a floor number for its second digit. For example, the cable range for the sixth floor in building 2 is 2610–2620.

Figure 6–1
Structured
AppleTalk
cable ranges.

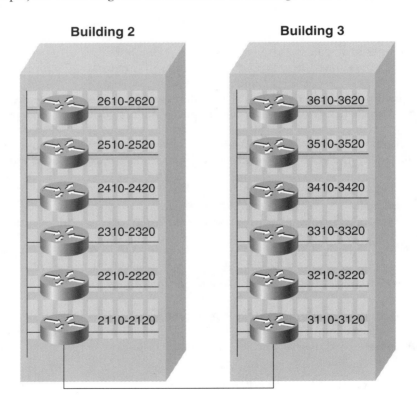

In Novell NetWare networks, each network segment is assigned a 4-byte hexadecimal number. In the past, some networking books used humorous words for Novell network segments, such as FEEDFACE and C0FFEE. Many network administrators adopted these funny network numbers only to find that they make troubleshooting difficult. It is a better idea to use meaningful numbers that include a campus, building, or floor number. When troubleshooting problems, if a protocol analyzer indicates a particular network is failing, you can go to the correct building and floor to troubleshoot the problem, if you have assigned meaningful network numbers.

For mixed-protocol environments, some administrators encode the IP network or subnet in AppleTalk and IPX network numbers. For example, an IPX network number could be 1011 to correspond with the IP network number 10.1.1.0. This facilitates troubleshooting.

Administering Addresses by a Central Authority

A corporate information systems (IS) or enterprise networking department should develop a global model for network-layer addressing. As the network designer, you should help the IS department develop the model. The model should identify network numbers for the core of the enterprise network, and blocks of subnets for the distribution and access layers. Depending on the organizational structure of the enterprise, network managers within each region or branch office can further divide the subnets.

In an IP environment, a central authority for the enterprise network can request a block of addresses from an Internet Service Provider (ISP) or from the Internet Assigned Numbers Authority (IANA). The block should be big enough to accommodate growth.

When addresses are assigned by an ISP, be sure to request from the ISP a block of addresses that is big enough to accommodate scalability goals. Some ISPs are running out of addresses and cannot give out large blocks. If this is the case, find a different ISP that can accommodate your planned growth. Otherwise, you might have to switch to a new ISP later, which would require renumbering existing networks. Renumbering can be very labor-intensive.

An alternative is to use private addresses, which are covered in the section, "Using Private Addresses in an IP Environment," later in this chapter. Private addresses make it easier to scale a network without being concerned about an ISP's capability to assign a large block of addresses.

Distributing Authority for Addressing

One of the first steps in developing an addressing and naming model is to determine who will implement the model. Which network administrators will actually assign addresses and configure devices? If addressing and configuration will be carried out by inexperienced network administrators, you should keep the model simple.

If there is a shortage of network administrators, (which there is in many organizations), then simplicity is important as well as minimizing the amount of configuration required. In these situations, dynamic addressing is a good recommendation. Dynamic addressing, such as the Dynamic Host Configuration Protocol (DHCP) for IP environments, allows each end system to learn its address automatically. Very little, if any, configuration is necessary.

If network administrators in regional and branch offices are inexperienced, you might consider not delegating authority for addressing and naming. A lot of small and medium size companies maintain strict control of addressing and naming at a corporate (centralized) level.

Using Dynamic Addressing for End Systems

Dynamic addressing reduces the configuration tasks required to connect end systems to an internetwork. Dynamic addressing also supports users who change offices frequently, travel, or work at home occasionally. With dynamic addressing, a station can automatically learn which network segment it is currently attached to, and adjust its network-layer address accordingly.

Dynamic addressing is built into desktop protocols such as AppleTalk and Novell NetWare. The designers of these protocols recognized the need to minimize configuration tasks so inexperienced users could set up small internetworks. The IP protocols, on the other hand, were designed to run on minicomputers managed by experienced system administrators, and did not originally support dynamic addressing. In recent years, however, the importance of dynamic addressing has been recognized, and many companies use DHCP to minimize configuration tasks for IP hosts. DHCP is covered in this section after a short description of dynamic addressing in AppleTalk and NetWare environments.

AppleTalk Dynamic Addressing

An AppleTalk network-layer station address consists of a 16-bit network number and an 8-bit node ID. The address is written as network.node, for example, *2210.15* means station 15 on network 2210. When an AppleTalk station boots, it dynamically chooses its 24-bit network-layer address, based partially on information it requests from routers on the network segment. A network manager configures routers with a cable range and one or more zones for each network segment. End systems require no configuration.

Once an AppleTalk station has chosen a network-layer address, it saves this information in battery-backed-up RAM, which is also called *parameter RAM*, or *PRAM*. When an AppleTalk station boots, it checks to see if it has an address in PRAM. If it does, it uses that address (after confirming that the address is still unique). Using the same address after a reboot facilitates network management. Without this feature, it would be more difficult to manage AppleTalk stations, because a station would receive a new address each time it booted.

An AppleTalk station communicates with a router to determine the cable range for its network segment. Some AppleTalk networks are so small and so isolated, that they do not include a router. For those networks, the protocol reserves a special range of network numbers, called the *startup range*. The startup range in hexadecimal is FF00–FFFE. The startup range is also used when a station first boots, if the station has no network number in PRAM.

An AppleTalk Phase 2 station uses Address Resolution Protocol (AARP) and Zone Information Protocol (ZIP) packets to determine its address. The process that an AppleTalk Phase 2 station uses to determine its dynamic address is documented in Appendix A, "Characterizing Network Traffic When Workstations Boot."

Novell NetWare Dynamic Addressing

A NetWare network-layer station address consists of a 4-byte network number and a 6-byte node ID. The 6-byte node ID is the same as the station's media-access control (MAC) address on its network interface card (NIC). Because a NetWare station uses its MAC address for its node ID, no configuration of the node ID is required. (Incidentally, the fact that the network-layer node ID and MAC address are the same means that no address-resolution protocol is required.)

A network manager configures routers and servers on a NetWare network with the 4-byte network number for a network segment. When a NetWare station boots, it sends a *get-nearest-server packet*. The servers that respond to this message inform the station of the network number for the local network segment. (If there are no servers on the station's segment, a router responds to the get-nearest-server request. Routers can usually be configured to delay their responses to avoid preempting a busy server's right to respond first.)

IP Dynamic Addressing

An IP network-layer station address is 4 bytes in length and consists of a prefix and host part. (IP version 6 will increase the length.) The address is usually written in dotted-decimal notation, for example, 192.168.10.1 means host 1 on network 192.168.10.0. Stations in an IP environment are called *hosts*, although the word *host* traditionally meant a large mainframe in IBM environments.

When the IP protocols were first developed, a network administrator was required to configure each host with its unique IP address. In the mid-1980s, protocols were developed to support diskless stations dynamically learning an address, which was necessary because a diskless station has no storage for saving a configuration. These protocols included the Reverse Address Resolution Protocol (RARP) and BOOTP. BOOTP has evolved into DHCP, which has gained considerable popularity in the late 1990s.

RARP is limited in scope; the only information returned to a station using RARP is its IP address. BOOTP is more sophisticated than RARP, and optionally returns additional information, including the address of a default router, the name of a boot file to download, and 64 bytes of vendor-specific information.

The Dynamic Host Configuration Protocol

DHCP is based on BOOTP. BOOTP hosts can interoperate with DHCP hosts, although DHCP adds many enhancements to BOOTP, including a larger vendor-specific information field (called the *options field* in DHCP) and the automatic allocation of reusable network-layer addresses. DHCP has bypassed BOOTP in popularity, probably because it is easier to configure. Unlike BOOTP, DHCP does not require a network administrator to maintain a MAC-to-IP address table.

DHCP uses a client/server model. Servers allocate network-layer addresses and save information about which addresses have been allocated. Clients dynamically request configuration parameters from servers. The goal of DHCP is that clients should require no manual configuration. In addition, the network manager should not have to enter any per-client configuration parameters into servers.

DHCP supports three methods for IP address allocation:

- **Automatic allocation.** A DHCP server assigns a permanent IP address to a client.

- **Dynamic allocation.** A DHCP server assigns an IP address to a client for a limited period of time.

- **Manual allocation.** A network administrator assigns a permanent IP address to a client, and DHCP is used simply to convey the assigned address to the client. (Manual allocation is rarely used because it requires per-client configuration, which automatic and dynamic allocations do not require.)

Dynamic allocation is the most popular method, partly because its reallocation feature supports environments where hosts are not online all the time, and there are more hosts than addresses. With dynamic allocation, a client requests the use of an address for a limited period of time. The period of time is called a *lease*.

The allocation mechanism guarantees not to reallocate that address within the requested time, and attempts to return the same network-layer address each time the client requests an address. The client may extend its lease with subsequent requests. The client may choose to relinquish its lease by sending a DHCP release message to the server.

The allocation mechanism can reuse an address if the lease for the address has expired. As a consistency check, the allocating server should probe the reused address before allocating the address. It can do this with an Internet Control Message Protocol (ICMP) echo request (also known as a *ping packet*). The client should also probe the newly-received address. It can do this with a ping packet or an Address Resolution Protocol (ARP) request.

When a client boots, it broadcasts a DHCP discover message on its local subnet. A station that has previously received a network-layer address and lease can include them in the DHCP discover message to suggest that they be used again. A router can pass the DHCP discover message on to DHCP servers not on the same physical subnet to avoid a requirement that a DHCP server reside on each subnet. (The router acts as a DHCP relay agent.)

Each server responds to the DHCP request with a DHCP offer message that includes an available network-layer address in the *your address (yiaddr)* field. The DHCP offer message can include additional configuration parameters in the options field.

After the client receives DHCP offer messages from one or more servers, the client chooses one server from which to request configuration parameters. The client broadcasts a DHCP request message that includes the *server identifier* option to indicate which server it has selected. This DHCP request message is broadcast and relayed through routers if necessary.

The server selected in the DHCP request message commits the configuration parameters for the client to persistent storage and responds with a DHCP ACK message, containing the configuration parameters for the requesting client.

If a client receives no DHCP offer or DHCP ACK messages, the client times out and retransmits the DHCP discover and request messages. To avoid synchronicity and excessive network traffic, the client uses a randomized exponential backoff algorithm to determine the delay between retransmissions. The delay between retransmissions should be chosen to allow sufficient time for replies from the server, based on the characteristics of the network between the client and server. For example, on a 10-Mbps Ethernet network, the delay before the first retransmission should be 4 seconds, randomized by the value of a uniform random number chosen from the range −1 to +1. The delay before the next retransmission should be 8 seconds, randomized by the value of a uniform number chosen from the range −1 to +1. The retransmission delay should be doubled with subsequent retransmissions up to a maximum of 64 seconds.

Using Private Addresses in an IP Environment

Private IP addresses are addresses that an enterprise network administrator assigns to internal networks and hosts without any coordination from an ISP or the Internet Assigned Numbers Authority (IANA). An ISP or the IANA provides *public addresses* for Web servers or other servers that external users access, but public addresses are not necessary for internal hosts and networks. Internal hosts that need access to a limited set of outside services, such as e-mail, FTP, or Web servers, can be handled by a gateway, such as a network address translation (NAT) gateway. NAT is covered later in this chapter.

In Request for Comments (RFC) 1918, the Internet Engineering Task Force (IETF) has reserved the following numbers for addressing nodes on internal private networks:

- 10.0.0.0–10.255.255.255

- 172.16.0.0–172.31.255.255

- 192.168.0.0–192.168.255.255

One advantage of private network numbers is security. Private network numbers are not advertised to the Internet. In fact, private network numbers *must not* be advertised to the Internet because they are not globally unique. By not advertising private internal network numbers, a modicum of security is achieved. (Additional security, including a firewall topology, should also be designed, as discussed in the previous chapter and in Chapter 8.)

Private addressing also helps meet goals for adaptability and flexibility. Using private addressing makes is easier to change ISPs in the future. If private addressing has been used, when moving to a new ISP, the only address changes required are in the router or firewall providing NAT services and in any public servers. You should recommend private addressing to customers who want the flexibility of easily switching to a different ISP in the future.

Another advantage of private network numbers is that an enterprise network can advertise just one network number, or a small block of network numbers, to the Internet. It is good practice to avoid advertising many network numbers to the Internet. One of the goals of modern Internet practices is that Internet routers should not need to manage huge routing tables. As an enterprise network grows, the network manager can assign private addresses to new networks, rather than requesting additional public network numbers from an ISP or the IANA. This avoids increasing the size of Internet routing tables.

Private network numbers let a network designer reserve scarce Internet addresses for public servers. During the mid-1990s, as the Internet became commercialized and popularized, a scare rippled through the Internet community regarding the shortage of addresses. Dire predictions were made that no more addresses would be available by the turn of the century. Because of this scare, many companies (and many ISPs) were given a small set of addresses that needed to be carefully managed to avoid depletion. These companies recognize the value of private addresses for internal networks.

NOTES

The shortage of Internet addresses was mainly due to the way IP addresses were divided into classes. Although the IP address space is fixed in size and will become depleted at some point, its 4-byte size is theoretically large enough to address over 4 billion nodes. The method used to divide the address space into classes meant that many addresses were wasted, however. Approximately 50 percent of the address space was used for Class A host addresses. Another 12 percent was used for Class C host addresses.

With the invention of classless addressing, the threat of running out of addresses is less imminent. Classless addressing is covered in the section, "Using a Hierarchical Model for Assigning Network-Layer Addresses."

Caveats with Private Addressing

Although the benefits of private addressing outweigh the disadvantages, it is important to be aware of the drawbacks. One drawback is that outsourcing network management is difficult. When a company delegates network management responsibility to an outside company, the outside company typically sets up network consoles at its own site that communicate with internetworking devices inside the client's network. With private addressing, however, the consoles cannot reach the client's devices, because no routes to internal networks are advertised to the outside. The outsourcing company might require that consoles and personnel be placed within the internal network, or that an out-of-band network management system be deployed, which would raise the price of network management.

Another drawback for private addressing is the difficulty of communicating with partners, vendors, suppliers, and so on. Because the partner companies are also probably using private addresses, building extranets becomes more difficult. Also, companies that merge with each other face a difficult chore of renumbering any duplicate addresses caused by both companies using the same private addresses.

One other caveat to keep in mind when using private addresses is that it is easy to forget to use a structured model with the private addresses. Enterprise network managers, who were once starved for addresses that were carefully doled out by ISPs and the IANA, get excited when they move to private addressing and have all of network 10.0.0.0 at their disposal.

The excitement should not overshadow the need to assign the new address space in a structured, hierarchical fashion. Hierarchical addressing facilitates route summarization within the enterprise network, which decreases bandwidth consumption by routing protocols, reduces processing on routers, and enhances network resiliency.

Network Address Translation

Network address translation (NAT) is an IP mechanism that is described in RFC 1631 for converting addresses from an inside network to addresses that are appropriate for an outside network, and vice-versa. NAT is useful when hosts that need access to Internet services have private addresses. NAT functionality can be implemented in a separate appliance, router, or firewall.

The NAT administrator configures a pool of outside addresses that can be used for translation. When an inside host sends a packet, the source address is translated dynamically to an address from the pool of outside addresses. NAT also has a provision for static addresses for servers that need a fixed address, for example, a Web or mail server that must always map to the same well-known address.

Some NAT products also offer port translation for mapping several addresses to the same address. With *port translation*, all traffic from an enterprise has the same address. Port numbers are used to distinguish separate conversations. Port translation reduces the number of required outside addresses.

When using NAT, all traffic between an enterprise network and the Internet must go through the NAT gateway. For this reason, you should make sure the NAT gateway has superior throughput and low delay, particularly if enterprise users depend on Internet video or voice applications. The NAT gateway should have a fast processor that can examine and change packets very quickly. Keep in mind that, in addition to modifying IP addresses, a NAT gateway must modify the IP, TCP, and UDP checksums. (The checksums for TCP and UDP cover a pseudo header that contains source and destination IP addresses.)

In many cases, NAT must also modify IP addresses that occur inside the data part of a packet. IP addresses can appear in ICMP, FTP, DNS, and other types of packets. Because NAT has the job of translating something so basic as network-layer addresses, it can be tricky to guarantee correct behavior with all applications. A NAT gateway should be thoroughly tested in a pilot environment before it is generally deployed.

USING A HIERARCHICAL MODEL
FOR ASSIGNING ADDRESSES

Hierarchical addressing is a model for applying structure to addresses so that numbers in the left part of an address refer to large blocks of networks or nodes, and numbers in the right part of an address refer to individual networks or nodes. Hierarchical addressing facilitates *hierarchical routing*, which is a model for distributing knowledge of a network topology among internetwork routers. With hierarchical routing, no single router needs to understand the complete topology. This chapter focuses on hierarchical addressing and routing for IP environments, but the concepts apply to other environments also.

Why Use a Hierarchical Model for Addressing and Routing?

Chapter 5, "Designing a Network Topology," talked about the importance of hierarchy in topology design. The benefits of hierarchy in an addressing and routing model are the same as those for a topology model:

- Support for easy troubleshooting, upgrades, and manageability

- Optimized performance

- Faster routing-protocol convergence

- Scalability

- Stability

- Fewer network resources needed (CPU, memory, buffers, bandwidth, and so on)

Hierarchical addressing permits the summarization (aggregation) of network numbers. *Summarization* allows a router to group many network numbers when advertising its routing table. Summarization enhances network performance and stability. Hierarchical addressing also facilitates *variable-length subnet masking (VLSM)*. With VLSM, a network can be divided into subnets of different sizes, which helps optimize available address space.

Hierarchical Routing

Hierarchical routing means that knowledge of the network topology and configuration is localized. No single router needs to understand how to get to each other network segment. Hierarchical routing requires that a network administrator assign addresses in a hierarchical fashion. IP addressing and routing have been somewhat hierarchical for a long time, but in recent years, as the Internet and enterprise intranets have grown, it has become necessary to add more hierarchy.

To understand hierarchical routing in simple terms, consider the telephone system. The telephone system has used hierarchical routing for years. When you dial 541-555-1212 from a phone in Michigan, the phone switch in Michigan does not know how to reach this specific number in Oregon. The switch in Michigan simply knows that the number is not in Michigan and forwards the call to a national phone company. A switch at the national phone company knows that 541 is for Southern Oregon, but does not know specifically where calls to 555 should go. A switch in Oregon determines which central-office switch handles the 555 prefix, and that switch routes the call to 1212.

With data networking, similar decisions are made as a packet travels across a routed network. However, in traditional IP networks, the decisions could not be quite as local as the decisions in the telephone example. Until recently, IP addresses for the Internet were assigned in a non-hierarchical fashion. For example, two companies in Oregon might have widely different Class C network numbers, despite the fact that they both use the same upstream provider to reach the Internet. This meant that the provider had to tell all other Internet sites about both Oregon companies. So, unlike the phone system example, a router in Michigan knew how to reach specific networks in Oregon.

Classless Inter-Domain Routing

In the mid-1990s, the IETF and IANA realized that the lack of a hierarchical model for assigning network numbers in the Internet was a severe scalability problem. Internet routing tables were growing exponentially, and the amount of overhead to process and transmit the tables was significant. To constrain routing overhead, it became clear that the Internet must adopt a hierarchical addressing and routing scheme.

To solve the routing overhead problem, the Internet adopted the *Classless Inter-Domain Routing (CIDR)* method for summarizing routes. CIDR specifies that IP network addresses should be assigned in blocks, and that routers in the Internet should group routes together to cut down on the quantity of routing information shared by Internet routers.

RFC 2050 provides guidelines for IP address allocation by regional and local Internet registries and ISPs. RFC 2050 states that:

> An Internet Provider obtains a block of address space from an address registry, and then assigns to its customers addresses from within that block based on each customer requirement. The result of this process is that routes to many customers will be aggregated together, and will appear to other providers as a single route. For route aggregation to be effective, Internet providers encourage customers joining their network to use the provider's block, and thus renumber their computers. Such encouragement may become a requirement in the future.

At the same time that the IETF and IANA addressed the problem of non-hierarchical routing, they also addressed the problem of IP address depletion. As mentioned in a previous section, the system of assigning addresses in classes meant that many addresses were going to waste. The IETF developed classless addressing, which provides more flexibility in specifying the length of the prefix part of an IP network number.

Classless Routing Versus Classful Routing

As shown in Figure 6–2, an IP address contains a prefix part and a host part. Routers use the prefix to determine the path for a destination address that is not local. Routers use the host part to reach local hosts.

Figure 6–2
The two parts of an IP address.

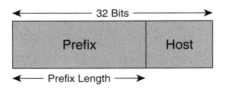

A prefix identifies a block of host numbers and is used for routing to that block. Traditional routing, also known as *classful routing*, does not transmit any information about the prefix length. With classful routing, hosts and routers calculate the prefix length by looking at the first few bits of an address to determine its class. The first few bits for Class A through C addresses are as follows:

Class A	First bit = 0	Prefix is 8 bits	First octet is 1–126
Class B	First 2 bits = 10	Prefix is 16 bits	First octet is 128–191
Class C	First 3 bits = 110	Prefix is 24 bits	First octet is 192–223

In early IP implementations, IP hosts and routers understood only three prefix lengths: 8, 16, and 24. This became a limitation as networks grew, so subnetting was introduced. With *subnets*, a host (or router) can be configured to understand that the local prefix length is extended. This configuration is accomplished with a subnet mask. For example, routers and hosts can be configured to understand that network 10.0.0.0 is subnetted into 254 subnets by using a subnet mask of 255.255.0.0.

A new notation that has gained popularity in recent years indicates the prefix length with a length field, following a slash. For example, in the address 10.1.0.1/16, the 16 indicates that the prefix is 16 bits long, which means the same as the subnet mask 255.255.0.0.

Traditional IP hosts and routers had a limited capability to understand prefix lengths and subnets. They understood the length for local configurations, but not for remote configurations. Classful routing did not transmit any information about the prefix length. The prefix length was calculated from the information about the address class provided in the first few bits of an address, as mentioned earlier.

Classless routing protocols, on the other hand, transmit a prefix length with an IP address. This allows classless routing protocols to group networks into one entry and use the prefix length to specify which networks are grouped. Classless routing protocols also accept any arbitrary prefix length, rather then only accepting lengths of 8, 16, or 24, which the classful system dictated.

Classless routing protocols include Routing Information Protocol (RIP) version 2, Enhanced Interior Gateway Routing Protocol (Enhanced IGRP), Open Shortest Path First (OSPF), Border Gateway Routing Protocol (BGP), and Intermediate System-to-Intermediate System (IS-IS).

Classful routing protocols include RIP version 1, and the Interior Gateway Routing Protocol (IGRP).

Route Summarization (Aggregation)

When advertising routes into another major network, classful routing protocols automatically summarize subnets. They only advertise a route to a Class A, B, or C network, instead of routes to subnets. Because classful routers and hosts do not understand non-local prefix lengths and subnets, there is no reason to advertise information about prefix lengths. The automatic summarization into a major class network has some disadvantages, for example, discontiguous subnets are not supported.

(Discontiguous subnets were mentioned in Chapter 3; they are covered in more detail later in this chapter in the section "Discontiguous Subnets.")

Classless routing protocols advertise a route and a prefix length. If addresses are assigned in a hierarchical fashion, a classless routing protocol can be configured to aggregate subnets into one route, thus reducing routing overhead. The importance of route summarization on the Internet was already discussed. It is also important to summarize (aggregate) routes on an enterprise network. Route summarization reduces the size of routing tables, which minimizes bandwidth consumption and processing on routers. Route summarization also means that problems within one area of the network do not tend to spread to other areas.

Route Summarization Example

This section covers a route summarization example that is based on the network shown in Figure 6–3. Looking at Figure 6–3, you can see that a network administrator assigned network numbers 172.16.0.0–172.19.0.0 to networks in a branch office.

Figure 6–3
*Route summa-
rization exam-
ple.*

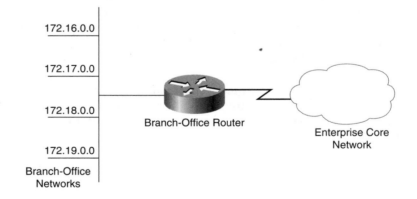

The branch-office router in Figure 6–3 can summarize its local network numbers and report that it has 172.16.0.0/14 behind it. By advertising this single route, the router is saying, "Route packets to me if the destination has the first 14 bits set to 172.16." The router is reporting a route to all networks where the first 14 bits are equal to 10101100 000100 in binary.

To understand the summarization in this example, you should convert the number 172 to binary, which results in the binary number 10101100. You should also convert the numbers 16 through 19 to binary, as shown in the following table.

Second Octet in Decimal	Second Octet in Binary
16	00010000
17	00010001
18	00010010
19	00010011

Notice that the left-most 6 bits for the numbers 16 through 19 are identical. This is what makes route summarization with a prefix length of 14 possible in this example. The first 8 bits for the networks are identical (all the networks have 172 for the first octet) and the next 6 bits are also identical.

Route Summarization Tips

For route summarization to work correctly, the following requirements must be met:

- Multiple IP addresses must share the same left-most bits.

- Routers must base their routing decisions on a 32-bit IP address and prefix length that can be up to 32 bits. (A *host-specific route* has a 32-bit prefix.)

- Routing protocols must carry the prefix length with 32-bit addresses.

Although classless addressing and routing are somewhat new concepts for IP network designers and administrators, they are not complicated concepts. By spending some time analyzing network numbers (and converting the addresses to binary), you can see the simplicity and elegance of classless addressing and route summarization.

When you look at a block of subnets, you can determine if the addresses can be summarized by using the following rules:

- The number of subnets to be summarized must be a power of 2, for example, 2, 4, 8, 16, 32, and so on.

- The relevant octet in the first address in the block to be summarized must be a multiple of the number of subnets.

Let's consider one more example. The following network numbers are defined at a branch office. Can they be summarized?

- 10.108.48.0
- 10.108.49.0
- 10.108.50.0
- 10.108.51.0
- 10.108.52.0
- 10.108.53.0
- 10.108.54.0
- 10.108.55.0

The number of subnets is 8, which is a power of 2, so the first condition is met.

The relevant octet (third in this case) is 48, which is a multiple of the number of subnets. So, the second condition is met. The subnets can be summarized as 10.108.48.0/21. (Convert the numbers to binary to understand the prefix length of 21.)

Discontiguous Subnets

As mentioned earlier, classful routing protocols automatically summarize subnets. One side-effect of this is that discontiguous subnets are not supported. Subnets must be next to each other, that is, contiguous. Figure 6–4 shows an enterprise network with discontiguous subnets.

With a classful routing protocol such as RIP Version 1 or IGRP, Router A in Figure 6–4 advertises that it can get to network 10.0.0.0. Router B ignores this advertisement, because it can already get to network 10.0.0.0. It is directly attached to network 10.0.0.0. (The opposite is also true: Router B advertises that it can get to network 10.0.0.0, but Router A ignores this information.) This means that the routers cannot reach remote subnets of network 10.0.0.0.

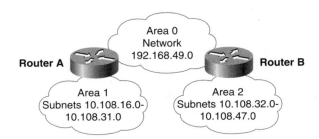

Figure 6–4
A network with discontiguous subnets.

To solve this problem, a classless routing protocol can be used. With a classless routing protocol, Router A advertises that it can get to networks 10.108.16.0/20. Router B advertises that it can get to networks 10.108.32.0/20. (To understand why the prefix length is 20, convert the network numbers to binary.) Because classless routing protocols understand prefixes of any length (not just 8, 16, or 24), the routers in Figure 6–4 can route to discontiguous subnets, assuming they are running a classless routing protocol, such as OSPF or Enhanced IGRP.

NOTES

To configure the devices in the previous example with an old-style subnet mask instead of a prefix length, use a mask of 255.255.240.0. The first four bits of the third octet are set to ones. A trick for determining the value of the relevant octet in a subnet mask is to subtract the number of summarized subnets from 256. In this example, there are 16 summarized subnets, so the relevant octet is 256–16, or 240.

Mobile Hosts

Classless routing and discontiguous subnets support mobile hosts. A *mobile host*, in this context, is a host that moves from one network to another and has a statically-defined IP address. A network administrator can move a mobile host and configure a router with a host-specific route to specify that traffic for the host should be routed through that router.

For example, in Figure 6–5, host 10.108.16.1 has moved to a different network. Even though Router A advertises that network 10.108.16.0/20 is behind it, Router B can advertise that 10.108.16.1/32 is behind it.

When making a routing decision, classless routing protocols match the longest prefix. The routers in the example have in their tables both 10.108.16.0/20 and 10.108.16.1/32. When switching a packet, the routers use the longest prefix available that is appropriate for the destination address in the packet.

Figure 6–5
A mobile host.

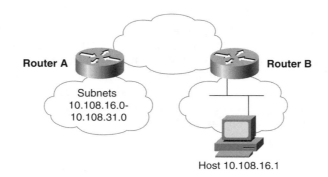

NOTES

In the previous example, a better design would be to use DHCP so that hosts can be moved without requiring any reconfiguration on the hosts or routers. The example is simply used to explain the longest-prefix-match concept. It is not meant to be a design recommendation.

Variable-Length Subnet Masking

Using a classless routing protocol means that you can have different sizes of subnets within a single network. Varying the size of subnets is also known as *variable-length subnet masking*, or *VLSM*. VLSM relies on providing prefix length information explicitly with each use of an address. The length of the prefix is evaluated independently at each place it is used. The capability to have a different prefix length at different points supports efficiency and flexibility in the use of the IP address space. Instead of each subnet being the same size, you can have both big and small subnets.

One use for small subnets is point-to-point WAN links that only have two devices (one router on each end of the link). Such a link can use a subnet mask of 255.255.255.252, because only two devices need addresses. The two devices can be numbered 01 and 10.

NOTES

A disadvantage of using a separate subnet for each WAN link is that each subnet adds an entry to the routing table. With some vendors' routers, you do not need to number the serial ports on a point-to-point WAN link, which obviates the need for small WAN point-to-point subnets. One drawback with unnumbered ports, however, is that you cannot ping them, which makes troubleshooting more difficult. But if SNMP or other network management tools can identify port problems, then the capability to ping a WAN port is not essential. Unnumbered WAN ports are a better solution than small WAN point-to-point subnets in this case.

With VLSM, it is important to avoid inadvertently overlapping blocks of addresses. The best way to avoid this is to first subnet the address space by using a general-purpose subnet mask. For example, you could subnet a Class B major network with an 24-bit subnet mask. Most subnets can use this mask, which is suitable for the average workgroup. If small subnets are needed, pick one of the general-purpose subnets, and subnet it further, using a longer subnet mask (prefix). (Be sure to avoid a prefix that is so long that it does not accommodate growth.) If the small subnets are grouped, routing information can be summarized.

DESIGNING A MODEL FOR NAMING

Names play an essential role in meeting a customer's goals for usability. Short, meaningful names enhance user productivity and simplify network management. A good naming model also strengthens the performance and availability of a network. The goal of this section is to help you design naming models for multiprotocol internetworks that will meet your customer's goals for usability, manageability, performance, and availability.

Names are assigned to many types of resources in a typical internetwork—routers, servers, hosts, printers, and other resources. This section covers the naming of devices and networks. Providing names for users, groups, accounts, and passwords is not covered, although some of the guidelines for naming devices apply to these items also.

A good naming model should let a user transparently access a service by name rather than address. Because networking protocols require an address, the user's system should map the name to an address. The method for mapping a name to an address can be either dynamic, using some sort of naming protocol, or static, for example, a file on the user's system that lists all names and their associated addresses. Usually, a dynamic method is preferable, despite the additional network traffic caused by dynamic naming protocols.

When developing a naming model, you should consider the following questions:

- What types of entities need names? Servers, routers, printers, hosts, AppleTalk zones, others?

- Do end systems need names? Will the end systems offer any services, such as personal Web serving?

- What is the structure of a name? Does a portion of the name identify the type of device?

- How are names stored, managed, and accessed?

- Who assigns names?

- How do hosts map a name to an address? Will a dynamic or static system be provided?

- How does a host learn its own name?

- If dynamic addressing is used, will the names also be dynamic and change when an address changes?

- Should the naming system use a peer-to-peer or client/server model?

- If name servers will be used, how much redundancy (mirroring) will be required?

- Will the name database be distributed among many servers?

- How will the selected naming system affect network traffic?

- How will the selected naming system affect security?

Distributing Authority for Naming

During the early stages of designing a naming model, you should consider the question of who will actually assign names. Will the name space be completely controlled by a centralized authority, or will the naming of some devices be carried out by decentralized agents? Will a corporate IS department name devices at regional and branch offices, or can departmental administrators implement naming at those sites? Will users be allowed to name their own systems, or are all names assigned by network administrators? The disadvantage of distributing authority for naming is that names become harder to control and manage. But if all groups and users agree on, and practice, the same policies, there are many advantages to distributing authority for naming.

The obvious advantage is that no department is burdened with the job of assigning and maintaining all names. Other advantages include performance and scalability. If each name server manages a portion of the name space instead of the whole name space, the requirements for memory and processing power on the servers are lessened. Also, if clients have access to a local name server instead of depending on a centralized server, many names can be resolved to addresses locally, without causing traffic on the internetwork. Local servers can cache information about remote devices, to further reduce network traffic.

Guidelines for Assigning Names

To maximize usability, names should be short, meaningful, unambiguous, and distinct. A user should easily recognize which names go with which devices. A good practice is to include in a name some sort of indication of the device's type. For example, you can suffix router names with the characters *rtr*, switches with *sw*, servers with *svr*, and so on. Using meaningful suffixes decreases ambiguity for end users, and helps managers more easily extract device names from network management tools.

Names can also include a location code. Some network designers use airport codes in their naming models. For example, all names in San Francisco start with SFO, all names in Oakland start with OAK, and so on. The location code could be a number instead, but most people remember letters better than numbers.

Try to avoid names that have unusual characters, for example hyphens, underscores, asterisks, and so on, even if the naming protocol allows these characters (which many do). These characters are hard to type and can cause applications and protocols to behave in unexpected ways. Unusual characters might mean something special to a protocol. For example, the dollar sign when used as the last character in a NetBIOS name means that the name does not appear in network browser lists or in response to NetBIOS network-survey commands. NetBIOS names with a dollar sign at the end are for administrative use only.

It is also best if names are case-insensitive, since people usually cannot remember which case to use. Names that require a user to remember mixed cases, for example DBServer, are not a good idea. They are hard to type and some protocols might be case-insensitive anyway and transmit the name as all lowercase or all uppercase, losing the significance of the mixed case.

You should also avoid spaces in names. Spaces confuse users and might not work correctly with some applications or protocols. For Windows 3.x and DOS users, you should keep names at eight characters or less in case applications or protocols are confined by the DOS restriction on the size of file names. This rule should not be hard to follow, because names should generally be eight characters or less anyway.

If a device has more than one interface and more than one address, you should map all the addresses to one common name. For example, on a multiport router with multiple IP addresses, assign the same name to all the router's IP addresses. This way network management software does not assume that a multiport device is actually more than one device.

NOTES

Security policy may contradict some of these recommendations for naming. Names that are easily recognized by users are easily recognized by attackers also. For key devices and data sources (for example, routers and servers), it is often a good idea to use long, cryptic names. In some cases, names are used only by system software and not by users, so usability is not affected. In other cases, tradeoffs must be made between usability and security goals.

Assigning Names in an AppleTalk Environment

In an AppleTalk environment, you assign names to shared servers and printers. You also name end systems when personal file sharing or personal Web hosting are enabled. The AppleTalk Name Binding Protocol (NBP) maps names to addresses. An NBP name has the format

object:type@zone

As an example, consider the name Sales:AFPServer@SFO. A Macintosh user finds the *Sales* AppleTalk Filing Protocol (AFP) file server in the *SFO* zone by opening a *Chooser Window*. In the Chooser Window, the user selects the *SFO* zone, and clicks on the icon for the *Sales* server. (The user does not see names in the unfriendly object:type@zone format.)

As a network designer, you should encourage AppleTalk users and managers to use meaningful names. Macintosh users and administrators like to be creative with their naming, but you should explain that creative names can actually decrease user- friendliness and make management and troubleshooting more difficult. Administrators and users should avoid cute names as they can be more confusing than informative.

In an AppleTalk internetwork, in addition to naming servers and printers, you also assign names to zones. A *zone* is a collection of nodes that share information (similar to a virtual LAN [VLAN]). AppleTalk supports multiple zones in a network segment and multiple network segments in a zone.

NOTES

In most cases, it is not necessary to assign more than one zone name to a single segment. Multiple zones on a segment logically divide very large segments with hundreds of services. But most AppleTalk networks do not have hundreds of services on one segment, so multiple zone names on one segment are generally not necessary.

There are a few reasons you might want to group multiple network segments into one zone:

- You can reduce the number of zones that appear in the Chooser Window, which is important in very large AppleTalk internetworks.

- You can make it easier for a group that is geographically dispersed to find its servers and printers.

- You can group administrative or corporate servers, even when the servers are on different segments.

- You can use one zone name for all point-to-point WAN links to remote sites.

Remote point-to-point WAN links have no services on them, so the zone name should be something unfriendly that discourages lookups in the zone. A zone name like ZZZRemote is a good choice because it looks unfriendly and sorts to the bottom of the zone list in the Chooser Window. It is a good idea to minimize lookups in geographically-dispersed zones, because the lookups spread across the internetwork, causing extra traffic.

When assigning zone names, make sure that the names are meaningful to enhance troubleshooting and the user's experience. A user needs to recognize which zone has local services. For example, if a user wants to print a document to a local printer, the user needs to know that the local zone is something like "Building5_Floor3" to avoid selecting a printer that is not physically nearby. It can be annoying to print a document and then not be able to find the printer!

Assigning Names in a Novell NetWare Environment

In a Novell NetWare environment, you assign names to resources such as volumes on a file server, shared printers, print queues, printer servers, and possibly other servers such as modem, fax, or database servers. Generally, there is no need to assign names to end systems. With NetWare 4.x, you can make use of the NetWare Directory Services (NDS), which is a global resource-naming system and set of protocols. NDS uses a distributed database approach to naming, whereby portions of the database reside on many servers, thus reducing the possibility of one central server failing and affecting all users.

Assigning Names in a NetBIOS Environment

NetBIOS is a session-layer protocol that includes functions for naming devices, which ensures the uniqueness of names, and finding named services. NetBIOS was developed by IBM and Sytek in the 1980s for use on PC networks. It gained popularity in the late 1980s as a way of connecting PCs using software from IBM, Microsoft, and 3Com corporations. It is still widely used in Windows and Windows NT environments.

There are many implementations of the NetBIOS protocol, including *NetBEUI* for bridged or switched environments, *NWLink* for Novell NetWare environments, and NetBIOS over TCP/IP, which is also known as *NetBT.* (NetBIOS over TCP/IP is also sometimes called *NBT.*)

NetBIOS in a Bridged or Switched Environment (NetBEUI)

NetBIOS was originally implemented as session-layer software that runs on top of the driver for a NIC. This implementation of NetBIOS is called *NetBEUI* and is only appropriate for bridged or switched networks (because it has no network layer).

The NetBEUI implementation of NetBIOS makes extensive use of broadcast packets for naming functions. When a station running NetBEUI starts up, it broadcasts *check-name queries* to make sure its name is unique. (The check-name query is sometimes called an *add-name query.*) A station can have as many as 32 names if it is running many applications, and it sends broadcast packets to check each of these names. The station also broadcasts one or more *find-name queries* to find other NetBIOS clients and servers by name.

Although many large-scale bridged NetBEUI networks are still in existence, most of them are destined for upgrades to new versions of NetBIOS. Because of the high level of broadcast traffic in a NetBEUI environment, large-scale NetBEUI networks exhibit performance and resiliency problems. The option to segment the network with routers does not work for NetBEUI, because NetBEUI has no network layer and is not routable. So many companies are migrating their NetBEUI environments to NWLink or NetBT.

NetBIOS in a Novell NetWare Environment (NWLink)

Companies that have applications that use NetBIOS in a Novell NetWare internetwork can use the NWLink implementation of the NetBIOS protocol. With NWLink,

NetBIOS runs on top of Novell's Sequenced Packet Exchange (SPX) and Internetwork Packet Exchange (IPX) protocols. NWLink uses *type-20 broadcast packets* to send name registration and lookup requests. To forward these packets through a Cisco router, use the `ipx type-20 propagation` command on each interface. (Configure each interface to receive and transmit type-20 packets.)

NetBIOS in a TCP/IP Environment (NetBT)

NetBT has gained popularity as a way of sharing files among Microsoft Windows and Windows NT clients in a TCP/IP internetwork. In a NetBT environment, there are four options for name registration and lookup:

- Broadcasts

- Lmhosts files

- Windows Internet Name Service (WINS)

- Domain Name System (DNS)

A combination of WINS and DNS is also supported.

Registering and Resolving Names with Broadcasts

Because NetBT is based on NetBIOS, it makes extensive use of broadcast packets by default. Broadcast packets are used to announce named services, find named services, and elect a *master browser* in a Windows NT environment.

Using broadcasts is not the preferred method for implementing naming functions in a TCP/IP environment, however, because of the performance implications and because routers do not forward broadcast packets by default. (A router can be configured to forward NetBT broadcasts, which go to UDP port 137, but this is not an optimal solution.)

Registering and Resolving Names with Imhosts Files

To avoid clients having to send broadcast frames to look for named services, a network administrator can place an lmhosts file on each station. The *lmhosts file* is an ASCII text file that contains a list of names and their respective IP addresses. The lmhosts file is similar to the hosts file on UNIX TCP/IP devices, although it includes some Windows NT-specific functionality.

Registering and Resolving Names with WINS Servers

lmhosts files are not dynamic and require a lot of maintenance. As a network grows, lmhosts files should be removed in favor of using WINS or DNS servers for dynamic resolution of NetBIOS names to IP addresses. When a PC is configured with a WINS server, the PC sends a message directly to the WINS server to resolve a name, instead of using the lmhosts file or sending broadcast packets. The PC also sends a message to the WINS server when it boots to make sure its own name is unique.

In a NetBT environment, your network design customers can plan to configure PCs with the address of a WINS server in the Network Control Panel. Alternately, to avoid configuring each PC with the address of a WINS server, a PC can receive the address of a WINS server in the Options field of a DHCP response.

To ensure that a PC can reach a WINS server, you can establish redundant WINS servers, and configure the PCs (or DHCP servers) with a primary and secondary WINS server. To use redundant servers, you must plan to synchronize the WINS databases on the servers. This is accomplished by establishing *WINS partners*. If the redundant WINS servers are on opposite sides of a slow WAN link, synchronization should occur infrequently or after business hours. For example, WINS severs on different continents connected via a 64-Kbps link should probably only update each other once every 12 hours.

Integrating WINS and the Domain Name System (DNS)

In a NetBT environment, hosts have both a NetBIOS and an IP host name. Typically these names are the same, but they do not have to be. IP host names are mapped to addresses using the Domain Name System (DNS). DNS is a standard Internet service and is covered in the next section, which covers naming in a generic IP environment. (This section covers naming in a NetBT environment.) It is expected that over time, naming in a Windows environment will be accomplished soley with DNS, and WINS will become obsolete.

In Windows NT 4.x, Microsoft's implementation of DNS is tightly integrated with WINS. This allows non-WINS clients to resolve NetBIOS names by querying a DNS server. Microsoft also supports dynamic host names, which are necessary when DHCP is used for dynamic addressing. With the DNS/WINS integration, a DNS server can query a WINS server to determine if the WINS server has learned a dynamic name. This avoids having to configure names in a DNS server, which is difficult with dynamic names.

Assigning Names in an IP Environment

Naming in an IP environment is accomplished by configuring hosts files, DNS servers, or Network Information Service (NIS) servers. DNS is used on the Internet, and has also gained widespread popularity for managing names in enterprise networks. It is the recommended naming system for modern networks.

A hosts file tells a UNIX workstation how to convert a host name into an IP address. A network administrator maintains a hosts file on each workstation in the internetwork. Both DNS and NIS were developed to allow a network manager to centralize the naming of devices, using a distributed database approach, instead of a flat file that resides on each system.

Sun Microsystems developed NIS to allow a UNIX network administrator to centralize the management of names and other configuration parameters. An administrator can use NIS to maintain names, user and password information, Ethernet addresses, mail aliases, group definitions, and protocol names and numbers. NIS is quite common, but will probably become less common as the Internet standard for naming (DNS) gains momentum.

The Domain Name System

DNS was developed in the early 1980s when it became clear that managing a hosts file containing the names and addresses of all the systems on the Internet would no longer work. As the Internet hosts file grew, it became difficult to maintain, store, and transmit to other hosts.

DNS is a distributed database that provides a hierarchical naming system. A DNS name has two parts: a host name and a domain name. For example, in information.priscilla.com, information is the host, and priscilla.com is the domain. The following chart shows some of the most common top-level domains.

Domain	Description
.edu	Educational institutions

Domain	Description
.gov	Government agencies
.net	Network providers
.com	Commercial companies
.org	Non-profit organizations

There are also many geographical top-level domains, for example .uk for the United Kingdom, and .de for Germany. Work is currently underway to develop some new top-level domains, such as .store for retail stores and .vend for other types of vendors. Increasing the options for top-level domains may help prevent the many disputes that occur over the right to use popular and marketable names.

To register a domain name, you must fill out forms available from the Internet Network Information Center (InterNIC) agency of the U.S. government and pay a small fee. The process for registering a domain name will probably change in the near future. The U.S. government has recently recognized the need to open the process to private organizations that can compete with each other on pricing and service. The U.S. government also wishes to remove itself from any disputes about popular names. The international community is especially anxious to see the top-level names managed by some agency other than a U.S. government agency.

The DNS architecture distributes the knowledge of names so that no single system has to know all names. The InterNIC currently has authority for top-level domains. (This will probably change in the near future.) The InterNIC delegates authority for names in the lower layers of the hierarchy. Each layer of the hierarchy can also delegate authority. For example, a corporate IS department might manage high-level names, such as www.company.com, but delegate authority to the marketing department for names in the marketing.company.com sub-domain. Delegation allows DNS to be autonomously managed at each layer, which increases scalability and helps keep names meaningful.

DNS uses a client/server model. When a client needs to send a packet to a named station, *resolver software* on the client sends a name query to a local DNS server. If the local server cannot resolve the name, it queries other servers on behalf of the resolver. When the local name server receives a response, it replies to the resolver and caches information for future requests. The length of time that a server should cache information received from other servers is entered into the DNS database by a network administrator. Long time intervals decrease network traffic but can also make it difficult to change a name. The old name might be cached on thousands of servers in the Internet.

The management of DNS names and servers is a complex task. For more information on managing DNS names in a UNIX environment, see the classic book by Paul Albitz and Cricket Liu called *DNS and BIND*. It is published by O'Reilly & Associates, Inc. The second edition of the book includes basic information about managing DNS on Windows NT systems, in addition to detailed information about DNS on UNIX systems.

Dynamic DNS Names

With many DHCP implementations, when a host requests an IP address from a DHCP server, the host also receives a dynamic host name, something like pc23.dynamic.priscilla.com. A dynamic name is not appropriate for some applications. For example, Web servers, FTP servers, Internet telephony applications, and push applications rely on static host names. To reach a Web server, a user types in a Universal Resource Locator (URL) that is based on the server's domain name. If the name changes dynamically, it becomes impossible to reach the server. With Internet telephony applications, a user needs to tell people the host name to use when placing a call to the user's system.

For these types of applications, it is important to have a DNS implementation that can associate a static name with a dynamic address. This can be accomplished in a variety of ways. Although there is currently no standard for dynamic DNS (DDNS), the IETF is working on one, and many vendors have developed creative solutions to the problems associated with names in a DHCP environment.

SUMMARY

This chapter provided guidelines for assigning addresses and names in a multiprotocol internetwork environment. The chapter illustrated the importance of using a structured model for addressing and naming to make it easier to understand network maps, operate network management software, recognize devices in protocol analyzer traces, and meet a customer's goals for usability.

Structured addresses and names facilitate network optimization because they make it easier to code network filters on firewalls, routers, and switches. Structured addresses also help you implement route summarization, which decreases bandwidth utilization, processing on routers, and network instability.

This chapter also discussed distributing authority for addressing and naming to avoid one department having to manage all addresses and names. Another way to simplify addressing and naming tasks is to use dynamic addressing and naming. Dynamic addressing, for example DHCP for IP environments, allows each end system to learn its address automatically. DHCP is recommended for the addressing of end systems in a campus network design.

Addressing and naming are essential elements of the logical design phase of the top-down network design process. If designed correctly, addressing and naming models can strengthen your ability to satisfy a customers' needs. They can also help you decide which routing and bridging protocols to select, which is covered in the next chapter.

CHAPTER 7

Selecting Bridging, Switching, and Routing Protocols

The goal of this chapter is to help you select the right bridging, switching, and routing protocols for your network design customer. The selections you make will depend on your customer's business and technical goals. To help you select the right protocols for your customer, the chapter covers the following attributes of bridging, switching, and routing protocols:

- Network traffic characteristics

- Bandwidth, memory, and CPU usage

- The approximate number of peer routers or switches supported

- The capability to quickly adapt to changes in an internetwork

- The capability to authenticate route updates for security reasons

At this point in the network design process, you have created a network design topology and have developed some idea of where switches and routers will reside, but you haven't selected any actual switch or router products. An understanding of the bridging, switching, and routing protocols that a switch or router must support will help you select the best product for the job.

This chapter begins with a generic discussion about decision-making to help you develop a systematic process for selecting solutions for both the logical and physical components of a network design. Making sound decisions regarding protocols and technologies is a crucial network design skill that this chapter can help you develop.

A discussion of bridging protocols follows the section on decision-making. The bridging section covers transparent bridging, source-route bridging and switching, mixed-media bridging, and switching protocols for transporting Virtual LAN (VLAN) information.

A section on routing protocols follows the bridging section. The routing section provides techniques for comparing and contrasting routing protocols, and includes information on Internet Protocol (IP), AppleTalk, Novell NetWare, and IBM Systems Network Architecture (SNA) routing. The section also discusses methods for migrating AppleTalk, Novell NetWare, and SNA networks to standards-based TCP/IP networking. The chapter concludes with a table that summarizes the comparison of routing protocols.

Making Decisions as Part of the Top-Down Network Design Process

The next few chapters provide guidelines for selecting network design solutions for a customer. The decisions you make regarding protocols and technologies should be based on the information you have gathered on your customer's business and technical goals.

Researchers studying decision models say that one of the most important aspects of making a sound decision is having a good list of goals. In her book, *The Can-Do Manager*, published by the American Management Association, Tess Kirby says that there are four factors involved in making sound decisions:

- Goals must be established.

- Many options should be explored.

- The consequences of the decision should be investigated.

- Contingency plans should be made.

To match options with goals, you can make a *decision table*, such as the one in Table 7–1. Table 7–1 shows a decision table that matches routing protocols to a fictional customer's business and technical goals. You can develop a similar table for bridging protocols, campus-design technologies, enterprise-design technologies, WAN protocols, and so on. To develop the table, place options in the left-most column and your customer's major goals at the top. Place the goals in priority order, starting with critical goals.

Table 7–1   Example Decision Table

	Critical Goals			Other Goals		
	Adaptability—must adapt to changes in a large internetwork within seconds	Must scale to a large size (hundreds of routers)	Must be an industry standard and compatible with existing equipment	Should not create a lot of traffic	Should run on inexpensive routers	Should be easy to configure and manage
BGP	X*	X	X	8	7	7
OSPF	X	X	X	8	8	8
IS-IS	X	X	X	8	6	6
IGRP	X	X				
Enhanced IGRP	X	X				
RIP			X			

* X = Meets critical criteria. 1 = Lowest. 10 = Highest.

You can fill in Table 7–1 first by simply putting an X in each option that meets a critical goal. Any options that do not meet critical goals can immediately be eliminated. Other options can be evaluated on how well they meet other goals, on a scale from 1 to 10.

Once a decision is made, you should troubleshoot the decision. Ask yourself the following:

- If this option is chosen, what could go wrong?

- Has this option been tried before (possibly with other customers)? If so, what problems occurred?

- How will the customer react to this decision?

- What are the contingency plans if the customer does not approve of the decision?

This decision-making process can by used during both the logical and physical network-design phases. You can use this process to help you select protocols, technologies, and devices that will meet a customer's requirements.

SELECTING BRIDGING AND SWITCHING METHODS

Decision-making with regards to bridging and switching methods is simple, because the options are limited. If your network design includes Ethernet bridges and switches, you will most likely use transparent bridging with the spanning-tree protocol. You might also need a protocol for connecting switches that supports virtual LANs (VLANs). This protocol could be an adaptation of the Institute of Electrical and Electronic Engineers (IEEE) 802.10 protocol, the IEEE 802.1q protocol, or the Cisco Inter-Switch Link (ISL) protocol.

With Token Ring networks, your options include source-route bridging (SRB), source-route transparent (SRT) bridging, and source-route switching (SRS). To connect Token Ring and Ethernet LANs (or other dissimilar LANs), you can use translational or encapsulating bridging.

This section discusses options for switching and bridging, including the features and disadvantages of the options. The goal is to help you decide which is the best option for your network design customer, and help you recognize the scalability constraints inherent in bridging and switching technologies in comparison to routing technologies. For detailed information on bridging and switching protocols, see the *Internetworking Technologies Handbook*, published by Cisco Press/MTP.

Characterizing Bridging and Switching Methods

The next few paragraphs apply to both bridges and switches. The generic term *bridge* is used to mean both a bridge and a data-link-layer switch.

Bridges operate at Layers 1 and 2 of the OSI reference model. They determine how to forward a frame based on information in the Layer-2 header of the frame. Unlike a router, a bridge does not look at Layer-3 information or any upper layers. A bridge segments bandwidth domains so that devices on opposite sides of a bridge do not compete with each other for media access control. A bridge does not forward Ethernet collisions or MAC frames in a Token Ring network.

Although a bridge segments bandwidth domains, it does not segment broadcast domains (unless programmed by filters to do so). A bridge sends broadcast frames out every port. This is a scalability issue that was already discussed in Part I of this book. To avoid excessive broadcast traffic, bridged and switched networks should be segmented with routers or divided into VLANs, as was documented in Table 4–8, "The Maximum Size of a Broadcast Domain."

Bridges usually connect like networks, but it is possible to connect unlike networks also, using translational or encapsulating bridging. For example, *remote bridges* use encapsulating bridging to connect LANs via a WAN link.

Switches became popular in the mid-1990s as an inexpensive way of partitioning LANs without incurring the latency associated with bridges. Switches take advantage of fast integrated circuits to offer very low latency. A switch behaves essentially just like a bridge except that it is faster. Switches usually have a higher port density than bridges and a lower cost per port. Because of these features, and the low latency of switches, switches are more common than bridges these days.

A bridge is a store-and-forward device. *Store-and-forward* means that the bridge receives a complete frame, determines which outgoing port to use, prepares the frame for the outgoing port, calculates a CRC, and transmits the frame once the medium is free on the outgoing port.

Switches have the capability to do store-and-forward processing or cut-through processing. With *cut-through processing*, a switch quickly looks at the destination address (the first field in a LAN frame), determines the outgoing port, and immediately starts sending bits to the outgoing port. This is one of the reasons that switches offer lower latency than traditional bridges.

A disadvantage with cut-through processing is that it forwards illegal frames (for example, Ethernet runts), and frames with CRC errors. On a network that is prone to runts and errors, cut-through processing should not be used. Some switches have the capability to automatically move from cut-through mode to store-and-forward mode when an error threshold is reached. This feature is called *adaptive cut-through switching* by some vendors.

NOTES

In this book, the term *switch* refers to a data-link-layer device, unless otherwise specified. Some vendors use the term *switch* in a more generic way. The distinction between switches and routers is becoming blurred because many switches support a routing module, and most routers can handle bridging and switching protocols. Vendors call their products *Layer-3 switches*, *routing switches*, *switching routers*, and *multi-layer switches*.

In general, a Layer-3 switch, routing switch, or switching router is a device that can handle both data-link-layer and network-layer switching (forwarding) of frames. A multi-layer switch is a router that understands bridging protocols, routing protocols, and upper-layer protocols. Some routers look into Layer 4 and other layers in a packet to determine if any special options should be applied when forwarding a packet to its destination port.

Modern routers can forward (switch) packets extremely quickly. Some vendors add the word *switch* to their router product names to emphasize that the routers are as fast (or almost as fast) as data-link layer switches. Modern routers use high-speed internal data paths and parallel processors, all essential to high-speed switching.

Transparent Bridging

Transparent bridging is most common in Ethernet environments, although it is available for other types of LANs also. A *transparent bridge* (switch) connects one or more LAN segments so that end systems on different segments can communicate with each other transparently. An end system sends a frame to a destination without knowing whether the destination is local or on the other side of a bridge. Because all nodes hear all frames in a LAN, a bridge can pick up the frame and forward it if necessary.

To learn how to forward frames, a transparent bridge listens to all frames and determines which stations reside on which segments. The bridge learns the location of devices by looking at the source address in each frame. The bridge develops a *switching table* such as the one shown in Table 7–2.

Table 7–2   Switching Table on a Bridge or Switch

MAC Address	Port
08-00-07-06-41-B9	1
00-00-0C-60-7C-01	2
00-80-24-07-8C-02	3

When a frame arrives at a bridge, the bridge looks at the destination address in the frame and compares it to entries in the switching table. If the bridge has learned where the destination station resides (by looking at source addresses in previous frames), it can forward the frame to the correct port. A transparent bridge sends (floods) frames with an unknown destination address and all multicast/broadcast frames out every port (except the port on which the frame was received). This is a scalability constraint that was already discussed in Part I of this book.

As discussed in Chapter 5, "Designing a Network Topology," transparent bridges and switches implement the spanning-tree algorithm to avoid loops in a topology. The IEEE 802.1d document specifies the algorithm for dynamically "pruning" a topology into a spanning tree. The spanning tree has one root bridge and a set of bridge ports. The protocol dynamically selects bridge ports to include in the spanning-tree topology by determining the lowest-cost paths to the root bridge. Bridge ports that are not part of the tree are disabled so that there is one and only one active path between any two stations. The lowest-cost path is usually the highest-bandwidth path, although the cost is configurable.

Transparent bridges send Bridge Protocol Data Unit (BPDU) frames to each other to build and maintain the spanning tree. The bridges send BPDU frames to a multicast address every two seconds. The amount of traffic caused by BPDU frames can be a scalability constraint on large networks with many switches and bridges. The 2-second timer can be lengthened, but if it is, bridges take a longer time to redevelop the spanning tree when changes occur.

Source-Route Bridging

IBM developed source-route bridging (SRB) for Token Ring networks in the 1980s. In the early 1990s, IBM presented the SRB protocols to the IEEE. The protocols became the source-routing-transparent (SRT) standard, which is documented in Annex C of the IEEE 802.1d document. An SRT bridge can act like a transparent bridge or a source-routing bridge, depending on whether source-routing information is included in a frame.

Bridging is not transparent in a LAN that uses pure SRB. To reach a remote station, a source node must place a *routing-information field* in the frame between the MAC header and the Logical Link Control (LLC) header, as shown in Figure 7–1. The source node sets the first bit of its source address to indicate that the routing-information field is present.

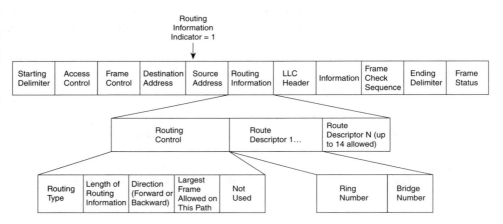

With SRB, a source node finds another node by sending *explorer frames*. Scalability in Token Ring networks is affected by the type of explorer frame the source sends. An explorer frame can be one of the following:

- **All-routes explorer.** The source node specifies that the explorer frame should take all possible paths. The source node usually specifies that the response should take just one path back.

- **Single-route explorer.** The source node specifies that the explorer frame should take just one path and that the response should take either all paths or just one path back.

When single-route explorer frames are used in a network that implements SRT, the bridges can use the spanning-tree algorithm to determine a single path to a destination ring. If the spanning-tree algorithm is not used, then the network administrator must manually choose which bridge should forward single-route explorer frames when there are redundant bridges connecting two rings. This can be hard to maintain and is a scalability issue.

The main scalability issue for source-route bridging, however, is the amount of traffic that can arrive on the destination station's ring when all-routes explorer frames are used. In Figure 7–2, the client sends one all-routes explorer frame to find the server. Because there are redundant bridges, the server receives four frames.

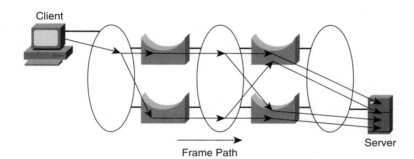

Client

Frame Path

Server

Figure 7–2
An all-routes explorer frame in a redundant Token Ring network.

To contain all-routes explorer traffic, source-route bridged networks should be limited in size or migrated to transparent bridging. Routers can be included in the design to isolate broadcast traffic. If applications use a non-routable protocol, then you should recommend implementing the non-routable protocol on top of a network-layer protocol. For example, NetBIOS applications can use NWLink in NetWare environments, and NetBT in TCP/IP environments.

Source-Route Switching

Source-route switching (SRS) is based on SRT bridging. SRS forwards a frame that has no routing-information field the same way transparent bridging does. All rings that are source-route switched have the same ring number and the switch learns the MAC addresses of devices on those rings.

In addition to learning MAC addresses for local devices, the switch also learns source-routing information for devices on the other side of SRB bridges. When a source-routed frame enters the switch, the switch learns the route descriptor (ring number, bridge number) for the hop closest to the switch. Future frames with the same route descriptor are forwarded only to the correct ring.

Source-route switching provides the following benefits:

- Rings can be segmented without having to add new ring numbers, which simplifies configuration and network documentation.

- A source-route bridged network can be incrementally upgraded to transparent bridging with minimal disruption or re-configuration.

- A switch does not need to learn the MAC addresses of devices on the other side of source-route bridges, which reduces processing and memory requirements.

- A switch can support parallel source-routing paths, which SRT does not support.

- A switch can support duplicate MAC addresses for stations that reside on different LAN segments.

Duplicate MAC addresses are often used in SNA environments. Some SNA network administrators assign the same MAC address to two SNA gateways that are on different rings to support PCs automatically rolling over to a new gateway when a gateway fails. Duplicate MAC addresses are not supported by most SRT-bridging implementations, but they are supported in SRS (as long as the duplicates are on the source-routing part of the network and not the transparently-bridged part of the network).

Mixed-Media Bridging

Some network designs include a mixture of Token Ring, Fiber Distributed Data Interface (FDDI), and Ethernet bridging. For example, in a campus design, an FDDI backbone might connect multiple Ethernet segments using Ethernet/FDDI switches. For mixed-media bridging, you can use encapsulating or translational bridging.

Encapsulating bridging is simpler than translational bridging, but is only appropriate for some network topologies. An *encapsulating bridge* encapsulates an Ethernet frame inside an FDDI (or Token Ring or WAN) frame, for traversal across a backbone network that has no end systems. Figure 7–3 shows a topology that uses encapsulating bridges.

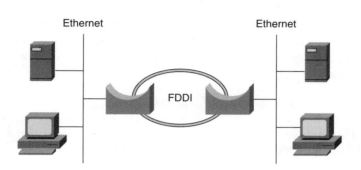

Figure 7–3
Encapsulating bridging.

If you need to support end systems (for example, servers) on the backbone network, then you must use translational bridging. *Translational bridging* translates from one data-link-layer protocol to another. Figure 7–4 shows a topology that uses translational bridges.

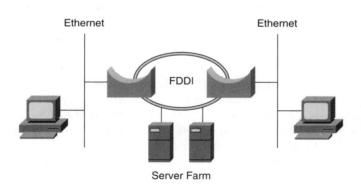

Figure 7–4
Translational bridging.

There are significant challenges associated with translating Ethernet frames to Token Ring or FDDI frames. Some of the problems are as follows:

- **Incompatible bit ordering.** Ethernet transmits the low-order bit of each byte in the header first. Token Ring and FDDI transmit the high-order bit of each byte in the header first. A translational bridge must reverse the bits. Otherwise, Ethernet devices cannot recognize the MAC addresses of Token Ring or FDDI devices, and vice versa.

- **Embedded MAC addresses.** In some cases, MAC addresses are carried in the data portion of a frame. For example, the Address Resolution Protocol (ARP) places MAC addresses in the data part of the frame. Conversion of addresses that appear in the data portion of a frame is difficult because it must be handled on a case-by-case basis.

- **Incompatible maximum transfer unit (MTU) sizes.** Token Ring and FDDI support much larger frames than Ethernet, which supports a frame of 1,500 bytes. Packets received from a Token Ring or FDDI segment that are larger than 1,500 bytes must either be dropped or fragmented.

- **Handling of exclusive Token Ring and FDDI functions.** Certain Token Ring and FDDI bits and functions have no corollary in Ethernet. For example, Ethernet transparent bridges do not inherently understand explorer frames.

- **No real standardization.** With the exception of the SRT standard, which handles some of the issues associated with mixing transparent and source-route bridging, no standards body has championed the standardization of translational bridging. Most vendors support translational bridging, but their methods for supporting it might not be compatible with other vendors' methods.

Although FDDI is a common choice for backbone networks in campus network designs, to avoid the problems associated with translating between Ethernet and FDDI frames, you should recommend using 100-Mbps Ethernet or Gigabit Ethernet on backbone segments, instead of FDDI. 100-Mbps Ethernet and Gigabit Ethernet use the same frame type as 10-Mbps Ethernet, which reduces the potential for problems. Upgrading from FDDI to 100-Mbps Ethernet or Gigabit Ethernet is straight-forward because the Ethernet technologies use the same physical cabling and physical-medium-dependent (PMD) protocols as FDDI. Chapter 9 covers campus network design in more detail.

Switching Protocols for Transporting VLAN Information

Before moving to a discussion of Layer-3 routing protocols, it is important to cover some additional Layer-2 protocols that can be deployed in switched networks that use VLAN technologies.

When VLANs are implemented in a switched network, the switches need a method to make sure intra-VLAN traffic goes to the correct segments. To benefit from the advantages of VLANs, the switches need to ensure that traffic destined for a particular VLAN goes to that VLAN and not to any other VLAN.

This can be accomplished by tagging frames with VLAN information. Cisco Systems, Inc., developed two tagging methods:

- An adaptation of the IEEE 802.10 security protocol

- The Inter-Switch Link (ISL) protocol

Cisco has also proposed these solutions to the IEEE, which is implementing a standard VLAN tagging specification in the IEEE 802.1q document.

Cisco also developed the *VLAN Trunk Protocol (VTP)*, which helps automate VLAN tagging in complex and diverse switched networks. The next few sections discuss these protocols.

IEEE 802.10

The IEEE 802.10 document is a security specification that Cisco and other vendors have adopted as a way of placing a VLAN identification (VLAN ID) in a frame. An 802.10 switch that receives a frame from a source station inserts a VLAN ID between the MAC and LLC headers of the frame. The VLAN ID allows switches and routers to selectively forward packets to ports with the same VLAN ID. The VLAN ID is removed from the frame when the frame is forwarded to the destination segment.

Figure 7–5 shows a typical implementation of 802.10 with Ethernet/FDDI switches. In this example, the VLAN ID allows the switches to ensure that traffic for VLAN 10 only goes to Segments A and D, and traffic for VLAN 20 only goes to Segments B and C.

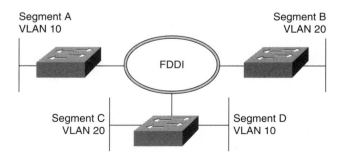

Figure 7–5

An Ethernet/ FDDI switched network with IEEE 802.10 VLAN tagging.

Inter-Switch Link Protocol

The *Inter-Switch Link (ISL) protocol* is another method for maintaining VLAN information as traffic goes between switches. Kalpana, Inc., (which was acquired by Cisco Systems, Inc.) developed ISL to carry VLAN information on a 100-Mbps Ethernet switch-to-switch or switch-to-router link. ISL can be used to carry multiple VLANs on a link between access- and distribution-layer switches in a campus network design.

An ISL link is called a trunk. A *trunk* is a physical link that carries the traffic of multiple VLANs between two switches or between a switch and a router, thereby allowing VLANs to extend across switches. Before placing a frame on the trunk, an ISL switch identifies a frame as belonging to a VLAN by adding a field containing a VLAN ID. Frames from different VLANs are then multiplexed across the trunk. File servers and other application-layer servers can also use ISL to participate in multiple VLANs if network interface cards (NICs) that have ISL VLAN intelligence are used.

VLAN Trunk Protocol

Some networks have a combination of different media types, including FDDI, 10-Mbps Ethernet, 100-Mbps Ethernet, and ATM. It should be possible for a VLAN to span these different technologies, and it should not be necessary to create a dedicated VLAN for each physical link. To meet these requirements, Cisco created the *VLAN Trunk Protocol (VTP)* which automatically configures a VLAN across a campus network, regardless of the media types that make up the campus network. VTP also allows network managers to physically move users while allowing the users to maintain their VLAN association.

VTP is a switch-to-switch, and switch-to-router VLAN management protocol that exchanges VLAN configuration changes as they are made to the network. VTP manages the addition, deletion, and renaming of VLANs on a campus-wide basis without requiring manual intervention at each switch. VTP further reduces manual configuration by automatically configuring a new switch or router with existing VLAN information when the new switch or router is added to the network.

SELECTING ROUTING PROTOCOLS

A *routing protocol* lets a router dynamically learn how to reach other networks and exchange this information with other routers or hosts. Selecting routing protocols for your network design customer is somewhat harder than selecting bridging protocols, because there are so many options. The decision is made easier if you can use a decision table, such as the one shown in Table 7–1. Armed with a solid understanding of your customer's goals and information on the characteristics of different routing protocols, you can make a sound decision about which routing protocols to recommend.

Characterizing Routing Protocols

All routing protocols have the same general goal: to share network reachability information among routers. Routing protocols achieve this goal in a variety of ways. Some routing protocols send a complete routing table to other routers. Other routing protocols send specific information on the status of directly connected links. Some routing protocols send periodic hello packets to maintain their status with peer routers. Some routing protocols include advanced information such as a subnet mask or prefix length with route information. Most routing protocols share dynamic (learned) information, but in some cases, static configuration information is more appropriate.

Routing protocols differ in their scalability and performance characteristics. Many routing protocols were designed for small internetworks. Some routing protocols work best in a static environment and have a hard time converging to a new topology when changes occur. Some routing protocols are meant for connecting interior campus networks, and others are meant for connecting different enterprises. The next few sections provide more information on the different characteristics of routing protocols. Table 7–4 at the end of this chapter summarizes the comparison of various routing protocols.

Distance-Vector Versus Link-State Routing Protocols

Routing protocols fall into two major classes: distance-vector protocols and link-state protocols. This chapter covers distance-vector protocols first.

The following protocols are distance-vector protocols (or derivatives of distance-vector protocols):

- IP Routing Information Protocol (RIP) Version 1 and 2

- IP Interior Gateway Routing Protocol (IGRP)

- Novell NetWare Internetwork Packet Exchange Routing Information Protocol (IPX RIP)

- AppleTalk Routing Table Maintenance Protocol (RTMP)

- AppleTalk Update-Based Routing Protocol (AURP)

- IP Enhanced IGRP (an advanced distance-vector protocol)

- IP Border Gateway Protocol (BGP) (a path-vector routing protocol)

The term *vector* means direction or course. A *distance vector* is a course that also includes information on the length of the course. Many distance-vector routing protocols specify the length of the course with a hop count. A *hop count* specifies the number of routers that must be traversed to reach a destination network. (For some protocols, *hop count* means the number of links, rather than the number of routers.)

A distance-vector routing protocol maintains (and transmits) a routing table that lists known networks and the distance to each network. Table 7–3 shows a typical distance-vector routing table.

Table 7–3   Distance-Vector Routing Table

Network	Distance (in Hops)	Send To (Next Hop)
10.0.0.0	0 (directly connected)	Port 1
172.16.0.0	0 (directly connected)	Port 2
172.17.0.0	1	172.16.0.2
172.18.0.0	2	172.16.0.2
192.168.1.0	1	10.0.0.2
192.168.2.0	2	10.0.0.2

A distance-vector routing protocol sends its routing table to all neighbors. It sends a broadcast packet that reaches all other routers on the local segment (and any hosts that use routing information). Distance-vector protocols can send the entire table each time, or they can simply send updates after the first transmission and only occasionally send the complete routing table.

Split Horizon, Hold-Down, and Poison-Reverse
Features of Distance-Vector Protocols

A router running a distance-vector protocol sends its routing table out each of its ports on a periodic basis. If the protocol supports the *split-horizon technique*, the router sends only routes that are reachable via other ports. This reduces the size of the update and, more importantly, improves the accuracy of routing information. With split horizon, a router does not tell another router information that is better learned locally.

Most distance-vector protocols also implement a *hold-down timer* so that new information about a route to a suspect network is not believed right away, in case the information is based on stale data. Hold-down timers are a standard way to avoid loops that can happen during convergence. To understand the loop problem, consider the network shown in Figure 7–6.

Router A   Router B

172.16.0.0   192.168.2.0

Figure 7–6
Partial distance-vector routing tables on Router A and Router B.

Router A's Routing Table		
Network	Distance	Send To
172.16.0.0	0	Port 1
192.168.2.0	1	Router B

Router B's Routing Table		
Network	Distance	Send To
192.168.2.0	0	Port 1
172.16.0.0	1	Router A

When routers broadcast their routing tables, they simply send the Network and Distance columns of the table. They do not send the Send To (Next-Hop) column, which is one of the causes of the loop problem.

The sequence of events that can lead to a routing loop is as follows:

1. Router A's connection to Network 172.16.0.0 fails.

2. Router A removes Network 172.16.0.0 from its routing table.

3. Based on previous announcements from Router A, Router B broadcasts its routing table saying that Router B can reach network 172.16.0.0.

4. Router A adds Network 172.16.0.0 to its routing table with a Send To (Next-Hop) value of Router B and a distance of 2.

5. Router A receives a frame for a host on network 172.16.0.0.

6. Router A sends the frame to Router B.

7. Router B sends the frame to Router A.

The frame loops back and forth from Router A to Router B until the IP time-to-live value expires. (*Time-to-live* is a field in the IP header of an IP packet that is decremented each time a router processes the frame.)

To make matters worse, without split-horizon, at some point Router A sends a route update saying it can get to Network 172.16.0.0, causing Router B to update the route in its table with a distance of 3. Both Router A and Router B continue to send route updates until finally the distance field reaches infinity. (Routing protocols arbitrarily define a distance that means infinity. For example, 16 means infinity for RIP.) When the distance reaches infinity, the routers remove the route.

The route-update problem is called the *count-to-infinity problem*. A hold-down function tells a router not to add or update information for a route that has recently been removed, until a hold-down timer expires. In the example, if Router A uses hold-down, it does not add the route for network 172.16.0.0 that Router B sends. Split horizon also solves the problem in the example, because if Router B uses split horizon, it does not tell Router A about a route to 172.16.0.0.

Poison-reverse messages are another way of speeding convergence and avoiding loops. With poison-reverse, when a router notices a problem with a route, it can immediately send a route update that specifies that the destination is no longer reachable. Most protocols do this by specifying the distance as infinity.

Link-State Routing Protocols

Link-state routing protocols do not exchange routing tables. Instead, routers running a link-state routing protocol exchange information about the status of their directly connected links. Each router learns enough information from peer routers to build its own routing table. A link-state router sends a multicast packet advertising its link states on a periodic basic. Other routers forward the multicast packet to peer routers in the internetwork.

The following protocols are link-state routing protocols:

- IP Open Shortest Path First (OSPF)

- IP Intermediate System-to-Intermediate System (IS-IS)

- NetWare Link Services Protocol (NLSP)

Link-state protocols usually converge more quickly than distance-vector protocols and are less prone to routing loops. On the other hand, link-state protocols require more CPU power and memory, and can be more expensive to implement and support. Link-state protocols are harder to troubleshoot than distance-vector protocols. With distance-vector routing, updates can be easily interpreted with a protocol analyzer. This makes debugging easy. (Unfortunately, it also makes it easy for a hacker to understand the protocol and compromise it, especially if the protocol does not support authentication.)

Routing Protocol Metrics

Routing protocols use *metrics* to determine which path is preferable when more than one path is available. Routing protocols vary on which metrics are supported. Traditional distance-vector routing protocols used hop count only. Newer protocols can also take into account delay, bandwidth, reliability, and other factors. Metrics can affect scalability. For example RIP only supports 15 hops. Metrics can also affect network performance. A router that only uses hop count for its metric misses the opportunity to select a route that has more hops but also more bandwidth than another route.

Hierarchical Versus Non-Hierarchical Routing Protocols

Some routing protocols do not support hierarchy. All routers have the same tasks, and every router is a peer of every other router. Routing protocols that support hierarchy, on the other hand, assign different tasks to routers, and group routers in areas, autonomous systems, or domains. In a hierarchical arrangement, some routers communicate with local routers in the same area, and other routers have the job of connecting areas, domains, or autonomous systems. A router that connects an area to other areas can summarize routes for its local area. Summarization enhances stability because routers are shielded from problems not in their own area.

Interior Versus Exterior Routing Protocols

Routing protocols can also be characterized by where they are used. Interior routing protocols, such as RIP, OSPF, and IGRP, are used by routers within the same enterprise or autonomous system. Exterior routing protocols, such as BGP, perform routing between multiple autonomous systems. BGP is used on the Internet by peer routers in different autonomous systems to maintain a consistent view of the Internet's topology.

Classful Versus Classless Routing Protocols

The previous chapter discussed the differences between IP classful and classless routing protocols. To summarize the concepts in Chapter 6, a classful routing protocol, such as RIP or IGRP, always considers the IP network class. Address summarization is automatic by major network number. This means that discontiguous subnets are not visible to each other, and variable-length subnet masking (VLSM) is not supported. These issues are discussed in more detail later in this chapter.

Classless protocols, on the other hand, transmit prefix-length or subnet-mask information with IP network addresses. With classless routing protocols, the IP address space can be mapped so that discontiguous subnets and VLSM are supported. The IP address space should be mapped carefully so that subnets are arranged in contiguous blocks, allowing route updates to be summarized at area boundaries.

Dynamic Versus Static and Default Routing

In some cases, it is not necessary to use a routing protocol. Static routes are often used to connect to a stub network. A *stub network* is a part of an internetwork that can only be reached by one path. An example of a stub network is a company that connects to the Internet via a single link to an Internet service provider (ISP). The ISP can have a static route to the company. It is not necessary to run a routing protocol between the company and the ISP. Internally, the company might run a routing protocol to connect intranet sites, but to reach Internet sites, internal routers can simply be configured with a default route that points to the ISP.

Scalability Constraints for Routing Protocols

When selecting a routing protocol for a customer, you should consider your customer's goals for scaling the network to a large size, and investigate the following questions for each routing protocol. Each of the questions addresses a scalability constraint for routing protocols.

- Are there any limits placed on metrics?

- How quickly can the routing protocol converge when upgrades or changes occur? Link-state protocols tend to converge more quickly than distance-vector protocols. Convergence is discussed in more detail in the next section.

- How often are routing updates or link-state advertisements transmitted? Is the frequency of updates a function of a timer, or are updates triggered by an event, such as a link failure?

- How much data is transmitted in a routing update? The whole table? Just changes? Is split horizon used?

- How much bandwidth is used to send routing updates? (See Table 4–7, "Bandwidth Used by Routing Protocols," to answer this question for distance-vector routing protocols.) Bandwidth utilization is particularly relevant for low-bandwidth serial links.

- How widely are routing updates distributed? To neighbors? To a bounded area? To all routers in the autonomous system?

- How much CPU utilization is required to process routing updates or link-state advertisements?

- Are static and default routes supported?

- Is route summarization supported?

These questions can be answered by watching routing protocol behavior with a protocol analyzer and by studying the relevant specifications or Request For Comments (RFCs). The next few sections in this chapter can also help you understand routing protocol behavior better. For more information on routing protocols, you can also read the *Internetworking Technologies Handbook*, published by Cisco Press/MTP.

Routing Protocols Convergence

Convergence is the time it takes for routers to arrive at a consistent understanding of the internetwork topology after a change takes place. A change can be a network segment or router failing, or a new segment or router joining the internetwork. To understand the importance of quick convergence for your particular customer, you should develop an understanding of the likelihood of frequent changes on the customer's network. Are there links that tend to fail often? Is the customer's network always "under construction" either for enhancements or because of reliability problems?

Because packets may not be reliably routed to all destinations while convergence is taking place, convergence time is a critical design constraint. The convergence process should complete within a few seconds for time-sensitive applications, such as voice applications and SNA-based applications. When SNA is transported across an IP internetwork, a fast-converging protocol such as OSPF is recommended. Link-state protocols were designed to converge quickly. Some newer distance-vector protocols, such as Enhanced IGRP, were also designed for quick convergence.

A router starts the convergence process when it notices that a link to one of its peer routers has failed. A Cisco router sends *keepalive frames* every 10 seconds (by default) to help it determine the state of a link. On a point-to-point WAN link, a Cisco router sends keepalive frames to the router at the other end of the link. On LANs, a Cisco router sends keepalive frames to a multicast address.

If a serial link fails, a router can start the convergence process immediately if it notices the Carrier Detect (CD) signal drop. Otherwise, a router starts the convergence after sending two or three keepalive frames and not receiving a response. On a Token Ring or FDDI network, a router can start the convergence process almost immediately if it notices the beaconing process indicating a network segment is down. On an Ethernet network, if the router's own transceiver fails, it can start the convergence process immediately. Otherwise, the router starts the convergence process after it has been unable to send two or three keepalive frames.

If the routing protocol uses hello packets and the hello timer is shorter than the keepalive timer, then the routing protocol can start convergence sooner. Another factor that influences convergence time is load balancing. If a routing table includes multiple paths to a destination, traffic can immediately take other paths when a path fails. Load balancing was discussed in more detail in Chapter 5, "Designing a Network Topology."

IP Routing

The most common IP routing protocols are RIP, IGRP, Enhanced IGRP, OSPF, and BGP. The following sections describe some of the performance and scalability characteristics of these protocols to help you select the correct protocols for your network design customer.

Routing Information Protocol

The IP *Routing Information Protocol (RIP)* was the first standard routing protocol developed for TCP/IP environments. RIP was developed originally for the Xerox Network System (XNS) protocols and was adopted by the IP community in the early

1980s. RIP is still commonly used as an interior routing protocol, probably because it is easy to configure, and runs on routers from every major vendor. RIP Version 1 is documented in RFC 1058. RIP Version 2 is documented in RFC 1723.

RIP is a distance-vector protocol that features simplicity and ease-of-troubleshooting. RIP broadcasts its routing table every 30 seconds. RIP allows 25 routes per packet, so on large networks, multiple packets are required to send the whole routing table. Bandwidth utilization is an issue on large RIP networks that include low-bandwidth links. To avoid routing loops during convergence, most implementations of RIP include split horizon and a hold-down timer.

RIP uses a single routing metric (hop count) to measure the distance to a destination network. This limitation should be considered when designing networks that use RIP. The limitation means that if multiple paths to a destination exist, RIP only maintains the path with the fewest hops, even if other paths have a higher aggregate bandwidth, lower aggregate delay, less congestion, and so on.

Another limitation of RIP is that the hop count can not go above 15. If a router receives a routing update that specifies that a destination is 16 hops away, the router purges that destination from its routing table. A hop-count of 16 means the distance to the destination is infinity, in other words, the destination is unreachable.

The Internet Engineering Task Force (IETF) developed RIP Version 2 to address some of the scalability and performance problems with RIP Version 1. RIP Version 2 adds the following fields to route entries within a routing table:

- **Route tag.** Distinguishes internal routes that are within the RIP routing domain from external routes that have been imported from another routing protocol or a different autonomous system.

- **Subnet mask.** Contains the subnet mask that is applied to the IP address to yield the non-host (prefix) portion of the address.

- **Next hop.** Specifies the immediate next-hop IP address to which packets to the destination in the route entry should be forwarded.

Route tags facilitate merging RIP and non-RIP networks. Including the subnet mask in a route entry provides support for classless routing. The purpose of the next-hop field is to eliminate packets being routed through extra hops. Specifying a value of 0.0.0.0 in the next-hop field indicates that routing should be via the originator of the

RIP update. Specifying a different value than 0.0.0.0 is useful when RIP is not in use on all routers in a network. See Appendix A of RFC 1723 for an example.

RIP Version 2 also supports simple authentication to foil hackers sending routing updates. The authentication scheme uses the space of a route entry. This means that there can be only 24 route entries in a message when authentication is used. Currently, the only authentication supported is a simple plain-text password.

Interior Gateway Routing Protocol

Cisco Systems, Inc. developed the distance-vector *Interior Gateway Routing Protocol (IGRP)* in the mid-1980s to meet the needs of customers requiring a robust and scalable interior routing protocol. Many customers migrated their RIP networks to IGRP to overcome RIP's 15-hop limitation and reliance on just one metric (hop count). IGRP's 90-second update timer for sending route updates was also more attractive than RIP's 30-second update timer for customers concerned about bandwidth utilization.

IGRP uses a composite metric based on the following factors:

- **Bandwidth.** The bandwidth of the lowest-bandwidth segment on the path. A network administrator can configure bandwidth or use the default value, which is based on the type of link. (Configuration is recommended for high-speed WAN links if the default bandwidth value is less than the actual speed.)

- **Delay.** A sum of all the delays for outgoing interfaces in the path. Each delay is inversely proportional to the bandwidth of each outgoing interface. Delay is not dynamically calculated.

- **Reliability.** The worst reliability on any link. By default, reliability is not used unless the metric weights command is configured, in which case reliability is dynamically calculated based on the ability to send and receive keepalive packets.

- **Load.** The heaviest load on any link. By default, load is not used unless the metric weights command is configured, in which case load is dynamically calculated.

IGRP allows load balancing over equal-metric paths and non-equal-metric paths. The IGRP *variance feature* means that if one path is three times better than another, the better path can be used three times more than the other path. (Only routes with metrics that are within a certain range of the best route can be used as multiple paths. See Cisco's configuration documentation for more information.)

IGRP has a better algorithm for advertising and selecting a default route than RIP does. RIP allows a network administrator to configure one default route, which is identified as network 0.0.0.0. IGRP, on the other hand, allows real networks to be flagged as candidates for being a default. Periodically, IGRP scans all candidate default routes and chooses the one with the lowest metric to be the actual default route. This feature allows more flexibility and better performance than RIP's static default route.

To reduce convergence time, IGRP supports triggered updates. A router sends a *triggered update*, which is a new routing table, in response to a change, for example, the failure of a link. Upon receipt of a triggered update, other routers can also send triggered updates. A failure causes a wave of update messages to propagate throughout the network, thus speeding convergence time and reducing the risk of loops.

NOTES

It is possible that a router that has not yet received a triggered update could issue a regular update at just the wrong time, causing a bad route to be reinserted into neighbors' routing tables. To avoid this problem, IGRP uses a hold-down timer. The default hold-down timer is 280 seconds, which is long enough to allow a wave of triggered updates to span across a large internetwork. The hold-down timer can be decreased (or even eliminated) to speed up convergence, especially since IGRP also implements split horizon and poison reverse as additional precautions against loops. Poison-reverse updates are sent if a route metric increases by a factor of 1.1. or greater, indicating a possible loop that hasn't been resolved by other loop-avoidance methods.

Enhanced Interior Gateway Routing Protocol

Cisco developed the *Enhanced Interior Gateway Routing Protocol (Enhanced IGRP)* in the early 1990s to meet the needs of enterprise customers with large, complex, multiprotocol internetworks. Enhanced IGRP is compatible with IGRP and provides an automatic redistribution mechanism to allow IGRP routes to be imported into Enhanced IGRP, and vice versa. Enhanced IGRP can also redistribute routes for RIP, IS-IS, BGP, and OSPF. In addition, Enhanced IGRP offers support for AppleTalk and Novell routing, and can redistribute RTMP and IPX RIP routes, and IPX Service Advertising Protocol (SAP) updates.

One of the main goals of Enhanced IGRP is to offer very quick convergence on large networks. To meet this goal, the designers of Enhanced IGRP adopted the *diffusing-update algorithm (DUAL)* that Dr. J. J. Garcia-Luna-Aceves developed at SRI International. DUAL specifies a method for routers to store neighbors' routing information so that the routers can switch to alternate routes very quickly. Routers can also query other routers to learn alternate routes and send hello packets to determine the reachability of neighbors. DUAL guarantees a loop-free topology, so there is no need for a hold-down mechanism, which is another feature that minimizes convergence time.

Because of the features of DUAL, Enhanced IGRP uses significantly less bandwidth than IGRP or other distance-vector protocols. A router using DUAL develops its routing table using the concept of a feasible successor. A *feasible successor* is a neighboring router that has the least-cost path to a destination.

When a router detects that a link has failed, if a feasible successor has an alternate route, the router switches to the alternate route immediately, without causing any network traffic. If there is no successor, the router sends a query to neighbors. The query propagates across the network until a new route is found.

An Enhanced IGRP router develops a *topology table* that contains all destinations advertised by neighboring routers. Each entry in the table contains a destination and a list of neighbors that have advertised the destination. For each neighbor, the entry includes the metric that the neighbor advertised for that destination. A router computes its own metric for the destination by using each neighbor's metric in combination with the local metric the router uses to reach the neighbor. The router compares metrics and determines the lowest-cost path to a destination and a feasible successor to use in case the lowest-cost path fails.

Enhanced IGRP can scale to thousands of routing nodes. To ensure good performance in large internetworks, Enhanced IGRP should be used on networks with simple hierarchical topologies. In May 1996, Cisco introduced a new version of Enhanced IGRP that fixed problems customers were encountering in large mesh networks with many low-bandwidth and high-delay circuits. If you recommend Enhanced IGRP to your network design customer, make sure the customer is not using a version of the Cisco Internetwork Operating System (IOS) software that was released before May 1996.

Open Shortest Path First

In the late 1980s, the IETF recognized the need to develop an interior link-state routing protocol to meet the needs of large enterprise networks that were constrained by the limitations of RIP. The *Open Shortest Path First (OSPF)* routing protocol is a result of the IETF's work. OSPF is defined in RFC 2178.

The advantages of OSPF are as follows:

- OSPF is an open standard supported by many vendors.

- OSPF converges quickly.

- OSPF authenticates protocol exchanges to meet security goals.

- OSPF supports discontiguous subnets and VLSM.

- OSPF sends multicast frames, rather than broadcast frames, which reduces CPU utilization on LAN hosts (if the hosts have NICs capable of filtering multicasts).

- OSPF networks can be designed in hierarchical areas, which reduces memory and CPU requirements on routers.

- OSPF does not use a lot of bandwidth.

To minimize bandwidth utilization, OSPF propagates only changes. Other network traffic is limited to database-synchronization traffic that occurs infrequently (every 30 minutes), and hello packets that establish neighbor adjacencies and are used to elect a designated router on LANs.

An OSPF router multicasts link-state advertisements (LSAs) to all other routers within the same hierarchical area. The LSA advertises the status of attached interfaces and the cost of sending a data packet on the interface. (Cost is OSPF's metric.)

OSPF routers accumulate link-state information to calculate the shortest path to a destination network. The calculation is called the *shortest-path first (SPF)* algorithm, or the *Dijkstra algorithm*, after the computer scientist who developed the algorithm. The result of the calculation is a database of the topology, called the *link-state database*. Each router in an area has an identical database.

All routers run the same algorithm, in parallel. From the link-state database, each router constructs a tree of shortest paths, with itself as the root of the tree. The shortest-path tree provides the route to each destination. Externally-derived routing information appears on the tree as leaves. When several equal-cost routes to a destination exist, traffic is distributed equally among them.

According to RFC 2178, the cost of a route is described by "a single dimensionless metric" that is "configurable by a system administrator." A cost is associated with the output side of each router interface. The lower the cost, the more likely the interface is to be used to forward data traffic. A cost is also associated with externally-derived routes (for example, routes learned from a different routing protocol).

On a Cisco router, the cost of an interface defaults to 100,000,000 divided by the bandwidth for the interface. For example, both FDDI and 100-Mbps Ethernet have a cost of 1. The cost can be manually configured. Usually it is best if both ends of a link use the same cost. If a Cisco router is at one end of a link and a non-Cisco router is at the other end, you might need to manually configure the cost. Because OSPF defines the cost metric so broadly, vendors are not required to agree on how the cost is defined.

NOTES

As of this writing, Cisco did not allow a cost of less than 1 for links with a higher speed than 100 Mbps. (The parameter for the `ip ospf cost` command is an integer between 1 and 65,535.) In an internetwork with high-speed links of 100 Mbps or higher, you can set the cost to 1 on the high-speed links and set the cost to an integer greater than 1 on slower links.

OSPF allows sets of networks to be grouped into areas. The topology of an area is hidden from the rest of the autonomous system. By hiding the topology of an area, routing traffic is reduced. Also, routing within the area is determined only by the area's own topology, providing the area protection from bad routing data. By dividing routers into areas, the memory and CPU requirements for each router are limited. Experience has shown that each area can have approximately 50 routers. (Depending on what else the routers are doing, this number can possibly be increased, especially if a simple hierarchical topology is used, and links are generally stable.)

A contiguous backbone area, called *Area 0*, is required when an OSPF network is divided into areas. Every other area connects to Area 0 via an *area border router (ABR)*, as shown in Figure 7–7. All traffic between areas must travel through Area 0. Area 0 should have high availability, throughput, and bandwidth. Area 0 should be easy to manage and troubleshoot. A set of routers in a rack connected via a high-speed LAN makes a good Area 0 for many customers.

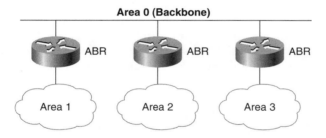

Figure 7–7
OSPF areas connected via area border routers (ABRs).

When designing an OSPF network, make sure to assign network numbers in blocks that can be summarized. An ABR should summarize routes behind it to avoid routers in the backbone and other areas having to know details about a particular area. The summarization must be configured on Cisco routers with the area-range command.

An ABR that connects a stub network can be configured to inject a default route into the stub area for all external networks that are outside the autonomous system or are learned from other routing protocols. The router can also be configured to inject a default route for internal summarized or non-summarized routes to other areas. If a router injects a default route for all routes, Cisco calls the area a *totally stubby area*. Cisco also supports *not-so stubby areas*, which allows the redistribution of external routes into OSPF in an otherwise stubby area.

Because of the requirement that OSPF be structured in areas and the recommendation that routes be summarized, it can be difficult to migrate an existing network to OSPF. Also, enlarging an existing OSPF network can be challenging. If a network is subject to rapid change or growth, OSPF might not be the best choice. For most networks, however, OSPF is a good choice because of its low-bandwidth utilization, scalability, and compatibility with multiple vendors. For more information on OSPF, see the "OSPF Design Guide" on Cisco's Web site.

Border Gateway Protocol

The IETF developed the *Border Gateway Protocol (BGP)* to replace the now-obsolete Exterior Gateway Protocol (EGP) as the standard exterior routing protocol for the Internet. BGP solves problems that EGP had with reliability and scalability. BGP4, the current version of BGP, is specified in RFC 1771.

Internal BGP (iBGP) can be used at a large company to route between domains. *External BGP (eBGP)* is often used to multihome an enterprise's connection to the Internet. It is a common misconception that multihoming requires BGP, but this is not true. Depending on a customer's goals and the flexibility of their Internet service providers' policies, you can multihome with default routes, as discussed in Chapter 5, "Designing a Network Topology."

Running eBGP and iBGP can be challenging, requiring an understanding of the complex BGP protocol. BGP should be recommended only to companies that have senior network engineers, and a good relationship with their ISPs. Also, a full Internet routing table is at least 50,000 routes (and continues to increase as the Internet expands). Substantial bandwidth is required to receive the table, and considerable processing power is required in all routers receiving the table. BGP should only be recommended to companies with high-bandwidth Internet connection(s) and routers with lots of processing power and memory.

The main goal of BGP is to allow routers to exchange information on paths to destination networks. Each BGP router maintains a routing table that lists all feasible paths to a particular network. BGP routers exchange routing information upon initial startup, and then send incremental updates, using the TCP protocol for reliable delivery of BGP packets. An update specifies *path attributes*, which include the origin of the path information, a sequence of autonomous-system path segments, and next-hop information.

When a BGP router receives updates from multiple autonomous systems that describe different paths to the same destination, the router must choose the single best path for reaching that destination. Once chosen, BGP propagates the best path to its neighbors. The decision is based on the value of attributes in the update (such as next hop, administrative weights, local preference, the origin of the route, and path length), and other BGP-configurable factors. See the "BGP4 Case Studies/Tutorial" on Cisco's Web site for more information on BGP's algorithm for selecting the best path. Also see Bassam Halabi's book *Internet Routing Architectures*, published by Cisco Press/MTP, for more information on BGP in general.

AppleTalk Routing

AppleTalk networks have three options for routing:

- Routing Table Maintenance Protocol (RTMP)

- AppleTalk Update-Based Routing Protocol (AURP)

- Enhanced IGRP for AppleTalk

RTMP is the most common option because it is easy to configure and is supported by most vendors of multi-protocol routers. To reduce the amount of traffic caused by RTMP, large enterprises have the option of using AURP or Enhanced IGRP in the core of their internetworks.

Routing Table Maintenance Protocol

RTMP is the main routing protocol for the AppleTalk protocol suite. Contrary to many pictures that you see of the AppleTalk protocol suite, RTMP is not a transport-layer protocol. It is a typical distance-vector routing protocol. RTMP packets reside in the data portion of AppleTalk's network-layer protocol, the Datagram Delivery Protocol (DDP).

An RTMP router sends its routing table every 10 seconds, using split horizon. Apple Computer chose such a short timer to minimize convergence time on large internetworks and to support end systems learning about a router on their network very quickly. In reality, large AppleTalk networks do not converge very quickly, however. This is partly because of enhancements that reduce the possibility of *ZIP storms*, which are covered in more detail later.

RTMP works closely with the *Zone Information Protocol (ZIP)*. Contrary to common pictures of the AppleTalk protocol suite, ZIP is not a session-layer protocol, though some ZIP packets do reside inside an AppleTalk Transaction Protocol (ATP) transport-layer packet. Other ZIP packets reside inside DDP. ZIP manages zones and the mapping of zones to networks. A *zone* is a logical grouping of nodes. A network administrator assigns one or more zone names to a network segment. Multiple network segments per zone are also supported.

When an RTMP router receives a routing-table update from another router, it checks the update for any networks that it didn't know about already. If there is a new network, the router sends a *ZIP query* to the router that sent the update, asking for the zone name(s) for that network. The router that sent the update looks up the network in its *zone information table* and replies to the ZIP query. Contrary to popular myths about AppleTalk, both the query and the reply are unicast packets, not broadcast packets. (Also, it is not true that AppleTalk routers broadcast their zone information tables on a regular basis.)

As mentioned before, when a router learns about a new network, it sends a ZIP query to get the zone name(s) for the network. This process can cause a flurry of ZIP queries to fan out across the internetwork, as each router learns about the new network. The flurry of ZIP queries can happen quite quickly because RTMP routers send their routing tables every 10 seconds.

The flurry of ZIP queries and replies is not a serious issue if there is just one new network, but it can be a problem when there are many new networks, such as during an upgrade or recovery from a disaster. For this reason, a lot of router vendors have implemented the rule that a router does not advertise a network in its RTMP routing update until the ZIP query/reply sequence has completed and the zone name(s) for the network have been determined. This rule slows down ZIP flurries and can eliminate ZIP storms.

NOTES

ZIP storms were a somewhat common occurrence on AppleTalk networks in the 1980s and early 1990s. They were often the result of physical-layer problems that caused network segments to go up and down. They were also sometimes caused by poorly-implemented AppleTalk routers. The problem was that routers sometimes advertised corrupted routing tables because of a lack of memory-protection features.

A router receiving the spurious routing table recognized many new network numbers and sent ZIP queries for them. The router also included the new network numbers in its next RTMP route update. The bad network numbers spread across the network causing numerous ZIP queries and replies. This problem became known as a *ZIP storm*. (It should not be confused with a broadcast storm. The packets are not broadcast packets.)

When the router that sent the spurious routing table received ZIP queries, it generally did not respond, because it didn't recognize the corrupted network numbers either. This was actually a good thing, because it meant router vendors could protect themselves from ZIP storms by not including networks in RTMP updates until zone names were received (which were never received in the case of the corrupted network numbers).

One disadvantage to the fact that routers do not spread the word on new network numbers as quickly as they used to is that convergence is not as fast as it used to be. On large internetworks, it takes a few minutes for all routers to learn about a new network.

AppleTalk Update-Based Routing Protocol

RTMP sends a complete routing table (after applying the split horizon rule) every 10 seconds. It does not have a feature to send just updates. To reduce routing traffic in an AppleTalk environment, you can use the AppleTalk Update-Based Routing Protocol (AURP). You can use AURP on WAN links or in the core of a network where no AppleTalk end systems reside. RTMP should run on LANs where end systems reside because end systems need to see RTMP packets to determine the address of a router.

AURP has the following features:

- Reduced routing traffic on WAN links because only updates are sent

- Hop-count reduction to allow the creation of larger internetworks

- Remapping of remote network numbers to resolve numbering conflicts

- Internetwork clustering (summarization) to minimize routing traffic, and route CPU and memory requirements

- Tunneling through IP or other types of networks

- Basic security, including device and network hiding

Enhanced IGRP for AppleTalk

Another option for reducing AppleTalk routing data is to use Cisco's Enhanced IGRP for AppleTalk. You can use Enhanced IGRP on WAN links or in the core of a network. Enhanced IGRP automatically redistributes routes between itself and RTMP. RTMP should be used on LANs where end systems reside. Enhanced IGRP saves bandwidth because it only sends routing updates when changes occur. It also converges more quickly than RTMP, usually within one second. Unlike AURP, Enhanced IGRP does not offer hop-count reduction. End-to-end hop counts are maintained across the Enhanced IGRP core.

Migrating an AppleTalk Network to IP Routing

Many enterprise network managers are beginning to mandate that only IP protocols can run on backbone networks. Modern Macintosh computers ship with TCP/IP built in so they can participate in a IP-only network. However, departments that are familiar with AppleTalk's user-friendly services, such as AppleShare file and print services, may not want to completely migrate to TCP/IP services.

To meet the needs of these departments, Apple Computer sells AppleShare IP which provides AppleShare file sharing on a TCP/IP or AppleTalk network. (Print sharing on TCP/IP or AppleTalk will be supported in the future.) AppleShare IP also provides traditional TCP/IP capabilities, such as File Transfer Protocol (FTP), electronic mail, and World Wide Web services.

For customers with AppleShare implementations that cannot be upgraded to the AppleShare IP version, or for customers who do not want to spend the money to upgrade to AppleShare IP, Open Door Networks, Inc., sells the ShareWay IP Gateway, which brings TCP/IP accessibility to any AppleTalk Filing Protocol (AFP) server.

With the ShareWay IP Gateway, the built-in personal file sharing on Macintoshes can be made accessible on a TCP/IP intranet. Macintosh users can also use the gateway to share files over the Internet with other Macintosh users. In addition, the ShareWay IP Gateway makes third-party AFP services, such as those on Windows NT, Novell NetWare or UNIX, accessible from anywhere on an intranet or the Internet. With products such as AppleShare IP and the ShareWay IP Gateway, customers can begin to turn off AppleTalk protocols on their internetworks without losing the benefits of traditional AppleTalk services.

Novell NetWare Routing

Novell NetWare networks have three options for routing:

- Internetwork Packet Exchange Routing Information Protocol (IPX RIP)

- NetWare Link Services Protocol (NLSP)

- Enhanced IGRP for IPX

NLSP is newer than IPX RIP and is gaining popularity in large enterprises. IPX RIP is still very popular at many small companies. Enhanced IGRP for IPX is a good option for large IPX networks with Cisco routers.

Internetwork Packet Exchange Routing Information Protocol

IPX RIP is similar to IP RIP but differs in minor ways. IPX RIP uses ticks for its routing metric. *Ticks* specify the amount of delay on a path. One tick is approximately 1/18th of a second. IPX RIP considers a LAN to be one tick and a WAN to be 6 ticks by default. If two paths have an equal tick count, RIP uses hop count as a tie breaker. Ticks are generally not dynamically calculated on LANs, although some implementations do dynamically calculate ticks on WANs.

IPX RIP sends the complete routing table (after applying split horizon) every 60 seconds. Because of a limitation on the size of an IPX RIP packet, only 50 routes are allowed per update packet, so on large networks, multiple update packets are sent. IPX RIP also sends immediate updates when a link fails or when a new network is brought up.

IPX RIP works closely with the Service-Advertising Protocol (SAP). Network resources, such as file servers and print servers, use SAP to advertise their services every 60 seconds. Routers also keep track of services and send SAP advertisements every 60 seconds. Only seven services are allowed per SAP packet, so on some networks, numerous SAP packets are sent, even though split horizon is used. The amount of traffic caused by IPX RIP and SAP is a problem for slow links and routers with insufficient processing power and memory. (SAP filters can lessen the problem, although filters require CPU processing so are not appropriate on a router that already has high CPU usage. Setting an output SAP delay value on every port can also lessen the problem.)

NetWare Link Services Protocol

An option for reducing routing traffic in a Novell environment is to use the NetWare Link Services Protocol (NLSP). NLSP advertises routes and services incrementally. NLSP is similar to OSI's Intermediate System-to-Intermediate System (IS-IS) link-state protocol. Like IS-IS, NLSP is a link-state protocol that supports a routing hierarchy and route aggregation (summarization). NLSP features quick convergence that is usually faster than IPX RIP.

NLSP supports three levels of hierarchical routing. A Level 1 router connects networks within a routing area. A Level 2 router connects areas and also acts as a Level 1 router within its own area. A Level 3 router connects domains and also acts as a Level 2 router within its own domain.

NLSP has the following features:

- Sends routing and service information only when changes occur

- Sends multicast packets instead of broadcast packets on LANs

- Makes more intelligent routing decisions than IPX RIP because each router stores a complete map of its area

- Uses IPX header compression

- Supports a standardized management interface

Enhanced IGRP for IPX

Another option for reducing NetWare routing and service-advertising data is to use Enhanced IGRP for IPX. Enhanced IGRP reduces bandwidth utilization because it only sends routing updates when changes occur. It also converges more quickly than

IPX RIP, usually within one second. Enhanced IGRP automatically redistributes routes and services between itself and IPX RIP and SAP. Enhanced IGRP tracks the IPX RIP routing metric (ticks), as an external metric. An Enhanced IGRP backbone does not add to the tick metric. Enhanced IGRP also tracks hop count as an external metric. The backbone appears as two hops.

Migrating a NetWare Network to IP Routing

A previous section mentioned that many enterprise network managers are beginning to mandate that only IP protocols can run on backbone networks. Managers are eliminating desktop protocols, such as AppleTalk and Novell NetWare, from backbone networks, and from LANs, for that matter. For many years, Novell has supported a variety of methods for merging IP and IPX networks. Recently, Novell has started talking more about migrating an IPX network to an IP network.

Novell's Open Solutions Architecture (OSA) initiative represents the company's strategy to move all products and services to open protocols and standards. As part of this strategy, Novell customized NetWare 5 specifically for Internet and Java support. Novell ported Netscape's Web server software to the NetWare 5 platform, and developed tools to support network-application developers who are moving from C and C++ to Java.

NetWare 5 offers a *migration gateway* that links IP and IPX segments so that customers can access network information during the migration from IPX to IP. NetWare 5 also offers a *compatibility mode* that allows customers to run IPX applications even after migrating to an IP-only network. For more information on migrating from IPX to IP, you should go to Novell's Web site.

IBM Systems Network Architecture Routing

Traditional IBM Systems Network Architecture (SNA) environments are hierarchical. Mainframes and front-end processors (FEPs) provide resource allocation, routing, and network addressing. Peripheral nodes connect user devices to the network.

With the rise of personal computers, client/server computing, and multiprotocol internetworks, IBM recognized the need to evolve SNA into a less hierarchical architecture. IBM modernized the SNA protocols with the creation of Advanced Peer-to-Peer Networking (APPN) and Advanced Program-to-Program Computing (APPC). Both traditional SNA and APPN/APPC are used on SNA networks today.

Traditional SNA

In traditional SNA, a mainframe running Advanced Communication Facility/Virtual Telecommunication Access Method (ACM/VTAM) is responsible for establishing sessions and activating and deactivating resources. Communications controllers, such as FEPs, manage communications links, route data, and implement *path-control functions*. Mainframes and FEPs are called *sub-area nodes*. They form the top part of the hierarchy of nodes.

At the low end of the hierarchy, peripheral nodes control the input and output functions of attached devices such as terminals and PCs running terminal-emulation software. A *cluster controller*, which is also called an *establishment controller*, is a typical peripheral node.

The path control layer of the SNA protocol stack most resembles the routing and network-layer functions of standards-based protocols such as TCP/IP. The path-control layer is responsible for moving information between SNA nodes and making communications possible between nodes on different networks.

Advanced Peer-to-Peer Networking

IBM's Advanced Peer-to-Peer Networking (APPN) is an overhaul of the SNA protocols to support modern networks characterized by peer-to-peer communication among routers, workstations, and applications. In an APPN network, low-entry nodes, end nodes, and network nodes communicate in a less hierarchical fashion than was possible with traditional SNA.

A *low-entry node* is a legacy node that does not inherently understand APPN but can participate in APPN networking by using the services of an adjacent network node. An *end node* is an APPN-capable node that uses the routing services of an adjacent network node. A *network node* (for example, a router) manages resources for its end nodes and low-entry nodes, and maintains network topology and directory databases. A network node communicates dynamically with adjacent network nodes and end nodes to create and update the topology and directory databases.

APPN connects network nodes via links called *transmission groups (TGs)*. The topology database contains a complete picture of all network nodes and TGs, and also includes information for selecting routes with a particular class of service (CoS) For example, a route can be selected based on a TG's capacity. Network nodes send topology-database update (TDU) messages to update the topology database when changes occur. Changes include a node or link becoming active or inactive, a TG becoming congested, or other resources becoming limited.

Transporting SNA Traffic on a TCP/IP Network

In the past, SNA was carried on its own communications network that was separate from the multiprotocol internetwork that carried TCP/IP and other LAN-based protocols. These days, most enterprise network managers are looking for ways to merge these two networks to avoid the overhead of managing two different networks. Integrating an SNA network with a standards-based multiprotocol internetwork allows an enterprise to meet the following goals:

- Reduce operations costs

- Use a mainframe as a high-speed and high-capacity file server

- Upgrade a legacy SNA network to use modern, high-throughput routing and switching techniques

Because SNA is an IBM standard, Token Ring, which was also an IBM standard, was the natural protocol to select when migrating SNA to LANs in the late 1980s and early 1990s. Standalone 3270 terminals were replaced by PCs running 3270-terminal-emulation software. The PCs communicated with Token Ring–attached FEPs or third-party gateways.

As TCP/IP internetworks became ubiquitous, the need arose for SNA Token Ring devices to communicate with hosts on the other side of an IP internetwork. The main options for supporting SNA traffic on an IP internetwork are remote source-route bridging (RSRB) and data-link switching (DLSw).

Remote Source-Route Bridging

Remote source-route bridging (RSRB) is a method for tunneling SNA Token Ring data between peer routers. Packets can be encapsulated directly in a data-link header such as High-Level Data Link Control (HDLC) or Frame Relay, or they can be encapsulated in IP or TCP. TCP offers the best reliability.

With RSRB, SNA data travels from a Token Ring-attached PC, through an internetwork or point-to-point segment, to a remote FEP or mainframe. When the PC starts up, it sends a Logical Link Control (LLC) test frame to find the FEP. The frame is an all-routes explorer source-routed frame. To keep explorer traffic off the internetwork, you can locate the FEP on the PC's ring instead of on a remote ring. Alternately, you can use the *proxy explorer* feature of RSRB to allow a router to cache source-routing paths and convert explorer frames into specifically-routed frames, as shown in Figure 7–8.

Figure 7–8
*An RSRB or
DLSw network
with proxy
explorer
and LLC
termination.*

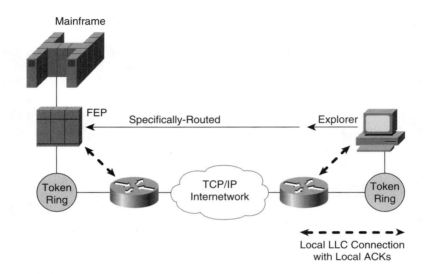

Data-Link Switching

Data-Link Switching (DLSw) is a standard way of carrying SNA and NetBIOS traffic in TCP packets for traversal across a TCP/IP internetwork. DLSw is specified in RFC 1795. Some enhancements to DLSw are described in RFC 2166.

DLSw is similar to RSRB but has the advantage of being an open, non-proprietary standard, which means that DLSw works across implementations from different router vendors. Like RSRB, DLSw supports reducing explorer packets, using a feature called *broadcast control of search packets*, which is similar to the RSRB proxy-explorer feature. DLSw also supports *LLC termination* functionality, which the next section describes.

Preventing Timeouts when Running SNA on a Multiprotocol Internetwork

In a multiprotocol internetwork, SNA runs above the connection-oriented (type 2) LLC protocol (LLC2). When a station sends an LLC2 frame, it expects a response within a timeframe defined by the LLC2 *T1 timer.* The default setting for the timer is 2 seconds, with 6 retries before a session is closed.

In the mid-1990s, when enterprise network managers started merging their SNA networks with their multiprotocol networks, many of them heard complaints from users about SNA session timeouts (which were actually LLC timeouts). Because SNA data is often critical to an enterprise's business mission, this problem was unacceptable. To solve the problem, protocol experts developed the *LLC termination* mechanism.

LLC termination prevents timeouts by terminating an LLC2 connection at a local router. The router handles LLC2 functions such as session establishment, reliability, error control, and flow control. Without the LLC termination mechanism, an LLC2 session is between remote devices that are on opposites sides of an internetwork. With LLC termination, the LLC2 session is between a device and a local router, which minimizes the chance that unpredictable delays in an internetwork will cause timeouts. Figure 7–8 shows a network that uses LLC termination. Both RSRB and DLSw support LLC termination (which is referred to as *Local ACK* in RSRB documentation from Cisco Systems).

In addition to using the LLC2-termination feature, it is also recommended that a fast-converging routing protocol be used on a TCP/IP internetwork that carries SNA traffic. Either OSPF or Enhanced IGRP are good choices. OSPF is the best choice if the customer requires an open standards-based protocol.

Using Multiple Routing and Bridging Protocols in an Internetwork

When selecting routing and bridging protocols for a customer, it is important to realize that you do not have to use the same routing and bridging protocols throughout the internetwork. The criteria for selecting protocols are different for different parts of an internetwork. Some protocols, for example, RIP and RTMP, work well at the access layer of a topology, but are not appropriate for the distribution or core layers.

To merge a new network with an old network, it is often necessary to run more than one routing or bridging protocol. In some cases, your network design might focus on a new design for the core and distribution layers and need to interoperate with existing access-layer routing and bridging protocols. As another example, when two companies merge, sometimes each company wishes to run a different routing protocol.

This chapter has already mentioned some techniques for running multiple routing or bridging protocols, including source-route transparent bridging, external routes in OSPF and RIP 2, and redistribution between routing protocols. This section summarizes some issues with redistribution and covers Integrated Routing and Bridging

(IRB), a Cisco IOS method for connecting bridged and routed networks in a single router.

Redistribution Between Routing Protocols

Redistribution allows a router to run more than one routing protocol and share routes among routing protocols. Implementing redistribution can be challenging because every routing protocol behaves differently and routing protocols cannot directly exchange information about routes, metrics, link states, and so on.

A network administrator must configure redistribution by specifying which protocols should insert routing information into other protocols' routing tables. The configuration should be done with care to avoid *feedback*. Feedback happens when a routing protocol learns about routes from another protocol and then advertises these routes back to the other routing protocol. For example, if a router is configured to redistribute between IGRP and RIP, the router must filter any routes that it learned from RIP before sending routing information back into the RIP network. This avoids any problems caused by the differences in metrics used by different routing protocols.

Another factor that makes redistribution challenging is the possibility that a router can learn about a destination via more than one routing protocol. Every routing protocol and every vendor handles this issue differently. Cisco assigns an *administrative distance* to routes learned from different sources. A lower administrative distance means that a route is preferred. For example, if a router learns about a route via both IGRP and RIP, the IGRP route is preferred because IGRP has a default administrative distance of 100 and RIP has a default administrative distance of 120. If a router also has a static route to the destination, then the static route is preferred, because the default administrative distance for a static route is 0 or 1 (depending on whether the static route is defined using an interface or an IP address). The default values for administrative distances can be changed.

NOTES

Cisco IOS software also supports a "floating static route" which is a static route that has a higher administrative distance than a dynamically-learned route. Floating static routes are available for IP, IPX, and AppleTalk. A floating static route is a statically-configured route that has a high administrative distance so that it can be overridden by dynamically-learned routing information. A floating static route can be used to create a "path of last resort" that is used only when no dynamic information is available. One important application of floating static routes is to provide backup routes in topologies where dial-on-demand (DDR) routing is used.

See Cisco's Web site for more information on floating static routes and setting the administrative distance for routes learned from different sources.

Integrated Routing and Bridging

For customers who need to merge bridged and routed networks, the Cisco IOS software offers support for IRB, which connects VLANs and bridged networks to routed networks within the same router.

An older Cisco IOS feature, called *Concurrent Routing and Bridging (CRB)*, supported routing and bridging within the same router, but it simply meant that you could connect bridged networks to other bridged networks and routed networks to other routed networks. IRB extends CRB by providing the capability to forward packets between bridged and routed interfaces via a software-based interface called the *bridged virtual interface (BVI)*.

One advantage of IRB is that a bridged IP subnet or VLAN can span a router. This can be useful when there is a shortage of IP subnet numbers and it is not practical to assign a different subnet number to each interface on a router. It can also be useful during migration from a bridged environment to a routed or VLAN environment.

A SUMMARY OF IP, APPLETALK, AND IPX ROUTING PROTOCOLS

Table 7–4 provides a comparison of various routing protocols to help you select a routing protocol based on a customer's goals for adaptability, scalability, affordability, security, and network performance.

Table 7–4   Routing Protocol Comparisons

	Distance-Vector or Link-State	Interior or Exterior	Classful or Classless	Metrics Suported	Scalability
RIP Version 1	Distance-vector	Interior	Classful	Hop count	15 hops
RIP Version 2	Distance-vector	Interior	Classless	Hop count	15 hops
IGRP	Distance-vector	Interior	Classful	Bandwidth, delay, reliability, load	255 hops (default is 100)
Enhanced IGRP	Advanced Distance–vector	Interior	Classless	Bandwidth, delay, reliability, load	1,000s of routers
OSPF	Link-state	Interior	Classless	Cost (100 million divided by bandwidth on Cisco routers)	About 50 routers per area, about 100 areas
BGP	Path-vector	Exterior	Classless	Value of path attributes and other configurable factors	1,000s of routers
IS-IS	Link-state	Interior	Classless	Configured path value, plus delay, expense, and errors	1,000s of routers
RTMP	Distance-vector	Interior	NA	Hop count	15 hops
AURP	Distance-vector	Interior or exterior	NA	Hop count	15 hops on each side
IPX RIP	Distance-vector	Interior	NA	Ticks and hop count	15 hops
NLSP	Link-state	Interior	NA	Cost (an integer between 1 and 63) and bandwidth	127 hops

Convergence Time	Resource Consumption	Supports Security? Authenticates Routes?	Ease of Design, Configuration, and Troubleshooting
Can be long (if no load balancing)	Memory: low CPU: low Bandwidth: high	No	Easy
Can be long (if no load balancing)	Memory: low CPU: low Bandwidth: high	Yes	Easy
Quick (uses triggered updates and poison reverse)	Memory: low CPU: low Bandwidth: high	No	Easy
Very quick (uses DUAL algorithm)	Memory: moderate CPU: low Bandwidth: low	Yes	Moderate
Quick (uses link-state advertisements and hello packets)	Memory: high CPU: high Bandwidth: low	Yes	Moderate
Quick (uses update and keepalive packets, and withdraws routes)	Memory: high CPU: high Bandwidth: low	Yes	Moderate
Quick (uses link-state advertisements)	Memory: high CPU: high Bandwidth: low	Yes	Moderate
Can be long	Memory: moderate CPU: moderate Bandwidth: high	No	Easy
Pretty quick (supports summarization)	Memory: low CPU: moderate Bandwidth: low	Yes	Moderate
Pretty quick (uses immediate updates)	Memory: moderate CPU: moderate Bandwidth: high	No	Easy
Quick (uses link-state packets and hierarchical routing)	Memory: high CPU: high Bandwidth: low	Yes	Moderate

SUMMARY

This chapter provided information to help you select the right bridging, switching, and routing protocols for your network design customer. The chapter covered scalability and performance characteristics of the protocols, and talked about how quickly protocols can adapt to changes.

Deciding on the right bridging, switching, and routing protocols for your customer will help you select the best switch and router products for the customer. For example, if you have decided that the design must support a routing protocol that can converge within seconds in a large internetwork, you will probably not recommend a router that only runs RIP.

This chapter began with a generic discussion about decision-making to help you develop a systematic process for selecting network design solutions. A discussion of bridging protocols followed, which covered transparent bridging, source-route bridging and switching, mixed-media bridging, and VLAN protocols. A section on routing protocols followed the bridging section. Table 7–4 summarizes the comparisons that were made of various routing protocols in the routing section.

Developing Network Security and Network Management Strategies

This chapter concludes the discussion on logical network design. Two of the most important aspects of logical network design are security and network management. Both security and management are often overlooked during the design of a network because they are considered operational issues rather than design issues. However, if you consider security and management in the beginning, you can avoid scalability and performance problems that occur when security and management are added to a design after the design is complete. You can also consider tradeoffs while still in the logical design phase, and plan a solution that can meet security, manageability, and other types of goals.

Security and network management designs should be completed before the start of the physical design phase in case they have an effect on the physical design. For example, do they increase capacity requirements? Do you need a separate data path for network management? Do you need all traffic to go through encryption and decryption devices? (You might need to reconsider your logical topology, also. Remember that top-down network design is an iterative process that allows you to revisit preliminary solutions as you develop increasingly detailed plans.)

The goal of this chapter is to help you work with your network design customer in the development of effective security and management strategies, and to help you select the right tools and products to implement the strategies. You can find details about security and management protocols in some of the books listed in the bibliography. One of the best references on security design is Request for Comments (RFC) 2196, "The Site Security Handbook."

NETWORK SECURITY DESIGN

Security is an especially hot topic for enterprise network designers these days because of increased Internet and extranet connections, increased electronic commerce on the Internet, and more telecommuters and mobile users accessing enterprise networks from remote sites.

To help you address the issues associated with increasing security requirements, this chapter lists the steps for developing a security strategy. This chapter also covers some common security techniques and some solutions for typical security challenges (such as securing the Internet connection, securing dial-up network access, securing network services, and securing user services).

The steps for security design are as follows:

1. Identify network assets.

2. Analyze security risks.

3. Analyze security requirements and tradeoffs.

4. Develop a security plan.

5. Define a security policy.

6. Develop procedures for applying security policies.

7. Develop a technical implementation strategy.

8. Achieve buy-in from users, managers, and technical staff.

9. Train users, managers, and technical staff.

10. Implement the technical strategy and security procedures.

11. Test the security and update it if any problems are found.

12. Maintain security by scheduling periodic independent audits, reading audit logs, responding to incidents, reading current literature and agency alerts, continuing to test and train, and updating the security plan and policy.

Identifying Network Assets and Risks

Chapter 2, "Analyzing Technical Goals and Constraints," discussed gathering information on a customer's goals for network security. As discussed in Chapter 2, analyzing goals involves identifying network assets and the risk that those assets could be sabotaged or inappropriately accessed. It also involves analyzing the consequences of risks.

Network assets can include network hosts (including the hosts' operating systems, applications, and data), internetworking devices (such as routers and switches), and network data that traverses the network. Less obvious, but still very important, assets include intellectual property, trade secrets, and a company's reputation.

Risks can range from hostile intruders to untrained users who download Internet applications that have viruses. Hostile intruders can steal data, change data, and cause service to be denied to legitimate users. (*Denial-of-service* attacks have become increasingly common in the last few years.) See Chapter 2 for more details on risk-analysis and requirements gathering.

Analyzing Security Tradeoffs

According to RFC 2196, "The Site Security Handbook,"

> One old truism in security is that the cost of protecting yourself against a threat should be less than the cost of recovering if the threat were to strike you. Cost in this context should be remembered to include losses expressed in real currency, reputation, trustworthiness, and other less obvious measures.

As is the case with most technical design requirements, achieving security goals means making tradeoffs. Tradeoffs must be made between security goals and goals for affordability, usability, performance, and availability. Also, security adds to the amount of management work because user login IDs, passwords, and audit logs must be maintained.

Security also affects network performance. Security features such as packet filters and data encryption consume CPU power and memory on hosts, routers, and servers. Encryption can use upwards of 15 percent of available CPU power on a router or server. Encryption can be implemented on dedicated devices instead of on shared routers or servers, but there is still an effect on network performance because of the delay that packets experience while they are being encrypted or decrypted.

Another tradeoff is that encryption can reduce network redundancy. If all traffic must go through an encryption device, the device becomes a single point of failure. This makes it hard to meet availability goals. It also makes it harder to offer load balancing. To maximize performance and minimize security complexity, a router that is running encryption probably should not also offer load balancing. Load balancing can still be used, but only if it is done transparently to the routers providing encryption. Devices in between the pair of routers offering encryption services can provide the load balancing.

Developing a Security Plan

One of the first steps in security design is developing a security plan. A *security plan* is a high-level document that proposes what an organization is going to do to meet security requirements. The plan specifies the time, people, and other resources that will be required to develop a security policy and achieve technical implementation of the policy. As the network designer, you can help your customer develop a plan that is practical and pertinent. The plan should be based on the customer's goals, and the analysis of network assets and risks.

A security plan should reference the network topology and include a list of network services that will be provided, for example, FTP, Web, e-mail, and so on. This list should specify who provides the services, who has access to the services, how access is provided, and who administers the services.

As the network designer, you can help the customer evaluate which services are definitely needed, based on the customer's business and technical goals. Sometimes new services are added unnecessarily, simply because they are the latest trend. Adding services might require new packet filters on routers and firewalls to protect the services, or additional user-authentication processes to limit access to the services, adding complexity to the security strategy. Overly complex security strategies should be avoided because they can be self-defeating. Complicated security strategies are hard to implement correctly without introducing unexpected security holes.

One of the most important aspects of the security plan is a specification of the people who must be involved in implementing network security:

- Will specialized security administrators be hired?

- How will end users and their managers get involved?

- How will end users, managers, and technical staff be trained on security policies and procedures?

For a security plan to be useful, it needs to have the support of all levels of employees within the organization. It is especially important that corporate management fully support the security plan. Technical staff at headquarters and remote sites should buy into the plan, as should end users.

Developing a Security Policy

According to RFC 2196, "The Site Security Handbook,"

> A security policy is a formal statement of the rules by which people who are given access to an organization's technology and information assets must abide.

A *security policy* informs users, managers, and technical staff of their obligations for protecting technology and information assets. The policy should specify the mechanisms by which these obligations can be met. As was the case with the security plan, the security policy should have buy-in from employees, managers, executives, and technical personnel.

Developing a security policy is the job of security and network administrators. The administrators get input from managers, users, network designers and engineers, and possibly legal counsel. As a network designer, you should work closely with the security administrators to understand how policies might affect the network design.

Once a security policy has been developed, with the engagement of users, staff, and management, it should be explained to all by top management. Many enterprises require personnel to sign a statement indicating that they have read, understood, and agreed to abide by a policy.

A security policy is a living document. Because organizations constantly change, security policies must be regularly updated to reflect new business directions and technological changes.

Components of a Security Policy

You should read RFC 2196 for detailed information on writing a security policy. In general a policy should include at least the following:

- An *access policy* that defines access rights and privileges. The access policy should provide guidelines for connecting external networks, connecting devices to a network, and adding new software to systems.

- An *accountability policy* that defines the responsibilities of users, operations staff, and management. The accountability policy should specify an audit capability, and provide guidelines on reporting security problems.

- An *authentication policy* that establishes trust through an effective password policy, and sets up guidelines for remote location authentication.

- *Computer-technology purchasing guidelines* that specify the requirements for acquiring, configuring, and auditing computer systems and networks for compliance with the policy.

Developing Security Procedures

Security procedures implement security policies. Procedures define configuration, login, audit, and maintenance processes. Security procedures should be written for end users, network administrators, and security administrators. Security procedures should specify how to handle incidents (that is, what to do and who to contact if an intrusion is detected). Security procedures can be communicated to users and administrators in instructor-led and self-paced training classes.

SECURITY MECHANISMS

This section describes some typical ingredients of secure network designs. You can select from these ingredients when designing solutions for common security challenges, which are described in the "Selecting Security Solutions" section later in this chapter.

Authentication

Authentication identifies who is requesting network services. The term *authentication* usually refers to authenticating users, but it could refer to verifying a software process also. For example, some routing protocols support *route authentication*, whereby a router must pass some criteria before another router accepts its routing updates.

Most security policies state that to access a network and its services, a user must enter a login ID and password that are authenticated by a security server. To maximize security, one-time (dynamic) passwords can be used. With one-time password systems, a user's password always changes. This is often accomplished with a security card. A *security card* is a physical device about the size of a credit card. The user types a personal identification number (PIN) into the card. (The *PIN* is an initial level of security that simply gives the user permission to use the card.) The card provides a one-time password that is used to access the corporate network for a limited time. The password is synchronized with a central security card server that resides on the network. Security cards are commonly used by telecommuters and mobile users. They are not usually used for LAN access.

Authorization

While authentication controls who can access network resources, *authorization* says what they can do once they have accessed the resources. Authorization grants privileges to processes and users. Authorization lets a security administrator control parts of a network, for example, directories and files on servers.

Authorization varies from user to user, partly depending on a user's department or job function. For example, a policy might state that only Human Resources employees should see salary records for people they don't manage. Explicitly listing the authorized activities of each user with respect to every resource is difficult, so techniques are used to simplify the process. For example, a network manager can create user groups for users with the same privileges.

Accounting (Auditing)

To effectively analyze the security of a network and to respond to security incidents, procedures should be established for collecting network activity data. Collecting data is called *accounting* or *auditing*.

For networks with strict security policies, audit data should include all attempts to achieve authentication and authorization by any person. It is especially important to log "anonymous" or "guest" access to public servers. The data should also log all attempts by users to change their access rights.

The collected data should include user and host names for login and logout attempts, and previous and new access rights for a change of access rights. Each entry in the audit log should be timestamped.

The audit process should not collect passwords. Collecting passwords creates a potential for a security breach if the audit records are improperly accessed. (Neither correct nor incorrect passwords should be collected. An incorrect password often differs from the valid password by only a single character or transposition of characters.)

A further extension of auditing is the concept of security assessment. With *security assessment*, the network is examined from within by professionals, trained in the vulnerabilities exploited by network invaders. Part of any security policy and audit procedure should be periodic assessments of the vulnerabilities in a network. The result should be a specific plan for correcting deficiencies, which may be as simple as retraining staff.

Data Encryption

Encryption is a process that scrambles data to protect it from being read by anyone but the intended receiver. An *encryption device* encrypts data before placing it on a network. A *decryption device* decrypts the data before passing it to an application. A router, server, end system, or dedicated device can act as an encryption or decryption device. Data that is encrypted is called *ciphered data* (or simply *encrypted data*). Data that is not encrypted is called *plain text* or *clear text*.

Encryption is a useful security feature for providing data confidentiality. It can also be used to identify the sender of data. Although authentication and authorization should also protect the confidentiality of data and identify senders, encryption is a good security feature to implement in case the other types of security fail.

There are performance tradeoffs associated with encryption, however, as mentioned in the "Analyzing Security Tradeoffs" section earlier in the chapter. Encryption should be used when a customer has analyzed security risks and identified severe consequences if data is not confidential and the identity of senders of data is not guaranteed. On internal networks and networks that use the Internet simply for Web browsing, e-mail, and file transfer, encryption is usually not necessary. For organizations that connect private sites via the Internet, using virtual private networking (VPN), encryption is recommended to protect the confidentiality of the organization's data.

Encryption has two parts:

- An *encryption algorithm* is a set of instructions to scramble and unscramble data.

- An *encryption key* is a code used by an algorithm to scramble and unscramble data.

Children sometimes play with encryption by using a simple algorithm such as "find the letter on the top row and use the letter on the bottom row instead," and a key that might look something like the following table:

A B C D E F G H I J K L M N O P Q R S T U V W X Y Z

I N B Y G L S P T A R W Q H X M D K F U O C Z VE J

In this example, LISA is encrypted as WTFI. The key only shows uppercase letters, but there are many other possibilities also, including lowercase letters, digits, and so on. Most algorithms are more complex than the one in the children's example to avoid having to maintain a key that includes a value for each possible character.

The goal of encryption is that even if the algorithm is known, without the appropriate key, an intruder can not interpret the message. This type of key is called a *secret key.* When both the sender and receiver use the same secret key, it is called a *symmetric key.* The Data Encryption Standard (DES) is the best known example of a symmetric key system. DES encryption is available for most routers and many server implementations.

Although secret keys are reasonably simple to implement between two devices, as the number of devices increases, the number of secret keys increases, which can be hard to manage. For example, a session between Station A and Station B uses a different key than a session between Station A and Station C, or a session between Station B and Station C, and so on. Asymmetric keys can solve this problem.

Public/Private Key Encryption

Public/private key encryption is the best known example of an asymmetric key system. With public/private key systems, each secure station on a network has a public key that is openly published or easily determined. All devices can use a station's public key to encrypt data to send to the station.

The receiving station decrypts the data using its own private key. Since no other device has the station's private key, no other device can decrypt the data, so data confidentiality is maintained. (Mathematicians and computer scientists have written computer programs that identify special numbers to use for the keys so that the same algorithm can be used by both the sender and receiver, even though different keys are used.) Figure 8–1 shows a public/private key system for data confidentiality.

Figure 8–1
Public/private key system for ensuring data confidentiality.

Public/private key systems provide both confidentiality and authentication features. Using asymmetric keys, a recipient can verify that a document really came from the user or host that it appears to come from. For example, let's say that you are sending your tax returns to the Internal Revenue Service (IRS). The IRS needs to know that the returns came from you and not from a hostile third party that wants to make it look like you owe more than you do.

You can encrypt your document or a part of your document with your private key, resulting in what is known as a *digital signature*. The IRS can decrypt the document, using your public key, as shown in Figure 8–2. If the decryption is successful, then the document came from you because nobody else should have your private key.

The digital signature feature of asymmetric keys can be used in conjunction with the feature for data confidentiality. After encrypting your document with your private key, you can also encrypt the document with the IRS's public key. The IRS decrypts the document twice. If the result is plain-text data, the IRS knows that the document came from you and that you meant for the document to go to the IRS and not anyone else.

Host A

Host B

Encrypted data

Encrypt data
using Host A's
Private Key

Decrypt data
using Host A's
Public Key

Figure 8–2
*Public/private
key system for
sending a digi-
tal signature.*

Some examples of asymmetric key systems include the Rivest, Shamir, and Adleman (RSA) standard, the Diffie-Hellman public key algorithm, and the Digital Signature Standard (DSS). Cisco Systems, Inc. ,uses the DSS standard to authenticate peer routers during the setup of an encrypted session. The peer routers use the Diffie-Hellman algorithm to send information on a secret key to use to encrypt data. The actual data is encrypted using the DES algorithm and the secret key.

Packet Filters

Packet filters can be set up on routers and servers to accept or deny packets from particular addresses or services. Packet filters augment authentication and authorization mechanisms. They help protect network resources from unauthorized use, theft, destruction, and denial-of-service (DoS) attacks.

A security policy should state whether packet filters implement one or the other of the following policies:

- Deny specific types of packets and accept all else

- Accept specific types of packets and deny all else

The first policy requires a thorough understanding of specific security threats and can be hard to implement. The second policy is easier to implement and more secure because the security administrator does not have to predict future attacks for which packets should be denied. The second policy is also easier to test because there is a finite set of accepted uses of the network. To do a good job implementing the second policy requires a good understanding of network requirements. The network designer should work with the security administrator to determine what types of packets should be accepted.

Cisco implements the second policy in their packet filters, which Cisco calls *access control lists (ACLs)*. An ACL on a router or switch running the Cisco Internetwork Operating System (IOS) software always has an implicit deny-all statement at the end. Specific accept statements are processed before the implicit deny-all statement. (The statement is implicit because the administrator does not have to actually enter it, though it is a good idea to enter it to make the behavior of the list more obvious.)

ACLs let you control whether network traffic is forwarded or blocked at interfaces on a router or switch. ACL definitions provide criteria that are applied to packets that enter or exit an interface. Typical criteria are the packet source address, the packet destination address, or the upper-layer protocol in the packet.

Because Cisco IOS software tests a packet against each criteria statement in the list until a match is found, ACLs should be designed with care to provide good performance. By studying traffic flow, you can design the list so that most packets match the earliest conditions. Fewer conditions to check per packet means better throughput. Good advice for ACLs is to order the list with the most general statements at the top and the most specific statements at the bottom, with the last statement being the general, implicit deny-all statement.

Firewalls

As discussed in Chapter 5, "Designing a Network Topology," a *firewall* is a system or combination of systems that enforces security policies at the boundary between two or more networks. A firewall can be a router with ACLs, a dedicated hardware box, or software running on a PC or UNIX system. Firewalls are especially important at the boundary between the enterprise network and the Internet.

Physical Security

Physical security refers to limiting access to key network resources by keeping the resources behind a locked door. Physical security also refers to protecting resources from natural disasters such as floods, fires, storms, and earthquakes. Because physical security is such an obvious requirement, it is easy to forget to plan for it, but it should never be overlooked or considered less important than other goals.

Depending on your particular network design customer, physical security should be installed to protect core routers, demarcation points, cabling, modems, servers, hosts, backup storage, and so on. Work with your customer during the early stages of the network design project to make sure equipment will be placed in computer rooms that have card key access and/or security guards. Computer rooms should also be equipped with uninterruptible power supplies, fire alarms, fire abatement mechanisms, and water removal systems. To protect equipment from earthquakes and high winds during storms, equipment should be installed in racks that attach to the floor or wall.

SELECTING SECURITY SOLUTIONS

The previous section described some typical ingredients of network security designs. This section provides some recipes for putting the ingredients together to meet the following security challenges:

- Securing the Internet connection

- Securing dial-up access

- Securing network services

- Securing user services

Securing the Internet Connection

The Internet connection should be secured with a set of overlapping security mechanisms, including firewalls, packet filters, physical security, audit logs, authentication, and authorization. Public servers, for example World Wide Web and possibly File Transfer Protocol (FTP) servers, can allow non-authenticated access, but all other servers should require authentication and authorization. Public servers should be placed on a free-trade-zone network that is protected from other networks via firewalls. Free-trade-zone networks were discussed in more detail in Chapter 5.

If a customer can afford two separate servers, security experts recommended that FTP services not run on the same server as Web services. FTP users have more opportunities for reading and possibly changing files than Web users do. A hacker could use FTP to damage a company's Web pages, thus damaging the company's image and possibly compromising Web-based electronic-commerce and other applications. Security experts recommend never allowing Internet access to Trivial File Transfer Protocol (TFTP) servers, because TFTP offers no authentication features.

Adding Common Gateway Interface (CGI) or other types of scripts to Web servers should be done with great care. Scripts should be thoroughly tested for security leaks. Electronic-commerce applications should be installed on Web servers only if the applications are compatible with the Secure Sockets Layer (SSL) standard.

E-mail servers have long been a source for intruder break-ins, probably because e-mail protocols and implementations have been around a long time and hackers can easily understand them. Also, by its very nature, an e-mail server must allow outsider access. To secure e-mail servers, network administrators should keep up to date on well-known bugs and security leaks by subscribing to mailing lists dedicated to security information.

Securing Internet Domain Name System Services

Domain Name System (DNS) servers should be carefully controlled and monitored. Name-to-address resolution is critical to the operation of any network. An attacker who can successfully control or impersonate a DNS server can wreak havoc on a network. DNS servers should be protected from security attacks using packet filters on routers, and versions of DNS software that incorporate security features.

Traditionally, DNS had no security capabilities. In particular, there was no way to verify information returned in a DNS response to a query. A hacker could hijack the query and return a counterfeit name-to-address mapping. Digital signatures and other security features are being added to the protocol to address this issue and other security concerns. See RFC 2065, "Domain Name System Security Extensions," for more information.

Logical Network Design and the Internet Connection

A good rule for enterprise networks is that the network should have well-defined exit and entry points. An organization that has only one Internet connection can manage Internet security problems more easily than an organization that has many Internet connections. Some very large organizations require more than one Internet connection for performance and redundancy reasons, however. This is fine as long as the connections are managed and monitored. Departments or users who add Internet connections without coordination from corporate network engineers should not be tolerated.

When selecting routing protocols for the Internet connection, to maximize security, you should select a protocol that offers route authentication such as RIP Version 2,

OSPF, or BGP4. Static and default routing is also a good option, because with static and default routing there are no routing updates that could be compromised. Internet routers should be equipped with packet filters to prevent DoS attacks.

When securing the Internet connection, Network Address Translation (NAT) can be used to protect internal network addressing schemes. As discussed in Chapter 6, NAT hides internal network numbers from outside networks. NAT translates internal network numbers when outside access is required.

Organizations that use Virtual Private Networking (VPN) services to connect private sites via the Internet should use NAT, firewalls, and data encryption. In VPN topologies, private data travels across the public Internet, so encryption is a must. The Layer 2 Tunneling Protocol (L2TP) is an emerging Internet Engineering Task Force (IETF) standard for tunneling private data over public networks.

The IP Security Protocol

The *IP Security Protocol (IPSec)* is a set of open standards that provides data confidentiality, data integrity, and authentication between participating peers at the IP layer. As IPSec gains industry acceptance, customers will require support for it in internetworking products that they purchase. Even though IPSec is relatively new, many router and server manufactures support it. IPSec is documented in RFCs 1825 through 1829.

IPSec enables a system to select security protocols and algorithms, and establish cryptographic keys. The Internet Key Exchange (IKE) protocol provides authentication of IPSec peers. It also negotiates IPSec keys and security associations. IKE uses the following technologies:

- **DES.** Encrypts packet data.

- **Diffie-Hellman.** Establishes a shared, secret, session key.

- **Message Digest 5 (MD5).** A hash algorithm that authenticates packet data.

- **Secure Hash Algorithm (SHA).** A hash algorithm that authenticates packet data.

- **RSA encrypted nonces.** Provides repudiation.

- **RSA signatures.** Provides non-repudiation.

NOTES

Repudiation is a security feature that prevents a third party from proving that a communication between two other parties took place. This is a desirable feature if you do not want your communication to be traceable.

Non-repudiation is the opposite of repudiation: a third party can prove that a communication between two other parties took place. Non-repudiation is desirable if you want to be able to trace your communications and prove that they occurred.

Securing Dial-Up Access

Security is critical for dial-up access and should consist of firewall technologies, physical security, authentication and authorization mechanisms, auditing, and possibly encryption. Authentication and authorization are the most important features for dial-up access security. One-time passwords with security cards make a lot of sense in this arena.

Remote users and remote routers that use the Point-to-Point Protocol (PPP) should be authenticated with the Challenge Handshake Authentication Protocol (CHAP). The Password Authentication Protocol (PAP), which offers less security than CHAP, is not recommended. The "Remote-Access Technologies" section of Chapter 10 covers PPP, CHAP, and PAP in more detail.

Another option for authentication, authorization, and accounting is the *Remote Authentication Dial-In User Server (RADIUS) protocol*. Livingston, Inc., developed RADIUS a few years ago; it has become an industry standard and is documented in RFC 2138. RADIUS gives an administrator the option of having a centralized database of user information. The database includes authentication and configuration information and specifies the type of service permitted by a user (for example, PPP, Telnet, rlogin, and so on). RADIUS is a client/server protocol. An access server acts as a client of a RADIUS server.

Dial-up services should be strictly controlled. Users should not be allowed to attach modems and analog lines to their own workstations or servers. (Some companies actually fire employees who do this.) It is helpful to have a single dial-in point (for example, a single large modem pool or access server) so that all users are authenticated in the same way. A different set of modems should be used for any dial-out services. Both dial-in and dial-out services should be authenticated.

If the modems and access servers support call-back (which most do), then call-back should be used. With *call-back*, when a user dials in and is authenticated, the system disconnects the call and calls back on a specified number. Call-back is useful because the system calls back the actual user, not a hacker who might be masquerading as the user. Call-back can easily be compromised, however, and should not be the only security mechanism used.

There are many operational security considerations with dial-up networks that are outside the scope of a design book, but suffice it to say that modems and access servers should be carefully configured and protected from hackers reconfiguring them. Modems should be programmed to reset to the standard configuration at the start and end of each call, and modems and access servers should terminate calls cleanly. Servers should force a logout if the user hangs up unexpectedly.

Securing Network Services

Many of the recommendations for securing the Internet connection apply to securing internal enterprise networks also. Internal network services can make use of authentication and authorization, packet filters, audit logs, physical security, encryption, and so on.

To protect internal network services, it is important to protect internetworking devices, such as routers and switches. Login IDs and passwords should be required for accessing these devices, whether the user accesses the device via a console port or via the network. A first-level password can be used for administrators that simply need to check the status of the devices. A second-level password should be used for administrators who have permission to view or change configurations.

If modem access to the console ports of internetworking devices is allowed, the modems must be secured just as standard dial-in user modems are, and the phone numbers should be unlisted and unrelated to the organization's main number(s). The phone numbers should also be changed when there is staff turnover.

For customers with numerous routers and switches, a protocol such as the *Terminal Access Controller Access Control System (TACACS)* can be used to manage large numbers of router and switch user IDs and passwords in a centralized database. TACACS also offers auditing features.

Limiting use of the Simple Network Management Protocol (SNMP) should be considered on enterprise networks for which security goals outweigh manageability goals. One of the main issues with SNMP is the set operation which allows a remote station to change management and configuration data. A new version of SNMP (SNMPv3) is under development that will support authentication for use with the set operation and other SNMP operations.

As was the case with Internet connections, internal networks should run the most secure versions of DNS, FTP, and Web software. Implementations of Network Information Services (NIS) and other types of naming and addressing servers should also be carefully selected based on the level of security offered.

Although it is obvious that services within a network (file servers, for example) should require authentication and authorization, it might be less obvious that the network itself should also require these security mechanisms. Before a user can get to the point of logging into servers, the user should first be required to login to the network.

Securing User Services

User services include end systems, applications, hosts, file servers, database servers, and other services. File and other servers should obviously offer authentication and authorization features. End systems can also offer these features if users are concerned about other people using their systems. Users should be encouraged to log out of sessions when leaving their desks for long periods of time, and to turn off their machines when leaving work, to protect against unauthorized people walking up to a system and accessing services and applications. Automatic logouts can also be deployed to automatically logout a session that has had no activity for a period of time.

Security policies and procedures should specify accepted practices regarding passwords: when they should be used, how they should be formatted, and how they can be changed. In general, passwords should include both letters and numbers, be at least six characters, not be a common word, and be changed often.

On servers, root password knowledge (or the non-UNIX equivalent) should be limited to a few people. Guest accounts should be avoided if possible. Protocols that support the concept of *trust* in other hosts should be used with caution. (Examples include rlogin and rsh on UNIX systems.) Hosts that permit guest accounts and support trusted hosts should be isolated from other hosts if possible.

Kerberos is an authentication system that provides user-to-host security for application-level protocols such as FTP and Telnet. If requested by the application, Kerberos can also provide encryption. Kerberos relies on a symmetric key database that uses a key distribution center (KDC) on a Kerberos server. See the Kerberos Frequently Asked Questions (FAQ) document, available at www.ov.com/misc/krb-faq.html, for the latest information on Kerberos.

A security policy should specify which applications are allowed to run on networked PCs, and guidelines restricting the downloading of unknown applications from the Internet or other sites. Security procedures should specify how users can install and update virus-protection software. Virus protection is one of the most important aspects of user-services security.

Depending on the network topology, user-services security might incorporate encryption. Encryption is sometimes done at servers and end systems, rather than within the network. Vendors such as Microsoft, Netscape, and Sun Microsystems offer encryption software for end systems, workstations, and servers.

To guarantee security at the user-services level, known security bugs in applications and network operating systems should be identified and fixed. Administrators should be required to keep up to date on the latest hacker tricks and viruses.

NETWORK MANAGEMENT DESIGN

A good network management design can help an organization achieve availability, performance, and security goals. Effective network management processes can help an organization measure how well design goals are being met and adjust network parameters if they are not being met. Network management also facilitates meeting scalability goals because it can help an organization analyze current network behavior, apply upgrades appropriately, and troubleshoot any problems with upgrades.

It is a good idea to approach network management design in the same way you approach any design project. Think about scalability, data formats, and cost/benefit tradeoffs. Network management systems can be very expensive. They can also have a negative effect on network performance.

Pay attention to the *Heisenberg Uncertainty Principle*, which states that the act of observing something can alter what is observed. Some network management systems poll remote stations on a regular basis. The amount of traffic caused by the polling can be significant. You should analyze your customer's requirements for polling timers and not arbitrarily use the defaults of a network management system.

Work with your customer to figure out which resources should be monitored and the metrics to use when measuring the performance of devices. Choose the data to collect carefully. Saving too much data can result in a requirement for a supercomputer to process and store the data. On the other hand, be careful not to throw away so much data that you are unable to use the remaining data to manage the network.

Plan the format that data should be saved in carefully. You should try to use general-purpose data formats. Assume that the data you collect might be used for different applications than the ones that you have in mind. As Kathryn Cramer says in her book, *Roads Home: Seven Pathways to Midlife Wisdom*:

> Remain open to possibilities other than what has been imagined.

Proactive Network Management

When helping your customer design network management strategies, you should encourage the practice of proactive network management. As more companies recognize the strategic importance of their internetworks, they are putting more emphasis on proactive management. *Proactive management* means checking the health of the network during normal operation in order to recognize potential problems, optimize performance, and plan upgrades.

Companies that practice proactive management collect statistics and conduct tests, such as response time measurements, on a routine basis. The statistics and test results can be used to communicate trends and network health to management and users. Network managers can write monthly or quarterly reports that document the quality of network service that has been delivered in the last period, measured against service goals. (The service goals are defined by the network design: availability, response time, throughput, usability, and so on.)

If your network design customer plans to implement proactive network management, which you should encourage, you should consider this objective when designing a network management strategy for your customer. Proactive network management is desirable, but can require that network management tools and processes be more sophisticated than with reactive network management.

Network Management Processes

Chapter 2, "Analyzing Technical Goals and Constraints," talked about analyzing a customer's goals for manageability of a network. In general, most customers have a need to develop network management processes that can help them manage the implementation and operation of the network, diagnose and fix problems, optimize performance, and plan enhancements.

The International Organization for Standardization (ISO) defines five types of network management processes:

- Performance management

- Fault management

- Configuration management

- Security management

- Accounting management

Performance Management

According to the ISO, performance management allows the measurement of network behavior and effectiveness. Performance management includes examining network application and protocol behavior, analyzing reachability, measuring response time, and recording network route changes. Performance management facilitates optimizing a network, meeting service-level agreements, and planning for expansion. Monitoring performance involves collecting data, processing some or all of the data, displaying the processed data, and archiving some or all of the data.

Two types of performance should be monitored:

- End-to-end performance management measures performance across an internetwork. It can measure availability, capacity, utilization, delay, delay variation, throughput, reachability, response time, errors, and the burstiness of traffic.

- Component performance measures the performance of individual links or devices. For example, throughput and utilization on a particular network segment can be measured. Additionally, routers and switches can be monitored for throughput (packets-per-second), memory and CPU usage, and errors.

Performance management often involves polling remote parts of the network to test reachability and measure response times. Response-time measurements consist of sending a ping packet and measuring the round-trip time (RTT) to send the packet and receive a response. The ping packet is actually an Internet Control Message Protocol (ICMP) echo packet.

On very large networks, reachability and RTT studies can be impractical. For example, on a network with 10,000 devices, some commercially available network management systems take hours to poll the devices, cause significant network traffic, and save more data than a human can process. Work with your customer to scale back goals for doing reachability and RTT studies if the goals are unrealistic.

Another performance management process is using protocol analyzers or SNMP tools to record traffic loads between important sources and destinations. The objective is to document the megabytes per second between pairs of autonomous systems, networks, hosts, or applications. Source/destination traffic-load documentation is useful for capacity planning, troubleshooting, and figuring out which routers should be peers in routing protocols that use a peering system, such as the Border Gateway Protocol (BGP). Source/destination traffic-load data is also useful if a service-level agreement includes throughput requirements.

Performance management can include processes for recording changes in routes between stations. Tracking route changes can be useful for troubleshooting reachability and performance problems. One way to document route changes is to use ICMP echo packets with the IP record-route option turned on. Be aware that turning on the record-route option might skew RTT measurements, however. The record-route option causes each router to put its address in the options field of the IP header, which can cause extra processing time. (Don't forget the Heisenberg Uncertainty Principle!) Plan to do route-change studies separately from RTT analyses. Another way to study route changes is with the IP trace-route command. trace-route is somewhat unreliable, however.

NOTES

trace-route is used to determine the IP routing path to a remote device. A trace-route packet is a User Datagram Protocol (UDP) "probe" packet sent to port 33434. trace-route works by taking advantage of the ICMP error message a router generates when a packet exceeds its time-to-live (TTL) value. TTL is a field in the IP header of an IP packet.

trace-route starts by sending a UDP probe packet with a TTL of one. This causes the first router in the path to discard the probe and send back a time-exceeded ICMP message. The trace-route command then sends several probes, increasing the TTL by one after a few packets have been sent at each TTL value. For example, it sends a few packets with TTL equal to 1, then a few packets with TTL equal to 2, then a few packets with TTL equal to 3, and so on, until the destination host is reached.

Each router in the path decrements the TTL. The router that decrements the TTL to 0 sends back the time-exceeded message. The final destination host sends back a destination unreachable (port-unreachable) ICMP message, because UDP port 33434 is not a well-known port. This process allows a user to see a message from every router in the path to the destination, and a message from the destination.

Unfortunately, trace-route is not dependable. Some routers do not send back time-exceeded messages. Some routers incorrectly use the TTL of the incoming packet to send the time-exceeded message, which does not work. Also, some systems do not send the port-unreachable message which means that trace-route waits for a long time before timing out. Finally, some service providers purposely change the results of trace-route to hide internal hops.

Fault Management

Fault management refers to detecting, isolating, diagnosing, and correcting problems. It also includes processes for reporting problems to end users and managers, and tracking trends related to problems. In some cases, fault management means developing workarounds until a problem can be fixed.

Network users expect quick and reliable fault resolution. They also expect to be kept informed about ongoing problems and to be given a timeframe for resolution. After a problem is resolved, they expect the problem to be tested and then documented in some sort of problem-tracking database. A variety of tools exist to meet these fault-management requirements, including monitoring tools that alert managers to problems, protocol analyzers for fault resolution, and help-desk software for documenting problems and alerting users of problems. Monitoring tools are often based on the SNMP and Remote Monitoring (RMON) standards, which are covered in more detail later in this chapter.

Configuration Management

Configuration management helps a network manager keep track of network devices and maintain information on how devices are configured. With configuration management, a network manager can define and save a default configuration for similar devices, modify the default configuration for specific devices, and load the configuration on devices. Configuration management also lets a manager maintain an inventory of network assets, and do version-logging. *Version-logging* refers to keeping track of the version of operating systems or applications running on network devices.

Configuration management facilitates change management. In the past, network administrators spent a lot of their time handling configurations for new employees and configuration changes for employees that moved. Encourage your network design customer to use dynamic configuration protocols and tools, such as the Dynamic Host Configuration Protocol (DHCP), to free up management time for more strategic tasks than moves, adds, and changes. A protocol such as the VLAN Trunking Protocol (VTP) is also beneficial, because it automatically keeps track of users' memberships in VLANs.

Security Management

Security management lets a network manager maintain and distribute passwords and other authentication and authorization information. Security management also includes processes for generating, distributing, and storing encryption keys.

One important aspect of security management is a process for collecting, storing, and examining security audit logs. As mentioned in the section, "Accounting (Auditing)," earlier in this chapter, audit logs should document logins and logouts (but not save passwords) and attempts by people to change their level of authorization.

Collecting audit data can result in a rapid accumulation of data. The required storage can be minimized by keeping data for a short period of time and summarizing the data. One drawback to keeping less data, however, is that it makes it harder to investigate security incidents. Compressing the data, instead of keeping less data, is often a better solution. It is also a good idea to encrypt audit logs. A hacker who accesses audit logs can cause a lot of damage to a network if the audit log is not encrypted.

A variety of tools exist for maintaining security logs, including Event Viewer on Windows NT machines, system logs (syslogs) on UNIX systems, and *C2 auditing* for detailed audit reports on UNIX systems. The U.S. Department of Defense defined C2 security, including auditing, as part of its guidelines for computer security in the 1980s.

Accounting Management

Accounting management facilitates usage-based billing, whereby individual departments or projects are charged for network services. Even in cases where there is no money exchange, accounting of network usage can be useful to catch departments or individuals who "abuse" the network. The abuse could be intentional, for example, a discontented employee or former employee causing network problems, or the abuse could be unintentional. (People playing network games do not intend to harm the network, but could cause excessive traffic nonetheless.) A practical reason to track unexpected traffic growth is so that the traffic can be considered during the next capacity-planning phase.

Network Management Architectures

This section discusses some typical decisions that must be made when selecting a network management architecture. A network management architecture consists of three major components:

- A managed device is a network node that collects and stores management information. Managed devices can be routers, servers, switches, bridges, hubs, end systems, or printers.

- An agent is network-management software that resides in a managed device. An agent tracks local management information and uses a protocol such as SNMP to send information to NMSs.

- A network-management system (NMS) runs applications to display management data, monitor and control managed devices, and communicate with agents. An NMS is generally a powerful workstation that has sophisticated graphics, memory, storage, and processing capabilities.

Figure 8–3 shows the relationship between managed devices, agents, and NMSs.

Figure 8–3
A network management architecture.

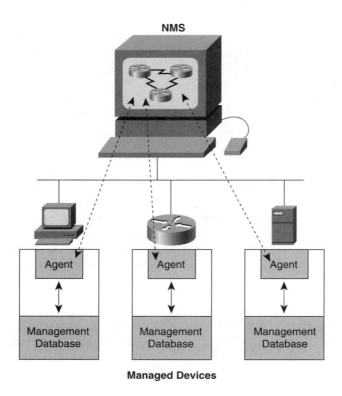

A network management architecture consists of managed devices, agents, and NMSs arranged in a topology that fits into the internetwork topology. The tasks for designing a network management architecture parallel the tasks for designing an internetwork. Traffic flow and load between NMSs and managed devices should be considered. A decision should be made regarding whether management traffic flows in-band (with other network traffic) or out-of-band (outside normal traffic flow). A redundant topology should be considered. A decision should be made regarding a centralized or distributed management topology.

In-Band Versus Out-of-Band Monitoring

With *in-band monitoring*, network management data travels across an internetwork using the same paths as user traffic. This makes the network management architecture easy to develop, but results in the dilemma that network management data is impacted by problems on the internetwork, making it harder to troubleshoot the problems. It is beneficial to be able to use management tools even when the internetwork is congested, failing, or under a security attack.

With *out-of-band monitoring*, network management data travels on different paths than user data. NMSs and agents are linked via circuits that are separate from the internetwork. The circuits can use dial-up, ISDN, Frame Relay, or other technologies. The separate circuits can be used all the time or they can be used as backup only when the primary internetwork path is broken.

Out-of-band monitoring makes the network design more complex and expensive. To keep the cost down, analog dial-up lines are often used for backup, rather than ISDN or Frame Relay circuits. Another tradeoff with out-of-band monitoring is that there are security risks associated with adding extra links between NMSs and agents. To reduce the risks, the links should be carefully controlled and only added if absolutely necessary. For analog modem links, the agent should use a call-back mechanism after the NMS calls the agent. (Call-back was covered in the "Securing Dial-Up Access" section earlier in the chapter.)

Centralized Versus Distributed Monitoring

In a centralized monitoring architecture, all NMSs reside in one area of the network, often in a corporate Network Operations Center (NOC). Agents are distributed across the internetwork and send data such as ping and SNMP responses to the centralized NMSs. The data is sent via out-of-band or in-band paths.

Distributed monitoring means that NMSs and agents are spread out across the internetwork. A hierarchical distributed arrangement can be used whereby distributed NMSs send data to sophisticated centralized NMSs using a manager-of-managers (MoM) architecture. A centralized system that manages distributed NMSs is sometimes called an *umbrella NMS*.

In a MoM architecture, distributed NMSs can filter data before sending it to the centralized stations, thus reducing the amount of network management data that flows on the internetwork. Another advantage with distributed management is that the distributed systems can often gather data even when parts of the internetwork are failing.

The disadvantage with distributed management is that the architecture is complex and hard to manage. It is more difficult to control security, contain the amount of data that is collected and stored, and keep track of management devices. A simple network management architecture that does not complicate the job of managing the network is generally a better solution.

Selecting Tools and Protocols for Network Management

Once you have discussed high-level network management processes with your customer, and developed a network management architecture, you can make some decisions on which network management protocols and tools to recommend to your customer. You can meet most customers' needs by recommending SNMP and RMON tools.

Simple Network Management Protocol

SNMP is supported in most commercial network management systems. SNMPv2 is gradually supplanting Version 1 because it increases vendor interoperability by more rigorously defining the specification. In addition, the SNMPv2 `get-bulk` operation adds support for the efficient retrieval of a block of parameters when gathering data from a table of parameters. Work is underway on SNMP Version 3 (SNMPv3). SNMPv3 offers better security, including authentication to protect against modification of information, and secure set operations for the remote configuration of SNMP managed devices.

SNMP consists of these components:

- RFC 1902 defines mechanisms for describing and naming parameters that are managed with SNMPv2. The mechanisms are called the *structure of managed information* or *SMI*.

- RFC 1905 defines protocol operations for SNMPv2.

- *Management information bases (MIBs)* define management parameters that are accessible via SNMP. Various RFCs define the core set of parameters for the Internet suite of protocols. The core set is called *MIB II*. Vendors can also define private MIBs.

SNMPv2 has seven types of packets:

- **Get Request.** Sent by an NMS to an agent to collect a management parameter.

- **Get-Next Request.** Sent by an NMS to collect the next parameter in a list or table of parameters.

- **Get-Bulk Request.** Sent by an NMS to retrieve large blocks of data, such as multiple rows in a table (not in SNMPv1).

- **Response.** Sent by an agent to an NMS in response to a request.

- **Set Request.** Sent by an NMS to an agent to configure a parameter on a managed device.

- **Trap.** Sent autonomously (not in response to a request) by an agent to an NMS to notify the NMS of an event.

- **Inform.** Sent by an NMS to notify another NMS of information in a MIB view that is remote to the receiving application (not in SNMPv1, supports MoM architectures).

Remote Monitoring (RMON)

The RMON MIB was developed by the IETF in the early 1990s to address shortcomings in the standard MIBs which lacked the ability to provide statistics on data-link and physical-layer parameters. The IETF originally developed the RMON MIB to provide Ethernet traffic statistics and fault diagnosis. In 1994, Token Ring statistics were added.

RMON agents gather statistics on CRC errors, Ethernet collisions, Token Ring soft errors, packet-size distribution, the number of packets in and out, and the rate of broadcast packets. The RMON alarm group lets a network manager set thresholds for network parameters and configure agents to automatically deliver alerts to NMSs. RMON also supports capturing packets (with filters if desired) and sending the captured packets to an NMS for protocol analysis.

RMON delivers information in nine groups of parameters. The groups for Ethernet networks are shown in Table 8–1.

Table 8–1   RMON Groups

Group	Description
Statistics	Tracks packets, octets, packet-size distribution, broadcasts, collisions, dropped packets, fragments, CRC/alignment errors, jabbers, and undersized and oversized packets.
History	Stores multiple samples of values from the Statistics group for the comparison of the current behavior of a selected variable to its performance over the specified period.
Alarms	Enables setting thresholds and sampling intervals on any statistic to create an alarm condition. Threshold values can be an absolute value, a rising or falling value, or a delta value.
Hosts	Provides a table for each active node that includes a variety of node statistics, including packets and octets in and out, multicast and broadcast packets in and out, and error counts.
Host Top N	Extends the host table to offer a user-defined study of sorted host statistics. Host Top N is calculated locally by the agent, thus reducing network traffic and processing on the NMS.
Matrix	Displays the amount of traffic and number of errors occurring between pairs of nodes within a segment.
Filters	Lets the user define specific packet-match filters and have them serve as a stop or start mechanism for packet-capture activity.
Packet Capture	Packets that pass the filters are captured and stored for further analysis. An NMS can request the capture buffer and analyze the packets.
Events	Lets the user create entries in a monitor log or generate SNMP traps from the agent to the NMS. Events can be initiated by a crossed threshold on a counter or by a packet-match count.

For Token Ring networks, the nine groups are enhanced to include the ability to track beacon, purge, soft error, and other Media Access Control (MAC) frames. The Token Ring groups let a manager determine the ring state, which station is the active monitor, a beacon fault domain, and a list of stations in ring order. The Ring Station Configuration Control group lets the manager remove stations from a ring using the 802.5 remove-station MAC frame.

RMON provides network managers with information about the health and performance of the network segment on which the RMON agent resides. RMON provides a view of the health of the whole segment, rather than the device-specific information that many non-RMON SNMP agents provide. The benefits or RMON are obvious, but the scope of RMON is limited because it focuses on data-link and physical-layer parameters. The IETF is currently working on an RMON2 standard that moves beyond segment information to supply information on the health and performance of network applications and end-to-end communications. RMON2 is described in RFC 2021.

Estimating Network Traffic Caused by Network Management

Once you have determined which management protocols will be used, you can estimate the amount of traffic caused by network management. Probably the main management protocol will be SNMP, though other options exist, such as:

- The Common Management Information Protocol (CMIP)

- The LAN Network Manager (LNM) standard for Token Ring networks

- The Cisco Discovery Protocol (CDP)

- ICMP pings

- IP trace-route commands

After selecting management protocols, you should determine which network and device characteristics will be managed. The goal is to determine what data an NMS will request from managed devices. This data could consist of reachability information, response-time measurements, network-layer address information, and data from the RMON MIB or other MIBs. Once you have determined what characteristics will be gathered from managed devices, you should then determine how often the NMS requests the data (this is called the polling interval).

To calculate a rough estimate of traffic load, you should multiply the number of management characteristics by the number of managed devices and divide by the polling interval. For example, if a network has 200 managed devices and each device is monitored for 10 characteristics, the resulting number of requests is

$$200 \times 10 = 2{,}000$$

The resulting number of responses is also

$$200 \times 10 = 2,000$$

If the polling interval is every 5 seconds and we assume that each request and response is a single 64-byte packet, the amount of network traffic is:

(4,000 requests and responses) × 64 bytes × 8 bits/byte = 2,048,000 bits every five seconds or 409,600 bps

In this example, on a shared 10-Mbps Ethernet, network management data would use 4 percent of the available network bandwidth, which is significant, but probably acceptable. A good rule of thumb is that management traffic should use less than 5 percent of a network's capacity.

NOTES

To get a more precise estimate of traffic load caused by management data, you should use a protocol analyzer. Many SNMP implementations ask for more than one characteristic in a request packet, which uses bandwidth more efficiently than was described in the example.

CiscoWorks Network Management Software

For your network design customers that have numerous Cisco products, Cisco provides the CiscoWorks series of network management applications. CiscoWorks uses SNMP to monitor and control devices on an internetwork. CiscoWorks applications can be integrated into several popular network management systems:

- HP OpenView on Solaris and HP-UX

- Sun Solstice Site Manager, Domain Manager, and Enterprise Manager

- Tivoli TME/10 NetView on AIX

CiscoWorks applications extend the industry-standard network management systems to facilitate checking the status of Cisco devices, maintaining device configurations and inventories, and troubleshooting device problems. CiscoWorks includes tools to help an administrator handle fault, performance, configuration, security, and accounting management. The tools include products for IBM SNA management as well as router and switch management.

Cisco StrataSphere Network Management Software

Cisco's StrataSphere network management system is an SNMP-based package that is designed specifically for WANs. The StrataSphere system lets a network manager monitor network usage, plan capacity requirements, optimize traffic flow, model and prototype network designs, and track network statistics.

StrataSphere helps network managers justify the costs of high-speed WAN networks and also allocate costs to users of the networks. StrataSphere also helps with network administration and operations tasks, which can be complex in a WAN environment with a high number of circuits and variety of services, for example an ATM WAN network.

StrataSphere tools include the StrataView Plus software, which is a suite of SNMP-based network management applications available for HP OpenView and NetView for AIX. StrataView Plus provides fault, configuration, and performance management. The StrataSphere tools also include the Modeler tool which lets network engineers design, modify, and analyze ATM and Frame Relay network topologies, based on existing network configuration data. The Modeler includes "what if" analysis for optimizing designs and for testing designs for adequate redundancy.

SUMMARY

Your goal as a network designer is to help your customer develop some strategies and processes for implementing security and management. You should also help your customer select tools and products to implement the strategies and processes.

Security is a major concern for most customers because of the increase in Internet connectivity and Internet applications, and because more users are accessing the enterprise network from remote sites. Management is also becoming a major concern as customers recognize the strategic importance of their internetworks.

This chapter provided information to help you select the right processes and tools to meet a customer's goals for network security and manageability. The tasks involved with security and management design parallel the tasks involved with overall network design: analyzing requirements and goals, making tradeoffs, characterizing network-management and security traffic flow, and developing an appropriate topology.

Both security and management are often overlooked during the design of a network because they are considered operational issues rather than design issues. However, by considering security and network management up front, instead of tacking them on at the end of the design process or after the network is already operational, your design will be more scalable and robust.

SUMMARY FOR PART II

This chapter concludes Part II of *Top-Down Network Design*. Part II concentrated on the logical design phase of the top-down network design methodology. During the logical design phase, a network designer develops a network topology based on knowledge gained about traffic flow and load in the requirements-analysis phase of network design. The designer also devises network-layer addressing and naming models, and selects bridging, switching, and routing protocols. The designer also develops security and network management strategies.

Developing a logical design is an important early step in network design. The logical design provides a network designer with a chance to focus on design goals, without delving too deeply into the details of the physical components of the network. By concentrating first on the logical architecture of the network, a designer can more accurately select technologies, capacities, and devices that will support the customer's goals. The logical design phase glues together the requirements-analysis phase, where traffic flow and technical and business goals are analyzed, and the physical design phase, where cabling, data-link-layer technologies, and devices are added to the final network architecture.

PART III

Physical Network Design

Selecting Technologies and Devices for Campus Networks

Physical network design involves the selection of LAN and WAN technologies for campus and enterprise network designs. During this phase of the top-down network design process, choices are made regarding cabling, physical and data-link-layer protocols, and internetworking devices (such as hubs, switches, and routers). A logical design, which Part II covered, forms the foundation for a physical design. In addition, business goals, technical requirements, network traffic characteristics, and traffic flows, all of which were discussed in Part I, influence a physical design.

A network designer has many options for LAN and WAN implementations. No single technology or device is the right answer for all circumstances. The goal of Part III is to give you information about the scalability, performance, affordability, and manageability characteristics of typical options, to help you make the right selections for your particular customer.

This chapter covers technologies for campus network designs. A *campus network* is a set of LAN segments and building networks in an area that is a few miles in diameter. The next chapter covers technologies for an enterprise network that includes WAN and remote-access services.

An effective design process is to develop campus solutions first, followed by remote-access and WAN solutions. Once you have designed a customer's campus networks, you can more effectively select WAN and remote-access technologies based on the bandwidth and performance requirements of traffic that flows from one campus to another.

This chapter begins with a discussion of LAN cabling-plant design, including cabling options for building and campus networks. The chapter then provides information on the following LAN technologies:

- Half- and full-duplex Ethernet

- 10-Mbps, 100-Mbps, and 1,000-Mbps (Gigabit) Ethernet

- Cisco's Fast EtherChannel

- Token Ring

- Fiber Distributed Data Interface (FDDI)

- Asynchronous Transfer Mode (ATM)

Near the end of the chapter, the section "Selecting Internetworking Devices for a Campus Network Design" provides some selection criteria you can use when selecting hubs, bridges, switches, and routers for a campus design.

The chapter concludes with an example of a campus network design that was developed for the Wandering Valley Community College.

NOTES

Though the example is a design for a college campus, it should not be assumed that campus network design only refers to college campuses. Many commercial businesses, government organizations, and other establishments have campus networks.

LAN CABLING PLANT DESIGN

Because cabling is more of an implementation issue than a design issue, it is not covered in detail in this book. However, the importance of developing a good cabling infrastructure should not be discounted. While other components of a network design generally have a lifetime of a few years before the technology changes, the cabling infrastructure often must last for many years. It is important to design and implement the cabling infrastructure carefully, keeping in mind availability and scalability goals, and the expected lifetime of the design.

In many cases, your network design must adapt to existing cabling. Chapter 3, "Characterizing the Existing Internetwork," discussed the process for documenting the cabling already in use in building and campus networks, including the following:

- Campus and building cabling topologies

- The types and lengths of cables between buildings

- The location of telecommunications closets and cross-connect rooms within buildings

- The types and lengths of cables for vertical cabling between floors

- The types and lengths of cables for horizontal cabling within floors

- The types and lengths of cables for work-area cabling going from telecommunications closets to workstations

Cabling Topologies

Companies such as AT&T, IBM, Digital Equipment Corporation (DEC), Hewlett-Packard, and Northern Telecom have all published cabling specifications and guidelines for developing a cabling topology. In addition, the Electronics Industry Association and the Telecommunications Industry Association publish the EIA/TIA guidelines for unshielded twisted-pair (UTP) cabling and installation. Though the guidelines from the different organizations differ slightly, the main goal of all of them is to help a network engineer develop a structured cabling system that is manageable and scalable.

Without going into detail on cabling topologies, a generalization can be made that two types of cabling schemes are possible:

- A *centralized cabling scheme* terminates most or all of the cable runs in one area of the design environment. A star topology is an example of a centralized system.

- A *distributed cabling scheme* terminates cable runs throughout the design environment. Ring, bus, and tree topologies are examples of distributed systems.

Building-Cabling Topologies

Within a building, either a centralized or distributed architecture can be used, depending on the size of the building. For small buildings, a centralized scheme with all cables terminating in a communications room on one floor is possible, as shown on the left side of Figure 9–1. A centralized scheme offers good manageability but does not scale. For larger buildings, a distributed topology is more appropriate. Many LAN technologies make an assumption that workstations are no more than 100 meters from a telecommunications closet where hubs or switches reside. For this reason, in a tall building with large floors, a distributed topology is more appropriate, as shown on the right side of Figure 9–1.

Campus-Cabling Topologies

The cabling that connects buildings is exposed to more physical hazards than the cabling within buildings. A construction worker might dig a trench between buildings and inadvertently cut cables. Flooding, ice storms, earthquakes and other natural disasters can also cause problems. In addition, cables might cross properties outside the control of the organization, making it hard to troubleshoot and fix problems. For these reasons, cables and cabling topologies should be selected carefully.

A distributed scheme offers better availability than a centralized scheme. The top part of Figure 9–2 shows a centralized topology. The bottom part of Figure 9–2 shows a distributed topology. The centralized topology in Figure 9–2 would experience a loss of all inter-building communication if the cable bundle between Buildings A and B were cut. With the distributed topology, inter-building communication could resume if a cable cut between Buildings A and B occurred.

In some environments, because of right-of-way issues or environmental obstructions such as creeks or swamps, it might not be practical to have multiple cable conduits on the campus as shown in the topology in the bottom part of Figure 9–2. In this case, if a clear line-of-sight is available, you can recommend a wireless technology, for example, a laser or microwave link between Buildings A and D.

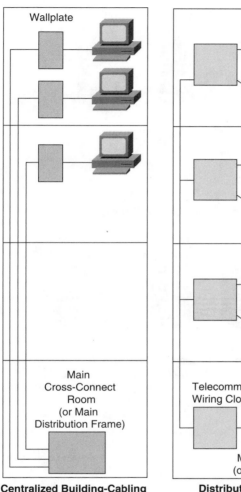

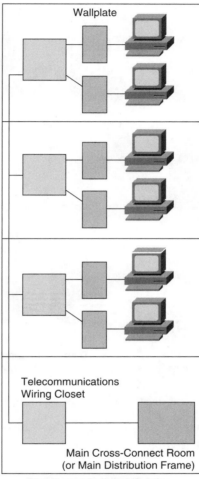

**Centralized Building-Cabling
Topology**

**Distributed Building-Cabling
Topology**

Figure 9–1
*Examples of
centralized
and distrib-
uted building-
cabling
topologies.*

One disadvantage of a distributed scheme is that management can be more difficult
than with a centralized scheme. Changes to a distributed cabling system are more
likely to require that a technician walk from building to building to implement the
changes. Availability versus manageability goals must be considered.

Figure 9–2
*Examples of
centralized
and distrib-
uted campus-
cabling
topologies.*

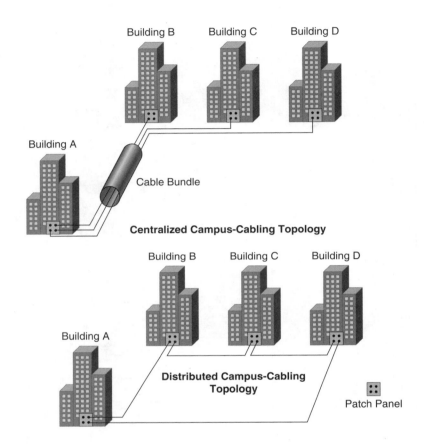

Centralized Campus-Cabling Topology

**Distributed Campus-Cabling
Topology**

Types of Cables

There are three major types of cables used in campus network implementations:

- Shielded copper, including shielded twisted pair (STP), coaxial (coax), and twin-axial (twinax) cables

- Unshielded copper (typically UTP) cables

- Fiber-optic cables

Coax cable was popular in the early days of LANs. Thick Ethernet (10Base5) used a double-shielded, 50-ohm coax cable that was about 0.4 inches in diameter, and thin Ethernet (10Base2 or "Cheapernet") used standard RG-58 cable that was about half that size. IBM terminals used 75-ohm coax cable, or, in some cases twinax cables. The cabling was usually installed in a bus topology and was hard to manage in large installations without multiport repeaters. With the introduction of standards for running LAN protocols on UTP cabling (such as 10BaseT Ethernet), coax cable became less popular. Coax and other types of shielded copper cabling are generally not recommended for new installations, except perhaps for short cable runs between devices in a telecommunications closet or computer room, or in cases where specific safety and shielding needs exist.

UTP is the typical wiring found in most buildings these days. It is generally the least expensive of the three types of cables. It also has the lowest transmission capabilities because it is subject to cross-talk, noise, and electromagnetic interference. Adherence to distance limitations minimizes the effects of these problems.

There are five categories of UTP cabling:

- Category 1 and 2 are not recommended for data transmissions because of their lack of support for high bandwidth requirements.

- Category 3 is tested to 16 MHz. Category 3 is often called *voice-grade cabling*, but it is widely used for data transmission also, particularly in 10BaseT Ethernet and 4-Mbps Token Ring networks.

- Category 4 is tested at 20 MHz, allowing it to run 16-Mbps Token Ring with a better safety margin than Category 3. Category 4 is not common, having been made obsolete by Category 5.

- Category 5 is tested at 100 MHz, allowing it to run high-speed protocols such as 100-Mbps Ethernet and FDDI.

Fiber-optic cables are quickly becoming a standard for new facilities. As the prices for cables and connection devices drop, it becomes practical to install fiber-optic cabling for vertical and horizontal wiring between telecommunications closets. Some companies also use fiber-optic cabling for work-area wiring, but the cost of network-interface cards (NICs) with fiber-optic support is still high, so that is not common yet. Fiber-optic cabling has been used between buildings for many years.

Fiber-optic cabling is not affected by cross-talk, noise, and electromagnetic interference, so it has the highest capacity of the three types of cables. With new technologies, such as Wave Division Multiplexing (WDM), a single strand of fiber-optic cabling can handle a capacity of 40 Gigabits/per second and beyond.

Fiber-optic cabling is either *single-mode* or *multi-mode*. Single-mode fiber has a smaller core diameter than multi-mode fiber. The small core ensures that only one ray of light is propagated. Without the distortion from other light rays, the signal travels a longer distance than with multi-mode fiber. Single-mode fiber requires a laser light source that is more expensive and harder to install than the LED light source used with multi-mode fiber. Single-mode interfaces for switches, routers, and workstations are more expensive than multi-mode interfaces.

LAN Technologies

This section covers data-link layer technologies that are available for LANs, including Ethernet, Token Ring, FDDI, and ATM. Ethernet is recommended for new campus networks because it provides superior scalability, manageability, and affordability. ATM also provides good scalability, but it is more complex and expensive than Ethernet.

Although work is being done on both 100-Mbps and Gigabit Token Ring, these technologies will mainly be used for upgrades to existing Token Ring networks rather than new networks. Work on 100-Mbps and Gigabit Ethernet began a few years before the Token Ring work, so there are many more product options for high-speed Ethernet compared to high-speed Token Ring.

There was talk a few years ago about a next-generation Gigabit FDDI, but the talk never materialized into standards or products. Although many FDDI installations still exist, especially in backbone networks, implementing 100-Mbps Ethernet on fiber-optic cabling is generally a more scalable and manageable solution than FDDI.

For a new network design that must merge with an existing design, which is the case for most network designs, there are some advantages to using the same LAN technologies that are already in use. For example, a customer might want the new network design to be based on Token Ring because network engineers, administrators, and technicians are already trained on existing Token Ring implementations. As another example, a customer might indicate that a new design must take advantage of existing FDDI concentrators in building-backbone networks to avoid spending money on new equipment.

Chapter 1, "Analyzing Business Goals and Constraints," discussed analyzing the following business constraints, all of which have an effect on the LAN technologies you should select:

- Biases (technology religion)

- Policies regarding approved technologies or vendors

- The customer's tolerance to risk

- Technical expertise of the staff and plans for staff education

- Budgeting and scheduling

Technical goals, as discussed in Chapter 2, "Analyzing Technical Goals and Constraints," also have a big impact on technology selections. The next few sections of this chapter demonstrate that LAN technologies vary in how well they can meet scalability, availability, manageability, adaptability, affordability, and other technical goals.

Chapter 2 recommended making a list of a customer's major technical goals. At this point in the design process, you should reference that list to make sure your technology selections are appropriate for your network design customer.

You should also take a look at Table 2–3, "Network Applications Technical Requirements," to determine if your customer has strict requirements regarding throughput, delay, and delay variation for any network applications. You should also consider the types of applications the customer plans to run on the network. Applications that allow users to share images, animated files, videos, and so on, are more bandwidth-hungry and delay-sensitive than text-based applications.

Table 4–4, "Network Applications Traffic Characteristics," can also help you select the right technologies for your customer. In that table you documented bandwidth and quality of service (QoS) requirements for applications. The next few sections will help you determine which solutions are appropriate for applications with demanding bandwidth and QoS requirements.

Ethernet

Ethernet is a physical and data-link-layer standard for the transmission of frames on a LAN. Since its invention in the 1970s by Xerox Corporation, Ethernet has gained widespread popularity and adapted to new demands for capacity, reliability, and low prices. The cost of an Ethernet port on a workstation or internetwork device is very low compared to other technologies. Many PC and workstation vendors build

Ethernet into the motherboard of the computer so that it is not necessary to purchase a separate NIC.

Ethernet is an appropriate technology choice for customers concerned with availability and manageability. An Ethernet LAN that is accurately provisioned to meet bandwidth requirements and outfitted with high-quality components, including NICs, cables, and internetworking devices, can meet even the most stringent demands for availability. Many troubleshooting tools, including cable testers, protocol analyzers, and hub-management applications, are available for isolating the occasional problems caused by cable breaks, electromagnetic interference, failed ports, or misbehaving NICs.

Ethernet and IEEE 802.3

DEC, Intel and Xerox published Version 2.0 of the Ethernet specification in 1982. Version 2.0, also known as the *DIX standard*, formed the basis for the work the Institute of Electrical and Electronic Engineers (IEEE) did on the 802.3 standard, which was finalized in 1983. Since then, 802.3 has evolved to support UTP and fiber-optic cabling, and faster transmission speeds.

Though there are some minor differences between the two technologies, the terms *Ethernet* and *802.3* are generally used synonymously. At the physical layer, 802.3 is the de facto standard. At the data link layer, both Ethernet Version 2.0 and 802.3 implementations are common.

NOTES

One important difference between Ethernet Version 2.0 and 802.3 is frame formats. 802.3 is usually used with an 802.2 Logical Link Control (LLC) header, except in early implementations of Novell NetWare. The 802.2 header includes a Destination Service Access Point (DSAP) and Source Service Access Point (SSAP) field to identify the receiving and sending processes. Ethernet Version 2.0 does not use 802.2 and instead includes an EtherType field to specify the sending/receiving process. These differences in frame format must be considered when configuring Ethernet devices. Figure 9–3 shows the frame formats.

Field Name	Preamble	Destination Address	Source Address	Ether Type	Information	Frame Check Sequence
Size in Bytes	8	6	6	2	46-1500	4

Ethernet Version 2.0 Frame Format

Field Name	Preamble	Destination Address	Source Address	Length	DSAP	SSAP	Control	Information	Frame Check Sequence
					LLC Header				
Size in Bytes	8	6	6	2	1	1	1	43-1497	4

IEEE 802.3 Frame Format

Figure 9–3
Ethernet Version 2.0 and IEEE 802.3 frame formats.

Ethernet Technology Choices

Ethernet is a scalable technology that has adapted to increasing capacity requirements. The following options for implementing Ethernet networks are available:

- Half- and full-duplex Ethernet

- 10-Mbps Ethernet

- 100-Mbps Ethernet

- 1000-Mbps (Gigabit) Ethernet

- Cisco's Fast EtherChannel

Each of these technologies is a possibility for the access, distribution, or core layers of a campus topology. Chapter 5, "Designing a Network Topology," talked about the access, distribution, and core layers of a hierarchical topology in more detail. Figure 5.7 showed a typical hierarchical topology for a campus network.

The choice of an Ethernet technology for the access layer depends on the location and size of user communities, bandwidth and QoS requirements for applications, broadcast and other protocol behavior, and traffic flow, as discussed in Chapter 4, "Characterizing Network Traffic." The choice of an Ethernet technology for the distribution and core layers depends on the network topology, the location of data stores, and traffic flow. The section called "Example of a Campus Network Design" at the end of this chapter provides an example of a network design that was accomplished by analyzing these factors.

Half-Duplex and Full-Duplex Ethernet

Ethernet was originally defined for a shared medium with stations using the *carrier sense multiple access/collision detection* (CSMA/CD) algorithm to regulate the sending of frames and the detection of collisions when two stations send at the same time.

With shared Ethernet, a station listens before it sends data. If the medium is already in use, the station defers its transmission until the medium is free. Shared Ethernet is *half-duplex*, meaning that a station is either transmitting or receiving traffic, but not both at once.

A point-to-point Ethernet link supports simultaneous transmitting and receiving, which is called *full-duplex Ethernet*. On a link between a switch port and a single station, for example, both the switch and the station can transmit at the same time. This is especially beneficial if the station is a server that processes requests from many users. The switch can transmit the next request at the same time the server is sending a response to a previous request. Full-duplex operation is also common in switch-to-switch links, allowing both switches to transmit to each other at the same time. The advantage of full-duplex Ethernet is that the transmission rate is theoretically double what it is on a half-duplex link.

NOTES

Full-duplex operation requires the cabling to dedicate one wire pair for transmitting and another for receiving. Full-duplex operation does not work on cables with only one path, for example, coax cable. Full-duplex also does not work with 100BaseT4 (100-Mbps Ethernet on Category-3 UTP). Unlike 10BaseT and 100BaseTX, with 100BaseT4, no separate dedicated transmit and receive pairs are present. 100BaseT4 uses three pairs for transmit and one pair for collision detection.

10-Mbps Ethernet

Although 100-Mbps Ethernet is beginning to replace 10-Mbps Ethernet, 10-Mbps Ethernet can still play a role in your network design, particularly at the access layer. For some customers 10-Mbps capacity is sufficient. For customers who have low bandwidth needs and a small budget, 10-Mbps Ethernet is an appropriate solution if the network does not need to scale to 100-Mbps in the near future.

NOTES

Many business applications do not benefit from an upgrade to 100-Mbps shared Ethernet. Inefficient applications that send many small frames generate more collisions on 100-Mbps Ethernet, actually decreasing throughput. Tests have shown a 9 percent decrease in throughput when a LAN with inefficient applications was migrated from shared 10-Mbps Ethernet to shared 100-Mbps Ethernet. For these applications, 100-Mbps should be reserved for the distribution or core layers. If 100-Mbps is desired at the access layer, possibly to support different applications, then full-duplex, switched 100-Mbps Ethernet should be deployed.

10-Mbps Ethernet components such as NICs, hubs, switches, and bridges are generally less expensive than 100-Mbps Ethernet components. (As more PCs are shipped with an auto-sensing NIC that supports either 10-or 100-Mbps, the price of NICs will become irrelevant, however.)

10-Mbps Ethernet can run on coax, UTP or fiber-optic cabling. Although coax cable is generally not selected for new networks, it might still be present in an existing network. Existing cable lengths must be considered when planning a new design that must interoperate with the existing network.

10-Mbps Ethernet supports both switched and shared networks. In a shared network, all devices compete for the same bandwidth and are in the same *bandwidth domain* (also known as the *Ethernet collision domain*). Physical-layer repeaters and hubs connect cables and users, but do not segment the collision domain. A switch or bridge, on the other hand, segments a collision domain into multiple domains. Each port on a switch defines one domain. The decision whether to use shared or switched architectures depends on bandwidth and performance requirements, and distance limitations.

One of the most significant design rules for Ethernet is that the round-trip propagation delay in one collision domain must not exceed the time it takes a sender to transmit 512 bits, which is 51.2 microseconds for 10-Mbps Ethernet. A single collision domain must be limited in size to make sure that a station sending a minimum-sized frame (64 bytes or 512 bits) can detect a collision reflecting back from the opposite side of the network while the station is still sending the frame. Otherwise, the station would be finished sending and not listening for a collision, thus losing the efficiency of Ethernet to detect a collision and quickly retransmit the frame.

To meet this rule, the farthest distance between two communicating systems must be limited. The number of repeaters (hubs) between the systems also must be limited, because repeaters add delay. The limitations for 10-Mbps Ethernet on coax and UTP cabling are shown in Table 9–1. The limitations for 10-Mbps Ethernet on fiber-optic cabling are shown in Table 9–2.

Table 9-1   Scalability Constraints for 10-Mbps Coax and UTP Ethernet

	10Base5	10Base2	10BaseT
Topology	Bus	Bus	Star
Type of cabling	Thick coax	Thin coax	UTP
Maximum cable length (in meters)	500	185	100 from hub to station
Maximum number of attachments per cable	100	30	2 (hub and station or hub and hub)
Maximum collision domain (in meters)	2,500	2,500	2,500
Maximum topology of a collision domain	Five segments, four repeaters, only three segments can have end systems	Five segments, four repeaters, only three segments can have end systems	Five segments, four repeaters, only three segments can have end systems

The original specification for running Ethernet on multi-mode fiber-optic cable was called the *Fiber-Optic Inter-Repeater Link (FOIRL) specification*. The newer 10BaseF specification is based on the FOIRL specification. It includes 10BaseFP, 10BaseFB, 10BaseFL, and a revised FOIRL standard. The new FOIRL differs from the old one in that it allows end-system connections in addition to repeaters and hubs. Table 9–2 shows scalability constraints for running 10-Mbps on multi-mode fiber-optic cabling.

Table 9–2 **Scalability Constraints for 10-Mbps Multi-Mode Fiber-Optic Ethernet**

	10BaseFP	10BaseFB	10BaseFL	Old FOIRL	New FOIRL
Topology	Star	Backbone or repeater system	Repeater-repeater link	Repeater-repeater link	Repeater-repeater link or star
Maximum cable length (in meters)	500	2,000	2,000	1,000	1,000
Allows end system connections?	Yes	No	No	No	Yes
Allows cascaded repeaters?	No	Yes	No	No	Yes
Maximum collision domain in meters	2,500	2,500	2,500	2,500	2,500

100-Mbps Ethernet

100-Mbps Ethernet, also known as *Fast Ethernet* and *100BaseT Ethernet*, is standardized in the IEEE 802.3u specification. It is very similar to 802.3 Ethernet, which is one of the reasons it is popular. For network engineers who have experience with 10-Mbps Ethernet, 100-Mbps Ethernet is easy to understand, install, configure, and troubleshoot. With some exceptions, 100-Mbps Ethernet is simply standard Ethernet, just ten times faster. In most cases, design parameters for 100-Mbps Ethernet are the same as 10-Mbps Ethernet, just multiplied or divided by 10.

100-Mbps Ethernet is defined for three physical implementations:

- 100BaseTX: Category-5 UTP cabling

- 100BaseT4: Category-3, -4, or -5 UTP cabling

- 100BaseFX: Multi-mode or single-mode fiber-optic cabling

100BaseTX is probably the most popular form of 100-Mbps Ethernet. 100BaseTX networks are easy to design and install because they use the same wire-pair and pin configurations as 10BaseT. Stations are connected to repeaters (hubs) or switches using Category-5 UTP cabling.

The IEEE designed 100BaseT4 to handle the large installed base of Category-3 cabling. 100BaseT4 uses four pairs (eight wires) of Category 3, 4, or 5 cable. 100BaseT4 sends a signal on three pairs of wire and uses the fourth pair for collision detection.

NOTES

100BaseT4 requires that four pairs (eight wires) be connected between a hub and a station. In some Category-3 installations, only two pairs (four wires) connect hubs and stations, because the cabling infrastructure was designed for 10BaseT, which only uses two pairs. This will make it difficult to upgrade to 100BaseT4 using the existing cabling.

As mentioned before, the round-trip propagation delay in one Ethernet collision domain must not exceed the time it takes a sender to transmit 512 bits, which is only 5.12 microseconds on 100-Mbps Ethernet. To make 100-Mbps Ethernet work, there are more severe distance limitations than those required for 10-Mbps Ethernet. The general rule is that a 100-Mbps Ethernet has a maximum diameter of 205 meters when UTP cabling is used, whereas 10-Mbps Ethernet has a maximum diameter of 2,500 meters. This may become a factor that determines where 100-Mbps and 10-Mbps Ethernet are used in a design.

Distance limitations for 100-Mbps Ethernet depend on the type of repeaters (hubs) that are used. In the IEEE 100BaseT specification, two types of repeaters are defined:

- *Class I repeaters* have a latency of 0.7 microseconds or less. Only one repeater hop is allowed.

- *Class II repeaters* have a latency of 0.46 microseconds or less. One or two repeater hops are allowed.

Table 9–3 shows the maximum size of a collision domain for 100-Mbps Ethernet depending on the type of repeater(s) in use and the type of cabling. Although not shown in the table, single-mode fiber is also possible. You should check with repeater and cabling manufacturers for exact distance limitations for single-mode fiber. Most vendors specify that when single-mode fiber is used in a switch-to-switch full-duplex connection, the maximum cable length is 10,000 meters or about six miles. The fact that such a long distance is allowed makes single-mode fiber attractive (though expensive) for large campus networks.

Table 9–3   Maximum Collision Domains for 100BaseT Ethernet

	Copper	Mixed Copper and Multi-mode Fiber	Multi-mode Fiber
DTE-DTE (or switch-switch)	100 meters	NA	412 meters (2,000 if full duplex)
One Class I repeater	200 meters	260 meters	272 meters
One Class II repeater	200 meters	308 meters	320 meters
Two Class II repeaters	205 meters	216 meters	228 meters

Figure 9–4 shows some typical ways that 100BaseT repeaters can be connected without breaking the distance rules.

Gigabit Ethernet

Gigabit Ethernet is defined in the IEEE 802.3z standard. It operates essentially like 100-Mbps Ethernet, except that it is 10 times faster. It uses CSMA/CD with support for one repeater per collision domain, and handles both half and full-duplex operations. It uses a standard 802.3 frame format and frame size. (Though some vendors are talking about implementing oversized *jumbo frames,* the IEEE 802.3z specification for Gigabit Ethernet does not change the frame size.)

Initially it is expected that Gigabit Ethernet will be implemented on fiber-optic cabling in building and campus backbone networks. Gigabit Ethernet can act as a *trunk network*, theoretically aggregating traffic from up to ten 100-Mbps Ethernet segments. Initial deployments will probably use full-duplex mode, connecting a

Figure 9–4
*Examples of
100BaseT
Ethernet
connections.*

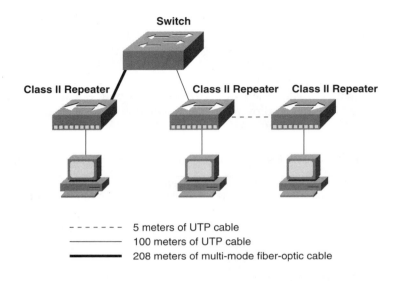

- - - - - - -   5 meters of UTP cable
——————   100 meters of UTP cable
▬▬▬▬▬▬▬   208 meters of multi-mode fiber-optic cable

switch to another switch or a switch to a router. Gigabit Ethernet will also be used on high-performance servers that require a large amount of bandwidth.

The 802.3z standard for Gigabit Ethernet specifies multi-mode and single-mode fiber-optic cabling, as well as shielded twinax copper cabling. Work is underway to standardize Gigabit Ethernet for copper UTP cabling. Table 9–4 shows the variations of Gigabit Ethernet:

Table 9–4   Gigabit Ethernet Specifications

	1000BaseSX	1000BaseLX	1000BaseCX	1000BaseT
Type of cabling	850-nanometer wavelength multi-mode fiber	1,300 nanometer wavelength multi-mode and single-mode fiber	Twinax	UTP
Distance limitations (in meters)	220–550, depending on the cable	550 for multi- mode and 5,000 for single-mode	25	100 between a hub and station; a total network diameter of 200 meters

1000BaseSX, also known as the *short-wavelength specification* (hence the S in the name), is appropriate for multi-mode horizontal cabling and backbone networks. For more information about exact cable lengths for 1000BaseSX, see the IEEE 802.3z specification or refer to the Web site of the Gigabit Ethernet Alliance at www.gigabit-ethernet.org.

1000BaseLX uses a longer wavelength (hence the L in the name), and supports both multi-mode and single-mode cabling. 1000BaseLX is appropriate for building and campus backbone networks.

1000BaseCX is appropriate for a telecommunications closet or computer room where the distance between devices is 25 meters or less. 1000BaseCX runs over 150-ohm balanced, shielded, twinax cable.

1000BaseT is intended for horizontal and work-area Category-5 UTP cabling. It is being defined by the 802.3ab task force, which is a subset of the 802.3z committee. 1000BaseT supports transmission over four pairs of Category-5 UTP cable, and covers a cabling distance of up to 100 meters, or a network diameter of 200 meters. Only one repeater is allowed.

Cisco's Fast EtherChannel

Cisco's Fast EtherChannel technology groups multiple 100-Mbps full-duplex links together to provide network designers a high-speed solution for campus backbone networks. Fast EtherChannel can be used between routers, switches, and servers on point-to-point links that require more bandwidth than a single 100-Mbps Ethernet can provide. Cisco provides Fast EtherChannel ports for many of its high-end switches and routers. Intel and other vendors make Fast EtherChannel NICs for servers.

Fast EtherChannel provides bandwidth aggregation in multiples of 200 Mbps. For example, network designers can group two full-duplex links into a 400-Mbps channel or group four links into a 800-Mbps channel. In the future, Fast EtherChannel will be able to group Gigabit Ethernet links also.

Fast EtherChannel distributes unicast, broadcast, and multicast traffic across the links in a channel, providing high-performance load-sharing and redundancy. In the event of a link failure, traffic is redirected to remaining links without user intervention.

NOTES

Fast EtherChannel selects a link within a channel by performing an XOR operation on the last two bits of the source and destination addresses in a frame. The XOR operation can result in one of four values that are mapped to the four possible links. (If only two links are used, then the XOR operation is done using only the last bit from each address). This method may not evenly balance traffic if a majority of traffic is between two hosts, such as two routers or two servers. However, for typical network traffic with a mix of senders and receivers, Fast EtherChannel provides high-performance load-balancing. To learn more about Fast EtherChannel, read the articles on the subject at Cisco's Web site.

Token Ring

Token Ring is a physical and data-link layer technology for connecting devices in a LAN in a logical ring that is physically cabled as a star. The IEEE specifies Token Ring in the IEEE 802.5 standards.

For new installations, Ethernet is recommended instead of Token Ring because Ethernet is less expensive, more scalable, and easier to manage. Despite a rich Token Ring Media Access Control (MAC) layer that monitors and reports ring errors, field experience shows that Token Ring is more susceptible to problems than Ethernet. It is more sensitive to delay, electromagnetic interference, noise, and cross-talk. Token Ring bridging and switching technologies are more complex than Ethernet solutions, and are more susceptible to problems.

Though Token Ring is probably not a good choice for a new network design, many options are available for updating existing Token Ring network designs. The IEEE and various vendors now support shared and switched Token Ring, half and full-duplex operations, and STP, UTP, and fiber-optic cabling. Speeds for Token Ring include 4-Mbps and 16-Mbps. The High-Speed Token Ring Alliance is working with the IEEE on a 100-Mbps Token Ring specification that will scale to 1 Gbps in the future. For more information on high-speed Token Ring, see the Alliance's Web site at www.hstra.com.

A Token Ring bandwidth domain can be segmented by using bridges or switches. The bridges and switches can use source-route bridging (SRB) or source-route switching (SRS) technologies, as discussed in Chapter 7, "Selecting Bridging, Switching, and Routing Protocols."

In a shared environment, Token Ring devices connect to physical-layer devices called *multistation access units (MAUs)* or *controlled access units (CAUs)*. According to the IEEE 802.5 specification, the maximum number of stations in a bandwidth domain should be limited to 250 to avoid too much delay as each station passes the token and frames to its downstream neighbor.

The IEEE does not specify maximum cable lengths for Token Ring. Vendors have planning guides that can be used to select proper cable lengths depending on the number of cables, the type of cables, the number of stations, and the number of MAUs or CAUs. The main goal of the planning guides is to make sure that delay characteristics of the network do not exceed IEEE specifications.

NOTES

The IEEE 802.5 MAC layer specifies timers that stations use to monitor the state of the ring. When a station sends a frame, it must see the frame return within the time specified by the return-to-repeat timer (TRR), which is 4 ms. Also, the station acting as the active monitor must see a token or frame every 10 ms, as specified by the valid transmission timer (TVX). Excessively long cables or too many MAUs or stations can mean that the timers expire, resulting in serious performance problems.

Fiber Distributed Data Interface

FDDI is an American National Standards Institute (ANSI) and International Organization for Standardization (ISO) standard for 100-Mbps transmission of data on fiber-optic cabling in a LAN or metropolitan area network (MAN). FDDI can also run on copper cables, as specified in the Copper-Distributed Data Interface (CDDI) specification.

FDDI uses a timed token-rotation protocol for its media access control that is some-what similar to Token Ring's protocol. Although FDDI was originally designed for a shared medium, switched FDDI is also supported.

Because FDDI is more expensive, more complex, and harder to install and manage than Ethernet, 100-Mbps switched Ethernet is generally recommended instead of FDDI for new installations, unless FDDI's greater distance limit is needed. But for many years FDDI was the best option for backbone networks and other high-bandwidth applications, because of its high capacity and support for long distances. Many FDDI networks still exist and some of them are expanding, so it is important to understand scalability constraints as shown in Table 9–5.

Table 9–5   Scalability Constraints for FDDI

	Multi-mode Fiber	Single-Mode Fiber	UTP
Topology	Dual ring, tree of concentrators, and other possibilities	Dual ring, tree of concentrators, and other possibilities	Star
Maximum cable length	2 km between stations	40 km between stations	100 meters from hub to station
Maximum number of attachments per segment	1,000 (500 dual-attached stations)	1,000 (500 dual-attached stations)	2 (hub and station or hub and hub)
Maximum network size	200 km	200 km	200 km

NOTES

The maximum length of a network is 200 km. Generally, a cable has two fibers with light traveling in opposite directions. If a two-fiber cable is used, the length of the cable interconnecting all stations should be at most 100 km.

Also, FDDI does not actually specify a maximum distance between stations. It specifies that the decibel (dB) power loss for the light signal between two stations cannot exceed -11 dB, which works out to the approximate distances shown in Table 9–5.

With FDDI, scalability constraints are necessary to make sure the timed token-rotation protocol works correctly. Each FDDI station maintains a *token-rotation timer (TRT)* that keeps track of the amount of time between arrivals of the token at the station. The time between arrivals is compared with an *operational token-rotation timer (OTRT)* that is established upon ring initialization. If the token arrives early or on time at a station, the TRT is reinitialized to zero. If the token arrives late, the TRT is not reinitialized, and the time expected before the next token arrival is shorter. If the token arrives late again, error-recovery procedures are started.

During ring initialization, stations negotiate the right to define the OTRT. The ring is initialized every time a station joins or leaves the ring. The station with the shortest *target token-rotation timer (TTRT)* wins the negotiation process and sets the OTRT to the station's TTRT. A station's TTRT is configurable, and defaults to anywhere from 4 to 165 ms, depending on a vendor's implementation. Stations with low TTRTs tend to be routers or servers that cannot afford to wait a long time for the token.

It might seem wise to make the OTRT as short as possible so stations see the token quickly. The problem with using a short OTRT is that it affects the *token-holding timer (THT)*, which specifies how long a station can hold the token to send data. A short OTRT results in short data frames. Selecting the right setting for the OTRT depends on which applications run on the FDDI network, and whether a short access-delay time is more important than the efficiency and low overhead associated with large frame sizes.

Campus ATM Networks

ATM can be used in WAN and campus networks. This chapter discusses ATM campus networks; the next chapter discusses ATM WAN networks. In a campus network, a designer can select ATM as a backbone technology for connecting LANs. The designer also has the option of recommending that workstations be equipped with ATM NICs and protocol stacks.

A few years ago some networking experts thought ATM would replace many LAN installations because of its scalability and support for QoS requirements. As Ethernet has been shown to be scalable also, and work has been done to support QoS on IP LAN/WAN networks, ATM in campus networks has lost favor with some experts. There is no "right" answer, however. ATM is the correct choice for some customers and not for others. Many organizations have implemented campus ATM networks and been satisfied with the results. Other organizations have steered away from ATM because of its complexity and the relatively high cost of ATM components.

ATM is a good choice for video conferencing, medical imaging, telephony, distance learning, and other applications that mix data, video, and voice, and require high bandwidth, low delay, and little or no delay jitter.

ATM supports end-to-end QoS guarantees (as long as the whole network is based on ATM and the workstations use an ATM protocol stack, rather than an IP or other protocol stack). With ATM, an end system can set up a virtual circuit with another ATM device on the other side of the ATM network and specify such QoS parameters as:

- Peak cell rate (PCR)

- Sustainable cell rate (SCR)

- Maximum burst size (MBS)

- Cell loss ratio (CLR)

- Cell transfer delay (CTD)

LAN/WAN networks generally cannot support end-to-end QoS functionality, though progress is being made on this for IP networks. Protocols such as the Resource Reservation Protocol (RSVP) and other work that the IETF Integrated Services Working Group is doing will result in IP networks that offer end-to-end QoS functionality. Chapter 4, "Characterizing Network Traffic," discussed the QoS functionality being developed by the Integrated Services Working Group.

At this time, ATM can support more bandwidth than Ethernet, which makes it a good selection for backbone networks and high-bandwidth applications. ATM supports OC-192 (10 Gbps) and can scale even beyond that speed as new technologies such as WDM become common.

In the Ethernet environment, Gigabit Ethernet has only recently been standardized. Faster speeds will no doubt be supported in the future, but they have not been standardized yet.

One disadvantage of ATM is that the overhead for transmitting ATM data is much higher than the overhead for transmitting traditional LAN data. The 5-byte header required in each 53-byte ATM cell equals 9.4 percent overhead. When segmentation and reassembly and ATM Adaptation Layer (AAL) functionality are added, the overhead can grow to 13 bytes or 24.5 percent.

One other factor to consider before selecting ATM is that security can be hard to implement. An ATM switch that only understands cells, and not packets, can not look into packets to check addresses and port numbers to implement packet filters. *Packet filters* are a typical method of protecting a network from illegal usage and access, as discussed in Chapter 8. A router or firewall that understands packets is necessary when implementing security with packet filters.

Because it is unlikely that a customer will upgrade an entire campus network to ATM, mixed ATM/LAN networks are often required when ATM is introduced into a campus design. Solutions for integrating ATM with existing protocols include LAN emulation (LANE) and Multiprotocol over ATM (MPOA). These technologies are described in the next few sections.

LAN Emulation

Although ATM can be used in LAN environments, it is quite different than most LAN protocols. ATM is a non-broadcast multiple-access (NBMA), connection-oriented, circuit-switching technology. Most LAN protocols are broadcast-multiple-access, connectionless, packet-switching technologies.

To make it possible for end systems that are running IP, Novell NetWare, AppleTalk, and other upper-layer protocols to function as if they were on a typical LAN, when in fact they are on an ATM network, the ATM Forum developed LAN Emulation (LANE). LANE is a standard for emulating LAN protocols such as Ethernet and Token Ring on an ATM network. LANE provides support for typical LAN functions, such as sending broadcast and multicast frames.

LANE can be introduced into a network design in a backbone network that connects Ethernet or Token Ring networks. This approach requires no changes to workstation configurations and minimizes the impact on end users. Alternatively, LANE can be used on workstations that have been upgraded with an ATM NIC. LANE provides an intermediate step when the ultimate plan is to migrate to native ATM applications or to a MPOA solution.

The ATM Forum published LANE version 1.0 in 1995. The ATM Forum is working on LANE version 2.0. The first part of LANE v.2, the LANE User-to-Network Interface (LUNI), was published in July 1997. The other part of LANE v.2, the LANE Network-to-Network Interface (LNNI), will be published in the future.

LUNI offers support for QoS, which LANE v.1 did not. In particular, LUNI offers support for the available bit rate (ABR) class of service. LUNI also offers better support for sending multicast frames. It provides protocol mechanisms to determine which members of an emulated LAN should receive specific multicast frames.

In a LANE environment, an end system is a *LANE client (LEC)*. LEC software handles data transmission and address resolution for an end system. A LEC is connected to a *LANE server (LES)* that provides an address resolution and registration facility.

A LEC registers its MAC addresses with the LES and indicates which multicast frames it wishes to receive. A LEC also queries its LES when it needs to resolve a MAC address to an ATM address. The LES responds directly to the LEC or forwards the query to other clients so they can respond.

A *LANE configuration server (LECS)* assigns individual LECs to particular emulated LANs. Based upon a configuration database and information provided by LECs and other devices, a LECS assigns a client to a particular emulated LAN service by giving that client the appropriate LES ATM address.

An emulated LAN must also include a *Broadcast and Unknown Server (BUS)* that sends traffic with an unknown destination address or multicast or broadcast destination address to clients within a particular emulated LAN. When an end system sends a broadcast, it sends it to the BUS first, and the BUS then sends the broadcast to the rest of the emulated LAN. A LEC learns the address of the BUS from a LES.

NOTES

Previous chapters have mentioned that broadcast traffic should be less than 20 percent of the traffic on a network. In the case of an emulated LAN, the percentage should probably be less than 10 percent to avoid overwhelming the BUS server. An exact percentage depends on the rate of broadcast traffic and which device is acting as the BUS. When purchasing a switch or router that will act as a BUS, ask the vendor to specify the packets per second (PPS) rate for forwarding broadcast and multicast packets.

Chapter 5 talked about the importance of deploying redundant LANE servers. LANE version 1.0 does not support redundant servers, but the LNNI part of LANE version

2.0 will support redundancy. Another option is to use the Cisco Simple Server Redundancy Protocol (SSRP) which provides support for redundant LANE servers.

Multiprotocol over ATM

MPOA is an ATM Forum standard that provides a framework for synthesizing bridging, switching, and routing with ATM in an environment of diverse protocols, network technologies, and IEEE 802.1 Virtual LANs (VLANs). MPOA standardizes the forwarding of Layer-3 packets between subnets in an ATM LANE environment.

In an IP, IPX, or AppleTalk network, subnets are often built using LAN technologies such as Ethernet, Token Ring, and VLANs. Routers allow communication between subnets. The LANE specification allows a subnet to be bridged across an ATM/LAN boundary, but requires that inter-subnet traffic be forwarded through routers. The goal of MPOA is to enhance LANE to allow the efficient and direct transfer of inter-subnet unicast data in a LANE environment.

MPOA makes use of the IETF Internetworking Over NBMA Networks (ION) Working Group's Next Hop Resolution Protocol (NHRP). NHRP enables the establishment of ATM virtual circuits across subnet boundaries.

Figure 9–5 shows an example of a network that could benefit from NHRP. In this example, the Portland site has two subnets connected to an ATM switch. Without NHRP, inter-subnet traffic must cross the ATM WAN link between Portland and Seattle because inter-subnet traffic must go through a router. With NHRP, the hosts on Subnet A and Subnet B can communicate directly through the ATM switch without going through the router.

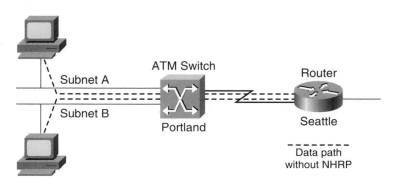

Figure 9–5
An ATM installation that could benefit from the Next Hop Resolution Protocol (NHRP).

SELECTING INTERNETWORKING DEVICES FOR A CAMPUS NETWORK DESIGN

At this point in the network design process, you have developed a network topology and should have an idea of which segments will be shared, switched, or routed. As covered in Chapter 5, "Designing a Network Topology," a *flat topology* is made up of hubs, bridges, and switches and is appropriate for small networks. A *hierarchical topology* is made up of bridges, switches, and routers and is more scalable and often more manageable than a flat topology.

Table 9–6 provides a review of the major differences between hubs (repeaters), bridges, switches, and routers.

Table 9–6   Comparing Hubs, Bridges, Switches, and Routers

	OSI Layers Implemented	How Bandwidth Domains Are Segmented	How Broadcast Domains Are Segmented	Typical Deployment	Typical Additional Features
Hub	1	All ports are in the same bandwidth domain	All ports are in the same broadcast domain	Connects individual devices in small LANs	Auto-partitioning to isolate misbehaving nodes
Bridge	1–2	Each port delineates a bandwidth domain	All ports are in the same broadcast domain	Connects networks	User-configured packet filtering
Data-Link Switch	1–2	Each port delineates a bandwidth domain	All ports are in the same broadcast domain	Connects individual devices or networks	Filtering, ATM capabilities, cut-through processing, multimedia (multicast) features
Router	1–3	Each port delineates a bandwidth domain	Each port delineates a broadcast domain	Connects networks	Filtering, firewalling, high-speed WAN links, compression, advanced queuing and forwarding processes, multimedia (multicast) features

Once you have designed a network topology and made some decisions regarding the placement and scope of shared, switched, and routed network segments, you should then recommend actual hubs, switches, bridges, and routers from various vendors. This section covers selection criteria you can use when making decisions.

Criteria for selecting internetworking devices in general include the following:

- The number of ports

- Processing speed

- Latency

- LAN technologies supported (10-, 100-, 1000-Mbps Ethernet; Token Ring; FDDI; ATM)

- Auto-sensing of speed (for example, 10 or 100 Mbps)

- Media (cabling) supported

- Ease of configuration

- Manageability (for example, support for SNMP and RMON)

- Cost

- Mean time between failure (MTBF) and mean time to repair (MTTR)

- Support for hot-swappable components

- Support for redundant power supplies

- Availability and quality of technical support

- Availability and quality of documentation

- Availability and quality of training (for complex switches and routers)

- Reputation and viability of the vendor

- Availability of independent test results that confirm the performance of the device

For bridges, the following criteria can be added:

- Bridging technologies supported (transparent bridging, spanning-tree algorithm, source-route bridging, remote bridging, and so on)

- WAN technologies supported

- The number of MAC addresses that a learning bridge can learn

- Filtering supported

For switches, the following criteria can be added:

- Throughput in packets per second (or cells per second for ATM)

- Support for cut-through switching

- Support for adaptive cut-through switching

- Auto-detection of half versus full-duplex operation

- VLAN technologies supported, such as the Virtual Trunking Protocol (VTP) or Inter-Switch Link (ISL) protocol

- Support for multimedia applications (for example, the ability to participate in the Internet Group Management Protocol [IGMP] to control the spread of multicast packets)

- The amount of memory available for switching tables, routing tables (if the switch has a routing module), and memory used by protocol routines

- Availability of a routing module

For routers (and switches with a routing module), the following criteria can be added:

- Network-layer protocols supported

- Routing protocols supported

- Support for multimedia applications (for example, support for RSVP, IP multicast, controlled-load, and guaranteed services)

- The ability to act as an ATM BUS, LECS, or LES and the performance of these functions

- Support for advanced queuing, switching, and other optimization features

- Support for compression (and compression performance if it is supported)

- Support for encryption (and encryption performance if it is supported)

- Support for packet filters and other advanced firewall features

AN EXAMPLE OF A CAMPUS NETWORK DESIGN

The goal of this section is to present a campus network design that was developed using the design methodology in this book. The section describes an actual network design that was developed for the Wandering Valley Community College. (The name of the college has been changed.) The example is based on a real network design. Some of the facts have been changed or simplified to preserve the privacy of the college, to protect the security of the college's network, and to make it possible to present a simple and easy-to-understand example.

Background Information for the Campus Network Design Project

Wandering Valley Community College (WVCC) is a small college in the western United States that is attended by about 400 full- and part-time students. The students do not live on campus. Approximately 30 professors teach courses in the fields of arts and humanities, business, social sciences, mathematics, computer science, the physical sciences, and health sciences. Many of the professors also have other jobs in the business community, and only about half of them have an office on campus. Approximately 15 administration personnel handle admissions, student records, and other operational functions. Three part-time network administrators manage the network.

The college wishes to attract and retain more students, many of whom leave the state to attend more prestigious colleges. The president of WVCC formed a Community Advisory Group whose mission was to determine why prospective students do not select WVCC. The group consisted of students, faculty, and business and civic leaders in the area. The group determined that many prospective students do not select WVCC because they perceive the computer facilities at WVCC to be inadequate.

Based on the advice of the Community Advisory Group, the president started the "Millennium Project" with the goal of upgrading the computer and networking facilities. The three network administrators and the Director of Operations for WVCC formed the Millenium Project Task Force.

The state government awarded the Millennium Project a $350,000 one-time grant to upgrade WVCC's computer labs and campus network. Although it is possible that more grants can be received in the future, this grant has to be spent within the school year. One challenge with the network design is that the school's budget does not call for more money to be spent on network administration and management, so the new design has to be manageable and simple.

Business and Technical Goals

The Community Advisory Group identified the following business goals for the Millennium Project:

- Increase the enrollment from 400 to 500 students by the year 2000

- Reduce the attrition rate from 30 to 15 percent by the year 2000

- Attract students who leave the state to attend colleges with more technological advantages

- Provide more and bigger computer labs on campus

- Allow students to attach their notebook computers to the campus network to reach campus and Internet services

- Maintain (or reduce if possible) the level of funding spent on network operations

The Millenium Project Task Force added the following technical goals:

- Centralize all services and servers to make the network easier to manage and more cost-effective. (Distributed servers will be tolerated but not managed, and traffic to and from these servers will not be accounted for when planning capacity.)

- Centralize the Internet connection and disallow distributed departmental Internet connections.

- Increase the bandwidth of the Internet connection to support new applications and the expanded use of current applications.

- Standardize on TCP/IP protocols for the campus network. Macintoshes will be tolerated but must use TCP/IP protocols or the AppleTalk Filing Protocol (AFP) running on top of TCP.

- Provide extra capacity at switches so users can attach their notebook PCs to the network.

- Install DHCP software on the Windows NT servers to support notebook PCs.

- Provide a network that offers a response time of approximately 1/10th of a second or less for interactive applications.

- Provide a campus network that is available approximately 99.90 percent of the time and offers a MTBF of 3,000 hours (about four months) and a MTTR of three hours (with a low standard deviation from these average numbers). Internet failures out of the control of the college will not count as failures.

- Provide security to protect the Internet connection and internal network from intruders.

- Provide a network that can scale to support future expanded usage of multimedia applications.

- Provide a network that uses state-of-the art technologies.

The network administrators on the Millenium Project Task Force have been criticized in the past by the Math/Science students and professors, and are looking forward to proving that they can develop a better network than the existing network. Getting support for the Millennium Project from the Math/Science users was not easy, and the administrators now need to deliver a network that performs well and has little downtime. The objective is to make sure the Math/Science students and professors do not revert to developing their own solutions.

Network Applications

The WVCC network is currently used for the following purposes:

- Writing papers and doing other homework, including printing the homework and saving the work on file servers

- Sending and receiving e-mail

- Surfing the Web using Netscape or Microsoft's Internet Explorer applications to access information, participate in chat rooms, play games, and use other typical Web services

- Accessing the library card-catalog

Students and professors in the School of Math and Sciences also use the following applications:

- **Weather modeling**. Meteorology students and professors are participating in a project to model weather patterns in conjunction with other colleges and universities in the state.

- **Telescope monitoring**. Astronomy students and professors have set up a PC to continually download graphical images from a telescope located at the state university.

Two new applications are planned:

- **Graphics upload**. The Art Department wishes to upload large graphics files to an off-campus print shop that can print large-scale images on a high-speed laser printer. The print shop prints artwork that is file-transferred to the shop via the Internet.

- **Distance learning**. The Computer Science department wishes to participate in a pilot distance-learning project with the state university. The state university will let WVCC students sign up to receive streaming video of a computer-science lecture course that is offered at the state university. The students can also participate in a real-time "chat room" while attending the class.

In addition to the applications used by the students and professors, the college administration personnel use the College Management System, which is a Novell NetWare client/server application that keeps track of class registrations and student records.

The Current Network at WVCC

Because so many students attend WVCC part-time, and because much of the faculty has other jobs, the assumption in the past has been that many of the students and professors use computing resources at home or at work and do not depend on the WVCC network. Although the Community Advisory Group indicated that this assumption is wrong, the current network reflects the assumption and consists of a few scattered computer labs and only one major lab in the Computing Center in the basement of the Library. The current campus network is shown in Figure 9–6.

All the LANs at WVCC use 10-Mbps Ethernet. Every building is equipped with Category-5 cabling and wallplates in the various offices, classrooms, and labs, though the cabling and wall-plates are not used yet in some of the buildings. To support users in the Administration Building, multi-mode fiber-optic cabling was pulled in the conduit between the Library and Sports Complex, and in the conduit between the Sports Complex and the Administration Building. (There is no direct conduit between the Library and the Administration Building.)

Users in the Library and in the Administration Building have Internet access, which is provided via a 56-Kbps Frame Relay link provided by the State Community College Network System.

The School of Math and Sciences grew impatient waiting for their request for Internet access to be granted by the network administrators, and contracted with a private Internet Service Provider (ISP) and the local telephone company to install their own 56-Kbps Frame-Relay link to the Internet, for which the network administration department pays.

Most of the computing power at WVCC is located in the Computing Center in the Library, which is shown in Figure 9–7. The college provides 10 Macintoshes and 25 PCs in the Computing Center for student use. A LAN switch in the Computing Center connects hubs, servers, printers, and the router that connects to the Internet. The router uses packet-filtering to act as a firewall. The router has a default route to the Internet and does not run a routing protocol.

Figure 9–6
The Wander-
ing Valley
Community
College's cur-
rent campus
network.

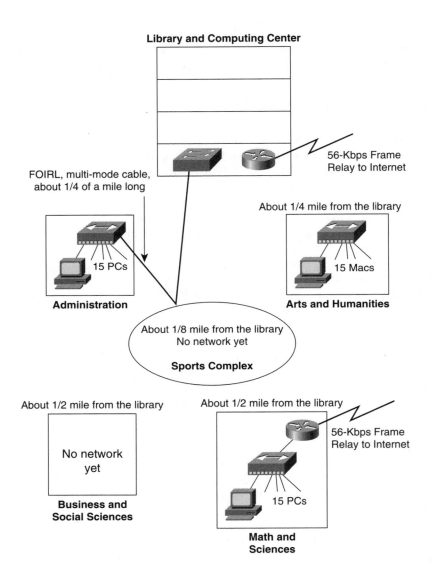

Figure 9–6
The Wandering Valley Community College's current campus network.

Each floor of the Library has a hub that connects five PCs that are used for public Internet access and checking the Library's card catalog.

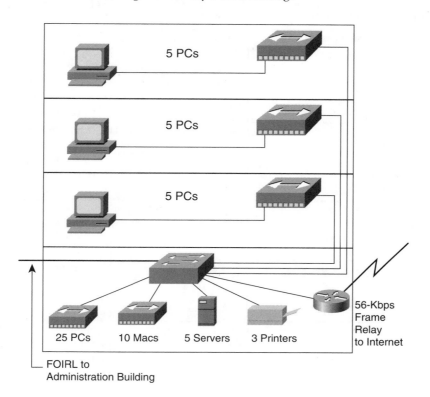

Figure 9–7
*The Wander-
ing Valley
Community
College's
Library and
Computing
Center build-
ing network.*

User Communities

Table 9–7 shows the user communities at WVCC. The expected growth of the communities is also included. Growth is expected for two reasons:

- New PCs and Macintoshes will be purchased

- Students will be allowed to plug their own notebook computers into the network

Table 9–7   WVCC User Communities

User Community Name	Size of Community (Number of Users)	Location(s) of Community	Application(s) Used by Community
PC users in Computing Center	25, will grow to 30	Basement of Library	Homework, e-mail, Web surfing, library card-catalog
Mac users in the Computing Center	10, will grow to 15	Basement of Library	Homework, e-mail, Web surfing, library card-catalog
Library patrons	15	Floors 1–3 of Library	E-mail, Web surfing, library card-catalog
Business/Social Sciences PC users	16 planned	Business and Social Sciences Building	Homework, e-mail, Web surfing, library card-catalog
Arts/Humanities Mac users	15, will grow to 24	Arts and Humanities Building	Homework, e-mail, Web surfing, library card-catalog, graphics upload
Arts/Humanities PC users	24 planned	Arts and Humanities Building	Homework, e-mail, Web surfing, library card-catalog, graphics upload
Math/Science PC users	15, will grow to 24	Math and Sciences Building	Homework, e-mail, Web surfing, library card-catalog, weather modeling, telescope monitoring, distance learning pilot
Administration PC users	15, will grow to 24	Administration Building	E-mail, Web surfing, library card-catalog, College Management System
Outside users	Unknown	Internet	Surfing the WVCC Web site

Data Stores (Servers)

Table 9–8 shows the data stores (servers) that have been identified at WVCC.

Table 9–8 WVCC Data Stores

Data Store	Location	Application(s)	Used by User Community (or Communities)
Library Card-Catalog Windows NT server	Computing Center	Library card-catalog	All
AppleShare IP file/print server	Computing Center	Homework	Mac users in the Computing Center, and in the future Mac users in Arts/Humanities
Windows NT file/print server	Computing Center	Homework	PC users in the Computing Center and in the future PCs in other buildings
Windows NT Web/ E-mail server	Computing Center	E-mail, Web surfing, (hosts the WVCC Web site)	PC users in the Computing Center and Administration, in the future all users (also includes outside users accessing WVCC Web site)
College Management System Novell server	Computing Center	College Management System	Administration
Upstream e-mail server	State Community College Network System	E-mail	Campus e-mail server sends and receives e-mail to this server

Traffic Characteristics of Network Applications

An analysis of the traffic characteristics of the applications was conducted. The analysis methods included capturing typical application sessions with a protocol analyzer, interviewing users about their current and planned uses of applications, and estimating the size of network objects transferred on the network using Table 4–5, "Approximate Size of Objects That Applications Transfer Across Networks." Table 4–6, "Traffic Overhead for Various Protocols," was also used to estimate extra bandwidth required by protocol headers.

It was determined that the homework, e-mail, Web surfing, library card-catalog, and College Management System applications have nominal bandwidth requirements and are not delay-sensitive. Although the Macintosh users plan to use the AppleTalk Filing Protocol (AFP) running on top of TCP/IP, it was determined by capturing network traffic with an analyzer that fears about excessive bandwidth usage caused by AFP were unfounded.

It was discovered that some of the students use e-mail attachments to submit homework assignments, and it was assumed that this will become more prevalent as more students and professors have network access. However, in most cases, the attachments are small, so e-mail was still considered a low-bandwidth application. Currently about 80 percent of the e-mail traffic is to and from Internet mail users, rather than being intra-campus mail. The percentage is expected to drop to around 60 percent once more students and professors receive WVCC e-mail accounts.

In the case of Web surfing, it was determined that most accesses are to Internet Web sites. Currently less than 2 percent of the HTTP traffic is between internal nodes and the college's local Web server. It was also determined that outsiders do not access the college Web site very frequently. A separate project is planned to update the college Web site to make it more appealing. It was assumed that in the future 10 percent of campus HTTP traffic will be local, and approximately 60-Kbps bandwidth will be required on the WAN link for outsiders accessing the WVCC Web site.

The Library card catalog system is based on an old terminal/host application, and though it has been updated to use Web technology and HTTP, it still behaves essentially like a terminal/host application and has very low-bandwidth requirements.

Users type in a few characters, such as **ti,** to specify a search by book title, and the server displays a list of book titles.

The College Management System has been upgraded to NetWare 4.1 and uses bandwidth efficiently because of the burst-mode protocol supported in Version 4.1. Because there is only one server, the amount of traffic caused by Novell's Service Advertising Protocol (SAP), which is an issue in some networks, was not an issue for this network design.

Network traffic caused by session initialization, as documented in Appendix A, "Characterizing Network Traffic When Workstations Boot," was taken into account when considering campus bandwidth requirements. Network traffic for the following "system" functions was also factored into the design:

- Host naming

- Dynamic addressing (DHCP)

- Network management

- Bridge Protocol Data Unit (BPDU) packets for maintaining the spanning tree on switches

Traffic Characteristics of New and Expanding Applications

Because the requirements for the applications mentioned above were minimal, analysis focused on new and expanding applications. Bandwidth requirements, QoS requirements, and broadcast and other protocol behavior were examined for the following applications:

- Weather-modeling

- Telescope-monitoring

- Graphics-upload

- Distance-learning

The users of the weather-modeling and telescope-monitoring applications wish to expand their usage of these applications, but are currently hindered by the amount of bandwidth available to the Internet. By using a protocol analyzer to characterize current bandwidth usage, and by talking to users about future plans, estimates were made about new requirements, and are included in Table 9–9, "Network Applications Traffic Characteristics and Traffic Flows."

For the graphics-upload application, an assumption (based on user interviews) was made that no more than one file per hour will be uploaded to the print shop. Although the graphics files are often huge (as big as 50 Mbytes), the users do not expect the file transfer to complete in less than approximately 5 to 10 minutes. The users plan to start the transfer and then work on something else or take a coffee break.

The distance-learning application is an asymmetric (one-way) streaming-video application. The state university uses digital video equipment to film the class lectures in real-time and send the video stream over the Internet, using the Real-Time Streaming Protocol (RTSP) and the Real-Time Protocol (RTP).

The remote students do not send any audio or video data; they simply have the ability to send text questions while the class is happening, using a chat-room Web page.

A user subscribes to the distance-learning class by accessing a Web server at the state university, entering a user name and password, and specifying how much bandwidth the user has available. The Web page currently does not let a user specify more than 56-Kbps of available bandwidth. (This is partly because there is an assumption that the remote students are using modems. In addition, the state university controls bandwidth usage on its WAN link by limiting how much bandwidth remote users can demand.) The fact that the state university limits bandwidth usage is beneficial for WVCC because it helps WVCC control its own bandwidth requirements.

At this time, the distance-learning service is a point-to-point system. Each user receives a unique 56-Kbps video stream from the video system at the state university. For this reason, WVCC plans to limit the number of users that can access the pilot distance-learning system to 10 students who are located in the Math and Sciences Building.

In the future, the distance-learning system will support IP multicast technologies. At that time, WVCC will expand support for the distance-learning service, and allow users anywhere on the campus to use the service.

A Summary of Traffic Characteristics and Traffic Flows

Table 9–9 summarizes the traffic characteristics and traffic flows for WVCC's current and planned network. The bandwidth calculations are based on peak usage and calculate a worst-case scenario. The bandwidth number in the Approximate Bandwidth column is an aggregate of the bandwidth requirements for all the users for that particular traffic flow. For example, all the PC users in the Computing Center use approximately 30-Kbps bandwidth for Application 1.

NOTES

For the low-bandwidth applications, it would have been acceptable to simply specify "nominal usage" in the table, but because more specific estimates were available from protocol analyzer traces and user interviews, they were included in the chart.

Once the "Network Applications Traffic Characteristics and Traffic Flows" chart was filled out, it became possible to represent cross-campus traffic flows in a graphical form, as shown in Figure 9–8.

Table 9–9   WVCC Network Applications Traffic Characteristics and Traffic Flows

	Name of Application	Type of Traffic Flow	Protocol(s) Used by Application	User Communities that Use Application
1	Homework	Client/Server	SMB/NetBT	PC users in Computing Center
			AFP over TCP	Mac users in Computing Center
			SMB/NetBT over TCP	PC users in Business/Social Sciences
			AFP over TCP	Mac users in Arts/ Humanities
			SMB/NetBT over TCP	PC users in Arts/Humanities
			SMB/NetBT over TCP	PC users in Math/Science
2	E-mail	Client/Server	SMTP and POP	Mac and PC users in Computing Center
				Library patrons
				PC users in Business/Social Sciences
				Mac and PC users in Arts/Humanities
				PC users in Math/Science
				Administration
		Server/Server	SMTP/POP over TCP	Windows NT Web/e-mail server
3	Web Surfing	Client/Server	HTTP over TCP	Mac and PC users in Computing Center
				Library patrons
				PC users in Business/ Social Sciences
				Mac and PC users in Arts/Humanities

Data Stores (Servers, Hosts, and so on)	Approximate Bandwidth Requirement for the Application	QoS Requirements
Windows NT file/print server	30 Kbps	Flexible
AppleShare IP file/print server	18 Kbps	Flexible
Windows NT file/print server	15 Kbps	Flexible
AppleShare IP file/print server	30 Kbps	Flexible
Windows NT file/print server	24 Kbps	Flexible
Windows NT file/print server	24 Kbps	Flexible
Windows NT Web/E-mail/DHCP server	30 Kbps	Flexible
Windows NT Web/E-mail/DHCP server	6 Kbps	Flexible
Windows NT Web/E-mail/DHCP server	10 Kbps	Flexible
Windows NT Web/E-mail/DHCP server	30 Kbps	Flexible
Windows NT Web/E-mail/DHCP server	16 Kbps	Flexible
Windows NT Web/E-mail/DHCP server	10 Kbps	Flexible
Upstream e-mail server at ISP	60 Kbps	Flexible
10% to WVCC Web site on the Windows NT e-mail/Web server, 90% to Internet sites	90 Kbps	Flexible
10% to WVCC Web site, 90% to Internet sites	30 Kbps	Flexible
10% to WVCC web site, 90% to Internet sites	30 Kbps	Flexible
10% to WVCC web site, 90% to Internet sites	96 Kbps	Flexible

Table 9-9   WVCC Network Applications Traffic Characteristics and Traffic Flows, Continued

				PC users in Math/Science Administration
		Client/Server	HTTP over TCP	Outside users
4	Library card-catalog	Client/Server	HTTP	All internal users
5	Weather modeling	Distributed Computing	Proprietary over TCP	Subset of Math/Science PC users
6	Telescope monitoring	Client/Server	HTTP	Subset of Math/Science PC users
7	Graphics upload	Client/Server	AFP over TCP, or FTP over TCP	Mac and PC users in Arts/Humanities
8	Distance learning	Client/Server	RTSP, RTP, TCP (future RSVP and IP multicast), HTTP for chat room	Subset of Math/Sciences PC users
9	College Management System	Client/Server	NetWare Core Protocol (NCP)	Administration

In addition to the cross-campus traffic flows, traffic flows inside the Library/Computing Center and to and from the Internet were documented. Inside the Library/Computing Center, traffic travels to and from the various servers at about the following rates:

Application 1	48 Kbps
Application 2	36 Kbps
Application 3	120 Kbps
Application 4	30 Kbps
Total	**234 Kbps**

10% to WVCC Web site, 90% to Internet sites	48 Kbps	Flexible
10% to WVCC Web site, 90% to Internet sites	48 Kbps	Flexible
WVCC Web site	60 Kbps	
Library Catalog Windows NT server	About 0.5 Kbps per user	Flexible
Servers on the Internet	120 Kbps	Flexible
Servers on the Internet	100 Kbps	Flexible
Server at print shop	200 Kbps	Flexible
Server at state university	600 Kbps	Controlled load (IETF terminology)
College Management System Novell Server	40 Kbps	Flexible

Traffic travels to and from the Internet at about the following rate:

Application 2	60 Kbps
Application 3	370 Kbps
Application 5	120 Kbps
Application 6	100 Kbps
Application 7	200 Kbps
Application 8	600 Kbps
Total	**1450 Kbps**

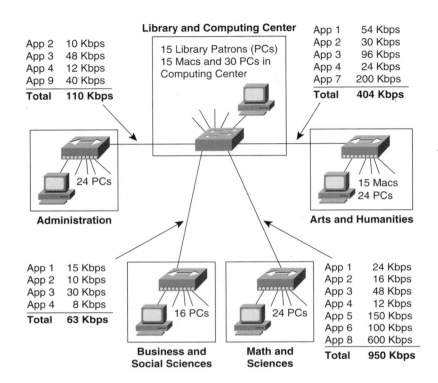

Figure 9–8
*Cross-campus
traffic flows
on the WVCC
campus net-
work.*

The Network Design for WVCC

After analyzing business and technical goals and studying the behavior of network applications, a hierarchical-mesh architecture with redundant links between buildings was selected for the logical topology at WVCC. The logical topology is shown in Figure 9–9.

In addition, the following decisions were made regarding the campus network:

- The network will use switched Ethernet. Though shared Ethernet would meet bandwidth requirements, switched Ethernet meets scalability goals and the objective of using state-of-the-art technology. A cost analysis indicates that switches are affordable.

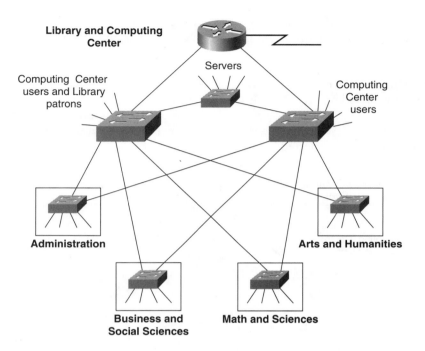

Library and Computing Center

Servers

Computing Center users and Library patrons

Computing Center users

Administration

Arts and Humanities

Business and Social Sciences

Math and Sciences

Figure 9–9
The hierarchical-mesh campus topology designed for WVCC.

- All devices will be part of the same broadcast domain for now. (The justification for this decision is that the total number of devices is less than the maximum specified in Table 4–8, "The Maximum Size of a Broadcast Domain.")

- All devices will be part of one IP subnet using the network address that the ISP administrators at the State Community College Network System assigned to the college. Addressing for PCs and Macintoshes will be accomplished with DHCP running on the Windows NT file/print and e-mail/Web servers.

- The switches will run the IEEE 802.1d spanning-tree protocol.

- The switches will support SNMP and RMON. A Windows-based network management software package will be purchased for the network administrators for monitoring the switches.

- The router will continue to act as a firewall using packet filtering. It will continue to support a default route to the Internet and will not run a routing protocol.

Once the logical network design was developed, some decisions were made regarding the capacity of links and which LAN technologies should be used, as shown in Figure 9–10. Vendors' switches were analyzed for port capacity, throughput, latency, and support for the relevant interface types and protocols. A variety of 24- and 48-port switches were selected.

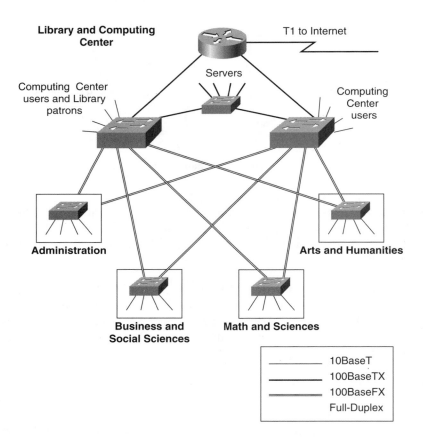

Figure 9–10
The physical network design for WVCC.

In addition, the following decisions were made regarding the physical network design:

- Buildings will be connected via 100BaseFX Ethernet. Because of the distances between building, the links must use full-duplex Ethernet. Though 10BaseFL or FOIRL Ethernet would meet bandwidth requirements, 100BaseFX was selected because it is more state-of-the-art and is supported on more switch platforms.

- Within buildings, 10-Mbps Ethernet switches will be used. (One exception is that the 15 Library patrons in floors 1-3 will still be connected via hubs, using the existing 10-Mbps Ethernet hubs.)

- All switches will have the ability to be upgraded with a routing module. The routing module can be added in the future to segment broadcast domains, as more multimedia applications are deployed.

- All switches will support IP multicast technologies to minimize the need to use broadcast and point-to-point technologies for multimedia applications in the future.

- The WAN link to the Internet will be upgraded to a 1.544 T1 link. The connection between the Math/Science building and the Internet will be dismantled.

- The router in the Computing Center will be upgraded to support two 100BaseTX ports and one T1 port with a built-in CSU/DSU unit. A redundant power supply will be added to the router, since the router represents a single point of failure.

- A centralized (star) physical topology will be used for the campus cabling. Existing underground cable conduits will be used, and multi-mode fiber-optic cabling will be added to the conduits. (Some of the conduits already have it.) The cabling will be off-the-shelf cabling that consists of 30 strands of fiber with a 62.5-micron core and 125-micron cladding, protected by a plastic sheath suitable for outdoor wear-and-tear.

The campus cabling design is shown in Figure 9–11.

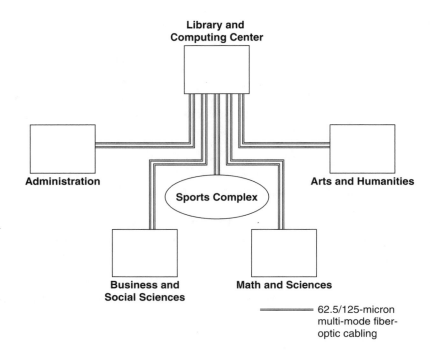

Figure 9–11
The campus cabling design for WVCC.

Library and
Computing Center

Administration

Sports Complex

Arts and Humanities

Business and
Social Sciences

Math and Sciences

══════ 62.5/125-micron
multi-mode fiber-
optic cabling

SUMMARY

This chapter covered the first step in the physical design phase of the top-down network design methodology: selecting technologies and devices for campus network designs. A physical design consists of cabling, Layer-2 protocol implementations, and network devices. The physical design depends on business objectives, technical requirements, traffic characteristics, and traffic flows, which Part I of this book discusses. The physical design builds on the logical design, which Part II discusses.

This chapter covered LAN cabling plant design and LAN technologies such as Ethernet, Fast EtherChannel, Token Ring, FDDI, and ATM. The chapter also provided some selection criteria you can use when choosing hubs, bridges, switches, and routers.

The chapter concluded with an example of a campus network design that was developed for the Wandering Valley Community College. Though the network design in the example is simple, and some decisions were more obvious than they would be for a more complex design, the example demonstrated the use of the following top-down network design steps:

- Analyzing requirements, including both business and technical goals, and any "workplace politics" that are relevant to technology choices

- Characterizing the existing network

- Identifying network applications and analyzing bandwidth and QoS requirements for the applications

- Analyzing traffic flows

- Designing a logical topology

- Selecting cabling and data-link layer technologies for building LAN segments

- Selecting cabling and LAN technologies for backbone and inter-building segments, based on the analysis of traffic flows and the aggregation of bandwidth requirements

CHAPTER 10

Selecting Technologies and Devices for Enterprise Networks

This chapter presents technologies for the remote-access and wide area network (WAN) components of an enterprise network design. The chapter discusses physical and data link layer protocols and enterprise network devices, such as remote-access servers, routers, and WAN switches.

The chapter begins with a discussion of the following remote-access technologies:

- The Point-to-Point Protocol (PPP)

- Integrated Services Digital Network (ISDN)

- Cable modems

- Digital Subscriber Line (DSL)

After discussing remote-access technologies, the chapter presents options for selecting WAN and remote-access capacities with the North American Digital Hierarchy, the European E system, or the Synchronous Digital Hierarchy (SDH). The chapter continues with a discussion of the following WAN technologies:

- Leased lines

- Synchronous Optical Network (SONET)

- Switched Multimegabit Data Service (SMDS)

- Frame Relay

- Asynchronous Transfer Mode (ATM)

The chapter concludes with an example of a WAN network design that was developed for a medium-sized company, Klamath Paper Products, Inc. The example indicates what technologies and devices were chosen for this customer, based on the customer's goals.

The technologies and devices you select for your particular network design customer will depend on bandwidth and quality of service (QoS) requirements, the network topology, business requirements and constraints, and technical goals (such as scalability, affordability, performance, and availability).

Increasing scale is a challenge facing many large enterprises. The ability to deploy and manage numerous dial-up, ISDN, Frame Relay, leased line, and ATM networks is an important requirement for many organizations. An analysis of traffic flow and load, as discussed in Chapter 4, "Characterizing Network Traffic," will help you accurately select capacities and devices for these customers.

For many organizations, a key design goal is to save money on the cost of WAN and remote-access circuits. Optimization techniques that reduce costs play an important role in most WAN and remote-access designs. Methods for merging separate voice, video, and data networks into a combined, cost-effective WAN also play an important role. These methods must handle the diverse QoS requirements of different applications. Chapter 4 discussed the importance of analyzing application QoS requirements to help you make the right selections from the WAN and remote-access options described in this chapter.

REMOTE-ACCESS TECHNOLOGIES

As organizations have become more mobile and geographically dispersed in the 1990s, remote-access technologies have become an important ingredient of many enterprise network designs. Enterprises use remote-access technologies to provide network access to telecommuters, employees in remote offices, and mobile workers who travel.

An analysis of the location of user communities and their applications should form the basis of your remote-access design. It is important to recognize the location and number of full- and part-time telecommuters, the extent that mobile users access the network, and the location and scope of remote offices. Remote offices include branch offices, sales offices, manufacturing sites, warehouses, retail stores, regional banks in the financial industry, and regional doctor's offices in the health-care industry. Remote offices are also sometimes located at a business partner's site, for example, a vendor or supplier.

Typically, remote workers use such applications as e-mail, Web browsing, sales order-entry, and calendar applications to schedule meetings. Other, more bandwidth-intensive applications include downloading software or software updates, exchanging files with corporate servers, providing product demonstrations, managing the network from home, and attending online classes.

Part-time telecommuters and mobile users who access the network less than two hours per day can generally use an analog modem line. Analog modem lines are also sometimes used for *asynchronous routing* when there is minimal traffic between a remote office and headquarters. Asynchronous routing uses Layer-3 protocols to connect two networks via a phone line.

Analog modems take a long time to connect and tend to have high latency and low speeds. (The highest speed available for analog modems today is 56 Kbps.) For customers who have requirements for higher speeds, lower latency, and faster connection-establishment times, analog modems can be replaced with routers that support ISDN, cable modems, or DSL modems. The following sections discuss these options and provide information on PPP, a protocol typically used with remote-access and other WAN technologies.

Point-to-Point Protocol

The Internet Engineering Task Force (IETF) developed PPP as a standard data-link-layer protocol for transporting various network-layer protocols across serial, point-to-point links. PPP can be used to connect a single remote user to a central office, or to connect a remote office with many users to a central office. PPP is used with ISDN, analog lines, digital leased lines, and other WAN technologies. PPP provides the following services:

- Network-layer protocol multiplexing

- Link configuration

- Link-quality testing

- Link-option negotiation

- Authentication

- Header compression

- Error detection

PPP has four functional layers:

- The physical layer is based on various international standards for serial communication, including EIA/TIA-232-C (formerly RS-232-C), EIA/TIA-422 (formerly RS-422), V.24, and V.35.

- The encapsulation of network-layer datagrams is based on the standard High-Level Data-Link Control (HDLC) protocol.

- The Link Control Protocol (LCP) is used for establishing, configuring, authenticating, and testing a data-link connection.

- A family of Network Control Protocols (NCPs) is used for establishing and configuring various network-layer protocols such as IP, IPX, AppleTalk, and DECnet.

Multilink PPP and Multichassis Multilink PPP

Multilink PPP (MPPP) adds support for channel aggregation to PPP. As mentioned in Chapter 5, "Designing a Network Topology," channel aggregation can be used for load-balancing and providing extra bandwidth. With channel aggregation, a device can automatically bring up additional channels as bandwidth requirements increase. Channel aggregation usually is used in an ISDN environment, but it can be used on other types of serial interfaces also. (A PC connected to two analog modems can use channel aggregation, for example.)

MPPP ensures that packets arrive in order at the receiving device. To accomplish this, MPPP encapsulates data in PPP and assigns a sequence number to datagrams. At the receiving device, PPP uses the sequence number to re-create the original data stream. Multiple channels appear as one logical link to upper-layer protocols.

Multichassis MPPP is a Cisco Systems, Inc., Internetwork Operating System (IOS) enhancement to MPPP that allows channel aggregation across multiple remote-access servers at a central site. Multichassis MPPP allows WAN administrators to group multiple access servers into a single *stack group*. User traffic can be split and reassembled across multiple access servers in the stack group.

Multichassis MPPP makes use of the *Stack Group Bidding Protocol (SGBP)*. SGBP defines a bidding process to allow access servers to elect a server to handle aggregation for an application. The server has the job of creating and managing a bundle of links for an application that requests channel aggregation.

SGBP bidding can be weighted so that CPU-intensive processes, such as bundle creation, fragmentation and reassembly of packets, compression, and encryption, are offloaded to routers designated as *offload servers*. You can deploy a high-end router, such as a Cisco 7500-series router, as an offload server. An Ethernet switch can connect members of the stack group and the offload server, as shown in Figure 10–1.

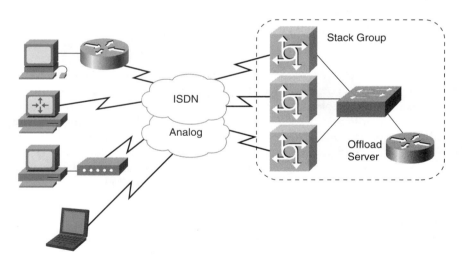

Figure 10–1
Multichassis multilink PPP stack group and offload server.

Password Authentication Protocol and Challenge Handshake Authentication Protocol

PPP supports two types of authentication:

- Password Authentication Protocol (PAP)

- Challenge Handshake Authentication Protocol (CHAP)

CHAP is more secure than PAP and is recommended. PAP can be used instead of CHAP if a remote station or remote server does not support CHAP, or if the extra configuration required for CHAP is considered a problem. In cases where security is less important than ease-of-configuration, PAP might be appropriate, but, in most cases, CHAP is recommended because of its superior protection from intruders.

With PAP, a user's password is sent as clear text. An intruder can use a protocol analyzer to capture the password and later use the password to break into the network.

CHAP provides protection against such attacks by verifying a remote node with a three-way handshake protocol and a variable challenge value that is unique and unpredictable. Verification happens upon link establishment and can be repeated any time during a session.

Figure 10–2 shows a CHAP sequence of events. When a remote node connects to an access server, the server sends back a challenge message with a challenge value that is based on an unpredictable random number. The remote station feeds the challenge value and the remote node's password through an algorithm, resulting in a one-way hashed challenge response. The remote node sends the hashed challenge response to the server, along with a user name that identifies the remote node. The server unhashes the challenge response and checks the response against a database of user names and passwords and sends back an "accept" or "deny" message.

Integrated Services Digital Network

PPP is often used with *Integrated Services Digital Network (ISDN)*, which is a digital data-transport service offered by regional telephone carriers. ISDN supports the transmission of text, graphics, video, music, voice, and other source material over telephone lines. PPP provides data encapsulation, link integrity, and authentication for ISDN.

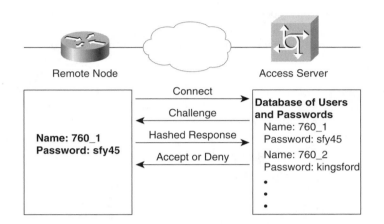

Remote Node

Access Server

	Connect	
	Challenge	**Database of Users and Passwords**
Name: 760_1	Hashed Response	Name: 760_1 Password: sfy45
Password: sfy45	Accept or Deny	Name: 760_2 Password: kingsford

Figure 10–2
Connection establishment with the Challenge Handshake Authentication Protocol (CHAP).

ISDN offers a cost-effective remote-access solution for telecommuters and remote offices that require higher transmission speeds and quicker connection establishment than analog dial-up links can offer. ISDN is also a good choice as a backup link for another type of link, for example, a Frame Relay link.

The cost of an ISDN circuit usually is based on a monthly fee plus usage time. Various options exist for saving money on an ISDN circuit. *Dial-on-demand routing (DDR)* lets a user keep an ISDN circuit idle until data must be transmitted to the remote site. *Snapshot routing* lets a router learn its routing table without periodic routing-table updates, thus allowing a circuit to remain idle for a long period of time. *Spoofing* allows a local router to respond to keepalive packets rather than sending the packets across the link. Keepalive packets are used in the Novell NetWare Core Protocol (NCP) and Sequenced Packet Exchange (SPX) protocols.

There are also various methods for aggregating ISDN bandwidth to meet the needs of applications with variable bandwidth requirements. For example, MPPP, which was covered in the PPP section earlier in this chapter, is often used to aggregate ISDN channels.

An ISDN circuit consists of 64-Kbps bearer (B) channels that carry user transmissions, and a signaling channel that carries control information, such as call setup and teardown signals. The signaling channel is called the *D channel*.

Figure 10–3 shows the two types of ISDN interfaces, which are as follows:

- The *Basic Rate Interface (BRI)* is two B channels and one 16-Kbps D channel.

- The *Primary Rate Interface (PRI)* is 23 B channels and one 64-Kbps D channel in the U.S., and 30 B channels and one 64-Kbps D channel in Europe and other parts of the world.

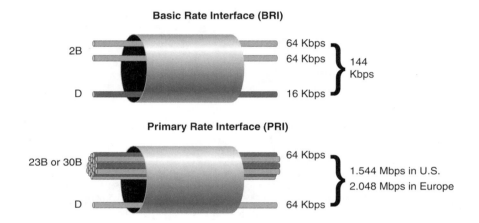

Telecommuters and remote offices typically use a device that supports BRI, for example, an ISDN BRI router. A central site, such as headquarters for a company, can use a PRI device to connect multiple telecommuters and remote offices. PRI offers an elegant solution for connecting many sites because it requires only one physical connection to support 23 (or 30) channels.

ISDN Components

ISDN components include terminals, terminal adapters (TAs), network-termination devices (NTs), line-termination equipment, and exchange-termination equipment. There are two types of ISDN terminals:

- ISDN-compliant terminals are called *terminal equipment type 1 (TE1)*.

- Non-ISDN terminals, that predate the ISDN standards, are called *terminal equipment type 2 (TE2)*.

There are also two types of NT devices:

- *NT1 devices* implement ISDN physical-layer functions and connect user devices to the ISDN facility.

- *NT2 devices* perform concentration services and implement Layer 2 and Layer 3 protocol functions. Equipment that provides NT2 functionality includes controllers and private branch exchanges (PBXs).

In the U.S. and Canada, ISDN enters the small office or home on a two-wire circuit at the *U reference point*, as shown in Figure 10–4. An NT1 interface converts the two-wire circuit into a four-wire circuit required by ISDN devices, such as ISDN phones and terminal adapters (TAs). An NT2 device typically is not used. Many routers have a built-in NT1 interface, which is sometimes called a *U option*. A router with a built-in NT1 is shown at the bottom of Figure 10–4.

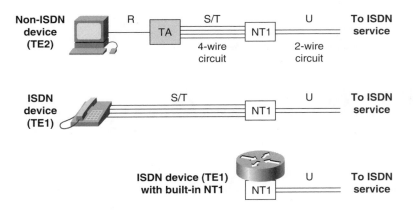

Figure 10–4
ISDN components and reference points in the U.S. and Canada.

ISDN specifies the following reference points (logical interfaces) shown in Figure 10–4:

- The *R* reference point defines the interface between a terminal equipment type 2 device (TE2) and a terminal adapter (TA).

- The *S* reference point defines the interface between a terminal equipment type 1 device (TE1) or TA, and an NT2.

- The *T* reference point defines the interface between an NT1 and NT2. In configurations with no NT2, an S/T interface connects an NT1 and TE1 or TA.

- The *U* reference point defines the interface between an NT1 and the ISDN service.

In Asia and Europe, the NT1 interface is considered part of the digital network and belongs to the telecommunications provider. Thus in Europe or Asia you would typically order a router with an *S/T option* and no built-in NT1. Figure 10–5 shows a European or Asian configuration.

Figure 10–5
ISDN compo-
nents and ref-
erence points
in Europe or
Asia.

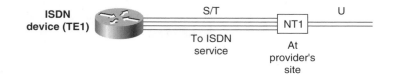

Cable Modem Remote Access

Another option for remote access is a cable modem. A *cable modem* operates over the coax cable that is used by cable TV (CATV) providers. Coax cable supports higher speeds than telephone lines, so cable-modem solutions are much faster than analog-modem solutions, and usually faster than ISDN solutions (depending on how many users share the cable).

Another benefit of cable modems is that no dialup is required. This is an advantage over analog modems that take a long time to dial and connect to a remote site.

NOTES

The term *cable modem* is somewhat misleading. A cable modem works more like a LAN interface than an analog modem.

Cable-network service providers offer *hybrid fiber/coax (HFC)* systems that connect CATV networks to the service-provider's high-speed fiber-optic network. The HFC systems allow users to connect their PCs or small LANs to the coax cable that enters their home or small office, and use this connection for high-speed access to the Internet or a central-site intranet.

Challenges Associated with Cable Modem Systems

Using cable modems for data transmission over household coax cable is a new technology, and there are still many challenges associated with implementing the technology. One challenge with transmitting data over CATV networks is that there are currently many standards that do not interoperate with each other, including the following:

- The Digital Audio Visual Council (DAVIC)/Digital Video Broadcasting (DVB) specification is a European standard that is being adopted in Asia and Australia and other parts of the world also.

- The Multimedia Cable Network System (MCNS)/Data Over Cable Service Interface Specification (DOCSIS) is a U.S. standard that is being adopted in other parts of the world also.

- The IP over Cable Data Network (IPCDN) Working Group of the Internet Engineering Task Force (IETF) is defining how IP will be supported on a CATV network.

- The Institute of Electrical and Electronics Engineers (IEEE) 802.14 working group is developing media access control (MAC) and physical-layer (PHY) standards for cable modems.

Another challenge with implementing a remote-access solution based on cable modems is that the CATV infrastructure was designed for broadcasting TV signals in just one direction—from the cable TV company to a person's home. Data transmission, however, is bidirectional. Data travels from the provider to the home (or small office) and from the home to the provider.

Because of the design of CATV networks, most cable-network services offer much more bandwidth for downstream traffic (from the service provider) than for upstream traffic (from the customer). An assumption is made that a lot of the data traveling from the home or small office consists of short acknowledgment packets and requires less bandwidth. This assumption is accurate for such applications as Web browsing, but might not be accurate for other applications that will be deployed in your network design. A cable modem solution is not the best answer for peer-to-peer applications or client/server applications in which the client sends lots of data.

A typical cable-network system offers 30–50 Mbps downstream and about 3 Mbps upstream. (Additional bandwidth is available for the cable TV signal; these numbers are for data transmission only.) Multiple users share the downstream and upstream bandwidth.

Downstream data is seen by all active cable modems. Each cable modem filters out traffic that is not destined for it. Upstream bandwidth is allocated using timeslots. There are three types of timeslots:

- A *reserved slot* is a timeslot that is available only to a particular cable modem. The head-end system at the provider's site allocates reserved timeslots to cable modems using a bandwidth allocation algorithm.

- A *contention slot* is a timeslot that is available to all cable modems. If two cable modems transmit in the same timeslot, the packets collide and the data is lost. The head-end system signals that no data was received, and the cable modems can try again after waiting a random amount of time. Contention slots are used for short data transmissions (including requests for a quantity of reserved slots for transmitting more data).

- A *ranging slot* is used for clock correction. The head-end system tells a cable modem to transmit during a ranging timeslot. The head-end system measures the time to receive the transmission, and gives the cable modem a small positive or negative correction value for its local clock.

If you plan to use a cable-modem solution for remote users or remote offices, be sure to query the service provider about the number of users that share a single cable and the types of applications they use. Provide the service provider with information about the bandwidth requirements of your users' applications, based on the analysis of traffic characteristics that you did as part of the requirements-analysis phase of the network design project.

Typically a service provider can give you an approximation of how much bandwidth is available per user of a cable-network system. Some systems also have the ability to guarantee a level of bandwidth for heavy-usage applications. If your users require more bandwidth than the service provider can offer, then you should investigate using a leased line or Frame Relay circuit instead of a cable modem.

Digital Subscriber Line Remote Access

Another technology that is gaining attention for remote access is *Digital Subscriber Line (DSL)*. Telephone companies offer DSL for high-speed data traffic over ordinary telephone wires.

With DSL, a home office or small office can connect a DSL modem or other device to a phone line and use this connection to reach a central-site intranet. In addition, some Internet Service Providers (ISPs) have arrangements with phone companies that let the providers offer their customers Internet access via a DSL modem.

DSL is similar to ISDN in that it is a technology that operates over existing telephone lines between a telephone switching station and a home or office. However, DSL uses sophisticated modulation schemes to offer much higher speeds than ISDN. DSL can support up to 32 Mbps for downstream traffic, and from 16 Kbps to 1.5 Mbps for upstream traffic.

DSL is sometimes called *xDSL* because of the many types of DSL technologies, including the following:

- Asymmetric DSL (ADSL)

- High-bit-rate DSL (HDSL)

- Very high-bit rate DSL (VDSL)

- Single-Line DSL (SDSL) (also known as *symmetric DSL*)

- Rate-Adaptive DSL (RADSL)

- ISDN DSL (IDSL)

- Consumer DSL (CDSL)

As the DSL industry matures, more technologies and acronyms will probably be added, and some of the acronyms will undoubtedly disappear. As of this writing, ADSL and HDSL are the most widely deployed DSL technologies. They are described in more detail in the next two sections.

Asymmetric Digital Subscriber Line

Much like cable modems, ADSL supports asymmetric bandwidth. More data can be sent downstream from the provider than can be sent from the customer to the provider.

An ADSL circuit has three channels:

- A high-speed downstream channel with speeds ranging from 1.5 to 9 Mbps

- A medium-speed duplex channel with speeds ranging from 16 Kbps to 640 Kbps

- A Plain Old Telephone Service (POTS) 64-Kbps channel for voice

Actual bandwidth rates depend on the type of DSL modem and many physical-layer factors, including the length of the circuit between the home or branch office and the telephone company, the wire gauge of the cable, the presence of bridged taps, and the presence of cross-talk or noise on the cable.

High-Bit-Rate Digital Subscriber Line

HDSL technology is symmetric, providing the same amount of bandwidth upstream as downstream: 1.544 Mbps over two wire pairs or 2.048 Mbps over three wire pairs. HDSL is the most mature of the DSL technologies. Telephone companies have offered HDSL service since the mid-1990s as a cost-effective alternative to a T1 or E1 circuit. HDSL is less expensive than T1 or E1 because it can run on poorer-quality lines without requiring any line conditioning.

Although HDSL's 12,000 to 15,000-foot operating distance is shorter than ADSL's maximum distance of 18,000 feet, telephone companies can install signal repeaters to extend HDSL's range. The repeaters might add to the cost of the service, but the cost is still generally significantly less than a T1 or E1 circuit.

SELECTING REMOTE-ACCESS DEVICES FOR AN ENTERPRISE NETWORK DESIGN

The previous sections discussed remote-access technologies. This section covers selecting devices to implement those technologies. Selecting remote-access devices for an enterprise network design involves choosing devices for remote users and for a central site. Remote users include telecommuters, users in remote offices, and mobile users. The central site could be the corporate headquarters of a company, the core network of a university that has branch campuses, a medical facility that connects doctors' offices, and so on.

Selecting Devices for Remote Users

Telecommuters and mobile users who access the central-site network less than two hours per day can use an analog modem. Modems should be selected carefully. Some modems are notoriously unreliable, especially when connecting to modems of a different brand or connecting to certain types of services. Before selecting modems, read articles in trade magazines and on the Web about the following modem characteristics:

- Reliability

- Interoperability with other brands of modems

- Interoperability with typical services

- Speed and throughput

- Latency

- Ease of setup

- Support for advanced features, such as compression and error-correction

- Cost

For customers who want higher speeds than an analog modem can offer, remote access can be accomplished with cable modems, DSL, or a small router that has an ISDN or other type of WAN port.

Criteria for selecting a router for remote sites includes:

- Support for protocols, such as IP, AppleTalk, IPX

- Support for a single remote user or a remote LAN

- Support for features that reduce line utilization, such as DDR, snapshot routing, and compression

- Support for channel aggregation

- Support for analog phone lines so that telephones and fax machines can share bandwidth with data

- Ease of configuration and management

- Security features

- Reliability

- Interoperability with typical services

- Cost

Selecting Devices for the Central Site

The central site generally includes remote-access servers that accept connection requests from remote sites, allowing multiple users to connect to the central-site network at the same time. There are five types of services provided by remote-access servers:

- **Remote-node services.** Allows PCs, Macintoshes, and X-terminals to connect to the central site and access network services as if they were directly connected to the network. The remote client can run Serial Line IP (SLIP), PPP, Xremote, AppleTalk Remote Access (ARA), or the NetWare IPXWAN protocol.

- **Terminal services.** Supports standard terminal services such as Telnet, rlogin for UNIX environments, Local Area Transport (LAT) for Digital Equipment Corporation (DEC) environments, X.25 packet assembler/disassembler (PAD) for accessing public X.25 networks, and TN3270, a virtual-terminal protocol for IBM 3270 applications.

- **Protocol translation services.** Lets terminals of one type access hosts using a different type of terminal service.

- **Asynchronous routing services.** Provides Layer-3 routing functionality to connect LANs via an asynchronous link.

- **Dialout services.** Allows desktop LAN users to share access-server modem ports for outbound asynchronous communications, eliminating the need for dedicated modems and phone lines for every desktop.

Criteria for selecting a central-site access server include the criteria listed above for a remote-site router, as well as the following additional criteria:

- The number of ports and types of ports

- Support for services (remote node, terminal, protocol translation, asynchronous routing, and dialout)

- Configuration flexibility and modularity: support for modems and ISDN, support for voice ports, support for cable modems or DSL ports, support for multichassis MPPP, and so on

- Support for network address translation (NAT) or port address translation (PAT) for hosts on remote networks

- Support for the Dynamic Host Configuration Protocol (DHCP) for hosts on remote networks

- Support for multimedia features and protocols, for example, the Resource Reservation Protocol (RSVP) and IP multicast

WAN TECHNOLOGIES

This section covers WAN technologies that are typical options for connecting geographically-dispersed sites in an enterprise network design. The section covers the most common and established WAN technologies, but the reader should also research new technologies as they gain industry acceptance. Wireless WAN technologies, for example, are not covered in this book, but are expected to greatly expand the options available for WAN (and remote-access) networks in the future. Low-orbit satellite, cellular, and radio-frequency wireless technologies will probably become popular options for voice, pager, and data services.

Recent changes in the WAN industry continue an evolution that began in the mid-1990s when the bandwidth and QoS requirements of corporations changed significantly due to new applications and expanded interconnectivity goals. As the need for WAN bandwidth accelerated, telephone companies upgraded their internal networks to use SONET and ATM technologies, and started offering new services to their customers, such as SMDS and Frame Relay. Today, an enterprise network architect has many options for WAN connectivity. The objective of this section is to present some of these options to help you select the right technologies for your customer.

Systems for Provisioning WAN Bandwidth

Regardless of the WAN technology you select, one critical network design step you must complete is selecting the amount of capacity that the WAN must provide. Selecting capacity is often called *provisioning*. Provisioning requires an analysis of traffic flows, as described in Chapter 4. This section provides an overview of the bandwidth capacities that are available to handle traffic flows of different sizes.

WAN bandwidth for copper cabling is provisioned in North America and many other parts of the world using the North American Digital Hierarchy, which is shown in Table 10–1. A channel in the hierarchy is called a *digital stream (DS)*. Digital streams are multiplexed together to form high-speed WAN circuits. DS-1 and DS-3 are the most commonly-used capacities.

Table 10-1   The North America Digital Hierarchy

Signal	Capacity	Number of DS-0s	Colloquial Name
DS-0	64 Kbps	1	Channel
DS-1	1.544 Mbps	24	T1
DS-1C	3.152 Mbps	48	T1C
DS-2	6.312 Mbps	96	T2
DS-3	44.736 Mbps	672	T3
DS-4	274.176 Mbps	4032	T4

In Europe, the Committee of European Postal and Telephone (CEPT) has defined a hierarchy called the *E system*, which is shown in Table 10–2.

Table 10–2   The Committee of European Postal and Telephone (CEPT) Hierarchy

Signal	Capacity	Number of E1s
E0	64 Kbps	N/A
E1	2.048 Mbps	1
E2	8.448 Mbps	4
E3	34.368 Mbps	16
E4	139.264 Mbps	64

The *Synchronous Digital Hierarchy (SDH)* is an international standard for data transmission over fiber-optic cables. SDH defines a standard rate of transmission of 51.84 Mbps, which is also called Synchronous Transport Signal level 1 or *STS-1*. Higher rates of transmission are a multiple of the basic STS-1 rate. The STS rates are the same as the SONET Optical Carrier (OC) levels, which are shown Table 10–3.

Table 10–3   The Synchronous Digital Hierarchy (SDH)

STS Rate	OC Level	Speed
STS-1	OC-1	51.84 Mbps
STS-3	OC-3	155.52 Mbps
STS-12	OC-12	622.08 Mbps
STS-24	OC-24	1.244 Gbps
STS-48	OC-48	2.488 Gbps
STS-96	OC-96	4.976 Gbps
STS-192	OC-192	9.952 Gbps

Leased Lines

The first WAN technology this chapter covers is the leased-line service offered by many telephone companies and other carriers. A *leased line* is a dedicated circuit that a customer leases from a carrier for a predetermined amount of time, usually for months or years. The line is dedicated to traffic for that customer and is used in a point-to-point topology between two sites on the customer's enterprise network. Speeds range from 64 Kbps (DS-0) to 45 Mbps (DS-3). Enterprises use leased lines for both voice and data traffic. Data traffic is typically encapsulated in a standard protocol such as PPP or HDLC.

Dedicated leased lines have the advantage that they are a mature and proven technology. Historically they had the disadvantage that they were very expensive, especially in some parts of Europe and Asia. As carriers upgrade their internal networks with more capacity, costs are dropping, however.

Leased lines also have the advantage over most other services that they are dedicated to a single customer. The customer does not share the capacity with anyone. Most newer systems, such as cable modems, DSL, ATM, and Frame Relay, are shared systems.

Leased lines tend to be overlooked as a potential WAN solution because they are not a new technology. In some situations, however, they are the best option for simple point-to-point links. Leased lines are a good choice if the topology is truly point-to-point (and not likely to become point-to-multipoint in the near future), the pricing offered by the local carrier is attractive, and applications do not require advanced QoS features that would be difficult to implement in a simple leased-line network.

Synchronous Optical Network

The next WAN technology this chapter covers is *Synchronous Optical Network (SONET)*, which is a physical-layer specification for high-speed synchronous transmission of packets or cells over fiber-optic cabling. SONET was proposed by Bellcore in the mid-1980s and is now an international standard. SONET uses the SDH system with STS-1 as its basic building block.

Service providers and carriers are making wide use of SONET in their internal networks. SONET is also gaining popularity within private networks to connect remote sites in a WAN or metropolitan-area network (MAN).

Both ATM and packet-based networks can be based on SONET. With packet transmission, SONET networks usually use PPP at the data-link layer and IP at the network layer. Packet Over SONET (POS) is expected to become quite popular as Internet and intranet traffic grows, and as new applications, such as voice over IP (VoIP), demand the high speed, low latency, and low error rates that SONET can offer.

One of the main goals of SONET and SDH was to define higher speeds than the ones used by the North American Digital Hierarchy and the European E systems, and to alleviate problems caused by incompatibilities in those systems. The creators of

SONET and SDH defined high-speed capacities, starting with the 51.84-Mbps STS-1, that were approved by both North American and European standards bodies.

Another goal of SONET was to support more efficient multiplexing and demultiplexing of individual signals. With SONET (SDH), it is easy to isolate one channel from a multiplexed circuit, for example, one phone call from a trunk line that carries numerous phone calls. With *plesiochronous systems*, such as the North American Digital Hierarchy and the European E system, isolating one channel is more difficult. Although isolating a 64-Kbps channel from a DS-1 circuit is straightforward, isolating a 64-Kbps channel from a DS-3 trunk requires demultiplexing to the DS-1 level first.

NOTES

The North American Digital Hierarchy and European E systems are called plesiochronous systems. *Plesio* means "almost" in Greek. A truly synchronous system, such as SONET, supports more efficient multiplexing and demultiplexing than a plesiochronous ("almost synchronous") system.

The SONET specification defines a four-layer protocol stack. The four layers have the following functions:

- The *photonic layer* specifies the physical characteristics of the optical equipment.

- The *section layer* specifies the frame format and the conversion of frames to optical signals.

- The *line layer* specifies synchronization and multiplexing onto SONET frames.

- The *path layer* specifies end-to-end transport.

Terminating multiplexers (implemented in switches or routers) provide user access to the SONET network. Terminating multiplexers turn electrical interfaces into optical signals and multiplex multiple payloads into the STS-N signals required for optical transport.

A SONET network is usually connected in a ring topology using two self-healing fiber paths. A path provides full-duplex communication and consists of a pair of fiber strands. One path acts as the full-time working transmission facility. The other path acts as a backup protection pair, remaining idle while the working path passes data. If an interruption occurs on the working path, data is automatically rerouted to the backup path within milliseconds. If both the working and protected pairs are cut, the ring wraps, and communication can still survive. Figure 10–6 shows a typical SONET network.

Figure 10–6
A redundant SONET ring.

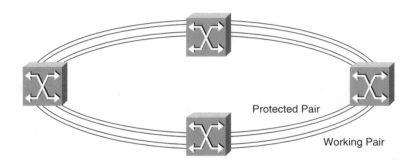

Protected Pair

Working Pair

Switched Multimegabit Data Service

SMDS is a physical and data link layer WAN technology that is an alternative to leased lines. Many telephone companies and other carriers in the U.S. and Europe offer SMDS. Because carriers in the U.S. tend to price SMDS higher than Frame Relay, however, SMDS is not a popular choice in the U.S.

SMDS runs on fiber or copper media. It transfers data between multiple subscribers in 53-byte cells at speeds of 1.544 Mbps (DS-1) and 45 Mbps (DS-3). The *SMDS Interface Protocol (SIP)* is used for communication between customer-premises equipment (CPE) and SMDS carrier equipment. SIP is based on the IEEE 802.6 Distributed Queue Dual Bus (DQDB) standard for cell-relay across MANs.

SMDS is usually positioned as a high-speed, low-latency, cost-effective solution for connecting LANs and MANs over a cell-relay WAN. SMDS was a forerunner of ATM, but differs from ATM in that it offers a connectionless service, thereby making the support of LAN protocols more straightforward.

Much like Frame Relay, a site that uses SMDS can have just one physical connection to the service-provider's network, but many logical connections to other sites. This type of service is much more economical than a network of many dedicated leased lines, and can generally offer lower latency than a complex partial-mesh network of leased lines.

As the number of connections increases, SMDS is arguably easier to administer than Frame Relay because of SMDS's support for any-to-any, connectionless communication. Nonetheless, in the U.S., Frame Relay has overtaken SMDS as the most popular alternative to expensive point-to-point WAN designs.

Frame Relay

Frame Relay is a high-performance WAN protocol that operates at the physical and data-link layers of the OSI reference model. Frame Relay emerged in the early 1990s as an enhancement to more complex packet-switched technologies such as X.25. Whereas X.25 is optimized for excellent reliability on physical circuits with a high error rate, Frame Relay was developed with the assumption that facilities are no longer as error-prone as they once were. This assumption allows Frame Relay to be more efficient and easier to implement than X.25.

Frame Relay offers a cost-effective method for connecting remote sites, typically at speeds from 64 Kbps to 1.544 Mbps. Frame Relay offers more granularity in the selection of bandwidth assignments than leased lines, and also includes features for dynamic bandwidth allocation and congestion control to support bursty traffic flows. Frame Relay has become a popular replacement for both X.25 and leased line networks because of its efficiency, flexible bandwidth support, and low latency.

Frame Relay Hub-and-Spoke Topologies and Subinterfaces

Frame Relay networks are often designed in a hub-and-spoke topology, such as the topology shown in Figure 10–7. A central-site router in this topology can have many logical connections to remote sites with only one physical connection to the WAN, thus simplifying installation and management. (Frame Relay is similar to SMDS in this respect.)

One problem with a hub-and-spoke topology is that split horizon can limit routing. With *split horizon*, distance-vector routing protocols do not repeat information out the interface it was received on. This means that devices on network 300 in Figure

10–7 cannot learn about devices on network 400, and vice versa, because the central-site router only advertises network 100 when it sends its routing table out the WAN interface.

Figure 10–7
*A Frame Relay
hub-and-spok
e topology.*

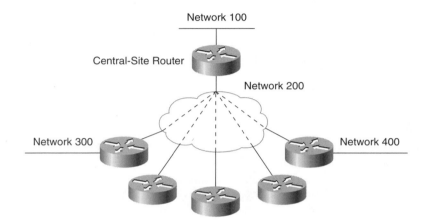

Some routing protocols support disabling the split horizon function. Split horizon is automatically disabled in a Frame Relay hub-and-spoke topology when Cisco's Interior Gateway Routing Protocol (IGRP) and Enhanced IGRP are used. Split horizon can be disabled for the IP Routing Information Protocol (RIP). However, some protocols, such as Novell's RIP and Service Advertising Protocol (SAP) and AppleTalk's Routing Table Maintenance Protocol (RTMP), require split horizon.

A solution to the split-horizon problem is to use a full-mesh design with physical circuits between each site. The drawback to this approach is cost. For example, in the network portrayed in Figure 10–7, a full mesh would comprise 15 circuits instead of 6. Since each circuit costs money, this would not be an optimum solution.

The other alternative is to use subinterfaces. A *subinterface* is a logical interface that is associated with a physical interface. In Figure 10–7, the central-site router could have five point-to-point subinterfaces defined, each communicating with one of the remote sites. With this solution, the central-site router applies the split horizon rule based on logical subinterfaces, instead of the physical interface, and includes remote sites in the routing updates it sends out the WAN interface.

One downside of using subinterfaces is that router configurations are more complex. Another disadvantage is that more network numbers are required. In Figure 10–7, the entire WAN "cloud" is network 200 when subinterfaces are not used. When subinterfaces are used, each circuit within the cloud requires a network number.

With subinterfaces, more broadcast traffic is propagated to the WAN and routers than without subinterfaces (where split horizon limits the broadcast routing traffic). The scope of a hub-and-spoke subinterface topology should be limited to ensure that broadcast traffic on each link is less than 20 percent of the total traffic, and no router is overwhelmed by broadcast traffic.

NOTES

By using the show processes command on a Cisco router, you can determine if a router's CPU utilization is too high because of broadcast processing. If the five-minute average CPU utilization is higher than 75 percent, analyze the output from the command to determine if the high utilization is caused by broadcast traffic, for example, routing protocol or service-advertising broadcast packets.

Frame Relay Congestion Control Mechanisms

Although Frame Relay devices generally do not use all of their available bandwidth all of the time, a Frame Relay device does have the ability to transmit data at its physical access rate for extended periods of time. For this reason, the Frame Relay standard includes congestion control mechanisms to ensure fair bandwidth allocation, and feedback mechanisms to inform user devices about the availability of network bandwidth.

The Frame Relay packet header includes a *discard eligibility (DE)* bit used to identify less important traffic that can be dropped when congestion occurs. In addition, Frame Relay includes two congestion-notification schemes:

- *Forward-explicit congestion notification (FECN)* informs the receiver of a frame that the frame traversed a path that is experiencing congestion.

- *Backward-explicit congestion notification (BECN)* informs a sender that congestion exists in the path that the sender is using.

Service providers are able to keep prices for their Frame Relay service reasonably low because of the bursty nature of the traffic typically offered to Frame Relay networks. The service provider generally oversubscribes its internal network, making the assumption that not all virtual circuits use all of their available bandwidth all of the time. Switches within the service provider's network can use the FECN and BECN mechanisms to notify end-system devices of any congestion problems. The resulting behavior at the end systems depends on which protocol and which implementation of the protocol is being used.

NOTES

Congestion control in a Transmission Control Protocol (TCP) application is usually independent of the FECN and BECN mechanisms. Upon packet loss, TCP decreases its transmit window size, effectively slowing its transmission rate. It then gradually increases the window size until congestion occurs again.

Frame Relay Bandwidth Allocation

Most Frame Relay networks provide some guarantee of bandwidth availability for each end point of a virtual circuit. The guarantee is expressed as the *committed information rate (CIR)*. The CIR specifies that as long as the data input by a device to the Frame Relay network is below or equal to the CIR, then the network will continue to forward data for that virtual circuit. If the data input rate exceeds the CIR, there is no longer any guarantee. The network might discard traffic beyond the CIR limit, although if there is sufficient bandwidth it might continue to forward traffic. CIR is measured over a time interval *T*.

In addition to specifying a CIR, many Frame Relay providers also let a customer specify a *committed burst size (Bc)* that specifies a maximum amount of data that the provider will transmit over the time interval T even after the CIR has been exceeded. The provider's Frame Relay switch is allowed to set the DE bit for frames at the Bc level.

Beyond the Bc, the provider can also support an *excess burst size (Be)* that specifies the maximum amount in excess of Bc that the network will attempt to transfer under normal circumstances during the time interval T. The switch sets the DE bit on these frames and has the right to discard the frames if the switch or network is congested.

Cisco System's Optimized Bandwidth Management algorithm for WAN switches (formerly known as ForeSight) controls congestion using a parameter called *peak information rate*, or *PIR*. PIR is the peak bandwidth that a connection can use during data bursts when there is excess bandwidth available and no congestion on the network connection.

PIR is related to Be, Bc, and a minimum information rate (MIR) as follows:

$$PIR = MIR \times (1 + Be/Bc)$$

MIR is used by the Optimized Bandwidth Management algorithm to represent the lowest information rate assigned when there is congestion on the network. This rate is reached only when there is congestion over an extended time. With MIR, a service provider can guarantee a customer a certain level of service, even when there is congestion on the network. This is theoretically superior to a simple CIR, which might not be accurate when there is congestion over a long period of time.

CIR, Be, Bc, PIR, and MIR should be selected with care, based on realistic, anticipated traffic rates and characteristics. In a hub-and-spoke design, such as the network in Figure 10–7, you can estimate the CIR for the central-site link by adding up the CIRs at each access site. The CIR at the central site should be at least equal to the sum of the remote-site CIRs, and generally should be higher to handle bursts.

TIPS

The access rate and CIR of the Frame Relay connection at the hub of a hub-and-spoke topology should be more than the sum of the CIRs at the remote sites and less than or equal to the sum of the burst capacities of the remote sites.

In actuality, a lot of service providers don't let you specify Be or Bc. Some providers don't let you specify CIR either. To keep things simple, some carriers base their Frame Relay offerings simply on a physical access speed. These carriers often offer a *zero*

CIR, which means that they make only a best effort to send your traffic. (The advantage of a zero CIR is that it is inexpensive.)

In cases when you are allowed to specify a CIR, make sure it is based on the analysis of traffic that you did as part of the requirements-analysis phase of the network design process. Consider application traffic as well as system traffic. In particular, be sure to estimate how much traffic will be caused by routing protocols. Using Table 4–7, "Bandwidth Used by Routing Protocols," you can determine how much bandwidth will be used based on the number of planned networks and the selected routing protocol. If the bandwidth seems too high, consider configuring route filters on routers, or selecting an update-based routing protocol or link-state protocol. Snapshot or static routing can also be used to save bandwidth.

Although it is recommended that the CIR and other parameters be based on a careful analysis of traffic, keep in mind that the CIR and other parameters are based on a probabilistic service. Although some carriers market the CIR as a true guarantee, carriers actually oversubscribe their networks and cannot guarantee that their customers will correctly react to congestion feedback mechanisms, which means that no customer's CIR or Bc is truly a guarantee.

Frame Relay/ATM Interworking

As ATM gains popularity, WANs that use both ATM and Frame Relay technologies are becoming more common. The term *Frame Relay/ATM Interworking* is used to describe the protocols and processes for connecting ATM and Frame Relay WANs. Interworking can be implemented in two different ways, depending on the goals of the network design:

- With *network interworking*, two or more Frame Relay networks are connected via an ATM core network. This is a common topology used by service providers who use ATM for their internal networks and offer Frame Relay to their customers.

- With *service interworking*, an ATM network connects to a Frame Relay network. This topology is less common, but might be used during a transition from Frame Relay to ATM or vice versa.

For more information on Frame Relay/ATM interworking, see the Frame Relay Forum's Web site at www.frforum.com.

ATM Wide Area Networks

Chapter 9, "Selecting Technologies and Devices for Campus Networks," discussed using ATM in a campus network. This chapter discusses using ATM as the core of a WAN enterprise network. Despite the complexity of ATM, ATM is a good choice for WAN backbone networks for customers with accelerating bandwidth requirements and applications with advanced QoS requirements.

ATM supports very high bandwidth requirements. When used on copper cabling, ATM can run at T3 or above speeds. When used on fiber-optic cabling, ATM supports speeds up to OC-192 (9.952 Gbps) and beyond, especially if technologies such as wave-division multiplexing (WDM) are used.

ATM facilitates the efficient sharing of bandwidth among applications with various QoS requirements. As discussed in Part I of this book, applications can theoretically share bandwidth more fairly in a cell-based system compared to a frame-based system, because in a frame-based system, large frames can monopolize bandwidth. In addition, with a connection-oriented technology such as ATM, an application can specify upon connection establishment the QoS it requires, including peak and minimum cell rates, a cell-loss ratio, and a cell-transfer delay.

A motivating factor for using ATM as a WAN core technology is to save money spent on monthly tariffs for WAN circuits. Because of the traffic management, dynamic bandwidth allocation, and congestion-control characteristics of ATM, customers can often have fewer WAN links with ATM than with older technologies, such as leased lines and Time Division Multiplexing (TDM).

NOTES

With synchronous TDM-based networks, applications are assigned to timeslots. An application can only transmit when its timeslot comes up, even if all other timeslots are empty. If an application has nothing to send during its timeslot, bandwidth during that timeslot is wasted. ATM, on the other hand, is asynchronous, which means that bandwidth is allocated on demand. High-bandwidth applications, for example, video applications, can make use of bandwidth that less demanding applications do not use.

Customers who in the past had separate voice, video, LAN-interconnect, and Systems Network Architecture (SNA) TDM-based WANs, can merge their networks into an ATM WAN that efficiently shares bandwidth among applications. In many cases, network consolidation can be achieved at the same time that new applications are implemented, for example, desktop video conferencing and IP telephony.

SELECTING DEVICES AND SERVICE PROVIDERS FOR AN ENTERPRISE WAN DESIGN

An enterprise WAN design is based on high-performance routers and WAN switches. This section covers selection criteria for those devices. It builds on information in Chapter 9, "Selecting Technologies and Devices for a Campus Network Design," which covered typical criteria for the selection of internetworking devices in general. The criteria in Chapter 9 (such as the number of ports, processing speed, media and technologies supported, MTTR and MTBF, and so on) apply to enterprise as well as campus devices.

Selecting Routers for an Enterprise WAN Design

Enterprise routers should offer high throughput, high availability, and advanced features to optimize the utilization of expensive WAN circuits. Selecting routers for an enterprise WAN network design is similar to selecting routers for a campus network design but often requires more care to avoid performance problems caused by an under-powered router that aggregates traffic from many networks.

When provisioning enterprise routers, keep in mind that in a hierarchical design, such as the designs discussed in Chapter 5, "Designing a Network Topology," a concentration of traffic from lower layers of the hierarchy aggregates at routers at the top of the hierarchy. This means you need to plan for adequate performance on the routers at the upper layers of the hierarchy.

Based on an analysis of traffic flow, you should select routers that provide the necessary WAN interfaces to support bandwidth requirements, provide an appropriate packets-per-second level, and have adequate memory and processing power to forward data and handle routing protocols. In addition, you should select routers that provide optimization features such as advanced switching and queuing techniques, traffic shaping, Random Early Detection (RED), and express forwarding. Chapter 12 discusses router optimization techniques in more detail.

Selecting WAN Switches for an Enterprise WAN Design

Much as LAN switching revolutionized campus network designs in the mid-1990s, WAN switching is changing WAN network designs. Multiservice WAN switches that handle ATM, Frame Relay, and remote-access technologies are gaining popularity in both service-provider and enterprise networks. These switches carry many types of network traffic, including TCP/IP and other LAN protocols, X.25, SNA, video, voice, and circuit-emulation traffic. They offer a variety of features that save costs compared to older telecommunications equipment, including statistical multiplexing, dynamic bandwidth allocation, voice activity detection (VAD), voice compression, and repetitive pattern suppression (RPS).

Service providers are building multiservice switched WANs that allow them to reduce operational costs, deploy new technologies, and sell new services to customers. Businesses and other organizations are building private multiservice switched WANs that allow them to save money on leased lines and more readily deploy new services. A private switched WAN that supports high capacities and dynamic bandwidth allocation can facilitate an organization deploying new services without having to purchase additional WAN capacity from a carrier.

WAN switches should support a variety of data types, interfaces, and services, and have features that optimize bandwidth utilization. They should have sufficient memory for buffers and queues, and sufficient processing power to handle the requisite amount of traffic and optimization features.

A WAN switch should have intelligent queue-handling algorithms that take into account the behavior of different types of applications. For example, consider the differences between voice and data applications. Although voice applications have stringent requirements regarding delay and delay variance, they tolerate some degree of cell loss in an ATM WAN.

Data applications, on the other hand, are more tolerant of delay than voice applications, but less tolerant of cell loss. With data applications, cell loss can cause data corruption and performance problems. (If one cell gets dropped in a TCP stream of bytes, the whole stream must be retransmitted.) When facing an overload condition, a WAN switch must handle different traffic types with intelligent queue-handling algorithms that can drop cells with minimal disruption to applications.

In addition to queues, buffers are also necessary on WAN switches to absorb traffic bursts from simultaneous connections. The switch must reallocate buffers as the traffic mix changes to provide performance guarantees for different types of traffic.

WAN switches should support features that facilitate redundancy and quick auto-rerouting in the case of failure. They should also offer automatic end-to-end connection management. With *automatic end-to-end connection management*, a route is selected based on the network topology, loading, and the geographical distance to the destination.

Selecting a WAN Service Provider

In addition to selecting technologies and devices for a WAN network design, you must also select service providers or carriers. The amount of interaction you have with a service provider depends on the network topology and the devices you have chosen. For a small WAN (actually a MAN), you might be able to install your own fiber-optic cabling and SONET network with little or no interaction with a carrier. For larger WANs, usually you must interact with a carrier to lease capacity from the carrier's network. If desired, you can outsource management of your WAN to the service provider. For example, in a Virtual Private Network (VPN) design, where enterprise sites are connected via a service-provider's network or the Internet, the provider manages the WAN.

One obvious criterion for selecting a service provider is the cost of services. Using cost as the main selection criterion, however, can make the choice difficult because providers offer distinct services and define terms and conditions differently. Also, for many network designs, cost is not the main criterion. The following criteria are often more important than cost:

- The extent of services and technologies offered by the provider

- The geographical areas covered by the provider

- Reliability and performance characteristics of the provider's internal network

- The level of security offered by the provider

- The level of technical support offered by the provider

When selecting a service provider, try to investigate the structure, security, and reliability of the provider's internal network to help you predict the reliability of your WAN, which depends on the provider's network. Learning about the provider's network can be challenging because providers generally do not share detailed information about their internal networks, but nonetheless talk to systems engineers and current customers of the provider to try to determine the following characteristics of the provider's network:

- The physical routing of network links

- Redundancy within the network

- The extent to which the provider relies on other providers for redundancy

- The level of oversubscription on the network

- Bandwidth allocation mechanisms used to guarantee application QoS requirements

- The types of switches that are used and the bandwidth-allocation and optimization features available on the switches

- The frequency and typical causes of network outages

- Security methods used to protect the network from intruders

- Security methods used to protect the privacy of a customer's data

- Disaster recovery plans in case of earthquakes, fires, hurricanes, asteroids that collide with satellites, or other natural or man-made disasters

Most service providers can furnish customers with a *service-level-agreement (SLA)* that defines the specific terms of the service and how the service will be measured and guaranteed. Many service providers are now offering refunds if the SLA terms are not met. Some SLAs address only network availability, which is not sufficient for many applications. An SLA should also address application performance, including latency and throughput.

An SLA should also specify the level of technical support that can be expected. Generally you should get a contract for 24-hour, 7-day support for a mission-critical WAN. In addition to specifying specific terms and conditions for support and service in an SLA, when negotiating a contract with a provider, try to get answers to the following support-related questions:

- What is the experience level of the installation and support staff?

- Does the support staff have experience with your particular protocols and applications?

- If necessary, can you request a dedicated single-point-of-contact support representative who will take responsibility for resolving all problems and questions?

- Have the provider's service standards received International Organization for Standards (ISO) 9002 certification?

- How difficult is it for a typical customer to provision and price new services?

- Does the provider offer a customer training program on services and pricing structures?

AN EXAMPLE OF A WAN DESIGN

This section presents a WAN design that was developed using some of the design steps in this book. The section describes an actual network design that was developed for Klamath Paper Products. (The name of the company has been changed.) The example is based on a real network design, but some of the facts have been changed to preserve the privacy of the company and protect the security of the company's network, and to make it possible to present a simple and easy-to-understand example.

Background Information for the WAN Design Project

Klamath Paper Products, Inc., manufactures paper and packaging products, including office paper, newsprint, cartons, and corrugated boxes. They also manufacture wood pulp and chemicals used in the manufacturing of pulp and paper.

Klamath Paper Products (which will be called Klamath from now on) has approximately 15 sites in the western United States. Headquarters are in Portland, Oregon. Klamath employs around 1,500 people and has customers all over the world, with a large customer base in Asia.

In the late 1990s, Klamath became concerned about reduced profit margins caused by fewer sales in Asia and the scarcity of lumber used to manufacture Klamath's products. Klamath recently completed a strategic re-engineering project that identified ways to increase profits by improving the efficiency of internal processes and making more use of recycled post-consumer paper in the production of new paper products.

As a result of the re-engineering project, the Conservation Initiative Task Force at Klamath plans to roll out an on-going distance-learning program that will train all employees on ways to conserve raw materials, use recycled materials, and work more efficiently. Executive management considers the new training program vital to the continued success of Klamath, and approved funding to equip the training rooms at most sites with digital video-conferencing systems.

Once Klamath installs the video-conferencing system and the WAN to support it, there are plans to offer classes to other companies in the wood and paper manufacturing industries. Klamath has recognized a business opportunity associated with the federal government's plan to help pay for workers in the timber industry to attend classes in modern methods for sustainable forest management and environmentally-sound lumber and paper production.

Business and Technical Goals

Klamath's main business goals for the WAN design project are as follows:

- Increase profits by implementing a WAN that will support the goals of the Conservation Initiative Task Force, in particular the new distance-learning program.

- Improve the performance of the existing WAN to support more efficient operations.

- Contain the rising costs associated with operating the existing WAN.

- Provide a network that will let employees more easily share ideas for further improving efficiency and increasing the use of recycled materials.

- Provide a new source of revenue from the timber-industry distance-learning program.

Engineers in the telecommunications and networking departments added the following technical goals:

- Update the capacity and QoS-capabilities of the existing WAN, which in its current state cannot support the new video-conferencing system.

- Design a network that uses currently-available technologies from the WAN service providers in the region.

- Provide a network that offers a response time of 1/10th of a second or less for interactive applications.

- Provide a network that is available 99.98 percent of the time and offers a MTBF of 4,000 hours (about 5.5 months) and a MTTR of one hour (with a low standard deviation from these average numbers).

- Improve the manageability of the network by simplifying the topology, which is currently a complex mesh of voice and data circuits.

- Design a network that will scale as new high-bandwidth applications are added in the future.

- Design a network that can support voice traffic in the future.

Network Applications

The new distance-learning application will use a two-way compressed digital video service based on the H.320 standards for video-conferencing. Each site with a training room will be equipped with a video camera and coder-decoder (CODEC) to convert from analog to digital signals.

Both synchronous and asynchronous distance learning will be supported. With *synchronous distance learning*, remote students attend classes taught by instructors at headquarters or other sites in "real-time." With *asynchronous distance learning*, students can check out a video class from a video server at headquarters and have the video transmitted to their site.

Other applications in use at Klamath include the following:

- The manufacturing support system is a terminal/host SNA application that runs on a mainframe in Portland. The system keeps track of manufacturing schedules and work orders. Members of the various manufacturing departments access the system from their PCs via TCP/IP-SNA gateways. This system is considered critical to Klamath's mission to deliver products by the dates that were promised to customers.

- The financial modeling system runs on TCP/IP and makes use of an Oracle database system that resides on UNIX machines in Portland. Financial analysts use applications on their PCs to access this system.

- The sales order-entry and tracking system runs on Novell NetWare servers. Sales and marketing personnel use their PCs to access this system.

- The graphics production system runs on Macintosh computers and uses AppleShare servers and printers.

- Most users also deploy a standard set of Windows 95 PC applications that include e-mail, calendaring, Web browsing, file sharing, and printing. These applications use TCP/IP and NetBIOS over TCP (NetBT).

User Communities

Table 10–4 shows a summarized view of the user communities at Klamath.

Table 10–4   Klamath User Communities

User Community Name	Size of Community (Number of Users)	Location(s) of Community	Application(s) Used by Community
Headquarters	350	Portland	All
Office paper manufacturing and sales	200	Seattle	All
Newsprint, cartons, and boxes manufacturing and sales	250	Spokane	All
Wood pulp and chemicals manufacturing and sales	150	Boise	All
Other smaller manufacturing and sales offices	25–75	Western U.S.	All

Data Stores (Servers)

Table 10–5 shows the data stores that were identified at Klamath.

Table 10–5   Klamath Data Stores

Data Store	Location	Application(s)	Used by User Community (or Communities)
Mainframe	Portland	Manufacturing Support System	All manufacturing sites
UNIX file servers	Two in Portland	Financial modeling	Finance departments in Portland, Seattle, Spokane, and Boise
Novell servers	Portland, Seattle, Spokane, Boise	Sales order-entry and tracking system	All sales sites
AppleShare servers	Portland, Seattle, Spokane, Boise	Graphics production	Graphics departments in Portland, Seattle, Spokane, and Boise
Video server (new)	Portland	Distance-learning	All

The Current Network

The current WAN consists of dedicated 64-Kbps data circuits that connect the 15 sites in a partial-mesh topology. Voice traffic is carried on separate 64-Kbps circuits. A WAN service provider leases the 64-Kbps lines to Klamath and also provides Internet access via a T1 circuit that connects a router at the Portland headquarters to a router at the provider's site. The router at the Portland headquarters acts as a packet-filtering firewall.

The core of the data network is a full-mesh of 64-Kbps circuits that connect the major sites, as shown in Figure 10–8. A router at each site connects Ethernet LANs to the WAN. The router in Portland is equipped with a Channel Interface Processor (CIP) that connects to the mainframe. The router encapsulates SNA traffic in TCP/IP for traversal across the WAN.

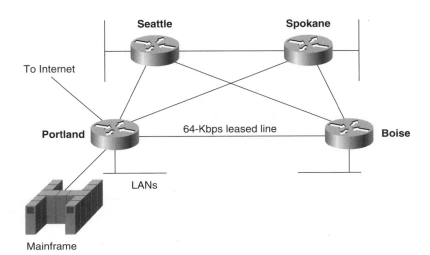

Seattle   Spokane

To Internet

Portland   64-Kbps leased line   Boise

LANs

Mainframe

Figure 10–8
*The existing
core WAN at
Klamath.*

Traffic Characteristics of the Existing WAN

As Klamath has grown over the years, network performance has degraded. Users report that the network is slow, especially during the busiest hour between 10 and 11 am. Users of the SNA manufacturing support system report that it sometimes takes two or three minutes for their screens to unlock after they enter information. Users of the Novell sales order-entry system and the TCP/IP financial modeling applications also report slow response times.

A WAN protocol analyzer was used at each of the major sites to measure current bandwidth usage on the 64-Kbps data circuits. It was determined that every circuit in Portland was approaching saturation, with an average utilization of 80 percent in a 10-minute window. WAN circuits between Seattle and Spokane, Spokane and Boise, and Boise and Seattle were also heavily used, with an average utilization in a 10-minute window of 70 percent.

Bandwidth utilization by protocol was also measured and is documented in Table 10–6. Table 10–6 is based on Table 3–3 in Chapter 3, "Characterizing the Existing Internetwork." *Relative usage* specifies how much of the bandwidth is used by the protocol in comparison to the total bandwidth currently in use. *Absolute usage* specifies how much of the actual capacity (64 Kbps) is used by the protocol.

Table 10–6 shows the results for the most heavily used Portland circuit. Though Net-BIOS and SNA traffic are carried inside TCP/IP packets, those protocols are categorized separately from the other TCP/IP applications, for example the e-mail and Web browsing applications.

Table 10–6   Bandwidth Utilization by Protocol

	Relative Network Broadcast/ Utilization	Absolute Network Utilization	Multicast Rate
IP	30 percent	15 Kbps	.5 Kbps
IPX	25 percent	13 Kbps	.7 Kbps
AppleTalk	8 percent	4 Kbps	.7 Kbps
NetBIOS	15 percent	8 Kbps	.6 Kbps
SNA	20 percent	10 Kbps	.3 Kbps
Other	2 percent	1 Kbps	.4 Kbps

The following conclusions were made regarding protocol and traffic characteristics:

- No single protocol was causing any serious problems.

- Although there were quite a few retransmissions, no applications appeared to retransmit too quickly.

- Applications appeared to have been optimized to use large frame sizes and large window sizes.

- Broadcast traffic accounted for about 5 percent of the network utilization and appeared to be normal routing and service-advertising protocol packets.

- The average error rate for the circuits was one CRC error per two million bytes of data (which is acceptable).

The status of the routers in the core of the network was also checked. The following Cisco Internetwork Operating System (IOS) commands, which were discussed in Chapter 3, "Characterizing the Existing Internetwork," were used to check the routers:

- The `show` `processes` command indicated no problems with CPU over-utilization.

- The `show buffers` command indicated no problems with buffers.

- The `show interfaces` command indicated that the routers were dropping frames from the output queue of the serial WAN ports at a rate of about 1 in 20 frames, or 5 percent. This appeared to be caused by too much network traffic destined for the 64-Kbps circuits, and was considered a problem.

The end result of the analysis of the existing core WAN was that the core WAN was congested due to too much traffic caused by normal application behavior.

The WAN Design for Klamath Paper Products

A decision table was used as part of the design process for Klamath. Klamath's major goals were consolidated and critical goals were placed at the top of the table, as shown in Table 10–7. Potential options were placed in the left-most column and evaluated on whether they met a critical goal.

NOTES

If all options had met all critical goals, then other goals could have been listed also to further the decision-making process. Options could have been evaluated on how well they met non-critical goals on a scale from 1 to 10, as shown in Table 7–1, "Example Decision Table." However, in the case of Klamath, it was not necessary to go beyond evaluating how well options met critical goals.

After analyzing business and technical goals, characterizing the existing core WAN, and analyzing the options available from the WAN service providers in the area, it was decided to update the WAN architecture to DS-1 (1.544 Mbps) leased lines and to use ATM to benefit from the QoS features of ATM.

Table 10–7   WAN Technologies Decision Table

	Critical Goals for the WAN Technology				
	Must have the capacity and QoS capabilities to support video training without disrupting SNA performance	Must use currently available technologies from WAN service providers in the region	Response time must be 1/10 of a second or less for interactive applications	Availability must be 99.98 percent or above	The long-term costs for operating the WAN must be contained
Add more 64-Kbps leased lines		X	X	X	
SONET	X		X	X	
SMDS			X	X	
Frame Relay		X		X	X
ATM	X	X	X	X	X

The two main contenders, besides ATM, were SONET and Frame Relay. SONET was ruled out because it was not yet available in all the cities in the core of Klamath's network. Frame Relay was seriously considered, but ATM was selected instead of Frame Relay because ATM was specifically designed to handle environments with diverse applications, such as the delay-sensitive video-conferencing and interactive manufacturing-support and financial-modeling applications at Klamath.

NOTES

With such optimization techniques as those covered in Chapter 12, "Optimizing Your Network Design," Frame Relay could probably meet Klamath's QoS goals. However, ATM was selected because it was designed to meet the requirements associated with networks that run both video and mission-critical data applications.

The current WAN service provider that leases the existing 64-Kbps circuits was selected as the service provider for the new ATM WAN. The current provider was selected because it offers the following advantages over other providers:

- A proven, albeit short, history of supplying highly-reliable DS-1 ATM services to customers

- Excellent pricing for DS-1 ATM that was comparable in price to the cost of adding numerous 64-Kbps circuits to meet capacity requirements

- The ability to allow Klamath to keep their current IP addressing scheme

- 24-hour support, 7-days a week, with a guaranteed MTTR of one hour

- A single point of contact who is responsible for Klamath's service

Each site will connect to the ATM network via an ATM WAN switch. An ATM switch was selected that supports a 1.544 or 45-Mbps connection for future scalability. The switch also has two OC-3 fiber connections that connect the router and video-conferencing equipment at each site.

The selected WAN switch can also handle voice traffic. In the future, the PBXs at each site will be connected to the WAN switch and Klamath's separate voice network will be dismantled. All voice, data, and video traffic will traverse the ATM network. This will simplify the topology of the current voice/data network and facilitate manageability. It will also allow Klamath to reduce the costs of operating separate data and voice networks and realize a quick return on the investment for the new WAN switches. Figure 10–9 shows the new core network.

SUMMARY

This chapter continues the discussion of physical network design that was started in the previous chapter. It covers selecting technologies and devices for enterprise network designs, with a focus on the remote-access and WAN components of an enterprise network.

Figure 10–9
*The new core
WAN at
Klamath.*

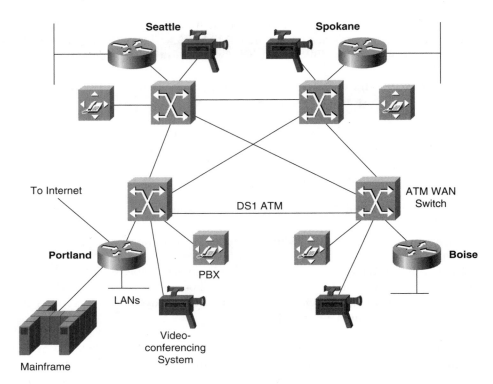

Remote-access technologies include PPP, ISDN, cable modems, and DSL. WAN technologies include the North American Digital Hierarchy, the European E system, SDH, leased lines, SONET, SMDS, Frame Relay, and ATM. There are many selection criteria you can use when choosing remote-access devices, enterprise routers, WAN switches, and a WAN service provider to implement these technologies. These criteria include the types of ports, protocols, and optimization and security features offered by the device or service provider.

The chapter concluded with an example of a WAN network design that was developed for Klamath Paper Products, Inc. To keep the example simple, not all steps of the top-down network design methodology were documented. The example demonstrated the use of the following steps:

- Analyzing requirements, including both business and technical goals

- Identifying existing and future network applications

- Identifying user communities and data stores

- Characterizing the existing network, including the existing topology, bandwidth utilization, bandwidth utilization by protocol, and network performance

- Selecting a WAN technology and service provider based on requirements and goals

SUMMARY FOR PART III

Chapter 10 concludes Part III, "Physical Network Design." Physical design involves the selection of media, technologies, and devices for campus and enterprise networks. A physical design consists of cabling, Layer-1 and Layer-2 protocol implementations, and network devices. The physical design depends on business objectives, technical requirements, traffic characteristics, and traffic flows, which Part I of this book discussed. The physical design builds on the logical design, which Part II discussed.

A network designer has many options for LAN and WAN technology choices for campus and enterprise networks. No single technology or device is the right answer for all circumstances. The goal of Part III was to present characteristics of typical options to help you make the right selections for your particular customer.

Part IV will cover the final steps in designing a network: Testing the network design, optimizing the network design, and documenting the design with a design proposal. Testing and optimizing a network design are two of the most significant steps in a systems-analysis approach to network design. Writing a comprehensive network design proposal that documents how the design fulfills business and technical goals is also a crucial step in the top-down network design methodology.

PART IV

Testing, Optimizing, and Documenting Your Network Design

CHAPTER 11

Testing Your Network Design

Part IV of *Top-Down Network Design* covers the final steps in network design—testing, optimizing, and documenting your design. This chapter discusses testing your design, which is a critical step in a systems-analysis approach to network design. Testing will help you prove to yourself and your network design customer that your solution meets business and technical goals.

The chapter covers using industry tests to predict the performance of network components. It also covers building and testing a prototype system, and using network-management and modeling tools to anticipate the end-to-end performance and quality of service (QoS) that your design will provide. The chapter concludes with an example of a design and testing project for an actual customer, Umqua Systems, Inc.

Testing a network design is a broad subject. This book covers the topic at a high level. Complete books could be written on network design testing. In fact, two recommended books that are relevant to network design testing include Raj Jain's *The Art of Computer Systems Performance Analysis*, and Robert Buchanan's *The Art of Testing Network Systems* (both published by John Wiley & Sons, Inc.).

Notice that both Jain and Buchanan use the word "art" in the titles of their books. Testing a network system, and predicting and measuring its performance, is in many ways an art rather than a science. For one thing, every system is different, so selecting the right testing methods and tools requires creativity, ingenuity, and a thorough understanding of the system to be evaluated. No single methodology or tool is right for every project or for every network designer.

Selecting the right testing procedures and tools depends on your goals for the testing project, which typically include the following:

- Verify that the design meets key business and technical goals.

- Validate LAN and WAN technology and device selections.

- Verify that a service provider provides the agreed-upon service.

- Identify any bottlenecks or connectivity problems.

- Test the redundancy of the network.

- Analyze the effects on performance of network-link failures.

- Determine optimization techniques that will be necessary to meet performance and other technical goals.

- Analyze the effects on performance of upgrading network links or devices ("what-if analysis").

- Prove that your design is better than a competing design (in cases where a customer plans to select one design from proposals provided by multiple vendors or consultants).

- Pass an "acceptance test" that gives you approval to go forward with the network implementation (and possibly get paid for completing the design phase of the project).

- Convince managers and coworkers that your design is effective.

- Identify any risks that might impede implementation, and plan for contingencies.

- Determine how much additional testing might be required. (For example, perhaps you will decide that the new system should first be deployed as a pilot and undergo more testing before being rolled out to all users.)

USING INDUSTRY TESTS

Vendors, independent test labs, and trade journals often publish information on the tests they have completed to verify the features and performance of particular network devices or network design scenarios. Some respected independent testing labs include the following:

- The Network Device Testing Laboratory run by Scott Bradner at Harvard University. Bradner's results are published on many vendors' Web pages, for example, Cisco Systems and 3Com Corporation.

- The Strategic Networks Consulting, Inc., (SNCI) lab. See SNCI's Web site at www.snci.com for more information.

- The Interoperability Lab at the University of New Hampshire (IOL). See IOL's Web site at www.iol.unh.edu for more information.

For simple network designs, sometimes you can rely on test results from vendors, independent labs, or trade journals to prove to your customer that your design will perform as intended. For example, if you have proposed a campus network design based solely on a particular vendor's switching technology, and an independent trade journal has verified the features and performance of the vendor's products, the journal's testing results might adequately convince your customer of the effectiveness of your design. For more complex network designs, you generally should do your own testing in addition to presenting to your customer any independent studies that will help you sell your case.

Test results published by vendors or independent parties, such as trade journals or testing labs, can be informative, but they can also be misleading. For one thing, vendors obviously make every effort to ensure that their products appear to perform better than their competitors' products. Keep in mind that some trade journals and labs are also reluctant to publish negative results about vendors' products because the vendors help pay their bills. (Vendors pay labs to run tests and publish advertisements in trade journals.)

In addition, most tests run by vendors, independent labs, and trade journals are component tests, rather than system tests. Component testing is generally not sufficient to measure the performance of a network design. Furthermore, the test configuration used by the vendor or testing lab almost certainly does not match your actual configuration. This means that the testing results may not be relevant to your particular design.

To understand how network components will behave in your configuration with your applications, network traffic, and unique requirements, building a prototype system or model of the network is usually necessary. The prototype or model will let you go beyond component testing and estimate the performance that the design will offer, including end-to-end delay, throughput, and availability.

BUILDING AND TESTING A PROTOTYPE NETWORK SYSTEM

The goal of this section is to help you itemize the tasks to build a prototype that verifies and demonstrates the behavior of a network system. A secondary goal is to help you determine how much of a network system must be implemented in a prototype to verify the design.

A *prototype* is an initial implementation of a new system that provides a model on which the final implementation will be patterned. A prototype allows a designer to validate the operation and performance of a new system. It should be functional, but does not need to be a full-scale implementation of the new system.

Determining the Scope of a Prototype System

Based on a clear understanding of your customer's goals, you should determine how much of the network system you must implement to convince your customer that the design will meet requirements. Since it is generally not practical to implement a complete, full-scale system, you should isolate which aspects of a network design are most important to your customer. Your prototype should verify important capabilities and functions that are at risk of not performing adequately. Risky functions can include complex, intricate functions, as well as functions where the design was highly influenced by business or technical constraints, and tradeoffs with conflicting goals.

The scope of a network prototype can depend on both technical and non-technical goals. You should pay attention to non-technical factors such as your customer's biases, business style, and history with network projects. For example, perhaps the customer already refused a network design because of its lack of manageability and usability features. The customer might be predisposed to look for these problems in your system. If this is the case, one goal of your prototype should be to develop a demonstration that showcases the manageability and usability benefits of your design.

Your ability to implement a prototype depends on available resources. Resources include people, equipment, money, and time. You should use sufficient resources to produce a valid test without requiring so many resources that the testing causes the project to go over budget, take too much time, or negatively affect network users.

A prototype can be implemented and tested in three different ways:

- As a test network in a lab

- Integrated into a production network but tested during off-hours

- Integrated into a production network and tested during normal business hours

It is a good idea to implement at least part of a prototype system on a test network before implementing it on a production network. This will allow you to work out bugs without impacting the productivity of workers who depend on the network. A test network can also help you evaluate products to determine if they perform as advertised, develop initial device configurations, and model the predicted performance and QoS that the fully-implemented network will provide. You can also use a test network to demonstrate your design and selected products to a customer.

Once a design has been accepted on a provisional basis, it is important to test an initial implementation of the design on a production network to identify possible bottlenecks or other problems. Initial tests can be done during off-hours to minimize possible problems, but final testing should be done during normal business hours to evaluate performance during normal load.

A few key tips to keep in mind when planning a "live" test are as follows:

- Warn users in advance about the timing of tests so they can expect some performance degradation, but ask the users to work as they typically do to avoid invalidating the test by abnormal behavior.

- Warn network administrators and other designers in advance to avoid the possibility that they could be running tests at the same time.

- Warn network managers in advance so they are not confused by unexpected alarms on network-management consoles, and so they can account for the testing when documenting baseline (normal) traffic load and availability statistics.

- If possible, run multiple, short (less than two-minute) tests to minimize user impact and lessen the effects on baseline measurements.

- Run tests that start with a small change and then incrementally increase the change.

- Monitor the results of tests and discontinue them when the objectives of the test are met, or if the production network is severely impacted or fails.

Writing a Test Plan for the Prototype System

Once you have decided on the scope of your prototype, you should write a plan that describes how you will test the prototype. The test plan should include each of the following topics, which the next few sections of this chapter describe in more detail:

- Test objectives and acceptance criteria

- The types of tests that will be run

- Network equipment and other resources required

- Testing scripts

- The timeline and milestones for the testing project

Developing Test Objectives and Acceptance Criteria

The first and most important step in writing a test plan is to list the objectives of the test(s). The objectives should be specific and concrete, and should include information on determining whether the test passed or failed. The following are some examples of specific objectives and acceptance criteria that were written for a particular customer:

- Measure the response time for Application XYZ during peak usage hours (between 10 and 11 a.m.). The acceptance criterion, per the network design proposal, is that the response time must be 1/2 a second or less.

- Measure the throughput for Application XYZ during peak usage hours (between 10 and 11 a.m.). The acceptance criterion, per the network design proposal, is that the throughput must be at least 2 Mbps.

- Measure the amount of time it takes for a user of the new Voice over IP (VoIP) system to hear a dial tone after picking up the telephone handset. The acceptance criterion is that the amount of time must be less than or equal to the amount of time for a user of the Private Branch Exchange (PBX) corporate telephone system.

Objectives and acceptance criteria should be based on a customer's business and technical goals for the network design, but may be more formally or specifically defined. The criteria for declaring that a test passed or failed must be clear and agreed upon by the tester and the customer. You should avoid a common problem where the test is completed, the testers and customers agree on the results, but disagree on the interpretation of the results.

Despite the fact that the underlying goal of your prototype might be to show that your system is better than a competitor's, you should avoid incorporating biases or preconceived notions about outcomes into test objectives (and test scripts). The test objective should simply be to measure the outcome, not prove that the outcome is in your favor.

Objectives and acceptance criteria can be based on a baseline measurement for the current network. For example, an objective might be to measure the collision rate on Ethernet Segment XYZ and compare the results to a baseline measurement. The acceptance criterion might be that there must be 20 percent fewer collisions than there are today. To be able to determine whether the criterion has been met, a baseline measurement must exist, as was discussed in Chapter 3, "Characterizing the Existing Internetwork." Chapter 3 also includes a Network-Health Checklist that can help you write objectives and acceptance criteria.

Determining the Types of Tests to Run

In general, tests should include performance, stress, and failure analyses. Performance analysis should examine the level of service that the system offers in terms of throughput, delay, delay variation, response time, and efficiency. Stress analysis should examine any degradation of service due to increased offered load on the network. Failure analysis should calculate network availability and accuracy, and analyze the causes of any network outages. Depending on a customer's business and technical goals, other tests that might be necessary are manageability, usability, adaptability, and security tests.

The specific types of tests to run against your particular prototype depend on the test objectives. Typical tests include the following:

- **Application response-time testing.** This type of test measures performance from a user's point of view and evaluates how much time a user must wait when executing typical operations that cause network activity. These operations include starting the application, switching between screens within the application, and file opens, reads, writes, searches, and closes. With this type of testing, the tester watches actual users or simulates user behavior with a simulation tool. The test should start with a predetermined number of users and then gradually increase the number of users to analyze any increases in response time due to additional load on the network or servers.

- **Throughput testing.** This type of test measures throughput for a particular application and/or throughput for multiple applications in Kilobytes or Megabytes per second. It can also measure throughput in terms of packets per second through a switching device (for example, a switch or router). As was the case with response-time testing, the test should begin with a number of users that is gradually increased.

- **Availability testing.** With availability testing, tests are run against the prototype system for 24 to 72 hours, under medium to heavy load. The rate of errors and failures are monitored.

- **Regression testing.** Regression testing makes sure the new system doesn't break any applications that were known to work and perform to a certain level before the new system was installed. Regression testing does not test new features or upgrades; instead, it focuses on existing applications. Regression testing should be comprehensive, and is usually automated to facilitate comprehensiveness.

Documenting the Network Equipment and Other Resources

A test plan should include a network topology drawing and a list of devices that will be required. The topology drawing should include major devices, addresses and names, network links, and some indication of the capacity of links. The topology drawing should also document any WAN or LAN links that must connect to the production network or to the Internet.

The list of devices should include hubs, switches, routers, workstations, servers, telephone-equipment simulators, modems, modem eliminators, cables, and so on. The list should document version numbers for hardware and software, and availability information. (Sometimes testing requires new equipment that might not be available yet, or equipment that for other reasons has a long lead time for procurement. If this is the case, it should be noted in the test plan.)

In addition to network equipment, a test plan should include a list of required testing tools. The "Tools for Testing a Network Design" section later in this chapter describes useful tools for testing a network design. Typical tools include network-management and monitoring tools, modeling and simulation tools, and QoS and service-level management tools.

The test plan should also list any applications that will increase testing efficiency, for example software distribution applications or remote-control programs that facilitate the configuring and reconfiguring of nodes during a test.

NOTES

In a Microsoft Windows environment, if your testing requires loading new software applications or versions on multiple systems, Microsoft's Systems Management Server (SMS) software can be a useful addition to the testing environment.

The test plan should document any other resources you will need, including the following:

- Scheduled time in a lab either at your site or the customer's site

- Help from coworkers or customer staff

- Help from users to test applications

- Network addresses and names

Writing Test Scripts

For each test you will run, write a test script that lists the steps to be taken to fulfill the test objective. The test script should identify which tool is used for each step, how the tool is used to make relevant measurements, and what information should be logged during the testing. The script should define initial values for parameters and how to vary those parameters during the testing procedure. (For example, the test script might include an initial traffic-load value and incremental increases for the load.)

Following is an example of a simple test script for the network-test environment shown in Figure 11–1.

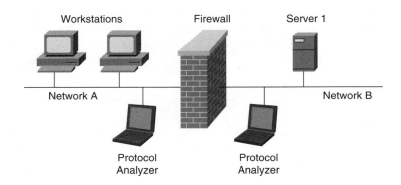

Figure 11–1
The test environment for the example test script.

Test objective: Assess the firewall's ability to block Application ABC traffic, during both light and moderately-heavy load conditions

Acceptance criterion: The firewall should block the TCP SYN request from every workstation on Network A that attempts to set up an Application-ABC session with Server 1 on Network B. The firewall should send each workstation a TCP RST (reset) packet.

Testing steps:

1. Start capturing network traffic on the protocol analyzer on Network A.

2. Start capturing network traffic on the protocol analyzer on Network B.

3. Run Application ABC on a workstation located on Network A and access Server 1 on Network B.

4. Stop capturing network traffic on the protocol analyzers.

5. Display data on Network A's protocol analyzer and verify that the analyzer captured a TCP SYN packet from the workstation. Verify that the network-layer destination address is Server 1 on Network B, and the destination port is port 1234 (the port number for Application ABC). Verify that the firewall responded to the workstation with a TCP RST packet.

6. Display data on Network B's protocol analyzer and verify that the analyzer did not capture any Application-ABC traffic from the workstation.

7. Log the results of the test in the project log file.

8. Save the protocol analyzer trace files to the project trace-file directory.

9. Gradually increase the workload on the firewall, by increasing the number of workstations on Network A one at a time, until 50 workstations are running Application ABC and attempting to reach Server 1. Repeat steps 1 through 8 after each workstation is added to the test.

Documenting the Project Timeline

For complex testing projects, the test plan should document the project timeline, including the start and finish date for the project, and major milestones. The timeline should list major tasks and the person who has been assigned to each task. The following list shows typical tasks, including some tasks that should have already been completed by the time the test plan is written:

- Write test objectives and acceptance criteria

- Design the network topology for the testing environment

- Determine what networking hardware and software will be necessary

- Place a purchase order for the hardware and software if necessary

- Determine which testing tools will be necessary

- Place a purchase order for the testing tools if necessary

- Determine other resources that will be necessary and arrange for their availability

- Write test scripts

- Install and configure hardware and software

- Start testing

- Log the results of the testing

- Review and analyze the results

- Reduce results data (if necessary)

- Present results to the customer

- Archive results

Implementing the Test Plan

Implementing the test plan is mostly a matter of following the test scripts and documenting your work. You should realize, however, that sometimes test scripts cannot be followed precisely, because it is difficult to consider all contingencies and potential problems when writing a script. For this reason, it is important to maintain logs, either electronically or in a paper notebook. (An electronic log is preferable because it enables easier searching for information in the log.)

In addition to keeping a log that documents collected test data and test results, it is a good idea to keep a daily activity log that documents progress and any changes that were necessary to the test scripts or equipment configurations. The daily activity log can also record any problems that were encountered and theories about what caused the problems. These theories might be helpful later when analyzing results (and they might help with future testing projects).

TOOLS FOR TESTING A NETWORK DESIGN

This section discusses the types of tools that can be used to test a network design. The section also recommends some specific tools.

In general, the types of tools you can use to test your network design include the following:

- Network-management and monitoring tools

- Modeling and simulation tools

- QoS and service-level management tools

Network-management and monitoring tools are usually used in a production environment to alert network managers to problems and significant network events, but they are also helpful when testing a network design. Network-management applications, such as the CiscoWorks offerings from Cisco Systems or HP OpenView from Hewlett-Packard, can alert you to problems on your test network. These types of tools usually run on a dedicated network-management station (NMS).

Network-management and monitoring software can also include applications that reside on network devices. For example, some network operating systems include software that monitors server CPU and memory usage, which can be useful when isolating performance problems in a new network design. As another example, many Cisco Internetwork Operating System (IOS) commands are useful tools for checking the performance of Cisco routers and switches in a test environment.

You can also use a protocol analyzer to monitor a new design. A *protocol analyzer* can help you analyze traffic behavior, errors, utilization, efficiency, and the rate of broadcast and multicast packets. You also can use a protocol analyzer to generate traffic. If it is impractical to purchase, install, and configure all the devices required to develop a large-scale prototype, you can purchase a subset of the devices and generate traffic to induce the load that would be present if all the devices were installed. This will give you an approximation of the behavior of the new system.

For a more sophisticated model of the new network system, you can use modeling and simulation tools. *Simulation* is the process of using software and mathematical models to analyze the behavior of a network without requiring an actual network. A *simulation tool* lets you develop a model of a network, estimate the performance of the network, and compare alternatives for implementing the network. A simulation tool is often preferable to implementing and measuring an extensive prototype system because it allows alternatives to be more easily compared.

A good simulation tool requires that the developers of the tool understand computer networking in addition to statistical analysis and modeling techniques. Because a complete simulation of a system would require the simulator to be more powerful than the sum of the components it is modeling, a sophisticated simulation tool allows the development of a model that factors in only those aspects of the network that have a significant impact on performance. Developing good simulation tools is an art.

Effective simulation tools include device libraries that model the behavior of major networking devices, for example, switches and routers. Because the performance limitations of switches and routers often arise from the way processes, buffers, and queues are implemented, switch and router models should take into account the architecture of the device.

Modeling switch and router behavior can be challenging, however, because every vendor has numerous optimization techniques and configuration options. One solution to this problem is that a simulation tool can incorporate measurements of actual network traffic, rather than relying solely on device libraries that model theoretical device behavior. This approach not only solves the problem of modeling complex devices, but also allows the tool to calibrate assumptions made about traffic load and characteristics. There is less reliance on the network designer to accurately predict traffic load, and more reliance on real measurements.

Most modeling and simulation tools on the market today base their results on user inputs about traffic characteristics and rudimentary queuing theory, rather than a measurement of actual traffic behavior. This will probably change as companies such as NetPredict lead the way in marketing new, sophisticated tools that allow a model to be calibrated (made more accurate) by the use of actual protocol-analyzer and network-management data.

Service-level management tools are an emerging type of tool that analyze end-to-end performance for network applications. NetPredictor from NetPredict, Inc. is a QoS and service-level management tool. Some tools, such as tools from VitalSigns Software, monitor real-time application performance. Other tools, such as tools from Optimal Networks, predict the performance of new applications before they are deployed. NetPredictor combines the capabilities of monitoring and prediction. NetPredictor is described in more detail in the next section.

Specific Tools for Testing a Network Design

This section recommends some specific tools that can be used to test your network design. In addition to the tools listed here you can also use many of the tools discussed in Chapter 3, "Characterizing the Existing Internetwork," and Chapter 8, "Developing Network Security and Network Management Strategies."

CiscoWorks Blue Internetwork Performance Monitor

Chapter 3 mentioned the CiscoWorks Blue Internetwork Performance Monitor, which is a network-management tool that locates bottlenecks, measures response time, and diagnoses latency problems. Working with features of the Cisco IOS software, the Internetwork Performance Monitor can identify the possible paths between two devices and display the performance for each of the hops in the paths.

The Internetwork Performance Monitor is particularly useful for testing performance in environments where Systems Network Architecture (SNA) traffic is transported over IP through a routed network to a Cisco Channel Interface Processor (CIP) or a front-end processor (FEP).

The Internetwork Performance Monitor has three components:

- Software processes in the Cisco IOS software that perform response-time measurements

- A graphical application that runs on an NMS and collects and stores data in various industry-standard relational database formats

- Software that runs on a mainframe that allows for response-time measurements from a router in the network to the mainframe

Cisco's Netsys Tools

Chapter 3 also mentioned the Cisco Netsys Service-Level Management Suite, which is a network-management tool that enables defining, monitoring, and assessing network connectivity, security, and performance.

The Netsys suite consists of four modules:

- The Netsys Connectivity Service Manager monitors network configuration data and verifies the availability of key network services.

- The Netsys Performance Service Manager lets you specify, analyze, and optimize network performance. This module supports modeling routing and traffic flow so you can analyze topologies, routing parameters, router configurations, and Cisco IOS software features.

- The Netsys LAN Service Manager complements the Connectivity Service Manager by adding LAN switching topology-viewing and diagnostic capabilities.

- The Netsys WAN Service Manager adds integrated WAN switching analysis and troubleshooting capabilities. It analyzes traffic to determine how your WAN is really being used, in comparison to the estimated loads it was designed to support. It also lets you analyze what-if scenarios to determine the effect of configuration changes and the behavior of the WAN when link problems are occurring.

Cisco's StrataSphere Modeling and Optimization Tools

Cisco Systems also offers WAN network-modeling tools as part of its StrataSphere Network-Management product suite. The StrataSphere Modeler supports basic network design and configuration verification. The StrataSphere Optimizer, used with

WANDL's *Network Planning and Analysis Tools (NPAT)*, which is described in the following section, provides an extended design and analysis capability for switched WANs.

WANDL's Network-Planning and Analysis Tools

WANDL, Inc., developed the NPAT software suite to help customers handle the design, planning, and management of large-scale WANs. WANDL's customers, who include carriers, Fortune 500 companies, and government organizations, use NPAT to plan and analyze networks ranging in size from 30 to more than 300 backbone nodes.

The WANDL tools support capacity planning, network testing, and optimization. They allow a user to test the redundancy of a network and analyze the effects of network outages. They facilitate analyzing alternatives for WAN technologies with sophisticated what-if-analysis tools. A unique feature of the WANDL tools is the ability to estimate monthly tariff charges for WAN circuits.

CACI Products

CACI COMNET III is a network simulation tool from CACI Products Company that provides an object-oriented approach to building a network model. Users graphically describe their proposed network and access animations and reports that show predicted LAN and WAN network performance. CACI COMNET III allows the user to experiment with diverse network alternatives before selecting an actual network design and network products.

Add-on modules for COMNET III, such as the Application Profiler, the Circuit-Switched Module, and the Satellite and Mobile Module, let users plan the roll out of new applications and technologies, including wireless networks.

COMNET Predictor works with COMNET III to allow a user to more quickly experiment with network upgrades before implementing them. Predictor lets the user import baseline data from network management and traffic-monitoring tools, and then specify the proposed test scenario. COMNET Predictor generates reports and charts illustrating how the proposed changes will affect network performance and where bottlenecks may appear. Predictor measures delay and utilization, and supports exporting data to COMNET III for detailed reports.

Make Systems' NetMaker XA

NetMaker XA from Make Systems is a well-respected suite of tools for network planning, analysis, and testing. Network designers of both small networks and large enterprise and carrier-class networks use NetMaker XA to inventory network devices and configurations, analyze applications and network traffic patterns, and evaluate tariff options.

NetMaker XA includes the following modules:

- *Visualizer* lets you discover and view your current network, and then edit information about the objects on your network.

- *Planner* lets you model what-if scenarios (such as changing the topology or capacity, or adding new users, applications, or devices). Planner supports plug-in device libraries.

- *Designer* supports building network diagrams and models, examining alternatives, and predicting network performance.

- *Interpreter* extracts and organizes information about traffic patterns, and facilitates incorporating data from protocol analyzers and other monitoring tools.

- *Analyzer* enables testing network reliability and disaster-recovery planning.

- *Accountant* helps you analyze the cost of various design options, and includes a tariff database.

NetPredict's NetPredictor

NetPredictor is a sophisticated service-level management tool that predicts and monitors the QoS provided by a network. NetPredictor analyzes the inter-related effects on network applications of end-to-end latency, load, and packet loss. It bases its analysis on a model of the network that is automatically calibrated by actual network-management and protocol-analyzer data.

NetPredictor facilitates the following design tasks:

- Determining what network and server resources are needed to deliver a required QoS level

- Predicting end-to-end performance prior to deploying new applications or technologies

- Developing service-level agreements (SLAs) based on verifiable performance predictions

- Monitoring actual performance and comparing it with expectations or SLAs

NetPredictor lets you model an existing network and then simulate replacing existing devices with other network components to determine how performance will change. The model can be based on knowledge about the network and applications that you input, and information from the device library. The model automatically adapts to data that NetPredictor captures from the actual network.

Model-adaptation approaches have been used extensively in many other industries, for example, the chemical-processing and aerospace industries. NetPredictor is the first product based on a model-adaptation approach for network management. The following example demonstrates how NetPredictor was used in an actual network design and testing scenario.

AN EXAMPLE OF A NETWORK DESIGN TESTING SCENARIO

This section discusses a network design and testing project that was completed for Umqua Systems, Inc., using some of the design steps described in this book and chapter. The example is based on a real network, but the name of the company has been changed, and some facts have been obscured to protect the privacy of the company.

Background Information for the Design and Testing Project at Umqua Systems, Inc.

Umqua Systems designs and manufactures specialized integrated circuits for the consumer electronics and digital-office markets. The design project for Umqua focused on the campus network that connects three buildings in close range to each other and one building about three miles away. The campus network connects approximately 400 engineering, sales, marketing, and finance employees.

Goals for the Design and Testing Project

Umqua had two main goals for the design and testing project:

- Determine the load and performance of the current network, with a focus on the FDDI backbone.

- Determine what will happen to network performance if 10 to 20 people run a new order-entry application based on database technology from Oracle Corporation.

Before this project was completed, Umqua network managers had little knowledge about the performance characteristics of their network. Due to a lack of understanding of the current network traffic, they were not able to plan and make proactive decisions to the extent that they wanted. Although the managers have good network-management tools, including HP OpenView, they primarily use the tools as a means of generating alarms when network nodes fail. They do not use the tools as a source of information about traffic distribution in the network.

This project focused on analyzing the current network traffic load and performance characteristics, and answered the question of whether the network has enough capacity to handle the new Oracle order-entry application.

Network Applications

The network applications currently in use on Umqua's campus network consist of typical office applications (such as e-mail, file sharing, and printing) and a computer-aided design (CAD) application for designing integrated circuits. The engineers who use the CAD system have two computers on their desks: a Windows 95 PC for office work and a Sun workstation that runs the CAD application. Other users have just a Windows 95 PC.

The analysis of current traffic concentrated on usage patterns for the CAD application. According to users, when small changes are made to an integrated circuit design, the changes are made to the CAD files that reside on the main file server in Building 1. When major edits are required, the files are transferred across the network to the engineer's local Sun workstation. These file transfers create a substantial portion of the workday traffic on the network. The files range in size from 1 to 20 Mbytes.

A file-synchronization process is run every night to ensure that all distributed versions of a CAD file are up-to-date. This application uses the UNIX rshell facility to check file modification dates and transfer files.

When checking dates, the rshell TCP packets are generally 64-72 bytes long. When transferring files, the rshell TCP packets carry 512 data bytes. (With headers, the packet size is 566 bytes.) Increasing the maximum TCP segment size to improve efficiency for these file transfers was discussed with Umqua, but they were reluctant to make a change for fear of breaking the elaborate synchronization system.

The analysis of applications also focused on the new Oracle order-entry system that will be used by ten to twenty employees in Building 4 to enter orders, process returned merchandise, and query order status using the structured-query language (SQL). Currently, these operations are handled via e-mail and paper forms. In the new system, blank forms are stored on a Novell server in Building 1. Order and return information is stored in a customized Oracle database that resides on another file server in Building 1.

The Current Network

The campus network at Umqua Systems consists of an FDDI backbone that connects Buildings 1 through 3, and two parallel DS-1 1.544 Mbps fiber-optic links that connect Buildings 4 and 1. Buildings 1 through 3 are separated by about 100 meters each, and Building 4 is about three miles away.

Access to other offices in the United States and Asia is through a channelized T1 link. Domestic offices are reached via a 64-Kbps Frame-Relay channel. A 128-Kbps dedicated channel reaches overseas locations. Internet access for the four local offices is through a separate 64-Kbps link in Building 2.

The Sun workstations used for the CAD application are mostly connected to 100BaseT Ethernet segments. The PCs are mostly connected to 10BaseT segments. All major file servers are on the FDDI backbone, including the Novell and Oracle database servers for the new order-entry system. Figure 11–2 shows the essential features of Umqua's network.

Figure 11–2
*The campus
network at
Umqua Sys-
tems, Inc.*

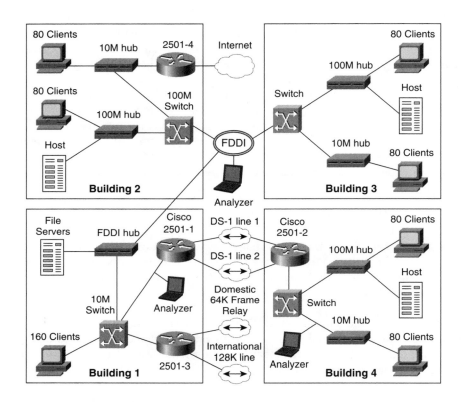

Testing Methods Used

A short test plan was written that documents the test objectives, acceptance criteria, testing equipment, and planned testing steps. NetPredict's NetPredictor tool was selected as the primary testing tool because it was uniquely able to meet the distinct objectives of measuring existing network performance and predicting performance when the new Oracle order-entry application is added.

A model of traffic load on the networks at Umqua was derived by talking to Umqua's network managers. The model was calibrated by measuring and examining actual traffic data. Table 11–1 shows the calibrated model, which includes estimated hourly average traffic loads. More detailed information about measured data is provided in the "Measured Data" section.

To calibrate the model, protocol-analyzer capabilities in NetPredictor were used to collect data from three network segments. Figure 11–2 shows the locations of the protocol analyzers that were placed on the following segments:

- The FDDI backbone

- A 10-Mbps Ethernet segment in Building 1

- A 10-Mbps Ethernet segment in Building 4

The analyzers collected data from approximately 4:30 p.m. on a Thursday to about 6 p.m. on the next Friday. The analyzers compiled detailed network-traffic statistics in minute-by-minute intervals over a 24-hour period.

The results were used to characterize load, calibrate the model, and study the network behavior of key systems. The analyzers also provided information on frame sizes, buffering techniques, efficiency, and throughput. In addition, the Umqua network managers provided key information about perceived latency, the sizes of files that are transferred across the network, and the configurations of the routers.

Measured Data

This section provides detailed information on the data collected with the analyzers, and some conclusions that were drawn from the data.

Load on the FDDI Backbone Network

Figure 11–3 shows traffic load on the FDDI backbone. Each data point in Figure 11–3 represents the average load for a minute on the FDDI network, as measured from 4:30 p.m. on Thursday to 5:00 p.m. on Friday. Figure 11–3 shows that the load is highest near the end of the workday, and demonstrates that the traffic load at night is quite small, about 2 percent of network utilization.

Table 11-1   Model of load distribution for Umqua Systems, Inc.

Building 2*			
# of client machines	160		
Average accessed file size	20	Mbytes	
Average activity per person	40	Mbytes/hr	
Total load initiated in building	6,400	Mbytes/hr	
Load on 10 Mbps Vs 100 Mbps	10%	90%	
Local load going out of building	67%		
Local 10 Mbps LAN load	640	Mbytes/hr	
Local 100 Mbps LAN load	5,760	Mbytes/hr	
Traffic from other buildings	3,008	Mbytes/hr	
Traffic to Building 1	80%	3,430.4	Mbytes/hr
Traffic to Building 3	20%	857.6	Mbytes/hr
Traffic to Building 4	0%	0	Mbytes/hr
10 Mbps LAN utilization	20.9%		
100 Mbps LAN utilization	18.8%		
Building 1			
# of client machines	160		
Average accessed file size	17	Mbytes	
Average activity per person	34	Mbytes/hr	
Total load initiated in building	5,440	Mbytes/hr	
Load on 10 Mbps Vs 100 Mbps	10%	90%	
Local load going out of building	65%		
Local 10 Mbps LAN load	544	Mbytes/hr	
Local 100 Mbps LAN load	4,896	Mbytes/hr	
Traffic from other buildings	3,540	Mbytes/hr	
Traffic to Building 2	80%	2,828.8	Mbytes/hr
Traffic to Building 3	20%	707.2	Mbytes/hr
Traffic to Building 4	0%	0	Mbytes/hr
10 Mbps LAN Utilization	20.0%		
100 Mbps LAN Utilization	18.0*		

* Note: Numbers in italics are computed numbers

Building 3			
# of client machines	160		
Average accessed file size	1	Mbytes	
Average activity per person	2	Mbytes/hr	
Total load initiated in building	320	Mbytes/hr	
Local load going out of building	80%		
Local 10 Mbps LAN load	320	Mbytes/hr	
Traffic from other buildings	1570	Mbytes/hr	
Traffic to Building 1	60%	153.6	Mbytes/hr
Traffic to Building 2	35%	89.6	Mbytes/hr
Traffic to Building 4	5%	12.8	Mbytes/hr
Assume two 10 Mbps LANs:			
Load on each 10 Mbps LAN	21.0%		
Building 4			
# of client machines	160		
Average accessed file size	2	Mbytes	
Average activity per person	4	Mbytes/hr	
Total load initiated in building	640	Mbytes/hr	
Load on 10 Mbps Vs 100 Mbps	15%	85%	
Local load going out of building	8%		
Local 10 Mbps LAN load	88.32	Mbytes/hr	
Local 100 Mbps LAN load	500.48	Mbytes/hr	
Traffic from other buildings	13	Mbytes/hr	
Traffic to Building 1	50%	25.6	Mbytes/hr
Traffic to Building 2	40%	20.48	Mbytes/hr
Traffic to Building 3	10%	5.12	Mbytes/hr
	Predicted	Measured	
10 Mbps LAN Utilization	2.0%	2.0%	
100 Mbps LAN Utilization	1.1%		
100 Mbps FDDI	18.0%	18.0%	
DS-1 Lines	4.6%	4.32%	

Figure 11–3
Load on the FDDI backbone as a percent of capacity in minute intervals.

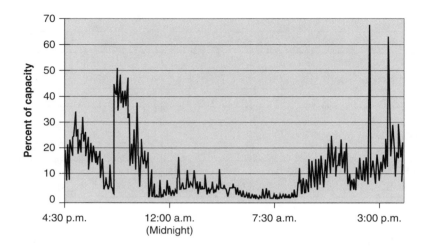

Figure 11–4 shows a *load-duration curve* that graphs the probability of a certain load occurring. The figure shows the distribution of the minute-by-minute average loads between 4 p.m. and 5 p.m. on Friday. The average load during this time was 15 to 20 percent of capacity; however, about 5 percent of the load data were above 25 percent. The NetPredictor software uses the load-duration curve to predict the probability of load and peak-load values for future conditions.

By analyzing detailed traffic-load data, it was discovered that network utilization on the FDDI network frequently reaches 100 percent when measured in 0.01-second intervals. Comparing minute averages to 0.01-second averages resulted in a peak-to-average ratio of about 20, which is a potential problem. When the average utilization in a minute interval is 15 percent, for example, it is possible the offered load to the network in 0.01-second intervals is 300 percent of capacity, which could cause noticeable delays for users.

The preliminary conclusion, however, is that there are no major adverse effects due to the FDDI network frequently reaching capacity for brief periods of time. This was confirmed by the lack of users complaining about performance on the network. However, further analysis should be done to determine the cause of the peaks and their potential for producing performance problems. NetPredictor has a peak-to-average representation of traffic burstiness to facilitate such analyses.

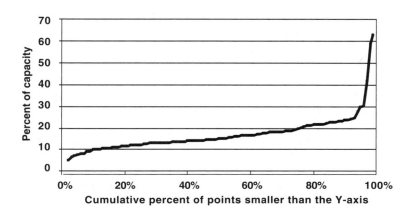

Figure 11–4
Load duration between 4 p.m. and 5 p.m. on the FDDI network.

Load on the DS-1 Circuits

As shown in Figure 11–5, traffic through the DS-1 lines was generally light, except for the nightly file synchronization that started around midnight and lasted about four hours.

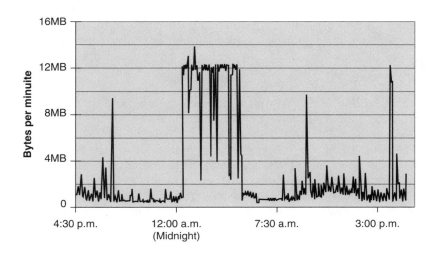

Figure 11–5
Load in bytes per minute in Building 1 near the router that connects to Building 4.

During normal work hours, the two DS-1 links appear to be below 10 percent capacity 90 percent of the time. Figure 11–5 shows that the DS-1 links are saturated, however, during the nightly file synchronization.

Based on link-performance data in NetPredictor, it was estimated that one DS-1 line can transfer about 9MB of data per minute, using TCP. Considering that Umqua has two DS-1 lines, this should have been sufficient. However, it was discovered that all the file-synchronization traffic was flowing across one of the DS-1 links. Load-balancing was not occurring for the IP traffic associated with the rshell TCP/IP file-synchronization application as expected.

It was determined that the router in Building 4 defaulted to *fast-switching* mode, which does not load balance when the IP destination address is always the same (which it was in this case). With fast switching, once the router learns which of its ports to use for a destination address, it always uses that port. Load balancing occurs for different destinations, but not for traffic destined for the same device. (The "Conclusions" section near the end of the chapter discusses this problem in more detail.)

Analysis of the New Order-Entry System

In an attempt to estimate the consequences of adding 10 users in Building 4 who will use the new Oracle order-entry system to access a database in Building 1, packet traces were collected during normal work hours for one Oracle user. From the captured data, it can be estimated that a typical order entry causes approximately 2MB of data traffic, broken down as follows:

- About 220KB of TCP/IP traffic between the user and the Oracle database server in Building 1 on the FDDI backbone.

- About 1.7MB of NetWare traffic between the user and the NetWare server in Building 1 on the FDDI backbone. This traffic consists of loading the application and downloading order-entry forms.

In less than three minutes, a test-user completed one full order-entry task (several screens) at an average network load of under 90 Kbps. This included downloading the application and forms from the NetWare server. The user's PC initially receives more data than it transmits, but once the application has started, traffic to and from the user's PC is more evenly matched.

The estimated traffic for continuous user work, once the application has loaded, is about 40 Kbps. For 10 users, therefore, an additional loading of 400 Kbps can be expected. The Oracle users will be in Building 4, which has both 10-Mbps and 100-Mbps Ethernet. In either case, the percentage of capacity is low—4 percent for 10-Mbps Ethernet, and 0.4 percent for 100-Mbps Ethernet.

Because the servers in Building 1 are on the FDDI backbone, the new application will also affect the LANs in Building 1 and the FDDI backbone, but not significantly. The extra load will have the most effect on the DS-1 lines, where it will increase the average load from 4.1 percent to about 17 percent.

Although the extra load is not expected to cause any noticeable performance problems, it was noted that the application is inefficient. The user's Oracle application currently generates SQL Select requests in clear text to the database server, after loading the requests from the forms server. These Selects are sizeable and add to network traffic twice—when the application starts and reads the Selects from the forms server, and when the Selects are executed. Although this behavior cannot easily be changed for Selects that are part of the standard Oracle order-entry application, it can be changed for the customized parts of the application.

Selects can be compiled into executable calls to the server so only the name of the executable command is read from the forms server and sent to the database server. The database server executes each command by expanding the predefined Selects. This technique (called *stored procedures*) reduces network traffic.

Delay Characteristics for the New Order-Entry System

In addition to understanding the extra load that the Oracle system will put on the network, Umqua was also interested in understanding the end-to-end delay characteristics of the application. Using NetPredictor, the delay when transmitting 5,000 bytes (40 Kbits) from Building 4 to Building 1 was predicted.

Figure 11–6 shows results produced by NetPredictor for the transmission of 5,000 bytes, including the time needed for the file server to respond and the travel time for the associated acknowledgment. As indicated by the leftmost bar in Figure 11–6, the expected total delay is between 64 ms (best performance) and 92 ms during burst conditions. This performance is considered to be more than adequate for productive work.

> **NOTES**
>
> The delay is based on default device-library data that assumes the server can accept a request, process it, and respond in 22 ms for each transaction. If the application turns out to be slow, the server's performance should be checked.

Figure 11–6
Components of delay when transmitting 5,000 bytes from Building 4 to Building 1.

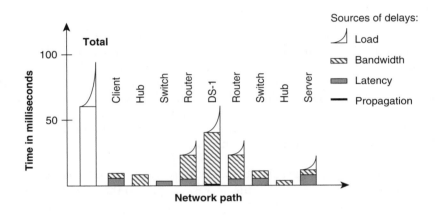

Individual bars in Figure 11–6 show the time each node expends transmitting the packets. The bars are structured to show the sources of delay at those nodes. Dynamic-load components are shaped as cumulative probability distributions, to indicate the probabilistic nature of load behavior. These probabilities are derived from load-duration curves, such as the example presented in Figure 11–4.

Conclusions

Based on the testing and data analysis performed for Umqua, the following conclusions were made:

- The network can easily accommodate 10–20 people in Building 4 using the new Oracle order-entry system, especially if the DS-1 routers between buildings are configured to load balance packet-by-packet, and some efficiency improvement in the SQL requests is made.

- The minute-by-minute average load on the FDDI backbone is currently about 15–20 percent of capacity most of the afternoon. Because of traffic bursts, however, the network frequently reaches full capacity, and the indication is that offered load exceeds capacity for short periods (as mentioned previously in the "Load on the FDDI Backbone Network" section). More analysis is needed to quantify the effects of this problem, but because no adverse effects have been identified so far, Umqua should probably not be concerned.

- The router in Building 4 that is feeding the DS-1 lines to Building 1 does not perform load balancing for IP traffic. Umqua should probably modify the configuration of the router to use process-switching instead of fast-switching (using the `no ip route-cache` command). The tradeoff is that process switching is slower than fast switching, but based on an analysis of traffic that the router must forward, it does not seem that this will be a problem.

- Because traffic is generally light on the DS-1 lines (except during file synchronization), Umqua might want to reconsider having two DS-1 lines to connect Buildings 4 and 1. (During normal work hours, the two DS-1 lines appear to be below 10 percent capacity 90 percent of the time.) If it is not necessary for the nightly file synchronization to complete quickly, Umqua should consider some other, more cost-effective connectivity that will still provide redundancy, for example, a dial-on-demand-routing (DDR) analog or ISDN link.

- No significant end-to-end delays were identified on Umqua's campus network. If some of the applications run over international links, then there may be delay problems for those users. That analysis has not yet been performed.

SUMMARY

Testing your network design is an important step in the design process that allows you to confirm that your design meets business and technical goals. By testing your design, you can verify that the solutions you have developed will provide the performance and QoS that your customer expects.

This chapter presented a systems-analysis approach to testing that includes writing concrete test objectives, verifiable acceptance criteria, test scripts, and test logs. The chapter also provided information on design and testing tools, including tools from Cisco Systems, WANDL, CACI Products Company, Make Systems, and NetPredict.

The chapter concluded with an example of an actual design and testing project completed for Umqua Systems, a manufacturer of specialized integrated circuits. The example demonstrated the value of using a systematic approach that includes measuring and modeling current and future performance characteristics with appropriate techniques and tools.

The next chapter talks about optimization techniques you can use to ensure that your design meets requirements. It is not uncommon during the testing phase to determine that an initial implementation of a design requires some manipulation to meet QoS requirements and other goals, such as scalability, availability, security, manageability, affordability, and so on. Based on the results of your network design testing, you can select and test optimization techniques, such as those described in the next chapter.

CHAPTER 12

Optimizing Your Network Design

Optimization is a critical design step for organizations that use high-bandwidth and delay-sensitive applications. To achieve business goals, these organizations expect their networks to use bandwidth efficiently, to control delay and jitter, and to support preferential service for essential applications. Internetworking vendors, such as Cisco Systems, and standards bodies, such as the Internet Engineering Task Force (IETF), offer numerous options to meet these expectations. This chapter introduces the reader to some of these options.

The chapter starts with a discussion of IP multicast techniques that minimize bandwidth utilization for multimedia applications. The chapter continues with a discussion of methods for optimizing network performance to meet quality of service (QoS) requirements. These methods allow applications to inform routers of their load and latency requirements, and let routers share QoS information amongst themselves and with policy servers.

The section "Cisco Internetwork Operating System Features for Optimizing Network Performance" describes an assortment of optimization techniques offered by Cisco, ranging from simple proxy services to advanced switching, queuing, and traffic shaping techniques. The chapter concludes with a section on Cisco WAN-switching optimization techniques.

OPTIMIZING BANDWIDTH USAGE
WITH IP MULTICAST TECHNOLOGIES

One of the main reasons optimization techniques are required on internetworks is the increasing use of high-bandwidth multiple-user, multimedia applications. Such applications as distance learning, videoconferencing, and collaborative computing have a need to send streams of data to multiple users, without using excessive amounts of bandwidth or causing performance problems on many systems.

The IETF has developed several IP multicast standards that optimize the transmission of multimedia and other types of traffic across an internetwork. The standards identify multicast addressing techniques that avoid the extra traffic caused by many unicast point-to-point or broadcast traffic streams. They also specify how routers learn which network segments should receive multicast streams, and how routers route multicast traffic.

Older multimedia applications that do not use multicast technologies, for instance the distance-learning application discussed in the Wandering Valley Community College example in Chapter 9, send a data stream to every user. Such applications use a unicast point-to-point method of handling multimedia traffic that wastes bandwidth.

An alternative to multiple point-to-point streams is to send a single stream and use a broadcast destination address. The obvious disadvantage with this technique is that the data stream goes to all devices, even devices for which no application is installed to handle the stream. This approach has a negative effect on performance for every device receiving the stream, including workstations, bridges, switches, and routers.

With IP multicast technologies, on the other hand, a single data stream is sent to only those stations that request the stream, thus optimizing bandwidth usage and reducing performance problems on end stations and internetworking devices.

Businesses, universities, and other organizations use IP multicast technologies for many information-dissemination applications, including online training classes, virtual meetings, and electronic newscasts.

In addition, IP multicast technologies are used in computer-simulation applications. An example is simulated military scenarios. Because it is impractical to prepare for large-scale battles with real equipment, some military institutions conduct training exercises with thousands of simulated planes, tanks, troops, weather satellites, and other devices. A plane or tank can register to receive weather and topology information for its current location by joining an IP multicast group for that location. As the plane moves, it leaves and joins new groups. This way the plane can avoid receiving information on the weather and topologies for all areas (which would be overwhelming), and instead receive information relevant only to its current location. This type of application must support multicast addressing and dynamic multicast group membership, which are discussed in the next few sections.

IP Multicast Addressing

IP multicasting transmits IP data to a group of hosts that are identified by a single Class-D IP address. In dotted-decimal notation, host group addresses range from 224.0.0.0 to 239.255.255.255. Network stations recognize an address as being a Class-D address because the first four bits must be 1110 in binary.

A multicast group is also identified by a MAC-layer multicast address. Using a MAC-layer multicast address optimizes network performance by allowing network interface cards (NICs) that are not part of a group to ignore a data stream that is not for them.

The Internet Assigned Numbers Authority (IANA) owns a block of MAC-layer addresses that are used for group multicast addresses. The range of addresses for Ethernet is 01:00:5E:00:00:00–01:00:5E:7F:FF:FF. When a station sends a frame to an IP group that is identified by a Class-D address, the station inserts the low-order 23 bits of the Class-D address into the low-order 23 bits of the MAC-layer destination address. The top 9 bits of the Class-D address are not used. The top 25 bits of the MAC address are 01:00:5E followed by a zero, or, in binary:

> 00000001 00000000 01011110 0

The Internet Group Management Protocol

In addition to defining group addresses, the IETF also defines the *Internet Group Management Protocol (IGMP)*, which allows a host to join a group and inform routers of the need to receive a particular data stream. IP hosts use IGMP to report their multicast group memberships to immediately-neighboring multicast routers.

When a user (or system process) starts an application that requires a host to join a multicast group, the host transmits a `membership-report` message to inform routers on the segment that traffic for the group should be multicast to the host's segment.

Although it is possible that the router is already sending data for the group to the host's segment, the specification states that a host should send a `membership-report` message in case it is the first member of the group on the network segment.

In addition to allowing hosts to join groups, IGMP specifies that a multicast router sends an IGMP query out every interface at regular intervals to see if any hosts belong to the group. A host responds by sending an IGMP `membership-report` message for each group in which it is still a member (based on the applications running on the host).

To lessen bandwidth utilization, hosts set a random timer before responding to queries. If the host sees another host respond for a group to which the host belongs, then the host cancels its response. The router does not need to know how many or which specific hosts on a segment belong to a group. It only needs to recognize that a group has at least one member on a segment, so that it sends traffic to that segment using the IP and MAC multicast addresses for the group.

RFC 2236 defines a new version of IGMP—*IGMPv2*. The main feature of IGMPv2 is the ability for a router to more quickly learn that the last host has left a group, which is important for high-bandwidth multicast groups and subnets with highly volatile group membership. When selecting routers as part of the physical-design phase of the top-down network-design process, you should make sure the routers support IGMPv2 (or will support it in the near future).

In addition to adding support for IGMPv2, vendors are working on supplements to IGMP to support IP multicasting in a switched environment. By default, a data-link-layer switch floods multicast frames out every port. One method to prevent the flooding of unnecessary multicasts is to allow a network administrator to configure filters. A more sophisticated method is to allow a switch to understand IGMP or a variant of it. Cisco Systems, for example, developed the *Cisco Group Management Protocol (CGMP)* to allow switches to participate in the process of determining which segments have hosts in a particular multicast group.

The Institute of Electrical and Electronics Engineers (IEEE) 802.1p standard, which is covered in more detail in the "IEEE 802.1p Specification" section, also defines methods for bridges and switches to dynamically filter multicast traffic to avoid flooding it to all ports.

Multicast Routing Protocols

In addition to determining which local network segments should receive traffic for particular multicast groups, a router must also learn how to route multicast traffic across an internetwork. Multicast routing protocols provide this function.

Multicast routing protocols extend the capabilities of a standard routing protocol, which learns paths to destination networks, to include the capability of learning paths to multicast destination addresses. A network designer currently has several options for multicast routing protocols. The following sections describe some of the most commonly-used options.

Multicast Open Shortest Path First

The *Multicast Open Shortest Path First (MOSPF) protocol*, defined in RFC 1584 and typically used in an OSPF environment, complements OSPF's capability to develop a link-state database that describes a network topology. MOSPF supplements the database with an additional type of link-state record for group memberships.

A router running MOSPF computes a shortest-path tree to all destinations within its area, and then uses advertised group-membership information to "prune" the branches of the tree that do not lead to any group members. This process allows the router to forward multicast packets only to those interfaces that belong to the pruned multicast tree. The end result is the amount of traffic traversing an internetwork is also "pruned."

MOSPF is optimized for an autonomous system that has a limited number of groups (although each group can be as large as necessary). MOSPF requires a router to perform the shortest-path computation for each new combination of sender and destination group. If there are many such combinations, a router's CPU can be overwhelmed by the number of computations.

One other caveat with MOSPF has to do with OSPF's support for dividing an autonomous system into areas. The advantage of areas, as discussed in Chapter 7, "Selecting Bridging, Switching, and Routing Protocols," is that no router needs to understand the complete topology of an autonomous system. A tradeoff is that multicast routing is inefficient in some cases.

If a source of multicast traffic is not in a router's area, the router can only build incomplete shortest-path trees between the source and group destinations. Information regarding the exact path between the router and the source is approximate, based on data in OSPF summary-link advertisements (or external-link advertisements if the source is in a different autonomous system).

Protocol-Independent Multicast

Protocol-Independent Multicast (PIM) is another option for multicast routing. Like MOSPF, PIM works in tandem with IGMP; it also works with a unicast routing protocol, such as OSPF, Routing Information Protocol (RIP), Cisco's Enhanced Interior Gateway Routing Protocol (Enhanced IGRP), and so on.

PIM has two modes: *dense mode* and *sparse mode*. The adjectives "dense" and "sparse" refer to the density of group members. Dense groups have many members. An example of a dense group is employees at a corporation who listen to the company president's quarterly report when it is multicast on the corporate intranet. A sparse group might be a much smaller group of employees who have signed up for a particular distance-learning course.

Dense-Mode Protocol-Independent Multicast

Dense-mode PIM is similar to an older dense-mode protocol, the Distance-Vector Multicast Routing Protocol (DVMRP), which is described in RFC 1075 and is a derivative of RIP. Both protocols use a reverse-path forwarding (RPF) mechanism to compute the shortest (reverse) path between a source and all possible recipients of a packet. Dense-mode PIM is simpler than DVMRP, however, because it does not require the computation of routing tables.

If a router running dense-mode PIM receives a multicast packet from a source to a group, it first verifies in the standard unicast routing table that the incoming interface is the one that it uses for sending unicast packets toward the source. If this is not the case, it drops the packet and sends back a prune message. If it is the case, the router forwards a copy of the packet on all interfaces for which it has not received a prune message for the source/group destination pair. If there are no such interfaces, it sends back a prune message.

The first packet for a group is flooded to all interfaces. Once this has occurred, however, routers listen to prune messages to help them develop a map of the network that lets them send multicast packets only to those networks that should receive the packets. The prune messages also let routers avoid loops that would cause more than one router to send a multicast packet to a segment.

Dense-mode PIM works best in environments with large multicast groups and a high likelihood that any given LAN has a group member, which limits the router's need to send prune messages. Because of the flooding of the first packet for a group, dense-mode does not make sense in environments where a few sparsely-located users wish to participate in a multicast application. In this case, sparse-mode PIM, which is described in the next section, is a better solution.

Sparse-Mode Protocol-Independent Multicast

Sparse-mode PIM is quite different than dense-mode PIM. Rather than allowing traffic to be sent everywhere and then pruned back where it is not needed, sparse-mode PIM defines a rendezvous point. The *rendezvous point* provides a registration service for a multicast group.

Sparse-mode PIM relies on IGMP, which lets a host join a group by sending a membership-report message, and detach from a group by sending a leave message. A designated router for a network segment tracks membership-report and leave messages on its segment, and periodically sends join and prune PIM messages to the rendezvous point. The join and prune messages are processed by all the routers between the designated router and the rendezvous point. The result is a distribution tree that reaches all group members and is centered at the rendezvous point.

The *distribution tree* for a multicast group is initially used for any source, but the sparse-mode PIM specification, RFC 2117, also provides a mechanism to let the rendezvous point develop source-specific trees to further the pruning of network traffic.

When a source initially sends data to a group, the designated router on the source's network unicasts register messages to the rendezvous point with the source's data packets encapsulated within. If the data rate is high, the rendezvous point can send join/prune messages back towards the source. This enables the source's data packets to follow a *source-specific shortest-path tree*, and eliminates the need for the packets to be encapsulated in register messages. Whether the packets arrive encapsulated or not, the rendezvous point forwards the source's decapsulated data packets down the distribution tree toward group members.

OPTIMIZING NETWORK PERFORMANCE TO MEET QUALITY OF SERVICE REQUIREMENTS

In addition to optimizing bandwidth usage by adding IP multicast features to a network design, you may determine that optimization is also needed to meet QoS requirements. The "Characterizing Quality of Service Requirements" section in Chapter 4 talked about specifying the QoS that an application requires. This section covers some techniques for meeting those requirements.

NOTES

The focus of this section is meeting QoS requirements in a TCP/IP internetwork. For more information on QoS in an ATM environment, see the "ATM Quality of Service Specifications" section in Chapter 4, and the "Prioritization and Traffic Management on WAN Switches" section later in this chapter.

As discussed in Chapter 4, the Integrated Services Working Group (ISWG) defines two types of services that offer QoS assurances beyond *best-effort service* (which offers no QoS assurances):

- The *controlled-load service* provides a client data flow with a QoS closely approximating the QoS that the flow would receive on an unloaded network. The controlled-load service is intended for applications that are highly sensitive to overload conditions.

- The *guaranteed service* provides firm bounds on end-to-end packet-queuing delays. Guaranteed service is intended for applications that need a guarantee that a packet will arrive no later than a certain time after it was transmitted by its source.

Many optimization options are available to accommodate applications with controlled-load or guaranteed-service requirements. The next few sections describe some of these options, starting with one that has been available for many years—the precedence and type-of-service functionality built into the IP frame.

IP Precedence and Type of Service

Although specialized features to support QoS have recently become a hot topic of conversation among network engineers and designers, the concept that a network must support applications with varying requirements for service is not new. In fact, the creators of IP incorporated support for different levels of precedence and types of service into the IP frame format when IP was first developed in the 1970s. Figure 12–1 shows the fields in the IP version-4 header, with an emphasis on the type-of-service byte near the beginning of the header.

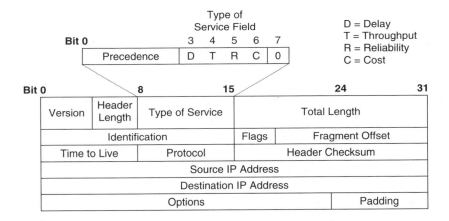

Figure 12–1
The Internet Protocol (IP) header.

The IP type-of-service byte specifies both precedence and type of service. *Precedence* helps a router determine which packet to send when several packets are queued for transmission to the same output interface. *Type of service* helps a router select a routing path when multiple paths are available.

The type-of-service byte is divided into two fields, (that are followed by a bit that is always set to zero):

- The 3-bit precedence field supports eight levels of priority

- The 4-bit type-of-service field supports four types of service

The IP Precedence Field

An application can use the *precedence field* to specify the importance of a packet. The importance can range from routine priority (the bits are set to 000) to high priority (the bits are set to 111).

One of the original uses envisioned for the precedence field was congestion control. By giving congestion-control packets a precedence of 7 (111 in binary), an application can specify that the congestion-control packets are more important than data packets, thus facilitating the effectiveness of the congestion-control mechanism. By selecting a precedence of 7, the application hopefully is ensuring that the congestion-control packets are not affected by the congestion that they are trying to control.

Precedence values 6 and 7 are reserved for network and internetwork control packets. The values 0–5 can be used for applications and user data. Some service providers offer a premium service that uses the precedence field to mark a customer's traffic as high-priority data. Many routers, and some hosts, support configuring the precedence value for applications. The precedence value is typically set to 5 for Voice over IP (VoIP) and other real-time applications.

The IP Type-of-Service Field

The *type-of-service field* helps a router select a route from a set of routes with different characteristics. A telephone circuit, for example, has low delay but limited throughput. A satellite link has high throughput; it also has high delay because of the distance to the satellite. A radio channel might be inexpensive, but error prone. Routing protocols attempt to determine the "best" route to a destination, but there are several definitions of "best": cheapest, fastest, most reliable, and so on. Some routing protocols, notably OSPF and BGP, support selecting a route based on the type of service that an application specifies.

The type-of-service field within the type-of-service byte in an IP header has four bits (refer to Figure 12–1):

- The *delay bit (D)* tells routers to minimize delay

- The *throughput bit (T)* tells routers to maximize throughput

- The *reliability bit (R)* tells routers to maximize reliability

- The *cost bit (C)* tells routers to minimize monetary cost

According to RFC 1349, an application can set one (and only one) of the four type-of-service bits to tell routers in the path to the destination how to handle the packet. A host can also use the type-of-service bits to decide which initial path to a local router to select. If all four bits are zero, then routine service is implied.

A router uses the type-of-service field to select a path that has the best chance of meeting an application's service requirements. The router is not required to offer any guarantees about service.

Interactive applications, such as Telnet and Rlogin, set the D bit. Voice and video applications can also set the D bit. When the D bit is set, a router should select a path that minimizes delay, for example, a dedicated high-speed leased line instead of a shared Frame Relay link.

File transfer applications, or any applications that send bulk data, set the T bit. Setting the T bit tells routers to select high-capacity links.

Routing protocols and network-management applications set the R bit. Setting the R bit tells routers to select fault-tolerant paths.

Applications for which neither delay nor throughput are critical—but a low monetary cost is important—set the C bit. The Network News Transfer Protocol (NNTP), which reads UseNet news, sets the C bit, presumably because reading news is not a critical activity and should not use a lot of monetary resources. The C bit was more recently defined than the other bits and is not widely used yet.

From a network designer's point of view, the importance of the IP precedence and type-of-service features of the IP header is the fact that the designer has the option of recommending applications that take advantage of this simple solution to meeting QoS requirements. In addition, the designer should also make sure the selected routing protocols and routers understand the bits in the precedence and type-of-service fields.

The Resource Reservation Protocol

The *Resource Reservation Protocol (RSVP)* is an alternative to the IP type-of-service and precedence capabilities inherent in the IP header. RSVP supports more sophisticated mechanisms for hosts to specify QoS requirements for individual traffic flows. RSVP can be deployed on LANs and intranets to support multimedia applications or other types of applications with strict QoS requirements.

Both the IP-header type-of-service capabilities and RSVP are examples of *QoS signaling protocols*. QoS signaling is a means of delivering QoS requirements across a network. The type-of-service byte in the IP header offers *in-band signaling*, meaning that bits within the frame header signal to routers how the frame should be handled. RSVP offers *out-of-band signaling*, meaning that hosts send additional frames, beyond data frames, to indicate that a certain QoS service is desired for a particular traffic flow.

RSVP is a setup protocol used by a host to request specific qualities of service from the network for particular application data streams or flows. RSVP is also used by routers to deliver QoS requests to other routers along the path of a flow. RSVP operates on top of IP version 4 or 6, occupying the place of a transport protocol in the protocol stack (although it does not transport application data).

RSVP is not a routing protocol; it operates in tandem with unicast and multicast routing protocols. Whereas a routing protocol determines where packets get forwarded, RSVP is concerned with the QoS those packets receive. RSVP consults the local unicast or multicast routing database to obtain routes. In the multicast case, for example, a host sends IGMP messages to join a multicast group and then sends RSVP messages to reserve resources along the delivery path(s) for that group.

According to the RSVP specification, a receiver is responsible for requesting a specific QoS, not a source. Putting the onus on the receiver lets RSVP more easily accommodate large groups, dynamic group membership, and heterogeneous receiver requirements.

An application residing on a receiver host passes a QoS request to the local RSVP process. The RSVP protocol then carries the request to all the nodes (routers and hosts) along the reverse data path(s) to the data source(s) (only as far as the router located where the receiver's data path joins the multicast distribution tree). RSVP requests should result in resources being reserved in each node along the path.

RSVP provides a general facility for creating and maintaining information on resource reservations across a mesh of unicast or multicast delivery paths. RSVP transfers QoS parameters, but does not define the parameters or the different types of services that an application can request. RSVP simply passes parameters to the appropriate traffic-control and policy-control modules for interpretation. As discussed in Chapter 4, the ISWG describes services in RFCs 2210–2216.

RSVP is a relatively new protocol, having been proposed by the IETF ISWG in RFC 2205 in September, 1997. Nonetheless, it is supported by most router vendors and many multimedia application developers, including Microsoft, Intel, and Sun.

As part of the requirements-analysis phase of the network-design process, you should have identified applications that can benefit from RSVP. You should have also selected routers to implement the design during the physical design phase. At this point in the design process, you should analyze your selections and take another look at the network topology to make sure routers that support RSVP are available to the applications that need it. For RSVP to be effective, each router on the path from a receiver to a source must support RSVP, including routers in redundant paths that may come into service during network outages or when the traffic load is high.

NOTES

Remember, network design is an iterative process that allows you to adjust your plans as you consider the details and ramifications of choices made so far.

When considering RSVP, be sure to read RFC 2208 (or any updates published after publication of this book). RFC 2208, "Resource Reservation Protocol Version 1 Applicability Statement," points out the problems with running RSVP on a backbone router that aggregates traffic from many networks. The processing and storage requirements for running RSVP on a router increase proportionally with the number of separate sessions and RSVP reservations. Supporting RSVP on a critical backbone router that handles many data streams can overtax the router, and is inadvisable.

Techniques are being developed that will aggregate streams that require a specific service at the "edge" of a backbone. Within the backbone, various less costly approaches can then be used to set aside resources for an aggregated stream. Until these techniques are developed, RSVP should be deployed on LANs and intranets where there is no need for any router to process numerous reservations.

RSVP is more suited for private intranets than the Internet or other public networks that cross multiple service providers' domains. Not only are there scalability issues associated with the amount of information that routers must maintain for each RSVP session, but there are also economic concerns. One service provider might be willing to provide resources (bandwidth and low delay, for example) that another service provider is not equipped to offer. A provider might not have the capacity to offer the services or the procedures to bill customers for them.

In addition, RSVP is best suited for long-duration flows, such as those present in video applications. About 60 percent of Internet traffic today consists of short-duration flows. For these reasons, RSVP is more appropriate for private networks than the Internet (although this may change in the future as applications on the Internet change and more progress is made on methods for providers to cooperate).

The Common Open Policy Service Protocol

As mentioned in the previous section, RSVP simply transports QoS requests and provides techniques for routers to maintain information about the state of resource reservations. For RSVP to be effective, it needs support from additional protocols that understand actual services and policies regarding the services. One such protocol is the *Common Open Policy Service (COPS) protocol*, which is currently under development by the IETF. (The IETF released a draft standard in March, 1998.)

COPS defines a simple client/server model for supporting policy control with QoS signaling protocols such as RSVP. The COPS draft specification describes a basic query-and-response protocol that can be used to exchange policy information between a policy server and its clients, which will typically be RSVP routers.

The COPS specification calls a policy server a *policy-decision point*, or *PDP*. It calls a client a *policy-enforcement point*, or *PEP*. The protocol lets a PEP send requests, updates, and deletes to a remote PDP, and lets the PDP return decisions to the PEP. In this fashion, RSVP-based routers can exchange information with centralized servers that store a network's QoS policies, and learn how to correctly handle flows for which resources have been reserved.

Though COPS is a new technology, by 1999, the client side will be supported by most major router vendors, and COPS servers will be available from companies such as IP Highway. (See www.iphighway.com for more information.) Cisco plans to support COPS on enterprise switches and routers to provide transport for both QoS and security policies.

IEEE 802.1p Specification

The IEEE 802.1p specification focuses on support for QoS on LANs. The 802.1p standard is a supplement to IEEE 802.1D, "Standard for Local Area Network MAC (Media Access Control) Bridges." It specifies mechanisms in bridges to expedite the delivery of time-critical traffic and to limit the extent of high-bandwidth multicast traffic within a bridged LAN. (The term *bridge* encompasses data-link-layer switches as well as traditional bridges.)

The IEEE 802.1p standard adds support for priority to LANs that do not support MAC priority methods. For example, Ethernet, unlike Token Ring and FDDI, has no inherent support for priority levels for frames.

IEEE 802.1p provides an in-band QoS signaling method for classifying traffic on the basis of MAC frame information. It also specifies an optional protocol mechanism in bridges to support end stations dynamically registering for time-critical frame-delivery or filtering services. Optional protocols between bridges to convey registration information in a bridged LAN are also supported.

IEEE 802.1p supports eight classes of service (COSs). A value of 0 means routine service, in other words, no priority. Different bridges within a LAN, and even different ports on bridges, can be configured for a different number of priority levels. In general, low-speed ports and backbone ports have the most need for multiple priority levels. A bridge should have a separate queue for each priority level used by a port.

NOTES

It could be argued that LANs do not need QoS features. LANs that have been migrated to switched technologies and high-speed MAC methods, such as 100-Mbps and Gigabit Ethernet, often have excess capacity. However, when backbone networks and uplinks segments to upper layers of a hierarchical topology are considered, it becomes clear that QoS methods are necessary on LANs as well as enterprise networks. As new networked multimedia applications become a central part of normal business practices, switched campus LANs can take advantage of 802.1p capabilities, in addition to the other capabilities already covered in this chapter.

IP Version 6

No discussion of QoS would be complete without a mention of IP Version 6, also known as *IPv6* and *IP next-generation* (or *IPng*). A detailed description of IPv6 is outside the scope of this book. However, it should be noted that in the next three to five years, many networks will be updated to IPv6 and will be able to take advantage of the inherent QoS features of the new version.

IPv6 enhances the capability of hosts and routers to implement varying levels of QoS for different traffic flows by including in the IPv6 header a flow-label field that identifies individual packet flows.

A source host assigns a flow label to each application flow. An IPv6-compatible router processes the IPv6 header of each packet and maintains a cache of flow information, indexed by source address and flow label. This process facilitates a router implementing QoS features for individual traffic flows.

In addition, the IPv6 header includes a 4-bit priority field that lets a source identify the desired delivery priority of its packets, relative to other packets from the same source. This field takes on the responsibility of the IP precedence bits from the IPv4 header.

Priority values are divided into two ranges:

- Values 0 through 7 are used to specify the priority of traffic for which the source is providing congestion control, for example, traffic that "backs off" in response to congestion, such as TCP traffic.

- Values 8 through 15 are used to specify the priority of traffic that does not back off in response to congestion, for example, real-time packets that are sent at a constant rate.

Table 12–1 shows recommended priority values for congestion-controlled traffic, per the IPv6 specification (RFC 1883), and some examples of applications and protocols that use the priority value.

Table 12–1   IPv6 Priority Values for Congestion-Controlled Traffic

Priority Value	Application Category	Example Application(s)
0	Uncharacterized traffic	Applications that do not support the priority scheme
1	"Filler" traffic	UseNet news
2	Unattended data transfer	E-mail

Table 12–1   IPv6 Priority Values for Congestion-Controlled Traffic, Continued

Priority Value	Application Category	Example Application(s)
3	Reserved	N/A
4	Attended bulk transfer	File Transfer Protocol (FTP), Network File System (NFS)
5	Reserved	NA
6	Interactive traffic	Telnet, X-Windows
7	Internet control traffic	Routing protocols, network management

For non-congestion-controlled traffic, the lowest priority value (8) should be used for those packets that the sender is most willing to have discarded under conditions of congestion, and the highest value (15) should be used for those packets that the sender is least willing to have discarded.

The Real-Time Protocol

The last QoS-enabling technology this section covers is the *Real-Time Protocol (RTP)*, which is a protocol used by multimedia applications. One of the main reasons for implementing QoS features in a network is to support real-time applications that send audio and video data streams. Such applications include distance learning, video conferencing, interactive distributed simulation tools, and interactive control and measurement tools. RTP, which is defined in RFC 1889, is a support protocol for such applications.

RTP provides end-to-end network transport functions suitable for transmitting real-time data over multicast or unicast network services. Applications typically run RTP on top of the User Datagram Protocol (UDP) to make use of UDP's multiplexing and checksum services. Working together with UDP, RTP implements Layer-4 (transport) functionality. (UDP is not required; RTP can be used with other suitable underlying network or transport protocols.)

The RTP packet header includes several fields that specify the attributes of the data carried in the RTP packet:

- The *payload type* indicates the format of the payload, for example, MPEG version 1 or 2 audio or video data, JPEG video, an H.261 video stream, and so on.

- The *sequence number* indicates the location of the packet in the data stream. The sequence number increments by one for each RTP data packet sent, and can be used by the receiver to detect packet loss and to restore packet sequence.

- The *timestamp* reflects the sampling instant of the first byte in the data packet.

- The *synchronization source (SSRC) field* identifies the source of a stream of RTP packets, for example, a microphone or video camera. All packets from a synchronization source form part of the same timing and sequence number space, so a receiver groups packets by SSRC for playback.

- The *contributing source (CSRC) list* identifies sources that have contributed to the payload in the packet. An example application is audio conferencing, where the CSRC field indicates all the talkers whose speech was combined to produce the outgoing packet.

RTP itself does not ensure the timely delivery of packets or provide QoS guarantees. It relies on lower-layer services to do so. RTP depends on RSVP to provide a mechanism for end systems and routers to specify and forward QoS requirements for an application. RTP also makes use of the *Real-Time Control Protocol (RTCP)*, which is an auxiliary control protocol that monitors data delivery, provides feedback on the QoS provided by the network, and optionally provides rudimentary session control.

NOTES

RTCP periodically sends information relevant to the calculation of packet-loss rate, packet-transmission delay, and delay jitter to all senders and receivers of a session. Applications use this data to characterize the current state of the network. Some applications can use the data to adjust their transmission rates and to help relieve congestion.

Numerous experimental and commercial applications currently use RTP, and RTP's popularity is expected to continue to grow. Nonetheless, the RTP specification (RFC 1889) includes a cautionary note about using RTP on intranets and the Internet, which are not yet capable of handling high-bandwidth applications without degrading the QoS of other network services. According to RFC 1889,

> Application documentation should clearly outline the limitations and possible operational impact of high-bandwidth real-time services on the Internet and other network services.

The network designer should check application documentation before recommending the deployment of an RTP-based application on a production network.

In addition, it is important to limit the use of RTP-based applications to networks that provide the necessary underlying support for QoS. This underlying support can be provided by techniques already discussed in this chapter, including IP multicast, IP type-of-service, and RSVP.

Finally, if possible, you should select routers that support RTP header compression. RTP header compression helps RTP run more efficiently and saves network bandwidth by compressing the RTP/UDP/IP header from 40 bytes to 2–5 bytes in a typical packet. This is especially beneficial for slow links and small packets (such as IP voice traffic), where the compression can reduce overhead and transmission delay significantly.

CISCO INTERNETWORK OPERATING SYSTEM FEATURES FOR OPTIMIZING NETWORK PERFORMANCE

The Cisco Internetwork Operating System (IOS) software provides a toolbox of optimization techniques to help you meet the challenges related to increasing traffic demands on campus and enterprise networks. The techniques range from proxy services that let you delegate specialized tasks to a router or switch, to advanced switching and queuing services to improve throughput and offer QoS functionality.

Proxy Services

Proxy services allow a router (or switch) to act as a surrogate for a service that is not available locally. Proxy services also support a router performing tasks beyond its typical duties to minimize delay and bandwidth usage. For example, a router can respond to keepalive packets on behalf of a remote device, rather than send the packets over a WAN or dial-up link.

NetWare servers running some versions of the NetWare Core Protocol (NCP), for example, send a keepalive message to all connected clients every 5 minutes. If clients are connected via dial-on-demand (DDR) circuits, the keepalive packets keep the DDR link active indefinitely. To avoid this problem, you can configure *IPX watchdog spoofing* on the router at the server end. This tells the router to respond to the keepalive messages locally, which allows the DDR link to be inactive for longer periods of time. *Novell Sequenced Packet Exchange (SPX) spoofing* does the same thing as IPX watchdog spoofing except for applications that use SPX instead of NCP.

In addition to responding to keepalives to reduce network traffic, a router can convert a frame type to a new type that causes less traffic, particularly in bridged environments. For example, a router or switch acting as a source-routing bridge can convert an *all-routes explorer* frame into a *single-route* frame, thus reducing the number of frames in a network that has many redundant paths. The router caches source routes to learn how to convert frames.

Proxy services also facilitate improved performance for applications that are time sensitive. Chapter 7, "Selecting Bridging, Switching, and Routing Protocols," talked about the *LLC-termination* mechanism, also known as *Local ACK*. LLC termination prevents timeouts by terminating an LLC type 2 (LLC2) connection at a local router. The router handles LLC2 functions such as session establishment, reliability, error control, and flow control. This prevents LLC2-based applications, for example SNA applications, from timing out when used on large routed networks with long round-trip delays.

One other feature of proxy services is the ability of a router to provide resource-discovery services on serverless LANs. Some examples of resource-discovery services a router can offer include the following:

- Forwarding resource-discovery broadcast frames (based on the configuration of a helper address), so that a client can reach a service on the other side of the router.

- Responding when there is no local Novell NetWare server to a get-nearest-server (GNS) request from a NetWare client.

- Responding when there is no local Banyan VINES server when a VINES client sends a broadcast asking a server to provide it with a network-layer address.

- Responding to an Address Resolution Protocol (ARP) request when a local IP station attempts to find the MAC address for a remote IP address. (This is known as *proxy ARP*.)

Switching Techniques

In addition to running routing protocols to develop a routing topology, and possibly implementing the proxy services discussed in the previous section, the major job of a router is to switch packets from incoming interfaces to outgoing interfaces. Switching involves receiving a packet, determining how to forward the packet based on the routing topology and QoS and policy requirements, and switching the packet to the right outgoing interface or interfaces. The speed at which a router can perform this task is a major factor in determining network performance in a routed network. Cisco supports many switching methods, with varying speeds and behaviors. This section describes some of these switching methods.

In general, you should use the fastest switching method available for an interface type and protocol (though there are some exceptions to this guideline, as mentioned in the next section in the discussion on fast switching). Using a speedy switching mode is especially important on backbone and core enterprise routers. Depending on the version of IOS software you are running, the fastest mode might need to be configured. (It is not always the default.)

NOTES

See Cisco's documentation for more information on the methods supported for various router platforms, protocols, and interfaces. Documentation for Cisco products is available online at www.cisco.com/univercd/home/home.htm.

This section starts by describing some older, but still used, technologies for Layer-3 switching, called the *classic methods for switching*, and continues with three newer technologies: NetFlow switching, Cisco express forwarding (CEF), and tag switching.

Classic Methods for Layer-3 Packet Switching

Process switching is the slowest of the switching methods. With process switching, when a packet arrives at an interface, the system processor is interrupted for the time it takes to copy the packet from the interface buffer to system memory. The processor looks up the Layer-3 destination address for the packet in the routing table to determine the exit interface. The packet is rewritten with the correct header for that interface and copied to the interface. At this time, an entry is also placed in the fast-switching cache so that subsequent packets for the destination address can use the same header. The first packet to a destination is always process switched.

Fast switching allows higher throughput by switching a packet using an entry in the fast-switching cache that was created when a previous packet to the same destination was processed. With fast switching, a packet is handled immediately, without scheduling an interrupt of the system processor.

NOTES

Fast switching is enabled by default for most protocols, but there are cases when it should be disabled, as discussed in the "Load on the DS-1 Circuits" section of the case study in Chapter 11, "Testing Your Network Design." In this example, fast switching was disabled to make sure traffic to the CAD file server was shared across two parallel DS-1 circuits. Before fast switching was disabled, the router learned the path to the server once, placed it in the cache, and never learned about the parallel path. Turning off fast switching made sense in this case because most of the traffic was to a single destination (the CAD file server).

Autonomous switching is available on Cisco 7000-series routers and uses an *autonomous-switching cache* located on interface processors. Autonomous switching provides faster packet switching by allowing the *ciscoBus controller* to switch packets independently, without having to interrupt the system processor.

Silicon switching is similar to autonomous switching, but speeds up autonomous switching through the use of a *silicon-switching cache* located on the Silicon Switch Processor (SSP) on some Cisco 7000-series routers.

Optimum switching is similar to fast switching, but is faster, due to an enhanced caching algorithm, and the optimized structure of the *optimum-switching cache*. Optimum switching is only available on routers equipped with a Route/Switch Processor (RSP).

Distributed switching is supported on routers that include Versatile Interface Processor (VIP) cards or other interface cards that can receive route information from the master RSP to make their own autonomous, multilayer switching decisions. Distributed switching supports very fast throughput because the switching process occurs on the interface card.

NetFlow Switching

NetFlow switching is a relatively new switching mode that is optimized for environments where services must be applied to packets to implement security, QoS features, and traffic accounting. An example of such an environment is the boundary between an enterprise network and the Internet.

NetFlow switching identifies traffic flows between hosts, and then quickly switches packets in these flows at the same time that it applies services. NetFlow switching also lets a network manager collect data on network usage to enable capacity planning and bill users based on network and application resource utilization. The data can be collected without slowing down the switching process.

To maximize network scalability, a good design practice is to use NetFlow switching on the periphery of a network to enable features such as traffic accounting, QoS functionality, and security, and to use an even faster switching mode in the core of the network. At the core of the network, the switching mode should forward packets based on easily-accessible information in the packet, and generally should not spend time applying services.

The next two switching modes covered in this section, *Cisco express forwarding (CEF)* and *tag switching*, are optimized for the core of a network for high performance, predictability, scalability, and resilience.

Cisco Express Forwarding

CEF is a Cisco-patented technique for switching packets very quickly across large backbone networks and the Internet. Rather than relying on the caching techniques used by classic switching methods, CEF depends on a *forwarding information base (FIB)*. The FIB allows CEF to be much less processor-intensive than other Layer-3 switching methods, because the FIB tables contain forwarding information for all routes in the routing tables (whereas a cache contains only a subset of routing information).

CEF evolved to accommodate Web-based applications and other interactive applications that are characterized by sessions of short duration to multiple destination addresses. CEF became necessary when it became clear that a cache-based system is not optimized for these types of applications. Consider a Web-surfing application, for example. When a user jumps to a new Web site, TCP opens a session with a new destination address. It is unlikely that the new destination is in the router's cache, unless it happens to be a destination the user, or other users, visited recently. This means that the packet is process switched, which is slow.

CEF improves switching speed, and avoids the overhead associated with a cache that continually changes, through the use of the FIB, which mirrors the entire contents of the IP routing table.

CEF technology takes advantage of the distributed architecture of the high-end Cisco routers, such as the Cisco 7500. *Distributed CEF (DCEF)* provides each of the Cisco 7500 VIPs with an identical on-card copy of the FIB database enabling them to autonomously perform CEF and therefore significantly increase aggregate throughput.

NOTES

For more information about CEF, see the white paper on the subject on Cisco's Web site at www.cisco.com/warp/public/732/tag/cef_wp.htm.

Tag Switching

Tag switching has a slightly different goal than the other switching methods covered. Whereas the other methods optimize the switching of a packet through a single router, tag switching optimizes packet-switching through a network of tag switches. (A *tag switch* is a router or switch that supports tag switching.)

Tag switching is an implementation of the IETF standard for *multiprotocol label switching (MPLS)*. The idea behind these algorithms is that by "labeling" or "tagging" the first packet in a flow of data, subsequent packets can be expedited to the final destination. Tagging minimizes the processing required of a router, and thus significantly reduces delay on packet and cell-based networks that include tag switches. In addition, packets can be tagged to travel along specified routes to implement load balancing, QoS, and other optimization features.

Tag information can be carried in a packet as a small header inserted between the Layer-2 and Layer-3 headers, or as part of the Layer-3 header, if the Layer-3 protocol supports it. (In IPv6, tag information can be included in the flow-label field.) Some Layer-2 implementations, such as ATM, support carrying the tag directly in the Layer-2 header.

An internetwork that uses tag switching has three major components as shown in Figure 12–2:

- *Tag edge routers*, located at the boundaries of a network, perform network-layer services and apply tags to packets.

- *Tag switches*, including routers and ATM or other Layer-2 switches, switch tagged packets based on the tags. The tag switches can also support traditional Layer-3 routing and Layer-2 switching.

- The *Tag Distribution Protocol (TDB)* distributes tag information between devices in a tag-switched network. Tag edge routers and switches use the tables generated by standard routing protocols to assign and distribute tag information via TDP.

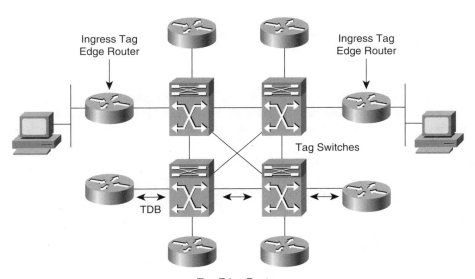

Ingress Tag
Edge Router

Ingress Tag
Edge Router

Tag Switches

TDB

Tag Edge Routers

Figure 12–2
The architecture of a network that uses tag switching.

When an ingress tag edge router receives a packet for forwarding across the tag network, it performs the following tasks:

- Analyzes the network-layer header

- Performs applicable network-layer services such as security, NetFlow accounting, QoS classification, and bandwidth management

- Selects a route for the packet from the routing tables

- Applies a tag and forwards the packet to the next-hop tag switch

When a tag switch receives a tagged packet, it switches the packet based solely on the tag, without re-analyzing the network-layer header. The switch uses the tag as an index into its *Tag Information Base (TIB)*. A TIB is a database of records that include the following elements:

- Incoming tag

- Outgoing tag

- Outgoing interface

- Outgoing link-level information

When a switch finds an entry in the TIB with the incoming tag equal to the tag carried in the packet, the switch replaces (swaps) the tag in the packet with the outgoing tag, replaces the link-level information (such as the MAC address) in the packet with the outgoing link-level information, and forwards the packet over the outgoing interface. This forwarding method can be used for both unicast and multicast traffic. A multicast entry in the TIB might have multiple entries for the outgoing information.

When a packet reaches a tag edge router at the egress point of a network, the tag is stripped off and the packet delivered. As can be seen, tag switching fuses the intelligence of routing with the performance of switching. This approach allows networks to scale to a large size and handle more traffic, users, media-rich data, and bandwidth-intensive applications.

A typical application for tag-switching is a large IP network built from a core of ATM switches surrounded by edge routers. In such a topology, the edge routers are mesh connected via virtual circuits through the ATM switches. If the routers are all peers of each other from a routing-protocol perspective, the topology can only scale to a limited number of routers before the routing protocols start having problems.

In a tag-switched network, however, because the ATM switches participate in the TDP, and because packets carry tags that specify path information, it is no longer necessary to configure virtual circuits between all the routers. The tag edge routers see far fewer routing-protocol peers, and hence the size of the network, measured in number of routers, can scale to a much larger size. This application of tag switching is especially beneficial for service providers that connect multiple customer IP networks through the provider's core ATM network.

In addition, service providers and enterprise networks can use tag-switching (regardless of whether the core network is based on ATM), to help solve the problem of uneven distribution of traffic among links, and to provide different classes of services to customers.

Queuing Services

The high-speed switching techniques discussed in the previous sections only go so far in optimizing a network that is experiencing congestion. Intelligent and fast queuing methods are also necessary. Queuing allows a network device to handle an overflow of traffic. Cisco IOS software supports the following queuing methods:

- First in, first out (FIFO) queuing

- Priority queuing

- Custom queuing

- Weighted fair queuing (WFQ)

First In, First Out Queuing

FIFO queuing provides basic store-and-forward functionality. It involves storing packets when the network is congested and forwarding them in the order they arrived when the network is no longer congested. FIFO has the advantage that it is the default queuing algorithm in some instances, so requires no configuration. FIFO has the disadvantage that it makes no decision about packet priority. The order of arrival determines the order a packet is processed and output.

FIFO provides no QoS functionality and no protection against an application using network resources in a way that negatively affects the performance of other applications. Bursty sources can cause high delays in delivering time-sensitive application traffic, and potentially defer network control and signaling messages. Long packets can cause unfair delays for applications that use short packets. For these reasons, Cisco has developed advanced queuing algorithms that provide more features than basic FIFO queuing, including priority queuing, custom queuing, and weighted-fair queuing (WFQ). These algorithms are described in the next few sections.

Priority Queuing

Priority queuing ensures that important traffic is processed first. It was designed to give strict priority to a critical application, and is particularly useful for time-sensitive protocols such as SNA. Packets can be prioritized based on many factors, including protocol, incoming interface, packet size, and source or destination address.

Priority queuing is especially appropriate in cases where WAN links are congested from time to time. If the WAN links are constantly congested, the customer should investigate protocol and application inefficiencies, consider using compression, or possibly upgrade to more bandwidth. If the WAN links are never congested, priority queuing is unnecessary. Because priority queuing requires extra processing and can cause performance problems for low-priority traffic, it should not be recommended unless necessary.

Priority queuing has four queues: high, medium, normal, and low. The high-priority queue is always emptied before the lower-priority queues are serviced, as shown in Figure 12–3.

Custom Queuing

Custom queuing was designed to allow a network to be shared among applications with different minimum bandwidth or latency requirements. Custom queuing assigns different amounts of queue space to different protocols and handles the queues in round-robin fashion. A particular protocol can be prioritized by assigning it more queue space. Custom queuing is more "fair" than priority queuing, although priority queuing is more powerful for prioritizing a single critical application.

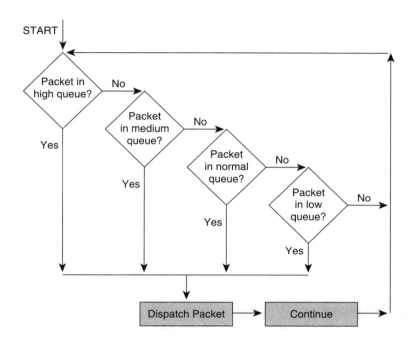

Figure 12–3
*The behavior
of priority
queuing.*

You can use custom queuing to provide guaranteed bandwidth at a potential congestion point. Custom queuing lets you assure each specified traffic type a fixed portion of available bandwidth, while at the same time avoid any application achieving more than a predetermined proportion of capacity when the link is under stress.

Custom queuing places a message in one of 17 queues. The router services queues 1 through 16 in round-robin order. (Queue 0 holds system messages, such as keepalive and signaling messages, and is emptied first.) A network administrator configures the transmission window size of each queue in bytes. Once the appropriate number of packets are transmitted from a queue such that the transmission window size has been reached, the next queue is checked, as shown in Figure 12–4.

Many businesses use custom queuing for SNA traffic. Because SNA is delay sensitive, one can set aside some portion of bandwidth, often 40 to 50 percent, for the SNA traffic to use during times of congestion.

Figure 12–4
*The behavior
of custom
queuing.*

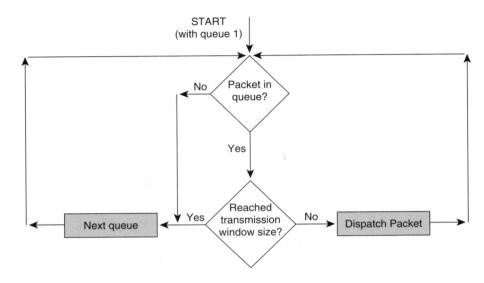

Weighted Fair Queuing

WFQ is a sophisticated set of algorithms designed to reduce delay variability and provide predictable throughput and response time for traffic flows. A goal of WFQ is to offer uniform service to light and heavy network users alike. WFQ ensures that the response time for low-volume applications is consistent with the response time for high-volume applications. Applications that send small packets are not unfairly starved of bandwidth by applications that send large packets.

WFQ is a flow-based queuing algorithm that recognizes a flow for an interactive application and schedules that application's traffic to the front of the queue to reduce response time. Low-volume traffic streams for interactive applications, which includes a large percentage of the applications on most networks, are allowed to transmit their entire offered loads in a timely fashion. High-volume traffic streams share the remaining capacity.

Unlike custom and priority queuing, WFQ adapts automatically to changing network traffic conditions and requires little to no configuration. It is the default queuing mode on most serial interfaces configured to run at or below E1 speeds (2.048 Mbps).

For applications that use the IP precedence field in the IP header, WFQ can allot bandwidth based on precedence. The algorithm allocates more bandwidth to conversations with higher precedence, and makes sure those conversations get served more quickly when congestion occurs. WFQ assigns a weight to each flow, which determines the transmit order for queued packets. IP precedence helps determine the weighting factor.

WFQ also works with RSVP. RSVP uses WFQ to allocate buffer space, schedule packets, and guarantee bandwidth based on resource reservations. Additionally, WFQ understands the discard eligibility bit (DE), and the forward explicit congestion notification (FECN) and backward explicit congestion notification (BECN) mechanisms in a Frame Relay network. Once congestion is identified, the weights used by WFQ are altered so that a conversation encountering congestion transmits less frequently.

Random Early Detection

The queuing mechanisms discussed in the previous sections are essentially congestion-management techniques. Although such techniques are necessary for controlling congestion, they fall short of avoiding congestion before it occurs. A new class of congestion-avoidance algorithms are gaining popularity.

One such algorithm is *random early detection (RED)*. RED works by monitoring traffic loads at points in a network and randomly discarding packets if congestion begins to increase. The result is that source nodes detect the dropped traffic and slow their transmission rate. RED is primarily designed to work with applications based on the Transmission Control Protocol (TCP).

Upon packet loss, a TCP session decreases its transmit window size, effectively slowing its transmission rate. It then gradually increases the window size until congestion occurs again. The term *porpoising* is sometimes used to refer to the closing and re-opening of windows.

Experience shows that if routers do not apply some sort of randomization to the dropping of packets, multiple TCP sessions tend to slow their transmission rate simultaneously. (The sessions take a *synchronized porpoise dive*.) Multiple applications lower and increase their transmission rate simultaneously, which means that bandwidth is not used effectively. When multiple applications slow down, bandwidth is wasted. When they increase their rate, they tend to increase bandwidth utilization to the point where congestion occurs again.

The advantage of RED is that it randomizes the dropping of packets, thus reducing the potential for multiple sessions synchronizing their behavior. RED is a good solution for a central-site router in a hub-and-spoke topology. RED distributes the dropping of packets across many of the spoke networks and avoids causing congestion problems for multiple application sessions from one site.

Weighted Random Early Detection

Weighted random early detection (WRED) is Cisco's implementation of RED. WRED combines the capabilities of the standard RED algorithm with IP precedence. This combination provides for preferential traffic handling for higher-priority packets. It selectively discards lower-priority traffic when an interface starts to get congested, rather than using simply a random method.

WRED can also adjust its behavior based on RSVP reservations. If an application registers for the ISWG controlled-load QoS service, WRED is made aware of this and adjusts its packet discarding accordingly.

In mid-1998, Cisco also announced support for *distributed weighted random early detection (D-WRED)*, a high-speed version of WRED that runs on the Versatile Interface Processors (VIPs) on a Cisco 7500 router.

Traffic Shaping

Another tool that is available to network designers using Cisco equipment is traffic shaping. *Traffic shaping* lets you manage and control network traffic to avoid bottlenecks and meet QoS requirements. It avoids congestion by reducing outbound traffic for a flow to a configured bit rate, while queuing bursts of traffic for that flow. In topologies with routers and links of varying capabilities, traffic can be shaped to avoid overwhelming a downstream router or link.

Traffic shaping is configured on a per-interface basis. The router administrator uses access control lists (ACLs) to select the traffic to shape. Traffic shaping works with a variety of Layer-2 technologies, including Frame Relay, ATM, Switched Multimegabit Data Service (SMDS), and Ethernet.

On a Frame Relay interface, you can configure traffic shaping to adapt dynamically to available bandwidth using the BECN mechanism. In addition, Cisco has a specific feature for Frame Relay networks called *Frame Relay traffic shaping* that supports optimization techniques specific to Frame Relay. For more information, see the "Configuring Frame Relay" section of Cisco's documentation.

Committed Access Rate

Cisco also supports a feature called *committed access rate (CAR)* that allows you to classify and police traffic on an incoming interface. CAR supports specifying policies regarding how traffic that exceeds a certain bandwidth allocation should be handled. CAR looks at traffic received on an interface (or a subset of that traffic selected by an ACL), compares its rate to a configured maximum, and then takes action based on the result. For example, it can drop a packet or change the IP precedence bits in the packet to indicate that the packet should be handled with less priority.

CISCO WAN SWITCHING OPTIMIZATION TECHNIQUES

This section briefly covers some techniques that can be deployed on Cisco WAN switches to optimize the handling of multiple types of traffic, including voice, video, and data. In most WAN environments, a key design goal is to reduce the cost of operating a WAN by using bandwidth intelligently. To meet this goal, customers seek solutions such as the ones in this section that can dynamically allocate bandwidth where it is needed, avoid using bandwidth unnecessarily, and prioritize, manage, and control bandwidth usage.

Voice Activity Detection

Voice activity detection (VAD) saves bandwidth by generating data only when someone is speaking. Voice conversations tend to be 60 percent silence, so VAD is an effective way to dynamically free up bandwidth. Cisco WAN switches combine VAD with standards-based digital voice compression to achieve 8:1 bandwidth savings. The extra bandwidth is dynamically reallocated to applications that need it.

Detecting that voice traffic is present takes some time, which means that speech is actually present before the speech detector function recognizes it. To accommodate this condition, the voice card in a WAN switch sends the first few packets of speech as high priority packets to minimize delay. This avoids cutting off the first few syllables of a conversation.

If your network design includes WAN switches that handle voice traffic, you should test the default settings for VAD to make sure they are appropriate for your network and users. Cisco's VAD implementation can be manipulated to ensure that there are no annoying side effects to the user. For example, a timer can be configured to specify how much time should elapse between the time that silence is detected and bandwidth is reallocated to other applications. By tweaking this timer, you can avoid users hearing any choppiness. A tradeoff can be made regarding how much bandwidth is freed up for other applications and the quality of voice conversations.

In addition, an adaptive voice feature can be configured that automatically disables VAD during periods when there is unused network bandwidth available, which allows transmission of compressed voice without any effects of VAD. As the extra bandwidth is allocated to other connections, VAD is dynamically enabled on all voice circuits to free up bandwidth.

To further improve user perception of a voice conversation, Cisco's implementation can insert a small amount of noise (called *pink noise*) to simulate background noise. Because total silence sounds wrong to many users, the voice card in the switch samples the background noise at the transmitting side and reproduces it at the receiving side.

Prioritization and Traffic Management on WAN Switches

Cisco WAN switches include a number of features that facilitate optimizing network performance by prioritizing traffic, and intelligently queuing, scheduling, and routing traffic. You should check Cisco's Web site for the latest information about the following WAN switch features:

- The *Advanced Class of Service (CoS) Management* software provides dedicated queues and queuing algorithms for the different sub-classes of service defined in a network. It supports per-virtual-circuit queuing and rate scheduling to ensure fairness among connections, and implements connection admission control on virtual circuits to manage traffic at ingress points on the network.

- The *Optimized Bandwidth Management* software is an implementation of version 4.0 of the ATM Forum Traffic Management Specification that enables a switch to continually monitor trunk utilization throughout the network, adjust bandwidth to all connections, proactively avoid queuing delays, and minimize cell loss.

- The *Automatic Routing Management* software provides end-to-end connection management services via a source-based routing algorithm. A source node (switch) selects a route based on the network topology, class of service, trunk loading, and the relative distance to the destination. Each node can independently determine a route, because topology and loading information are synchronized and distributed to nodes in the network. The Automatic Routing Management software also provides intelligent rerouting around trunk or hardware failures.

SUMMARY

To meet a customer's goals for network performance, scalability, availability, and manageability, you can recommend a variety of optimization techniques. Optimization provides the high bandwidth, low delay, and controlled jitter required by many critical business applications.

To minimize bandwidth utilization for multimedia applications that send large streams of data to many users, you can recommend IP multicast technologies. These technologies include multicast addressing, IGMP for allowing clients to join multicast groups, and various multicast routing protocols, such as MOSPF and PIM.

Multimedia and other applications that are sensitive to network congestion and delay can inform routers in the network of their QoS requirements using both in-band and out-of-band methods. An in-band method involves setting bits within packets to specify how the packet should be handled. For example, IPv4 includes the precedence and type of service bits, and IPv6 includes the priority field. IEEE 802.1 also has a way of specifying priority within data-link layer frames.

RSVP is an emerging out-of-band method for specifying QoS. It can be used with the Common Open Policy Service (COPS) protocol which standardizes the client/server communication between policy-enforcement points (PEPs), such as routers, and policy servers, also known as policy-decision points (PDPs).

Once a network has been upgraded to include QoS features, applications that use RTP can be deployed. RTP provides a transport-layer service suitable for transmitting real-time audio and video data over multicast or unicast network services.

Cisco Systems supplies a number of features for optimizing a network, including the following:

- Proxy services

- Advanced switching techniques, including NetFlow switching, express forwarding, and tag switching

- Advanced queuing services, including priority, custom, and weighted-fair queuing (WFQ)

- Random early detection (RED) and weighted random early detection (WRED)

- Traffic shaping

- Committed access rate (CAR)

- Voice activity detection

- WAN switching prioritization and traffic management

CHAPTER 13

Documenting Your Network Design

This chapter starts by providing advice on responding to a customer's request for proposal (RFP), and concludes with information on writing a design document when no RFP exists. The section "Contents of a Network Design Document" provides an outline of a typical design document, and specifies the topics that should be included in each part of the document. The section serves as a summary for *Top-Down Network Design* because it references each of the major steps of the top-down design methodology presented in this book.

At this point in the design process you should have a comprehensive design that is based on an analysis of your customer's business and technical goals, and includes both logical and physical components that have been tested and optimized. The next step in the process is to write a design document.

A *design document* describes your customer's requirements and explains how your design meets those requirements. It also documents the existing network, the logical and physical design, and the budget and expenses associated with the project.

It is also important that a design document contain plans for implementing the network, measuring the success of the implementation, and evolving the network design as new application requirements arise. The network designer's job is never complete. The process of analyzing requirements and developing design solutions begins again as soon as a design is implemented. Figure 13–1 shows the cyclical nature of the top-down network design process.

Figure 13–1
Network design and implementation cycle.

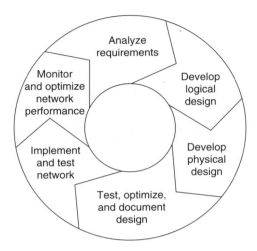

As mentioned in earlier chapters, in addition to being cyclical, network design is also iterative. Some steps take place during multiple phases of a design. Testing occurs during the design-validation phase and also during implementation. Optimization occurs while finalizing the design and also after implementation during the network-monitoring phase. Documentation is an ongoing effort. Documentation that is completed before the implementation stage can facilitate the approval process for a design, and help expedite the rollout of new technologies and applications.

RESPONDING TO A CUSTOMER'S REQUEST FOR PROPOSAL

An *RFP* lists a customer's design requirements and the types of solutions a network design must include. Organizations send RFPs to vendors and design consultants, and use the responses they receive to weed out suppliers that cannot meet requirements. RFP responses help organizations compare competing designs, product capabilities, pricing, and service and support alternatives.

Every RFP is different, but typically an RFP includes some or all of the following topics:

- Business goals for the project

- Scope of the project

- Information on the existing network and applications

- Information on new applications

- Technical requirements including scalability, availability, performance, security, manageability, usability, adaptability, and affordability

- Warranty requirements for products

- Environmental or architectural constraints that could affect implementation

- Training and support requirements

- Preliminary schedule with milestones and deliverables

- Legal contractual terms and conditions

Some organizations specify the required format for the RFP response. If this is the case, your initial design document should follow the customer's prescribed format and structure precisely. Organizations that specify a format may refuse to read responses that do not follow the requested format. In some cases, the customer may request a follow-up document where you can provide more detailed information on your logical and physical network design.

Some RFPs are in the form of a questionnaire. In this case, the questions should drive the proposal's organization. Embellishments that focus on key requirements and the selling points of your design can sometimes be added, unless the RFP specifically states that they should not be added.

Although every organization handles RFPs slightly differently, typically an RFP states that the response must include some or all of the following topics:

- A network topology for the new design

- Information on the protocols, technologies, and products that form the design

- An implementation plan

- A training plan

- Support and service information

- Prices and payment options

- Qualifications of the responding vendor or supplier

- Recommendations from other customers for whom the supplier has provided a solution

- Legal contractual terms and conditions

Despite the fact that a response to an RFP must stay within the guidelines specified by the customer, you should nonetheless use ingenuity to ensure that your response highlights the benefits of your design. Based on an analysis of your customer's business and technical goals, and the flow and characteristics of network traffic (as covered in Part I of this book), write your response so the reader can easily recognize that the design satisfies critical selection criteria.

When writing the response, be sure to consider the competition. Try to predict what other vendors or design consultants might propose so you can call attention to the aspects of your solution that are likely to be superior to competing designs. In addition, pay attention to your customer's "business style." Chapter 1 talked about the importance of understanding your customer's biases and any "office politics" or project history that could affect the perception of your design.

CONTENTS OF A NETWORK DESIGN DOCUMENT

When your design document does not have to follow a format dictated by an RFP, or when a customer requests a follow-up document to a basic RFP response, you should write a design document that fully describes your network design. The document should include the logical and physical components of the design, information on technologies and devices, and a proposal for implementing the design. The following sections describe the topics that should be included in a comprehensive design document.

Executive Summary

A comprehensive design document can be many pages in length. For this reason, it is essential that you include at the beginning of the document an Executive Summary that succinctly states the major points of the document. The Executive Summary should be no more than one page and should be targeted at the managers and key project participants who will decide whether to accept your design.

Although the Executive Summary can include some technical information, it should not provide technical details. The goal of the summary is to sell the decision-makers on the business benefits of your design. Technical information should be summarized and organized in order of the customer's highest-priority objectives for the design project.

Project Goal

This section should state the primary goal for the network design project. The goal should be business-oriented and related to an overall objective that the organization has to become more successful in its core business. The Project Goal section should be no more than one paragraph; it often can be written as a single sentence. Writing it carefully will give you a chance to make it obvious to the decision-makers reading the document that you understand the primary purpose and importance of the network design project.

An example of a project goal that was written for an actual design customer follows:

> The goal of this project is to develop a wide-area network (WAN) that will support new high-bandwidth and low-delay multimedia applications. The new applications are key to the successful implementation of new training programs for the sales force. The new WAN should facilitate the goal of increasing sales in the United States by 50 percent in the next fiscal year.

Project Scope

The Project Scope section provides information on the extent of the project, including a summary of the departments and networks that will be affected by the project. The Project Scope section specifies whether the project is for a new network or modifications to an existing network. It indicates whether the design is for a single network segment, a set of LANs, a building or campus network, a set of WAN or remote-access networks, or possibly the whole enterprise network.

An example of a Project Scope section follows:

> The scope of this project is to update the existing WAN that connects all major sales offices in the United States to corporate headquarters. The new WAN will be accessed by sales, marketing, and training employees. It is outside the scope of this project to update any LANs that these employees use. It is also outside the scope of this project to update the networks in satellite and telecommuter offices.

The scope of the project might intentionally not cover some matters. For example, fixing performance problems with a particular application might be intentionally outside the scope of the project. By stating up front the assumptions you made about the scope of the project, you can avoid any perception that your solution inadvertently fails to address certain concerns.

Design Requirements

Whereas the Project Goal section is generally very short, the Design Requirements section is your opportunity to list all the major business and technical requirements for the network design. The Design Requirements section should list the goals in priority order. Critical goals should be marked as such. To review some examples of design requirements, see the case studies in Chapters 9, 10, and 11.

Business Goals

Business goals explain the role the network design will play in helping an organization provide better products and services to its customers. Executives who read the design document will be more likely to accept the network design if they recognize from the Business Goals section that the network designer understands the organization's business mission.

Many network designers have a hard time writing the Business Goals section because they are more interested in technical goals. However, it is critical that you focus your network design document on the ability of your design to help a customer solve real-world business problems.

As discussed in Chapter 1, most businesses embark on a network design project to help them increase revenue, reduce operational costs and inefficiencies, and improve corporate communications. Other typical goals include building partnerships with other companies and expanding into worldwide markets. At this point in the network design process you should have a comprehensive understanding of your customer's business goals and be able to list them in the design document in priority order.

Technical Goals

The Technical Goals section documents the following goals discussed in Chapter 2:

- **Scalability.** How much growth a network design must support.

- **Availability.** The amount of time a network is available to users, often expressed as a percent uptime, or as a mean time between failure (MTBF) and mean time to repair (MTTR). Availability documentation can also include any information gathered on the monetary cost associated with network downtime.

- **Performance.** The customer's criteria for accepting the service level of a network, including its throughput, accuracy, efficiency, delay, delay variation (jitter), and response time. Specific throughput requirements for internetworking devices, in packets per second (PPS), can also be stated. Specific throughput requirements for applications should be included in the Applications section.

- **Security.** General and specific goals for protecting the organization's ability to conduct business without interference from intruders inappropriately accessing or damaging equipment, data, or operations. This section should also list the various security risks that the customer identified during the requirements-analysis phase of the design project.

- **Manageability.** General and specific goals for performance, fault, configuration, security and accounting management.

- **Usability.** The ease with which network users can access the network and its services. This section can include information on goals for simplifying user tasks related to network addressing, naming, and resource discovery.

- **Adaptability.** The ease with which a network design and implementation can adapt to network faults, changing traffic patterns, additional business or technical requirements, new business practices, and other changes.

- **Affordability.** General information on the importance of containing the costs associated with purchasing and operating network equipment and services. Specific budget information should be included in the Project Budget section.

The Technical Goals section should also describe any tradeoffs the customer is willing to make. For example, some customers might indicate that affordability can be sacrificed to meet strict availability goals, or usability can be sacrificed to meet strict security goals. As discussed in Chapter 2, including a chart that categorizes the comparative weights of goals can help the readers of a network design document understand some of the design choices that were made.

User Communities and Data Stores

This section lists major user communities, including their sizes, locations and the principal applications they use. You can use Table 4–1, "User Communities," to summarize information about user communities. This section should also list major data stores (servers and hosts) and their locations. Use Table 4–2, "Data Stores," to summarize information about data stores.

Network Applications

The Network Applications section lists and characterizes the new and existing network applications. Information about applications can be summarized in the "Network Applications Technical Requirements" chart shown in Table 2–3, and in the "Network Applications Traffic Characteristics" chart shown in Table 4–4. If you want, you can merge these two tables so that there is just one row for each application.

The case studies in Chapters 9, 10, and 11 provide good examples of the information regarding network applications, user communities, and data stores that should be included in a design document.

Current State of the Network

This section briefly describes the structure and performance of the existing network. It should include a high-level network map that identifies the location of major internetworking devices, data-processing and storage systems, and network segments. The high-level map should document the names and addresses of major devices and segments, and indicate the types and lengths of principal network segments. For very large internetworks, two or three high-level maps might be necessary. Detailed maps, however, should be placed in the Appendix rather than in this section.

The network maps should include logical as well as physical components, for example, the location and reach of any Virtual Private Networks (VPNs), virtual LANs (VLANs), firewall segments, server clusters, and so on. The maps should also characterize the logical topology of the internetwork and the networks that make up the internetwork. Network drawings, or text associated with drawings, should indicate whether networks are hierarchical or flat, structured or unstructured, layered or not, and so on. They should also indicate network geometry, for example, star, ring, bus, hub and spoke, or mesh.

The documentation of the current state of the network also briefly describes any strategies or standards your customer uses for network addressing and device naming. If the customer uses (or plans to use) address-summarization techniques, for example, this should be indicated in the design document.

A major portion of the "Current State of the Network" section of the network design document should be dedicated to an analysis of the health and performance of the present network. See Chapter 3, "Characterizing the Existing Internetwork," for more information on the documentation you should gather about the existing network.

Detailed reports (for example, one-minute network utilization charts) can be placed in the Appendix of the design document to avoid overwhelming the reader with too much information at this stage. It is important that the reader be able to quickly reach the Logical Design and Physical Design sections of the document, as those sections contain the essence of your design proposal.

Logical Design

The Logical Design section documents the following aspects of your network design:

- The network topology, including one or more drawings that illustrate the logical architecture of the new network

- A model for addressing network segments and devices

- A model for naming network devices

- A list of the routing, bridging, and switching protocols that have been selected to implement the design, and any specific implementation recommendations associated with those protocols

- Recommended security mechanisms and products, including a summary of security policies and procedures. (If a detailed security plan was developed as part of the network design, it can be submitted as an addendum to the design document.)

- Recommended network management architectures, processes, and products

- Design rationale, outlining why various choices were made, in light of the customer's goals and the current state of the network

---

NOTES

Not all designs include all these components. Based on your customer's requirements, you should recognize whether it is necessary to address all the issues included in the preceding list in your network design document.

Physical Design

The Physical Design section describes the features and recommended uses for the technologies and devices you selected to implement the design. It can include information for campus networks (as discussed in Chapter 9) and remote-access and wide area networks (as discussed in Chapter 10). This section can also include information about any service providers selected.

If appropriate, the Physical Design section should include information on the pricing for network devices and services. Sometimes pricing is negotiable and is not appropriate to include in the design document. In most cases, however, customers expect to see product and service pricing in the design document.

The Physical Design section should also contain information on the availability of products. If your design recommends products that are not yet shipping, you should document a predicted ship date, as provided by the product vendor.

Results of Network Design Testing

This section describes the results of the testing that you did to verify your network design. It is one of the most important portions of the design document because it gives you a chance to prove to your customer that your design will likely meet requirements for performance, security, usability, manageability, and so on. You can describe any prototype or pilot systems that you implemented and the following testing components:

- Test objectives

- Test acceptance criteria

- Testing tools

- Test scripts

- Results and observations

In the Results and Observations segment, be sure to include any optimization techniques you recommend be applied to the design to ensure that it meets requirements. Based on the results of your testing, you might recommend mechanisms for minimizing broadcast and multicast traffic, advanced features for meeting quality of service (QoS) requirements, and sophisticated router switching and queuing services. See Chapter 12 for more information on optimization techniques.

Implementation Plan

The Implementation Plan includes your recommendations for deploying the network design. The level of detail in this section varies from project to project, and depends on your relationship to your customer.

If you are a member of an Information Systems (IS) department that is responsible for the design and implementation of the new network, then this section should be quite detailed. If you are a sales engineer for a vendor of networking products, on the other hand, your role is probably to recommend solutions but not implement them, so this section should be short. (You should avoid appearing as if you are telling your customers how to do their jobs.)

The following topics are suitable for the Implementation Plan:

- A project schedule

- Plans with vendors or service providers for the installation of links, equipment, or services

- Plans or recommendations for outsourcing the implementation or management of the network

- A plan for communicating the design to end users, network administrators, and management. This section can also explain how implementation progress will be communicated (possibly via regularly-scheduled status meetings or e-mail messages).

- A training plan for network administrators and end users

- A plan for measuring the effectiveness of the design after it has been implemented

- A list of known risks that could delay the project

- A fallback plan if the network implementation fails

- A plan for evolving the network design as new application requirements and goals arise

Project Schedule

The Implementation Plan should include a project schedule or timeline. The level of detail you include in a schedule depends on your role on the project. In general, the schedule should at least include the dates and deliverables for major milestones. Table 13–1 shows an example of a high-level schedule that was developed by a sales engineer for an actual customer.

Table 13–1   High-level schedule developed for a network design customer

Date of completion	Milestone
June 1	Design completed and beta version of Design Document distributed to key executives, managers, network administrators, and end users
June 15	Comments on Design Document due
June 22	Final Design Document distributed
June 25	Installation of leased lines between all buildings completed by WAN service provider

Table 13–1   High-level schedule developed for a network design customer, Continued

Date of completion	Milestone
June 28–29	Network administrators trained on new system
June 30–July 1	End users trained on new system
July 6	Pilot implementation completed in Building 1
July 20	Feedback received on pilot from network administrators and end users
July 27	Implementation completed in Buildings 2–5
August 10	Feedback received on Buildings 2–5 implementation from network administrators and end users
August 17	Implementation completed in the rest of the buildings
Ongoing	New system monitored to verify that it meets goals

Project Budget

The Project Budget section should document the funds the customer has available for equipment purchases, maintenance and support agreements, service contracts, software licenses, training, and staffing. The budget can also include consulting fees and outsourcing expenses.

Return on Investment

In many cases the best way to sell a customer on a new network design is to convince the customer that the design will pay for itself in a reasonable time period. The network design document can include a *return-on-investment (ROI)* analysis that explains how quickly the design or new equipment will pay for itself.

Following is an example of an ROI that was completed for an actual customer, Customer ABC. The goal of this ROI analysis was to prove to the customer that the recommended WAN switching equipment will pay for itself very quickly because it will allow the customer to decrease the number of required T1 lines, and thus reduce the cost of leasing those lines from the local phone company.

| **ROI Analysis for Customer ABC** | Customer ABC is considering spending $1 million on new WAN switching equipment.

If Customer ABC does not spend the $1 million on equipment and instead puts the money into other investments for five years, Company ABC can earn approximately 5 percent interest, and the original $1 million would be worth $1.05 million. This means that the investment in the equipment should actually be considered $1.05 million.

An assumption was made that the WAN switching equipment will have a 5-year life span before it is obsolete. So, the cost per year for owning the equipment was calculated as $1.05 million divided by 5, or $210,000. The cost per month for owning the equipment is $210,000 divided by 12, or $17,500.

The monthly cost must be compared to the cost of owning the existing Time Division Multiplexers (TDMs) that comprise the current design. That cost is zero because the TDMs are old and fully paid-for and depreciated.

However, the cost of operating the old network must be compared to the cost of operating the new network. The new design will make it possible for Customer ABC to use 12 T1 lines instead of the 20 T1 lines required in the old design. Each line costs Customer ABC $1,500 per month. This means that 20 lines cost $30,000 per month, and 12 lines cost $18,000 per month.

The savings to Customer ABC with the new network design is $30,000–$18,000, or $12,000 per month. Considering that the cost for the new equipment is approximately $17,500 per month, a conclusion can be drawn that the equipment will pay for itself in its second month of use. |
|---|---|

Design Document Appendix

Most design documents include one or more appendixes that present supplemental information about the design and implementation. Supplemental information can include detailed topology maps, device configurations, network-addressing and naming details, and comprehensive results from the testing of the network design.

You can also include business information such as a list of contacts at the customer's site and in your organization, including e-mail addresses, phone numbers, beeper numbers, and physical addresses. Information on where to ship equipment and any special shipping requirements or procedures is a useful addition in some cases.

If necessary, the appendix can include exact information on pricing and payment options. Sometimes copies of purchase orders are included. The appendix can also contain legal and contractual terms and conditions, and non-disclosure agreements.

Some design documents include information about the company presenting the design proposal, including pages from annual reports, product catalogs, or recent press releases favorable to the company. The goal of this type of information is to make sure the reader understands that the company is qualified to develop and implement the proposed network design. If appropriate, this section can include recommendations from other customers for whom the company has provided a solution.

SUMMARY

When a customer provides an RFP, your network design proposal should follow the format prescribed in the RFP. When not bound by an RFP, or when a customer expects comprehensive design documentation, you should develop a document that describes requirements, the existing network, the logical and physical design, and the budget and expenses associated with implementing the design.

The design document should include an executive summary and a primary project goal. It should also document the network topology, any addressing and naming schemes you designed, security recommendations, and information about protocols, technologies, and products. Results of your network design testing can be included to convince your customer of the validity of your design.

It is also important that a design document contain a plan for implementing the network and measuring the success of the implementation. The plan should recommend network-management and monitoring processes that can confirm that the implementation meets requirements for performance, availability, security, manageability, usability, and affordability.

The plan should also mention a process for evolving the network design as new application requirements arise. Enterprise networks continue to change at a rapid rate as organizations increasingly rely on their networks to help them achieve critical business goals. A network design must keep pace with new applications that let organizations increase revenue, reduce operational costs, and communicate more effectively with customers, business partners, and employees. Organizations that have not yet implemented modern applications such as electronic commerce, IP telephony, and videoconferencing will likely want to deploy these or other new applications in the near future.

Vendors and standards bodies rapidly introduce new products and protocols to keep up with changing requirements. By following a systematic design process, you can keep pace with the evolving networking industry. With a focus on your customer's business and technical goals, you can develop solutions that accommodate changing technologies and requirements.

Many inexperienced network designers make the mistake of immediately jumping to the design step of selecting vendors and products. *Top-Down Network Design* has presented the benefits of first analyzing requirements and traffic flows, and then developing a logical design, followed by a physical design that specifies products and technologies. Using this approach will strengthen your competency as a network designer, and promote the success of your network design customers.

Appendixes

A

Characterizing Network Traffic When Workstations Boot

This appendix shows the network traffic caused by a workstation booting on a network and setting up a network session. Each table shows typical workstation behavior for a particular protocol. The following protocols are represented:

- Novell NetWare

- AppleTalk

- TCP/IP

- TCP/IP with the Dynamic Host Configuration Protocol (DHCP)

- NetBIOS (NetBEUI)

- NetBIOS with a Windows Internet Name Service (WINS) server

- SNA

The tables in this appendix show initialization packets and approximate packet sizes. On top of the packet size, you should add the data-link layer overhead, such as 802.3 with 802.2, 802.5 with 802.2, FDDI with 802.2, or other data-link layer overhead. Network-layer and transport-layer overhead are already included. Depending on the version of a protocol, the behavior on a particular network might be slightly different from the behavior shown in the tables.

NOVELL NETWARE PACKETS

Table A–1 shows the packets that a Novell NetWare client sends and receives when it boots.

Table A-1   Packets for NetWare Client Initialization

Packet Type	Source	Destination	Packet Size in Bytes	Number of Packets	Total Bytes
Get nearest server	Client	Broadcast	34	1	34
Get nearest server response	Server or router	Client	66	Depends on number of servers	66 if 1 server
Find network number	Client	Broadcast	40	1	40
Find network number response	Router	Client	40	1	40
Create connection	Client	Server	37	1	37
Create connection response	Server	Client	38	1	38
Negotiate buffer size	Client	Server	39	1	39
Negotiate buffer size response	Server	Client	40	1	40
Logout old connections	Client	Server	37	1	37
Logout response	Server	Client	38	1	38
Get server's clock	Client	Server	37	1	37
Get server's clock response	Server	Client	38	1	38
Download login.exe	Client	Server	50	Hundreds, depending on buffer size	Depends
Download login.exe response	Server	Client	Depends on buffer size	Hundreds, depending on buffer size	Depends
Login	Client	Server	37	1	37
Login response	Server	Client	38	1	38

AppleTalk Packets

Table A–2 shows the packets that an AppleTalk station sends and receives when it boots.

NOTES

An AppleTalk station that has already been on a network remembers its previous network number and node ID. It tries 10 times to verify that the network.node combination is still unique using the AppleTalk Address Resolution Protocol (AARP). If the AppleTalk station has never been on a network or if it has been moved, it sends 20 AARP multicasts: 10 multicasts with a provisional network number and 10 multicasts with a network number supplied by a router that responds to the ZIP GetNetInfo request. The example shows a station that has already been on a network.

Table A–2   Packets for AppleTalk Client Initialization

Packet Type	Source	Destination	Packet Size in Bytes	Number of Packets	Total Bytes
AARP for node ID	Client	Multicast	28	10	280
ZIP GetNetInfo	Client	Multicast	15	1	15
ZIP GetNetInfo response	Router(s)	Client	About 44	All routers respond	44 if one router
NBP broadcast request to check uniqueness of name	Client	Router	About 65	3	195
NBP forward request	Router	Other routers	Same	Same	Same
NBP lookup	Router	Multicast	Same	Same	Same

Table A–2   Packets for AppleTalk Client Initialization, Continued

Packet Type	Source	Destination	Packet Size in Bytes	Number of Packets	Total Bytes
If Chooser started:					
Get Zone List	Client	Router	12	1	12
Get Zone List reply	Router	Client	Depends on number and names of zones	1	Depends
NBP broadcast request for servers in zone	Client	Router	About 65	Once a second if Chooser is left open; decays after 45 seconds	About 3,000 if Chooser closed after 45 seconds
NBP forward request	Router	Other routers	About 65	Same	Same
NBP lookup	Router	Multicast	About 65	Same	Same
NBP reply	Server(s)	Client	About 65	Depends on number of servers	Depends
ASP open session and AFP login	Client	Server	Depends	4	About 130
ASP and AFP replies	Server	Client	Depends	2	About 90

TCP/IP PACKETS

Table A–3 shows the packets that a traditional TCP/IP station sends and receives when it boots. (Traditional means that the station is not running DHCP.)

Table A–3   Packets for Traditional TCP/IP Client Initialization

Packet Type	Source	Destination	Packet Size in Bytes	Number of Packets	Total Bytes
ARP to make sure its own address is unique (optional)	Client	Broadcast	28	1	28
ARP for any servers	Client	Broadcast	28	Depends on number of servers	Depends
ARP for router	Client	Broadcast	28	1	28
ARP response	Server(s) or router	Client	28	Depends on number of servers	Depends

TCP/IP DHCP Packets

Table A–4 shows the packets that a TCP/IP station running DHCP sends and receives when it boots. Although a DHCP client sends more packets than a traditional TCP/IP station when initializing, DHCP is still recommended. The benefits of dynamic configuration outweigh the disadvantages of extra traffic and extra broadcast packets.

NOTES

Normally, DHCP servers attempt to deliver *DHCP offer, DHCP ACK,* and *DHCP NAK* messages directly to the client using unicast delivery. Some client implementations are unable to receive such unicast IP datagrams until the implementation has been configured with a valid IP address. This leads to a deadlock in which the client's IP address cannot be delivered until the client has been configured with an IP address.

A client that cannot receive unicast IP datagrams until its protocol software has been configured with an IP address sets the broadcast bit in the *flags* field in any *DHCP discover* or *DHCP request* messages the client sends. The broadcast bit tells the DHCP server to broadcast any messages back to the client on the client's subnet. The following example shows a client that set the broadcast bit.

Table A–4   Packets for TCP/IP DHCP Client Initialization

Packet Type	Source	Destination	Packet Size in Bytes	Number of Packets	Total Bytes
DHCP discover	Client	Broadcast	328 (older versions used 576 bytes)	Once every few seconds until client hears from a DHCP server	Depends
DHCP offer	Server	Broadcast	328	1	328
DHCP request	Client	Broadcast	328 (older versions used 576 bytes)	1	576
DHCP ACK	Server	Broadcast	328	1	328
ARP to make sure its own address is unique	Client	Broadcast	28	3	84
ARP for any servers	Client	Broadcast	28	Depends on number of servers	Depends
ARP for router	Client	Broadcast	28	1	1
ARP response	Servers or router	Client	28	Depends on number of servers	Depends

NETBIOS (NETBEUI) PACKETS

Table A–5 shows the packets that a NetBIOS (NetBEUI) station sends and receives when it boots. In a Windows, Windows NT, LAN Manager, or LAN Server environment, Server Message Block (SMB) session-initialization packets follow the NetBIOS packets. The SMB packets are not shown.

Table A–5   Packets for NetBIOS (NetBEUI) Client Initialization

Packet Type	Source	Destination	Packet Size in Bytes	Number of Packets	Total Bytes
Check name (make sure own name is unique)	Client	Broadcast	44	6 for each name	264 if 1 name
Find name for each server	Client	Broadcast	44	Depends on number of servers	44 if 1 server
Find name response	Server(s)	Client	44	Depends	44 if 1 server
Session initialize for each server	Client	Server	14	Depends	14 if 1 server
Session confirm	Server	Client	14	Depends	14 if 1 server

NetBIOS with WINS Packets

Table A–6 shows the packets that a NetBIOS station configured with the address of a WINS server sends and receives when it boots. Using NetBIOS with a WINS server (instead of NetBEUI) is recommended because of the reduction in broadcast packets. In a Windows, Windows NT, LAN Manager, or LAN Server environment, SMB session-initialization packets follow the NetBIOS packets. The SMB packets are not shown.

Table A–6   Packets for NetBIOS with WINS Client Initialization

Packet Type	Source	Destination	Packet Size in Bytes	Number of Packets	Total Bytes
Register name	Client	WINS server	96	1 for each name	96 if 1 name
Register name response	WINS server	Client	90	1 for each name	90 if 1 name
Name query request for each server	Client	WINS Server	78	Depends on number of servers	78 if 1 server
Name query response	WINS Server	Client	90	Depends	90 if 1 server
Session initialize for each server	Client	Server	14	Depends	14 if 1 server
Session confirm	Server	Client	14	Depends	14 if 1 server

SNA PACKETS

Table A–7 shows the packets that a typical SNA station sends and receives when it boots. Note that the SNA example does not include any NetBIOS or other packets necessary to reach an SNA gateway, although the example is based on a Token Ring network that had a gateway.

Table A–7   Packets for SNA Client Initialization

Packet Type	Source	Destination	Packet Size in Bytes	Number of Packets	Total Bytes
LLC test	Client	Broadcast	3	1	3
LLC test response	Host or gateway	Client	3	1	3
LLC XID	Both	Both	3	2	6
LLC SABME	Host or gateway	Client	3	1	3
LLC SABME response	Client	Host or gateway	3	1	3
ACTPU	Host	Client	40	1	40
ACTPU response	Client	Host	51	1	51
ACTLU	Host	Client	34	1	34
ACTLU response	Client	Host	47	1	47

References and Recommended Reading

Albitz, P. and C. Liu. *DNS and BIND*, 2nd ed. Sebastopol, California: O'Reilly & Associates, Inc.; 1997.

ATM Forum. *LANE User-to-Network Interface (LUNI) Version 2.0*. Available at: ftp://ftp.atmforum.com/pub/approved-specs/af-lane-0084.000.pdf.

ATM Forum. *Traffic Management Specification Version 4.0*. Available at: ftp://ftp.atmforum.com/pub/approved-specs/af-tm-0056.000.pdf.

Black, U. *Frame Relay Networks: Specifications and Implementations,* 2nd ed. New York, New York: McGraw-Hill, Inc.; 1996.

Breyer, B. and S. Riley. *Switched and Fast Ethernet,* 2nd ed. Emeryville, California: Ziff-Davis Press; 1996.

Buchanan, R. *The Art of Testing Network Systems*. New York, New York: John Wiley & Sons, Inc.; 1996.

Comer, D.E. *Internetworking with TCP/IP: Principles, Protocols, and Architecture,* Vol. I, 3rd ed. Englewood Cliffs, New Jersey: Prentice Hall, Inc.; 1995.

Ford, M., H.K. Lew, S. Spanier, and T. Stevenson. *Internetworking Technologies Handbook*. Indianapolis, Indiana: Macmillan Technical Publishing; 1997.

Freeman, R.L. *Telecommunication System Engineering*, 3rd ed. New York, New York; John Wiley & Sons, Inc.; 1996.

Gane, C. and T. Sarson. *Structured Systems Analysis: Tools & Techniques*. New York, New York: Improved System Technologies; 1977.

Halabi, B. *Internet Routing Architectures*. Indianapolis, Indiana: Macmillan Technical Publishing; 1997.

Huitema, C. *Routing in the Internet*. Englewood Cliffs, New Jersey: Prentice Hall, Inc.; 1995.

Institute of Electrical and Electronics Engineers, Inc. *The 802 Standards for Local and Metropolitan Area Networks*. See www.ieee.org for the latest standards.

Internet Engineering Task Force (IETF). *Request for Comments (RFCs)*. See www.rfc-editor.org/ for the latest standards and draft standards.

Jain, R. *The Art of Computer Systems Performance Analysis: Techniques for Experimental Design, Measurement, Simulation, and Modeling*. New York, New York: John Wiley & Sons, Inc.; 1991.

Kirby, T. *The Can-Do Manager: How to Get Your Employees to Take Risks, Take Action, and Get Things Done*. New York, New York: American Management Association; 1989.

Lloyd-Evans, R. *Wide Area Network Performance and Optimization: Practical Strategies for Success*. Harlow, England: Addison-Wesley Publishing Company, Inc.; 1996.

McCabe, J.D. *Practical Computer Network Analysis and Design*. San Francisco, California: Morgan Kaufmann Publishers, Inc.; 1998.

McDysan, D.E. and D.L. Spohn. *ATM: Theory and Application*. New York, New York: McGraw-Hill, Inc.; 1994.

Miller, M.A. *Internetworking: A Guide to Network Communications LAN to LAN; LAN to WAN*, 2nd ed. New York, New York: IDG Books Worldwide, Inc.; 1995.

Miller, M.A. *Troubleshooting TCP/IP: Analyzing the Protocols of the Internet*, 2nd ed. New York, New York: IDG Books Worldwide, Inc.; 1996.

Mirchandani, S. and R. Khanna. *FDDI: Technology and Applications.* New York, New York: John Wiley & Sons, Inc.; 1993.

Perlman, R. *Interconnections: Bridges and Routers.* Reading, Massachusetts: Addison-Wesley Publishing Company, Inc.; 1992.

Rose, M.T. and K. McCloghrie. *How to Manage Your Network Using SNMP: The Networking Management Practicum.* Englewood Cliffs, New Jersey: Prentice Hall, Inc.; 1995.

Sidhu, G.S., R.F. Andrews, and A.B. Oppenheimer. *Inside AppleTalk,* 2nd ed. Reading, Massachusetts: Addison-Wesley Publishing Company, Inc.; 1990.

Spohn, D.L. *Data Network Design,* 2nd ed. New York, New York: McGraw-Hill, Inc.; 1997.

Spurgeon, C.E. *Practical Networking with Ethernet.* Boston, Massachusetts: International Thomson Computer Press; 1997.

Stallings, W. *Data and Computer Communications,* 5th ed. Englewood Cliffs, New Jersey: Prentice Hall, Inc.; 1997.

Stallings, W. *Local and Metropolitan Area Networks,* 4th ed. New York, New York: Macmillan Publishing Company; 1993.

Stevens, W.R. *TCP/IP Illustrated,* Vol. 1. Reading, Massachusetts: Addison-Wesley Publishing Company, Inc.; 1994.

Tanenbaum, A.S. *Computer Networks,* 3rd ed. Englewood Cliffs, New Jersey: Prentice Hall, Inc.; 1996.

Glossary

A

ABR—1. available bit rate. QoS class defined by the ATM Forum for ATM networks. ABR provides a feedback mechanism that lets traffic sources adapt their transmissions to changing network conditions to facilitate low cell loss and the fair sharing of available bandwidth. ABR provides no guarantees in terms of cell loss or delay. Compare with *CBR*, *UBR*, and *VBR*. 2. area border router. Router located on the border of one or more OSPF areas that connects those areas to the backbone network.

access control list—See *ACL*.

access layer—One of three layers in a hierarchical network topology, the access layer provides users on local segments access to the internetwork. Compare with *core layer* and *distribution layer*. See also *hierarchical network design*.

access server—See *remote-access server*.

accuracy—The amount of useful traffic that is correctly transmitted on a network, relative to total traffic. Accuracy is measured as a bit-error rate (BER), cell-error rate (CER), or as the number of frame errors compared to the total number of bytes transmitted. See also *BER* and *CER*.

ACL—access control list. List kept by a router to control access to or from the router for a number of services (for example, to prevent packets with a certain IP address from leaving a particular interface on the router).

active monitor—Device responsible for monitoring a Token Ring. The active monitor ensures that tokens are not lost and that frames do not circulate indefinitely.

adaptability—The ease with which a network design and implementation can adapt to network faults, changing traffic patterns, additional business or technical requirements, and other changes.

Address Resolution Protocol—See *ARP*.

administrative distance—Rating of the trustworthiness of a route in a routing table. A route with a low administrative distance is preferred over routes with higher administrative distances.

ADSL—asymmetric digital subscriber line. One of many DSL technologies. ADSL is designed to deliver more bandwidth downstream (from the provider to the customer site) than upstream. See also *DSL* and *HDSL*.

Advanced Peer-to-Peer Networking—See *APPN*.

Advanced Program-to-Program Communication—See *APPC*.

affordability—A common network design goal that specifies the importance of containing the costs associated with developing and implementing a network design, including the purchasing and operating of network equipment and services.

AFP—AppleTalk Filing Protocol. Application- and presentation-layer protocol that allows users to share data files and application programs that reside on a file server.

agent—In network management, a process that resides in a managed device and reports the values of specified variables to management stations.

APPC—Advanced Program-to-Program Communication. IBM SNA system software that allows high-speed communication between programs on different computers in a distributed computing environment.

AppleTalk—Series of communications protocols designed by Apple Computer that feature ease-of-use, dynamic addressing, and simplified resource discovery.

AppleTalk Filing Protocol—See *AFP*.

AppleTalk Update-Based Routing Protocol—See *AURP*.

application layer—Layer 7 of the OSI reference model. This layer provides services to application processes (such as electronic mail, file transfer, and terminal emulation) that are outside the OSI model. The application layer identifies and establishes the availability of intended communication partners (and the resources required to connect with them), synchronizes cooperating applications, and establishes agreement on procedures for error recovery and control of data integrity.

APPN—Advanced Peer-to-Peer Networking. Enhancement to the original IBM SNA architecture. APPN handles session establishment between peer nodes, dynamic transparent route calculation, and traffic prioritization for APPC traffic. See also *APPC*.

ARCNET—Attached Resource Computer Network. 2.5-Mbps token-bus LAN developed in the late 1970s and early 1980s by Datapoint Corporation.

area—Logical set of network segments and their attached devices. Areas are usually connected to other areas via routers.

area border router—See *ABR*.

ARP—Address Resolution Protocol. Internet protocol used to map an IP address to a MAC address. Defined in RFC 826. Compare with *RARP*. See also *proxy ARP*.

asymmetric digital subscriber line—See *ADSL*.

asymmetric encryption—An encryption technique where a different key is used to encrypt a message than is used to decrypt the message. Compare with *symmetric encryption*.

asynchronous routing—A function of a remote-access server that provides Layer-3 routing functionality to connect LANs via an asynchronous serial WAN link.

ATM—Asynchronous Transfer Mode. International standard for cell relay in which multiple service types (such as voice, video, or data) are conveyed in fixed-length (53-byte) cells.

ATM Forum—International organization jointly founded in 1991 by Cisco Systems, NET/ADAPTIVE, Northern Telecom, and Sprint that develops and promotes standards-based implementation agreements for ATM technology. The ATM Forum expands on official standards developed by international standards bodies, and develops implementation agreements in advance of official standards.

Attached Resource Computer Network—See *ARCNET*.

AURP—AppleTalk Update-Based Routing Protocol. AppleTalk routing protocol that minimizes routing-update traffic on WANs and provides a method of encapsulating AppleTalk traffic in the header of a foreign protocol.

authentication—In security, the verification of the identity of a person or process.

authorization—Securing a network by specifying which areas of the network (applications, devices, and so forth) a user is allowed to access.

autonomous system—Collection of networks or areas under a common administration sharing a common routing strategy.

availability—The amount of time a network is available to users, often expressed as a percent uptime, or as a mean time between failure (MTBF) and mean time to repair (MTTR). See also *MTBF* and *MTTR*.

available bit rate—See *ABR*.

B

backbone—A network that connects many other networks and acts as the primary path for traffic between those networks.

backup links—Physical redundant connections between network devices.

backward explicit congestion notification—See *BECN*.

bandwidth—See *capacity*.

bandwidth domain—In a LAN, the set of devices that share and compete for bandwidth. Bandwidth domains are bounded by switches, bridges, or routers. A hub or repeater does not bound a bandwidth domain. Also called a *collision domain* on Ethernet networks.

Banyan VINES—See *VINES*.

baseline—Characterization of the normal traffic flow and performance of a network, used as input to a new or enhanced design for the network.

Basic Rate Interface—See *BRI*.

beacon—Frame from a Token Ring or FDDI device indicating a serious problem with the ring, such as a broken cable.

BECN—backward explicit congestion notification. Bit set by a Frame Relay network in frames traveling in the opposite direction of frames encountering a congested path. Compare with *FECN*.

BER—bit error rate. Ratio of received bits that contain errors to the total number of received bits.

BERT—bit error rate tester. Device that determines the BER on a given communications channel.

BGP—Border Gateway Protocol. Inter-domain routing protocol that exchanges reachability information with other BGP systems. BGP Version 4 (BGP4) is the predominant inter-domain routing protocol used on the Internet.

BIND—Berkeley Internet Name Domain. Implementation of DNS developed and distributed by the University of California at Berkeley (United States).

bit error rate—See *BER*.

bit error rate tester—See *BERT*.

BOOTP—Bootstrap Protocol. Protocol used by a network node to determine the IP address of its interfaces in order to achieve network booting.

Border Gateway Protocol—See *BGP*.

BPDU—bridge protocol data unit. Spanning Tree Protocol hello packet that is sent out at configurable intervals to exchange information among bridges in a network.

BRI—Basic Rate Interface. ISDN interface composed of two bearer (B) channels for user data and one data (D) channel used for signaling. Compare with *PRI*.

bridge—Device that connects and passes frames between two network segments. Bridges operate at the data-link layer (Layer 2) of the OSI reference model. A bridge filters, forwards, or floods an incoming frame based on the MAC destination address of the frame.

bridge protocol data unit—See *BPDU*.

broadcast—Message that is sent to all nodes on a network. Compare with *multicast* and *unicast*.

broadcast address—Special address reserved for sending a message to all nodes. Generally, a broadcast address is a MAC destination address of all ones (FF:FF:FF:FF:FF:FF in hexadecimal). Compare with *multicast address* and *unicast address*.

Broadcast and Unknown Server—See *BUS*.

broadcast domain—The set of all devices that receives broadcast frames originating from any device within the set. Broadcast domains are bounded by routers (which do not forward broadcast frames). A switch or hub does not bound a broadcast domain.

broadcast storm—Undesirable network event in which many broadcasts are sent in quick succession across numerous network segments. A broadcast storm uses substantial network bandwidth, causes extra processing at network nodes, and can cause network time-outs.

building network—Multiple LANs within a building, usually connected to a building backbone network.

burst mode—Method of sending data in a Novell network that features flow control and the ability to send large bursts of data before stopping and waiting for an acknowledgment.

bursty traffic—Network traffic characterized by short intervals of intense activity with lulls between the intervals.

BUS—Broadcast and Unknown Server. Multicast server used in ELANs that floods traffic addressed to an unknown destination and forwards multicast and broadcast traffic to the appropriate clients. See also *ELAN*.

C

cable modem—A modem that operates over the coaxial cable that is used by cable TV providers. Because the coaxial cable provides greater bandwidth than telephone lines, a cable modem offers much faster access than an analog modem.

CAC—connection admission control. Set of actions taken by an ATM switch during connection setup that determines whether a connection's requested QoS violates the QoS guarantees for established connections.

caching—Form of replication in which information learned during a previous transaction is used to process later transactions.

campus network—A set of LAN segments and building networks in a geographical area that is a few miles in diameter.

capacity—The data-carrying capability of a circuit or network, measured in bits per second (bps). Because this book focuses on digital transmission technologies, it uses the terms *capacity* and *bandwidth* synonymously.

Carrier Detect—See *CD*.

carrier sense multiple access with collision detection—See *CSMA/CD*.

CBR—constant bit rate. QoS class defined by the ATM Forum for ATM networks. CBR is used for connections that depend on precise clocking to ensure undistorted delivery. Compare with *ABR*, *UBR*, and *VBR*.

CD—Carrier Detect. Signal that indicates whether an interface is active. Also, a signal generated by a modem indicating that a call has been connected.

CDP—Cisco Discovery Protocol. Device-discovery protocol that runs on Cisco-manufactured equipment including routers, remote-access servers, and switches. Using CDP, a device can advertise its existence to other devices and receive information about other devices on the same LAN or on the remote side of a WAN.

CDV—cell delay variation. In ATM, component of cell transfer delay (CTD) that is induced by buffering and cell scheduling. CDV is a QoS delay parameter associated with CBR and VBR service.

cell—Basic data unit for ATM switching and multiplexing. Cells contain identifiers that specify the data stream to which they belong. Each cell consists of a 5-byte header and 48 bytes of payload.

cell delay variation—See *CDV*.

cell error ratio—See *CER*.

cell loss ratio—See *CLR*.

cell transfer delay—See *CTD*.

CER—cell error ratio. In ATM, the ratio of transmitted cells that have errors to the total cells sent in a transmission for a specific period of time.

Challenge Handshake Authentication Protocol—See *CHAP*.

channel aggregation—A process wherein a device can automatically bring up multiple circuits as bandwidth requirements increase.

Channel Interface Processor—See *CIP*.

channel service unit—See *CSU*.

CHAP—Challenge Handshake Authentication Protocol. Security feature supported on links using PPP encapsulation that identifies the remote end of a PPP session using a handshake protocol and a variable challenge value that is unique and unpredictable. Compare with *PAP*.

CIDR—classless inter-domain routing. Technique supported by BGP4 and other routing protocols based on route summarization (aggregation). CIDR allows routers to group routes together to cut down on the quantity of routing information carried by the core routers.

CIP—Channel Interface Processor. Channel attachment interface for Cisco 7000 series routers. The CIP is used to connect a host mainframe to a control unit, eliminating the need for an FEP for channel attachment.

CIR—committed information rate. Rate at which a Frame Relay network agrees to transfer information under normal conditions, averaged over a minimum increment of time. CIR, measured in bits per second, is one of the key negotiated tariff metrics for a Frame Relay service.

circuit—Communications path between two or more points.

Cisco Discovery Protocol—See *CDP*.

Cisco IOS—Cisco Internetwork Operating System. Cisco system software that provides common functionality, scalability, and security for Cisco products. Cisco IOS supports a wide variety of protocols, media, services, and platforms.

classless inter-domain routing—See *CIDR*.

client—Node or software program that requests services from a server.

client/server—Distributed-computing network systems in which transaction responsibilities are divided into two parts: client and server. Clients rely on servers for services such as file storage, printing, and processing power.

CLR—cell loss ratio. In ATM, the ratio of discarded cells to cells that are successfully transmitted. CLR can be set as a QoS parameter when a connection is set up.

coaxial cable—Cable consisting of a hollow outer cylindrical conductor that surrounds a single inner wire conductor. Also known simply as *coax cable*.

CODEC—Coder-decoder. Device that typically uses pulse-code modulation to transform analog signals into a digital bit stream and digital signals back into analog.

collision—In Ethernet, the result of two nodes transmitting simultaneously.

collision domain—In Ethernet, the network area within which frames that have collided are propagated. Repeaters and hubs propagate collisions; LAN switches, bridges and routers do not. See also *bandwidth domain*.

committed information rate—See *CIR*.

Common Open Policy Service—See *COPS*.

compression—The running of data through an algorithm that reduces the space required to store or the bandwidth required to transmit the data.

congestion—A condition whereby network traffic has reached or is approaching network capacity.

connection admission control—See *CAC*.

connection-oriented—Data transfer that requires the establishment of a virtual circuit.

connectionless—Data transfer without the existence of a virtual circuit.

constant bit rate—See *CBR*.

convergence—Speed and ability of a group of internetworking devices running a specific routing protocol to agree on the topology of an internetwork after a change in that topology.

COPS—Common Open Policy Service. An IETF protocol that defines a client/server model for supporting policy control with QoS-reservation protocols such as RSVP.

core layer—The high-speed backbone of an internetwork in a hierarchical topology. The core layer should be highly reliable and adapt to changes quickly. Compare with *access layer* and *distribution layer*. See also *hierarchical network design*.

cost—Arbitrary value, typically based on hop count, media bandwidth, a configurable parameter, or other measures, that is used by routing protocols to determine the most favorable path to a particular destination. The lower the cost, the better the path. See also *routing metric*.

count to infinity—Problem that can occur in routing algorithms that are slow to converge, in which routers continuously increment the hop count to particular networks. Typically, some arbitrary hop-count limit is imposed to prevent this problem.

CRC—cyclic redundancy check. Error-checking technique in which the frame recipient calculates a remainder by dividing frame contents by a prime binary divisor and compares the calculated remainder to a value stored in the frame by the sending node.

CSMA/CD—carrier sense multiple access with collision detection. Media-access mechanism wherein devices determine if another device is already transmitting before starting their own transmissions. If no transmission is sensed for a specific period of time, a device can transmit. If multiple devices transmit at once, a collision occurs and is detected by all colliding devices. This collision subsequently delays retransmission from those devices for some random length of time. CSMA/CD is used by Ethernet and IEEE 802.3.

CSU—channel service unit. Digital interface device that connects end-user equipment to the local digital telephone loop. Often referred to together with DSU, as *CSU/DSU*.

CTD—cell transfer delay. In ATM, the elapsed time between a cell-exit event at the source UNI and the corresponding cell-entry event at the destination UNI for a particular connection.

custom queuing—Cisco IOS routing feature that assigns different amounts of queue space to different protocols and handles queues in a round-robin fashion. Custom queuing assures each specified traffic type a fixed portion of available bandwidth. Compare with *priority queuing*.

cut-through switching—Frame-switching approach that streams data through a switch so that the leading edge of a frame exits the switch at the output port before the frame finishes entering the input port. A device using cut-through switching forwards frames as soon as the destination address is looked up and the outgoing port determined. Compare with *store-and-forward switching*.

cyclic redundancy check—See *CRC*.

D

Data Encryption Standard—See *DES*.

data-link layer—Layer 2 of the OSI reference model. This layer provides reliable transit of data across a physical link. The data-link layer is concerned with physical addressing, network topology, line discipline, error notification, ordered delivery of frames, and flow control. The IEEE has divided this layer into two sublayers: the MAC sublayer and the LLC sublayer.

data-link switching—See *DLSw*.

data service unit—See *DSU*.

data store—An area in a network where application-layer data resides. A data store can be a server, a set of servers, a mainframe, a tape backup unit, a digital video library, or any device or component of an internetwork where large quantities of data are stored. Sometimes called a *data sink*.

data terminal equipment—See *DTE*.

datagram—Logical grouping of information sent as a network-layer unit over a transmission medium without prior establishment of a virtual circuit.

Datagram Delivery Protocol—See *DDP*.

DCE—data communications equipment or data circuit-terminating equipment. Devices and connections of a communications network that comprise the network end of the user-to-network interface. Modems and interface cards are examples of DCE. Compare with *DTE*.

DDP—Datagram Delivery Protocol. AppleTalk network-layer protocol that is responsible for the delivery of datagrams over an AppleTalk internetwork.

DDR—dial-on-demand routing. Technique whereby a router can automatically initiate and close a circuit-switched session as transmitting stations demand.

decapsulation—The reverse application of encapsulation. Decapsulation unwraps data from a protocol header that was added by a device or process before transmitting the data. Compare with *encapsulation*.

DECnet—Group of communications protocols developed and supported by Digital Equipment Corporation. DECnet/OSI (also called *DECnet Phase V*) is the most recent iteration, and supports both OSI protocols and proprietary Digital protocols.

decryption—The reverse application of an encryption algorithm to encrypted data, thereby restoring the data to its original, unencrypted state. See also *encryption*.

default gateway—See *default router*.

default route—Routing table entry that is used to direct frames for which a next hop is not explicitly listed in the routing table.

default router—IP address of a router configured on an end station to allow the station to get to the rest of the internetwork. Also called *default gateway*.

delay—1. Time between the initiation of a transaction by a sender and the first response received by the sender. 2. Time required to move a frame from source to destination over a given path.

delay variation—The amount of time average delay varies. See also *jitter*.

demultiplexing—Separating of multiple input streams that were multiplexed into a common physical signal back into multiple output streams. See also *multiplexing*.

denial-of-service—A security attack where an intruder disables a network service, making it unusable by legitimate users.

dense-mode PIM—One of two PIM operational modes. With dense-mode PIM, packets are forwarded on all outgoing interfaces until pruning occurs. Receivers are densely populated, and it is assumed that many downstream networks want to receive and will probably use multicast datagrams that are forwarded to them. See also *PIM,* *prune,* and *sparse-mode PIM*.

DES—Data Encryption Standard. Standard cryptographic algorithm developed by the U.S. National Bureau of Standards.

DHCP—Dynamic Host Configuration Protocol. Provides a mechanism for allocating IP addresses dynamically to minimize configuration and allow addresses to be reused when hosts no longer need them. Defined in RFC 2131.

dial-on-demand routing—See *DDR*.

Diffusing Update Algorithm—See *DUAL*.

digital signal level 1—See *DS-1*.

digital signature—String of bits appended to a message that provides authentication and data integrity.

digital subscriber line—See *DSL*.

discontiguous subnet—An IP subnet that is made up of two or more physical networks that are separated by routers.

distance learning—A training method wherein students attend a class from remote sites using videoconferencing or other digital or analog video and audio techniques.

Distance-Vector Multicast Routing Protocol—See *DVMRP*.

distance-vector routing algorithm—Class of routing algorithms that call for each router to send its routing table in periodic update packets to its neighbors. Compare with *link-state routing algorithm*.

distribution layer—Connects network services to the access layer in a hierarchical topology, and implements policies regarding security, traffic loading, and routing. Compare with *access layer* and *core layer*. See also *hierarchical network design*.

DLSw—data-link switching. Interoperability standard, described in RFC 1434, that provides a method for forwarding SNA and NetBIOS traffic over TCP/IP networks.

DNS—Domain Name System. System used in the Internet for translating names of network nodes into addresses.

DS-1—digital signal level 1. Framing specification used in transmitting digital signals at 1.544 Mbps on a WAN circuit.

DSL—digital subscriber line. Public network technology that delivers high bandwidth over conventional telephone wiring at limited distances. See also *ADSL* and *HDSL*.

DSU—data service unit. Device used in digital transmission that adapts the physical interface on a DTE device to a transmission facility such as T1 or E1. Often referred to together with CSU, as *CSU/DSU*. See also *CSU*.

DTE—data terminal equipment. Device at the user end of a user-network interface that serves as a data source, destination, or both. DTE connects to a data network through a DCE device (for example, a modem) and typically uses clocking signals generated by the DCE. DTE includes such devices as computers, internetworking devices, and multiplexers. Compare with *DCE*.

DUAL—Diffusing Update Algorithm. Convergence algorithm used in Enhanced IGRP that provides loop-free operation. DUAL allows routers involved in a topology change to synchronize, while not involving routers that are unaffected by the change. See also *Enhanced IGRP*.

DVMRP—Distance-Vector Multicast Routing Protocol. Multicast routing protocol, largely based on RIP. Packets are forwarded on all outgoing interfaces until pruning occurs. Defined in RFC 1075. See also *prune*.

Dynamic Host Configuration Protocol (DHCP)—See *DHCP*.

dynamic password—Security mechanism that incorporates a dynamically-generated password that can be used only once.

E

E1—Wide-area digital transmission scheme used predominantly in Europe that carries data at a rate of 2.048 Mbps. E1 lines can be leased for private use from common carriers.

efficiency—A measure of how much overhead is required to produce a certain amount of data throughput on a network. Overhead includes frame headers and trailers, acknowledgments, tokens and other MAC mechanisms, and flow-control mechanisms.

EIGRP— See *Enhanced Interior Gateway Routing Protocol.*

ELAN—emulated LAN. ATM network in which an Ethernet or Token Ring LAN is emulated using a client/server model. ELANs are composed of an LEC, an LES, a BUS, and an LECS. ELANs are defined by the LANE specification.

encapsulating bridging—A bridging method for connecting LANs across a network of a different type, for example, connecting Ethernet LANs via an FDDI backbone. The entire frame from one network is placed inside the frame used by the data-link layer protocol of the other network. Compare with *translational bridging.*

encapsulation—Wrapping of data in a particular protocol header.

encryption—Application of a specific algorithm to alter the appearance of data, making it incomprehensible to those who are not authorized to see the information. See also *decryption.*

encryption key—A code used by an encryption algorithm to scramble and unscramble data.

Enhanced Interior Gateway Routing Protocol— Advanced version of IGRP developed by Cisco. Provides superior convergence properties and operating efficiency, and combines the advantages of link-state protocols with those of distance-vector protocols.

enterprise network—Large and diverse internetwork connecting most major points in an organization. An enterprise network typically consists of building and campus networks, remote-access services, and one or more WANs.

Ethernet—LAN technology invented by Xerox Corporation and developed jointly by Xerox, Intel, and Digital Equipment Corporation. Ethernet networks use CSMA/CD and run over a variety of cable types at 10 Mbps. Ethernet is similar to IEEE 802.3.

explorer frame—Frame generated by an end station trying to find its way through a SRB network. The frame gathers a hop-by-hop description of a path through the network by being marked (updated) by each bridge that it traverses.

F

Fast Ethernet—Any of a number of 100-Mbps Ethernet specifications. Fast Ethernet offers a speed increase ten times that of the original IEEE 802.3 specification, while preserving such qualities as frame format, MAC mechanisms, and frame size.

FDDI—Fiber Distributed Data Interface. LAN standard specifying a 100-Mbps token-passing network using fiber-optic cable and a dual-ring architecture to provide redundancy.

FECN—forward explicit congestion notification. Bit set by a Frame Relay network to inform a device receiving the frame that congestion was experienced in the path from source to destination. Compare with *BECN*.

FEP—front-end processor. Device or board that provides network interface capabilities for a network segment or networked device. In SNA, typically an IBM 3745 device.

Fiber Distributed Data Interface—See *FDDI*.

fiber-optic cable—Physical medium capable of conducting modulated light transmission. Fiber-optic cable is not susceptible to electromagnetic interference, and is capable of high data rates.

fiber-optic inter-repeater link—See *FOIRL*.

FIFO—first in, first out. Method of sending traffic through a device whereby the first packet received is the first packet transmitted. Does not support prioritization.

File Transfer Protocol—See *FTP*.

filter—Generally, a process or device that screens network traffic for certain characteristics, such as a source address, destination address, or protocol, and determines whether to forward or discard that traffic based on the established criteria.

firewall—Router or remote-access server (or several routers or access servers) designated as a buffer between connected networks. A firewall uses access lists and other methods to ensure the security of a network.

first in, first out—See *FIFO*.

flat network design—A network design that has little or no hierarchy or modularity and is generally only appropriate for small shared or switched LANs.

flooding—Traffic-passing technique used by switches and bridges, in which traffic received on an interface is sent out all interfaces except the interface on which the information was received.

flow—Stream of data traveling between two endpoints across a network.

flow control—Technique for ensuring that a transmitting entity does not overwhelm a receiving entity with data. When the buffers on the receiving device are full, a message is sent to the sending device to suspend transmission until the data in the buffers has been processed.

FOIRL—fiber-optic inter-repeater link. Fiber-optic signaling methodology for transmitting Ethernet frames on fiber-optic cables, based on the IEEE 802.3 fiber-optic specification.

forward explicit congestion notification—See *FECN*.

forwarding—Process of sending a frame toward its ultimate destination by way of an internetworking device.

fragmentation—Process of breaking a packet into smaller units when transmitting over a network medium that cannot support the original size of the packet. See also *reassembly*.

frame—Logical grouping of information sent as a data-link layer unit over a transmission medium. Often refers to the header and trailer, used for synchronization and error control, that surround the user data contained in the unit.

Frame Relay—Industry-standard, switched data-link layer protocol that handles multiple virtual circuits between connected devices. Frame Relay is more efficient than X.25, the protocol for which it is generally considered a replacement. See also *X.25*.

front-end processor—See *FEP*.

FTP—File Transfer Protocol. Application protocol, part of the TCP/IP protocol stack, used for transferring files between network nodes. FTP is defined in RFC 959.

full duplex—Capability for simultaneous data transmission between a sending station and a receiving station. Compare with *half duplex*.

full mesh—Term describing a network in which devices are organized in a mesh topology, with each network node having either a physical circuit or a virtual circuit connecting it to every other network node. See also *mesh* and *partial mesh*.

G

Gigabit Ethernet—1000-Mbps LAN technologies specified in IEEE 802.3z. Gigabit Ethernet offers a speed increase 100 times that of the original IEEE 802.3 specification, while preserving such qualities as frame format, MAC mechanisms, and frame size.

goodput—Generally referring to the measurement of actual data successfully transmitted from the sender(s) to receiver(s). In an ATM network, this is often a more useful measurement than the number of ATM cells-per-second throughput of an ATM switch if that switch is experiencing cell loss that results in many incomplete, and therefore unusable, frames arriving at the recipient.

group address—See *multicast address*.

H

H.320—Suite of international standard specifications for videoconferencing over circuit-switched media such as ISDN, fractional T1, or switched-56 lines.

H.323—Extension of H.320 that enables videoconferencing over LANs and other packet-switched networks, as well as video over the Internet.

half duplex—Capability for data transmission in only one direction at a time between a sending station and a receiving station. Compare with *full duplex*.

handshaking—Process whereby two protocol entities synchronize during connection establishment.

hardware address—See *MAC address*.

hash—Resulting string of bits from a hash function.

hash function—A mathematical computation that results in a string of bits (digital code); the function is not reversible to produce the original input.

HDLC—High-Level Data Link Control. Synchronous data-link layer protocol for WAN links that specifies framing and error control.

HDSL—high-data-rate digital subscriber line. One of many DSL technologies. HDSL delivers 1.544 Mbps of bandwidth each way over two copper twisted pairs. See also *DSL* and *ADSL*.

hello packet—Packet that is used by networking devices for neighbor discovery and recovery, and to indicate that a device is still operating.

helper address—Address configured on a router interface to which broadcasts received on that interface will be sent.

hierarchical network design—A technique for designing scalable campus and enterprise network topologies using a layered, modular model. See also *access layer, core layer,* and *distribution layer.*

hierarchical routing—A model for distributing knowledge of a network topology among internetwork routers. With hierarchical routing, no single router needs to understand the complete topology. See also *route summarization.*

high-data-rate digital subscriber line—See *HDSL*.

High-Level Data Link Control—See *HDLC*.

holddown—State into which a route is placed so routers will neither advertise the route nor accept advertisements about the route for a specific length of time (the holddown period). Holddown is used to flush bad information about a route from all routers in the network. A route is typically placed in holddown when a link to that route fails.

hop—Term describing the passage of a data packet between two network nodes (for example, between two routers).

hop count—Routing metric used to measure the distance between a source and a destination in number of routers or hops between the source and destination.

HSRP—Hot Standby Router Protocol. Provides high network availability and transparent network topology changes. HSRP creates a Hot Standby router group with a lead router that services all packets sent to the Hot Standby address. The lead router is monitored by other routers in the group, and if it fails, one of these standby routers inherits the lead position and the Hot Standby group address.

hub—1. Generally, a term used to describe a device or network that serves as the center of a star or hub-and-spoke topology. 2. In Ethernet and IEEE 802.3, an Ethernet multiport repeater, sometimes referred to as a *concentrator*.

hub-and-spoke topology—A topology that consists of one central network and a set of remote networks each with one connection to the central network and no direct connections to each other. Traffic between remote networks goes through the hub network.

I

IANA—Internet Assigned Numbers Authority. Organization operated under the auspices of the ISOC that delegates authority for IP address-space allocation, domain-name assignment, and autonomous system number assignment to the NIC and other organizations. IANA also maintains a database of assigned protocol identifiers used in the TCP/IP protocol stack. See also *ISOC* and *NIC*.

ICMP—Internet Control Message Protocol. Network-layer TCP/IP protocol that reports errors and provides other information relevant to IP packet processing. Documented in RFC 792.

IEEE—Institute of Electrical and Electronics Engineers. Professional organization whose activities include the development of communications and network standards. IEEE LAN standards are the predominant LAN standards today.

IEEE 802.1d—IEEE specification that describes an algorithm that prevents bridging loops by creating a spanning tree.

IEEE 802.1p—IEEE LAN protocol for supporting QoS on LANs. Specifies mechanisms in bridges to expedite the delivery of time-critical traffic and to limit the extent of high-bandwidth multicast traffic within a bridged LAN.

IEEE 802.1q—IEEE LAN protocol for supporting VLANs across various media.

IEEE 802.2—IEEE LAN protocol that specifies an implementation of the LLC sublayer of the data-link layer. See also *LLC*.

IEEE 802.3—IEEE LAN protocol that specifies an implementation of the physical layer and the MAC sublayer of the data-link layer. IEEE 802.3 uses CSMA/CD access at a variety of speeds over a variety of physical media. IEEE 802.3 is similar to Ethernet.

IEEE 802.5—IEEE LAN protocol that specifies an implementation of the physical layer and MAC sublayer of the data-link layer. IEEE 802.5 uses token passing access at 4 or 16 Mbps over UTP or STP cabling and is similar to IBM Token Ring.

IETF—Internet Engineering Task Force. Task force consisting of numerous working groups responsible for developing Internet and TCP/IP standards.

IGMP—Internet Group Management Protocol. Used by IP hosts to report their multicast group memberships to an adjacent multicast router. Defined in RFC 1112.

IGRP—Interior Gateway Routing Protocol. An interior routing protocol developed by Cisco to address the problems associated with routing in large, heterogeneous networks. Compare with *Enhanced IGRP*.

infrared—Electromagnetic waves whose frequency range is above that of microwaves, but below that of the visible spectrum. Wireless LAN systems based on infrared technology represent an emerging technology.

Institute of Electrical and Electronics Engineers—See *IEEE*.

Integrated Services Digital Network—See *ISDN*.

Integrated Services Working Group—See *ISWG*.

integrity—Keeping data safe as it traverses the network.

Inter-Switch Link—See *ISL*.

interface—1. Connection between two systems or devices. 2. A port on a device.

Interior Gateway Routing Protocol—See *IGRP*.

Intermediate System-to-Intermediate System—See *IS-IS*.

International Organization for Standardization—See *ISO*.

Internet—Term used to refer to the largest global internetwork, connecting hundreds of thousands of networks worldwide using the TCP/IP protocol stack.

Internet Assigned Numbers Authority—See *IANA*.

Internet Control Message Protocol—See *ICMP*.

Internet Engineering Task Force—See *IETF*.

Internet Group Management Protocol—See *IGMP*.

Internet Protocol—See *IP*.

Internet service provider—See *ISP*.

Internet Society—See *ISOC*.

Internet telephony—Generic term used to describe various approaches to running voice traffic over IP networks, in particular, the Internet. See also *VoIP*.

internetwork—Collection of networks interconnected by routers.

Internetwork Packet Exchange—See *IPX*.

internetworking—General term used to refer to the industry and technologies devoted to connecting networks together.

IOS—See *Cisco IOS*.

IP—Internet Protocol. Network-layer protocol in the TCP/IP stack offering a connectionless internetwork service. IP provides features for addressing, type-of-service specification, fragmentation and reassembly, and security. Defined in RFC 791.

IP address—32-bit address assigned to hosts using TCP/IP. An IP address belongs to one of five classes (A, B, C, D, or E) and is written as four octets separated by periods (dotted decimal format). Each address consists of a network number, an optional sub-network number, and a host number.

IP multicast—Routing technique that allows IP traffic to be propagated from one source to a number of destinations. Rather than sending one packet to each destination, one packet is sent to a multicast group identified by a single IP destination group address.

IPSec—IP Security Protocol. A set of open standards that provides data confidentiality, data integrity, and authentication between participating peers at the IP layer. IPSec is documented in RFCs 1825 through 1829.

IPv6—IP version 6. Replacement for the current version of IP (version 4). IPv6 includes support for flow ID in the packet header, which can be used to identify flows. Formerly called *IPng* (next generation).

IPX—Internetwork Packet Exchange. Novell NetWare network-layer (Layer-3) protocol used for transferring data between servers and workstations.

ISDN—Integrated Services Digital Network. Communication protocol, offered by telephone companies, that permits telephone networks to carry data, voice, and other source traffic.

IS-IS—Intermediate System-to-Intermediate System. OSI link-state hierarchical routing protocol based on DECnet Phase V routing.

ISL—Inter-Switch Link. Cisco-proprietary protocol that maintains VLAN information as traffic flows between switches and routers.

ISO—International Organization for Standardization. International organization that is responsible for a wide range of standards, including those relevant to networking. ISO developed the OSI reference model, a popular networking reference model.

ISO 9000—Set of international quality-management standards defined by ISO. The standards, which are not specific to any country, industry, or product, allow companies to demonstrate that they have specific processes in place to maintain an effective quality system.

ISOC—Internet Society. International nonprofit organization, founded in 1992, that coordinates the evolution and use of the Internet.

ISP—Internet service provider. Company that provides Internet access to other companies and individuals.

ISWG—Integrated Services Working Group. Subset of the IETF dedicated to defining QoS mechanisms for the Internet and other TCP/IP-based networks.

J

jitter—Communication line distortion caused by the variation of a signal from its reference timing positions. See also *delay variation*.

K

keepalive message—Message sent by one network device to inform another network device that the virtual circuit between the two is still active.

Kerberos—An authentication system that provides user-to-host security for application-layer protocols such as FTP and Telnet.

key—See *encryption key*.

L

L2TP—Layer-2 Tunneling Protocol. An emerging IETF standard for tunneling private data over public networks.

LAN—local area network. High-speed, low-error data network covering a relatively small geographic area (up to a few thousand meters). LANs connect workstations, peripherals, terminals, and other devices in a single building or other geographically-limited area.

LAN Emulation—See *LANE*.

LAN Emulation Client—See *LEC*.

LAN Emulation Configuration Server—See *LECS*.

LAN Emulation Network-to-Network Interface—See *LNNI*.

LAN Emulation Server—See *LES*.

LAN Emulation User-to-Network Interface—See *LUNI*.

LANE—LAN Emulation. Technology that allows an ATM network to function as a LAN. See also *ELAN*.

LAT—local-area transport. A network virtual-terminal protocol developed by Digital Equipment Corporation.

late collision—An Ethernet collision that occurs after the first 64 bytes of a frame. Compare with *legal collision*. See also *collision* and *CSMA/CD*.

latency—1. Delay between the time a device requests access to a network and the time it is granted permission to transmit. 2. Delay between the time a device receives a frame and the time that frame is forwarded out the destination port.

Layer-2 Tunneling Protocol—See *L2TP*.

Layer-3 switch—Switch that filters and forwards packets based on MAC addresses and network addresses. Also referred to as *multilayer switch*.

leased line—Transmission line reserved by a communications carrier for the private use of a customer.

LEC—LAN emulation client. Entity in an end system that performs data forwarding, address resolution, and other control functions for a single end system within a single ELAN. An LEC also provides a standard LAN service interface to any higher-layer entity that interfaces to the LEC.

LECS—LAN emulation configuration server. Entity that assigns individual LANE clients to particular ELANs by directing them to the LES that corresponds to the ELAN.

legal collision—An Ethernet collision that occurs within the first 64 bytes of a frame. Compare with *late collision*. See also *collision* and *CSMA/CD*.

LES—LAN emulation server. Entity that implements the control functions for a particular ELAN.

link—Network communications channel consisting of a circuit or transmission path and all related equipment between a sender and a receiver.

link-state advertisement—See *LSA*.

link-state routing algorithm—Routing algorithm in which each router broadcasts or multicasts information regarding the cost of reaching its neighbors to all nodes in its area(s). Compare with *distance-vector routing algorithm*.

LLC—Logical Link Control. Higher of the two data-link layer sublayers defined by the IEEE. The LLC sublayer handles error control, flow control, framing, and the network-layer (Layer-3) service interface. Includes both connectionless and connection-oriented services. Also known as IEEE 802.2.

LLC2—Logical Link Control, type 2. Connection-oriented LLC.

LNNI—LAN Emulation Network-to-Network Interface. Supports communication between the server components within the ATM Forum LANE specification.

load balancing—In routing, the capability of a router to distribute traffic over all its network ports that are the same distance from the destination address. Sometimes called *load sharing* to indicate that most routing protocols do not evenly balance traffic.

local acknowledgment—Method whereby an intermediate network node, such as a router, responds to acknowledgments for a remote end host. Use of local acknowledgments reduces network overhead and, therefore, the risk of time-outs.

local area network—See *LAN*.

local-area transport—See *LAT*.

Logical Link Control—See *LLC*.

LSA—link-state advertisement. Multicast packet used by link-state protocols that contains information about neighbors and path costs. LSAs are used by the receiving routers to maintain their routing tables.

LUNI—LAN Emulation User-to-Network Interface. An ATM Forum standard for LAN emulation (LANE) on ATM networks. LUNI defines the interface between the LAN emulation client (LEC) and the LAN emulation server (LES).

M

MAC—Media Access Control. Lower of the two sublayers of the data-link layer defined by the IEEE. The MAC sublayer handles access to shared media, such as whether token passing or contention will be used.

MAC address—Standardized data-link layer address that is required for every port or device that connects to a LAN. Other devices in the network use these addresses to locate specific ports in the network. MAC addresses are six bytes long and include a 3-byte vendor code that is controlled by the IEEE. Also referred to as a *hardware address, MAC-layer address, or physical address.* Compare with *network address.*

MAN—metropolitan-area network. A network that spans a metropolitan area. Generally, a MAN spans a larger geographic area than a LAN, but a smaller geographic area than a WAN.

manageability—The ease with which a network can be managed and monitored, including the management of the network's performance, faults, configuration, security, and accounting capabilities.

Management Information Base—See *MIB.*

maximum burst size—See *MBS.*

maximum cell delay variation—See *MCDV.*

maximum cell transfer delay—See *MCTD.*

maximum transmission unit—See *MTU.*

MBS—maximum burst size. Parameter defined by the ATM Forum for ATM traffic management. MCR is defined for VBR transmissions.

MCDV—maximum cell delay variation. In an ATM network, the maximum two-point CDV objective across a link or node for the specified service category.

MCR—minimum cell rate. Parameter defined by the ATM Forum for ATM traffic management. MCR is defined for ABR transmissions.

MCTD—maximum cell transfer delay. In an ATM network, the sum of the MCDV and the fixed delay component across the link or node.

mean time between failure—See *MTBF.*

mean time to repair—See *MTTR.*

media—Plural of medium. The various physical environments through which transmission signals pass. Common network media include twisted-pair, coaxial, and fiber-optic cable; and the atmosphere (through which microwave, laser, and infrared transmission occurs).

Media Access Control—See *MAC.*

mesh—Network topology in which devices are organized with many, often redundant, interconnections strategically placed between network nodes. See also *full mesh* and *partial mesh.*

message digest—Value returned by a hash function. Also referred to as *hash.*

metric—See *routing metric.*

metropolitan-area network—See *MAN.*

MIB—Management Information Base. Database of network management information that is used and maintained by a network management protocol such as SNMP. The value of a MIB object can be changed or retrieved using SNMP commands, usually through a network management system (NMS). MIB objects are organized in a tree structure that includes public (standard) and private (proprietary) branches.

minimum cell rate—See *MCR.*

MLP—See *MPPP.*

MMP—See *Multichassis MPPP.*

MOSPF—Multicast Open Shortest Path First. Intra-domain multicast routing protocol used in OSPF networks. Extensions are applied to the base OSPF unicast protocol to support IP multicast routing. Defined in RFC 1584.

MPEG—Moving Picture Experts Group. Standard for compressing video. *MPEG1* is a bit-stream standard for compressed video and audio. The most common implementations of MPEG1 use less than T1 (1.5 Mbps) capacity. *MPEG2* is intended for higher quality video-on-demand applications and runs at data rates between 4 and 9 Mbps. *MPEG4* is a low-bit-rate compression algorithm intended for 64-Kbps connections. (*MPEG3* was proposed in 1991 for High-Definition Television [HDTV], but in 1992 it was realized that MPEG2 already met the requirements.)

MPOA—Multiprotocol Over ATM. ATM Forum standardization effort specifying the way that existing and future network-layer protocols such as IP, IPv6, AppleTalk, and IPX run over an ATM network with directly attached hosts, routers, and multi-layer LAN switches.

MPPP—Multilink PPP. Method of splitting, recombining, and sequencing datagrams across multiple PPP circuits. Sometimes abbreviated as *MLP* or simply *MP*.

MTBF—mean time between failure. The average time that elapses between network or system failures.

MTTR—mean time to repair. The average amount of time it takes to fix a network or system when it fails.

MTU—maximum transmission unit. Maximum frame size, in bytes, that a particular interface or medium can handle.

multicast—Message that is sent to a subset of nodes on a network. Compare with *broadcast* and *unicast*.

multicast address—Single address that refers to multiple network nodes. Also referred to as *group address*. Compare with *broadcast address* and *unicast address*.

multicast group—Dynamically determined group of IP hosts identified by a single IP multicast address.

Multicast Open Shortest Path First—See *MOSPF*.

multicast routing protocol—Routing protocol used to route multicast packets. See also *DVMRP, MOSPF,* and *PIM.*

multichassis MPPP—Extends MPPP support across multiple routers and remote-access servers. Multichassis MPPP enables multiple routers and access servers to operate as a single, large dial-up pool, with a single network address and access number. Multichassis MPPP correctly handles packet fragmenting and reassembly when a user connection is split between two physical access devices. Sometimes abbreviated *MMP*. See also *MPPP*.

multihoming—Attaching a host or network to multiple physical network segments.

multilayer-switch—Switch that filters and forwards packets based on MAC addresses and network addresses. Also referred to as *Layer-3 switch*.

Multilink PPP—See *MPPP*.

multimode fiber—Optical fiber supporting propagation of multiple frequencies of light. Compare with *single-mode fiber*.

multiplexing—Scheme that allows multiple logical signals to be transmitted simultaneously across a single physical channel. Compare with *demultiplexing*.

N

Name Binding Protocol—See *NBP*.

NAT—Network Address Translation. Mechanism for reducing the need for globally unique IP addresses. NAT allows an organization with addresses that are not globally unique to connect to the Internet by translating those addresses into globally-routable addresses.

NBMA—nonbroadcast multiaccess. Term describing a multiaccess network that does not inherently support broadcasting, for example, ATM.

NBP—Name Binding Protocol. AppleTalk protocol that translates a character-string name into the network-layer address of the corresponding client.

NetBIOS—Network Basic Input/Output System. API used by applications on a LAN to request services from lower-level network processes. These services include session establishment and termination, and information transfer. NetBIOS is used by network operating systems such as LAN Manager, LAN Server, Windows for Workgroups, and Windows NT.

NetFlow—A Cisco Systems optimization technique that identifies traffic flows and speeds the forwarding of traffic for a flow. When a flow is identified, the switching, security, QoS, and traffic-measurement services required for the flow are used to build an entry in a NetFlow cache. Subsequent packets in the flow are handled via a single streamlined task that references the cache.

NetWare—Popular distributed network-operating system developed by Novell. Provides transparent remote file access and numerous other distributed network services.

NetWare Link Services Protocol—See *NLSP*.

NetWare Loadable Module—See *NLM*.

network address—Network-layer address referring to a logical, rather than a physical, network device. Used by the network layer. Compare with *MAC address*.

Network Address Translation—See *NAT*.

Network File System—See *NFS*.

Network Information Center—See *NIC*.

network interface card—See *NIC*.

network layer—Layer 3 of the OSI reference model. This layer provides connectivity and path selection between two end systems. The network layer is the layer at which routing occurs.

network management system—See *NMS*.

network utilization—See *utilization*.

Network-to-Network Interface—See *NNI*.

Next Hop Resolution Protocol—See *NHRP*.

NFS—Network File System. A distributed file-system protocol suite developed by Sun Microsystems that allows remote file access across a network.

NHRP—Next Hop Resolution Protocol. Protocol used by routers to dynamically discover the MAC address of other routers and hosts connected to an NBMA network. These systems can then directly communicate without requiring traffic to use an intermediate hop, thus increasing performance in ATM, Frame Relay, and SMDS environments.

NIC—1. network interface card. Board that provides network-communication capabilities for a computer system. 2. Network Information Center. Organization that serves the Internet community by supplying addressing, naming, documentation, training, and other services.

NLM—NetWare Loadable Module. Individual program that can be loaded into memory on a NetWare server and function as part of the NetWare network operating system.

NLSP—NetWare Link Services Protocol. Link-state routing protocol based on IS-IS used in Novell networks.

NMS—network management system. System responsible for managing a network. An NMS is generally a powerful and well-equipped computer such as an engineering workstation. NMSs communicate with agents to help keep track of network statistics and resources.

NNI—Network-to-Network Interface. ATM Forum standard that defines the interface between two ATM switches that are both located in a private network, or are both located in a public network.

nonbroadcast multiaccess—See *NBMA*.

O

OC—Optical Carrier. Series of physical protocols (OC-1, OC-2, OC-3, and so on) defined for SONET optical signal transmissions. OC signal levels put STS frames onto fiber-optic lines at a variety of speeds. The base rate is 51.84 Mbps (OC-1); each signal level thereafter operates at a speed divisible by that number (thus, OC-3 runs at 155.52 Mbps). See also *SONET* and *STS-1*.

offered load—The sum of all the data all network nodes have ready to send at a particular time.

Open Shortest Path First—See *OSPF.*

OSI reference model—Open System Interconnection reference model. Network architectural model that consists of seven layers, each of which specifies particular network functions such as addressing, flow control, error control, encapsulation, and reliable message transfer. The OSI reference model is used universally as a method for teaching and understanding network functionality. See *application layer, data link layer, network layer, physical layer, presentation layer, session layer,* and *transport layer.*

OSPF—Open Shortest Path First. Link-state, hierarchical interior routing algorithm proposed as a successor to RIP in the Internet community. OSPF features include least-cost routing, multipath routing, and load balancing. Defined in RFC 2178.

P

packet—Logical grouping of information that includes a header containing control information and (usually) user data. Packets are most often used to refer to network-layer units of data.

packets per second—See *PPS.*

PAP—Password Authentication Protocol. Authentication protocol that allows PPP peers to authenticate one another. Unlike CHAP, PAP passes the password and host name or username in clear text (unencrypted). Compare with *CHAP.*

partial mesh—Term describing a network in which devices are organized in a mesh topology without requiring that every device have a direct connection to every other device. Compare with *full mesh.* See also *mesh.*

PBX—private branch exchange. Digital or analog telephone switchboard located on a subscriber premises and used to connect private and public telephone networks.

PCR—peak cell rate. Parameter defined by the ATM Forum for ATM traffic management. In CBR transmissions, a source can emit cells at the PCR at any time and for any duration and the negotiated QOS commitments should pertain.

phantom router—In HSRP, two or more routers share the same virtual IP address and virtual MAC address thus creating a third, non-physical router, called the *phantom router.* See also *HSRP.*

physical address—See *MAC address.*

physical layer—Layer 1 of the OSI reference model. The physical layer defines the electrical, mechanical, procedural, and functional specifications for activating, maintaining, and deactivating the physical link between end systems.

PIM—Protocol Independent Multicast. Multicast routing architecture that allows the addition of IP multicast routing on existing IP networks. PIM does not require a specific unicast routing protocol, and can be operated in two modes: dense mode and sparse mode. See also *dense-mode PIM* and *sparse-mode PIM*.

ping—1. ICMP echo message and its reply. Used in IP networks to test the reachability of a network device. 2. Generic term for an echo mechanism in any protocol stack.

plesiochronous transmission—Term describing digital signals that are sourced from different clocks of comparable accuracy and stability.

Point-to-Point Protocol—See *PPP*.

poison reverse updates—Routing updates that explicitly indicate that a network or subnet is unreachable, rather than implying that a network is unreachable by not including it in updates. Poison reverse updates are sent to defeat routing loops.

port—1. Interface on an internetworking device (such as a router). 2. In IP terminology, an upper-layer process that receives information from lower layers. Ports are numbered, and each numbered port is associated with a specific process.

PPP—Point-to-Point Protocol. Protocol that provides router-to-router and host-to-network connections over synchronous and asynchronous circuits. PPP was designed to work with several network-layer protocols, such as IP, IPv6, IPX, and AppleTalk.

PPS—packets per second. A measure of how quickly a switch or router can forward data.

precedence—Field in an IP header that indicates the priority of a packet. Precedence helps a router determine which packet to send when several packets are queued for transmission to the same output interface.

presentation layer—Layer 6 of the OSI reference model. This layer ensures that information sent by the application layer of one system is readable by the application layer of another.

PRI—Primary Rate Interface. ISDN interface to primary-rate access. Primary-rate access consists of a single 64-Kbps data (D) channel for signaling, plus 23 (T1) or 30 (E1) bearer (B) channels for user data. Compare with *BRI*.

priority queuing—Cisco IOS routing feature in which frames in an interface output queue are prioritized based on various characteristics such as packet and interface type. Compare with *custom queuing*.

private branch exchange—See *PBX*.

private key—Digital code used to decrypt/encrypt information and provide digital signatures. This key should be kept secret by the owner; it has a corresponding public key.

propagation delay—Time required for data to travel over a network, from its source to its ultimate destination.

protocol analyzer—Hardware or software device offering various network troubleshooting features, including protocol-specific packet decodes, specific preprogrammed troubleshooting tests, and traffic generation.

Protocol Independent Multicast—See *PIM*.

proxy ARP—Proxy Address Resolution Protocol. Variation of the ARP protocol, in which an intermediate device (for example, a router) sends an ARP response on behalf of an end node to the requesting host. Defined in RFC 1027.

proxy explorer—Technique that minimizes explorer-frame traffic propagating through an SRB network by creating an explorer-frame reply cache, the entries of which are reused when subsequent explorer frames need to find the same host.

prune—In an IP multicast environment the process wherein a router detects that there are no group members on one of its interfaces and stops sending a multicast stream out that interface.

public key—A digital code used to encrypt/decrypt information and verify digital signatures. This key can be made widely available; it has a corresponding private key.

pull—In client/server information-dissemination applications, requesting data from another computer or application. The Web is based on pull technology where a client uses a browser to request (pull) a Web page. Compare with *push*.

push—In client/server information-dissemination applications, sending data to a client without the client requesting it. Increasingly, companies are using push technologies to deliver customized data to users without the users explicitly requesting it. An example is customized news and stock information that is delivered on a daily basis. Compare with *pull*.

Q

QoS—quality of service. Measure of performance for a transmission system that reflects its transmission quality and service availability.

queue—1. Generally, an ordered list of elements waiting to be processed. 2. In routing, a backlog of packets waiting to be forwarded over a router interface.

R

RADIUS—Remote Authentication Dial-In User Server. Protocol and database for authenticating users, tracking connection times, and authorizing services permitted to users. A remote-access server acts as a client of a RADIUS server.

RARP—Reverse Address Resolution Protocol. Protocol in the TCP/IP stack that provides a method for a diskless station to determine its IP address when its MAC address is known. Compare with *ARP*.

Real-Time Control Protocol—See *RTCP*.

Real-Time Protocol—See *RTP*.

reassembly—The putting back together of an IP datagram at the destination after it has been fragmented either at the source or at an intermediate node. See also *fragmentation*.

recoverability—How quickly a network or computer system can recover from a problem.

redistribution—Allowing routing information discovered through one routing protocol to be distributed in the update messages of another routing protocol.

redundancy—The duplication of devices, services, or connections so that, in the event of a failure, the redundant devices, services, or connections can perform the work of those that failed.

reliability—The extent to which a network or computer system provides dependable, error-free service.

remote access—Analog and digital dial-in and dial-out technologies for reaching remote networks via remote-access servers.

Remote Authentication Dial-In User Server—See *RADIUS*.

Remote Monitoring—See *RMON*.

remote source-route bridging—See *RSRB*.

remote-access server—Communications server that connects remote nodes or LANs to an internetwork. Generally supports standard terminal services, such as Telnet, as well as remote-node, protocol-translation, and asynchronous-routing services.

remote-node services—A function of a remote-access server that allows PCs, Macintoshes, and X Window terminals to connect to a remote network and access network services as if they were directly connected to the network.

rendezvous point—Router specified in sparse-mode PIM implementations to track membership in multicast groups and to forward messages to known multicast group addresses. See also *sparse-mode PIM*.

repeater—Physical-layer device that regenerates and propagates electrical signals between two network segments.

repetitive pattern suppression—See *RPS*.

Request For Comments—See *RFC*.

resiliency—Capability of a network to withstand failures and still maintain network operation.

resource discovery—The processes and protocols that network users and applications employ to find network resources such as file, naming, and print servers.

Resource Reservation Protocol—See *RSVP*.

response time—The amount of time between a request for some network service and a response to the request.

Reverse Address Resolution Protocol—See *RARP*.

reverse-path forwarding—See *RPF.*

RFC—Request For Comments. Document series written by the IETF as the primary means for communicating information about the Internet and the TCP/IP protocols. RFCs are available online from numerous sources, including www.rfc-editor.org/.

ring poll—A process started by the active monitor in a Token Ring network wherein every ring station identifies itself. A station learns the identity of its upstream neighbor from this process.

ring purge frame—Frame sent by the active monitor in a Token Ring network to reinitialize the ring. The active monitor sends a ring purge frame when the token is lost.

RIP—Routing Information Protocol. Interior distance-vector routing protocol supplied with UNIX BSD systems and widely used in the early years of the Internet. Defined in RFC 1058 and RFC 1723.

RMON—remote monitoring. MIB agent specifications developed by the IETF that define functions for the remote monitoring of networked devices to facilitate statistics gathering, problem determination, and reporting.

round-trip time—See *RTT.*

route—Path through an internetwork.

route summarization—Consolidation of advertised addresses in routing protocols that causes a single summary route to be advertised instead of many individual routes.

router—Network-layer device that uses one or more metrics to determine the optimal path along which network traffic should be forwarded. Routers forward packets from one network to another based on network-layer information. Routers also perform network-layer services on the network.

Routing Information Protocol—See *RIP.*

routing metric—Method by which a routing algorithm determines that one route is better than another. This information is stored in routing tables. Metrics include bandwidth, communication cost, delay, hop count, load, MTU, path cost, and reliability. Sometimes referred to simply as a *metric.* See also *cost.*

routing table—Table stored in a router or some other internetworking device that keeps track of routes to particular network destinations and, in some cases, metrics associated with those routes.

Routing Table Maintenance Protocol—See *RTMP*.

routing update—Message sent from a router to indicate network reachability and associated cost information. Routing updates are typically sent at regular intervals and after a change in network topology.

RPF—reverse-path forwarding. Multicasting technique in which a multicast datagram is forwarded out all but the receiving interface, if the receiving interface is the one used to forward unicast datagrams to the source of the multicast datagram.

RPS—repetitive pattern suppression. An option for WAN data circuits that replaces repeating strings of data by a single occurrence of the string and a code that indicates to the far end how many repetitions of the string were in the original data.

RSRB—remote source-route bridging. A method for tunneling SNA or other Token Ring data between peer routers. Packets can be encapsulated directly in a data-link header such as High-Level Data Link Control (HDLC) or Frame Relay, or they can be encapsulated in IP or TCP. TCP offers the best reliability.

RSVP—Resource Reservation Protocol. A protocol that supports the reservation of resources across an IP network. Applications running on IP end systems can use RSVP to indicate to other nodes the nature (bandwidth, jitter, maximum burst, and so on) of the packet streams they wish to receive. Defined in RFC 2205.

RTCP—Real-Time Control Protocol. Protocol that monitors the QoS of an RTP connection and conveys information about the on-going session. See also *RTP*.

RTMP—Routing Table Maintenance Protocol. Distance-vector routing protocol developed by Apple Computer for use with the AppleTalk protocol suite. RTMP is similar in behavior to RIP.

RTP—Real-Time Protocol. IETF protocol that provides end-to-end network-transport functions for applications transmitting real-time data, such as audio, video, or simulation data, over multicast or unicast network services. RTP provides services such as payload type identification, sequence numbering, time-stamping, and data delivery.

RTT—round-trip time. Time required for a network communication to travel from the source to the destination and back. RTT includes the time required for the destination to process the message from the source and generate a reply.

runt frame—An Ethernet frame that is shorter than 64 bytes.

S

SAP—Service Advertising Protocol. IPX protocol that provides a means of informing network clients about available network resources and services via routers and servers.

scalability—Capacity of a network to keep pace with changes and growth.

SCR—sustainable cell rate. Parameter defined by the ATM Forum for ATM traffic management. For VBR connections, SCR determines the long-term average cell rate that can be transmitted. See also *VBR*.

SDH—Synchronous Digital Hierarchy. European standard that defines a set of rate and format standards that are transmitted using optical signals over fiber. SDH is similar to SONET, with a basic SDH rate of 51.84 Mbps, designated as STS-1.

Secure Socket Layer—See *SSL*.

segment—1. A single network that is based on a particular Layer-2 protocol and is bounded by repeaters, bridges, or switches. 2. Term used in the TCP specification to describe a single transport-layer unit of information.

Sequenced Packet Exchange—See *SPX*.

server—Node or software program that provides services to clients.

Service Advertising Protocol—See *SAP*.

session layer—Layer 5 of the OSI reference model. This layer establishes, manages, and terminates sessions between applications and manages data exchange between presentation-layer entities.

shielded twisted-pair—See *STP*.

shortest path first algorithm—See *SPF*.

Simple Mail Transfer Protocol—See *SMTP*.

Simple Network Management Protocol—See *SNMP*.

simulation—The process of using software and mathematical models to analyze the behavior of a system without requiring that an actual system be built.

single-mode fiber—Fiber-optic cabling with a narrow core that allows light to enter only at a single angle. Such cabling has higher bandwidth than multimode fiber, but requires a light source with a narrow spectral width (for example, a laser). See also *multimode fiber*.

SMDS—Switched Multimegabit Data Service. High-speed, packet-switched, datagram-based WAN networking technology offered by telephone companies.

SMTP—Simple Mail Transfer Protocol. Internet protocol providing e-mail services.

SNA—Systems Network Architecture. Large, complex, feature-rich network architecture developed in the 1970s by IBM for communication between terminals and mainframes.

SNMP—Simple Network Management Protocol. Network management protocol for TCP/IP networks. SNMP provides a means to monitor and control network devices, and to manage configurations, statistics collection, performance, and security.

SONET—Synchronous Optical Network. High-speed (up to 2.5 Gbps) synchronous network specification developed by Bellcore and designed to run on optical fiber. STS-1 is the basic building block of SONET. Approved as an international standard in 1988. See also *STS-1*.

source-route bridging—See *SRB*.

source-route switching—See *SRS*.

source-route transparent bridging—See *SRT*.

spanning tree—Loop-free subset of a network topology.

Spanning Tree Protocol—Bridge protocol that utilizes the spanning-tree algorithm, enabling a learning bridge to dynamically work around loops in a network topology by creating a spanning tree. Bridges exchange BPDU messages with other bridges to detect loops, and then remove the loops by shutting down selected bridge interfaces.

spanning-tree algorithm—Algorithm used by the Spanning Tree Protocol to create a spanning tree.

sparse-mode PIM—One of two PIM operational modes. Sparse-mode PIM tries to constrain data distribution so that a minimal number of routers in a network receive irrelevant data. Packets are sent only if they are explicitly requested at the rendezvous point. In sparse mode, receivers are widely distributed, and the assumption is that downstream networks do not necessarily use the multicast datagrams that are sent to them. Defined in RFC 2117. See also *dense-mode PIM*, *PIM*, and *rendezvous point*.

SPF—shortest path first algorithm. Routing algorithm that iterates on length of path to determine a shortest-path spanning tree. Commonly used in link-state routing algorithms. Sometimes called Dijkstra's algorithm.

split-horizon updates—Routing technique in which information about routes is prevented from exiting the router interface through which that information was received. Split-horizon updates are useful in preventing routing loops.

spoofing—1. Scheme used by routers to cause a host to treat an interface as if it were up and supporting a session. The router spoofs replies to keepalive messages from the host in order to convince the host that the session still exists. Spoofing is useful in routing environments such as DDR, in which a circuit-switched link is taken down when there is no traffic to be sent across it in order to save toll charges. See also *DDR*. 2. Action of a packet illegally claiming to be from an address from which it was not actually sent. Spoofing is designed to foil network security mechanisms such as filters and access lists.

SPX—Sequenced Packet Exchange. Reliable, connection-oriented protocol that supplements the datagram service provided by IPX in the NetWare protocol suite.

SQL—Structured Query Language. International standard language for defining and accessing relational databases.

SRB—source-route bridging. Method of bridging originated by IBM and popular in Token Ring networks. In an SRB network, a source end station determines the route to a destination by sending an explorer frame. Compare with *transparent bridging*.

SRS—source-route switching. Enhancement to SRB that uses high-speed switching techniques.

SRT—source-route transparent bridging. Bridging scheme that merges the two most prevalent bridging strategies: SRB and transparent bridging. SRT employs both technologies in one bridge or switch to satisfy the needs of all end nodes. No translation between bridging protocols is necessary.

SSL—Secure Socket Layer. Encryption technology for the Web used to provide secure transactions such as the transmission of credit card numbers for electronic commerce applications.

static route—Route that is explicitly configured and entered into a routing table.

store-and-forward switching—Frame-switching technique in which frames are completely processed before being forwarded out the appropriate port. This processing includes calculating the CRC and checking the destination address. In addition, frames must be temporarily stored until network resources (such as an unused link) are available to forward the frame. Compare with *cut-through switching*.

STP—shielded twisted-pair. Two- or four-pair wiring medium used in a variety of networks. STP cabling has a layer of shielded insulation to reduce noise and interference. Compare with *UTP*.

STS-1—Synchronous Transport Signal level 1. Basic building-block signal of SONET, operating at 51.84 Mbps. Faster SONET rates are defined as STS-*n*, where *n* is a multiple of 51.84 Mbps. See also *SONET*.

subinterface—A virtual interface on a single physical interface.

subnet—See *subnetwork*.

subnet address—Portion of an IP address that is specified as the subnetwork by the subnet mask.

subnet mask—32-bit address mask used in IP to indicate the bits of an IP address that are being used for the subnet address.

subnetwork—In IP networks, a network sharing a particular subnet address. Subnetworks are networks that are arbitrarily segmented by a network administrator in order to provide a multilevel, hierarchical routing structure while shielding the subnetwork from the addressing complexity of attached networks.

sustainable cell rate—See *SCR.*

switch—1. Network device that filters, forwards, and floods frames based on the MAC destination address of each frame. A switch operates at the data-link layer of the OSI model. 2. A generic term for an electronic or mechanical device that connects devices or networks, and relays data between devices or networks.

Switched Multimegabit Data Service—See *SMDS.*

symmetric encryption—Encryption method that provides data confidentiality. When two end stations use symmetric encryption, they must agree on the algorithm to use and on the encryption key they will share. Compare with *asymmetric encryption.*

Synchronous Digital Hierarchy—See *SDH.*

Synchronous Optical Network—See *SONET.*

T

T1—Digital WAN facility provided by telephone companies in the United States. T1 transmits DS-1-formatted data at 1.544 Mbps. T1 lines can be leased for private use.

TA—terminal adapter. Device used to connect an interface to an ISDN service.

TACACS—Terminal Access Controller Access Control System. Authentication protocol that provides remote access authentication and related services, such as event logging. User passwords are administered in a central database rather than in individual routers, providing a scalable network-security solution.

tag switching—High-performance, packet-forwarding technology that integrates network layer (Layer 3) routing and data link layer (Layer 2) switching and provides scalable, high-speed switching in a network core. Tag switching is based on the concept of label swapping, in which packets or cells are assigned short, fixed-length labels that tell switching nodes how data should be forwarded.

tandem switching system—See *TSS.*

TCP—Transmission Control Protocol. Connection-oriented transport-layer protocol that provides reliable full-duplex data transmission. TCP is part of the TCP/IP protocol stack.

TDM—1. time-division multiplexer. A device that implements time-division multiplexing. 2. time-division multiplexing. Technique in which information from multiple channels can be allocated bandwidth on a single wire based on pre-assigned time slots.

TDR—time-domain reflectometer. Device capable of sending signals through a network medium to check cable continuity and other attributes. TDRs are used to find physical-layer network problems.

TE—terminal equipment. Any ISDN device that can be attached to a network, such as a telephone, fax, or computer. ISDN-compliant terminals are called *terminal equipment type 1 (TE1)*. Non-ISDN-compliant terminals, that predate the ISDN standards, are called *terminal equipment type 2 (TE2)*.

Telnet—Standard terminal emulation protocol in the TCP/IP protocol stack. Telnet is used for remote terminal connection, enabling users to log in to remote systems and use resources as if they were connected to a local system. Telnet is defined in RFC 854.

Terminal Access Controller Access System—See *TACACS*.

terminal adapter—See *TA*.

terminal equipment—See *TE*.

throughput—Rate of information arriving at, and possibly passing through, a particular point in a network system.

time domain reflectometer—See *TDR*.

Time To Live—See *TTL*.

time-division multiplexer—See *TDM*.

time-division multiplexing—See *TDM*.

token—Frame that contains control information. Possession of the token allows a network device to transmit data onto the network.

token passing—Access method by which network devices access a physical medium in an orderly fashion based on possession of a small frame called a token.

token ring—Any network or technology that uses token passing for its access method. Examples include FDDI and Token Ring.

Token Ring—Token-passing LAN developed and supported by IBM. Token Ring runs at 4 or 16 Mbps over a ring topology. Token Ring was standardized in the IEEE 802.5 specification.

top-down network design—A network-design methodology that calls for analyzing business and technical requirements and developing a logical design, including a topology and protocols, before selecting products and devices to implement the physical design.

topology—Logical arrangement of network nodes and media within a networking structure.

trace-route—Program available on many systems that traces the path a packet takes to a destination. It is mostly used to debug routing problems between hosts.

traffic shaping—Use of queues to limit surges that can congest a network. Data is buffered and then sent into the network in regulated amounts to ensure that the traffic will fit within the promised traffic envelope for the particular connection. Traffic shaping is used in ATM, Frame Relay, and other types of networks.

translational bridging—Bridging between networks with dissimilar MAC sublayer protocols. MAC information is translated into the format of the destination network at the bridge. Compare with *encapsulating bridging*.

Transmission Control Protocol—See *TCP*.

transparent bridging—Bridging scheme often used in Ethernet and IEEE 802.3 networks in which bridges pass frames along one hop at a time based on tables associating end nodes with bridge ports. Transparent bridging is so named because the presence of bridges is transparent to network end nodes. Compare with *SRB*.

transport layer—Layer 4 of the OSI reference model. This layer is responsible for reliable network communication between end nodes. The transport layer provides mechanisms for the establishment, maintenance, and termination of virtual circuits; transport fault detection and recovery; and information flow control.

TTL—Time To Live. Field in an IP header that indicates how long a packet is considered valid.

TSS—tandem switching system. An intermediate switch that interconnects circuits from the switch of one telephone company central office to the switch of a second central office in the same exchange.

twisted pair—A commonly-used transmission medium consisting of 22 to 26 gauge insulated copper wire. Can be either shielded (STP) or unshielded (UTP).

type of service—1. A byte in an IP header that indicates precedence and type of service. See also *precedence*. 2. Four-bit field within the type-of-service byte in an IP header that helps a router select a routing path when multiple paths are available. A source node can specify whether low delay, high throughput, high reliability, or low monetary cost is desired.

U

UBR—unspecified bit rate. QoS class defined by the ATM Forum for ATM networks. UBR allows any amount of data up to a specified maximum to be sent across the network, but there are no guarantees in terms of cell loss rate and delay. Compare with *ABR*, *CBR*, and *VBR*.

UDP—User Datagram Protocol. Connectionless transport layer protocol in the TCP/IP protocol stack. UDP is a simple protocol that exchanges datagrams without acknowledgments or guaranteed delivery, requiring that error processing and retransmission be handled by other protocols. UDP is defined in RFC 768.

UNI—User-Network Interface. ATM Forum specification that defines an interoperability standard for the interface between ATM-based products (a router or an ATM switch) located in a private network and the ATM switches located within the public carrier networks.

unicast—Message that is sent to a single network node. Compare with *broadcast* and *multicast*.

unicast address—Address specifying a single network node. Compare with *broadcast address* and *multicast address*.

UNIX—Operating system developed in 1969 at Bell Laboratories. UNIX has gone through several iterations since its inception. These include UNIX 4.3 BSD (Berkeley Standard Distribution), developed at the University of California at Berkeley, and UNIX System V, Release 4.0, developed by AT&T.

unshielded twisted-pair—See *UTP*.

unspecified bit rate—See *UBR*.

UPC—usage parameter control. In ATM, the set of actions taken by the network to monitor and control traffic at the end-system access point.

usability—The ease with which network users can access a network and its services, including the ease of network addressing, naming, and resource discovery.

usage parameter control—See *UPC*.

user community—A set of network users that employ a particular application or set of applications and have similar network-design goals.

User Datagram Protocol—See *UDP*.

utilization—The percent of total available capacity in use on a network or circuit.

UTP—unshielded twisted-pair. Two or four-pair wire medium used in a variety of networks. Lacks shielding and is subject to electrical noise and interference. Compare with *STP*.

V

VAD—voice activity detection. A technology that compresses voice traffic by not sending packets in the absence of speech. Other types of traffic can use the extra bandwidth saved.

variable bit rate—See *VBR*.

variable-length subnet mask—See *VLSM*.

variance—1. In statistics, a measurement of how widely data disperses from the mean. 2. In Cisco System routers, a routing feature that allows IGRP and Enhanced

IGRP to load balance traffic across multiple paths that do not have the same bandwidth, but whose bandwidth varies by some small amount that is configurable

VBR—variable bit rate. QoS class defined by the ATM Forum for ATM networks. VBR is subdivided into a Real Time (RT) class and Non-Real Time (NRT) class. VBR (RT) is used for connections in which there is a fixed timing relationship between samples. VBR (NRT) is used for connections in which there is no fixed timing relationship between samples, but that still need a guaranteed QoS. Compare with *ABR*, *CBR*, and *UBR*.

videoconferencing—Conducting a conference between two or more participants at different sites by using networking devices and protocols to transmit digital audio and video data. Generally each participant has a video camera and microphone and equipment to transform analog signals into a digital bit stream for traversal across a LAN or WAN.

VINES—Virtual Integrated Network Service. Network operating system developed and marketed by Banyan Systems.

virtual circuit—Logical circuit created to ensure reliable communication between two network devices.

virtual LAN—See *VLAN*.

virtual private network—See *VPN*.

virtual private networking—See *VPN*.

VLAN—virtual LAN. Group of devices on one or more LANs that are configured (using management software) so that they can communicate as if they were attached to the same wire, when in fact they are located on a number of different LAN segments.

VLAN trunk—A single physical link that supports more than one VLAN.

VLAN Trunk Protocol—See *VTP*.

VLSM—variable-length subnet mask. Ability to specify a different subnet mask for the same network number on different subnets. VLSM can help optimize available address space.

voice activity detection—See *VAD*.

VoIP—voice over IP. Protocols and products that enable the transmission of telephone calls over IP networks.

VPN—1. virtual private network. A network that implements virtual private networking. 2. virtual private networking. Set of processes and protocols that enables an organization to securely interconnect sites that are part of a private network via a public network, such as a service-provider's network or the Internet.

VTP—VLAN Trunk Protocol. A Cisco switch-to-switch, and switch-to-router VLAN management protocol that exchanges VLAN configuration changes as they are made to a network.

W

WAN—wide area network. Data communications network that serves users across a broad geographic area and often uses transmission devices provided by common carriers.

watchdog packet—Used to ensure that a client is still connected to a NetWare server. If the server has not received a packet from a client for a certain period of time, it sends the client a series of watchdog packets. If the station fails to respond to a pre-defined number of watchdog packets, the server concludes that the station is no longer connected and clears the connection for that station.

watchdog spoofing—Subset of spoofing that refers specifically to a router acting for a NetWare client by sending watchdog packets to a NetWare server to keep the session between client and server active.

WDM—wave division multiplexing. A type of multiplexing developed for use on fiber-optic cables. WDM modulates each of several data streams onto a different part of the light spectrum.

Web—Short for the World Wide Web (WWW). A large network of Internet servers that provides hypertext and other services to terminals running client applications, such as browsers.

WFQ—weighted fair queuing. Congestion-management algorithm that identifies conversations (in the form of traffic flows), separates packets that belong to each conversation, and ensures that capacity is shared fairly between these individual conversations.

wide area network—See *WAN*.

window—A protocol data structure that stores outgoing data and generally allows a sender to send a set of packets before an acknowledgment arrives.

windowing—Using windows as a flow-control mechanism when sending data.

wire speed—The theoretical maximum throughput of a network or circuit.

wiring closet—Specially designed room used for wiring a data or voice network. Wiring closets serve as a central junction point for the wiring and wiring equipment that is used for interconnecting devices.

WWW—World Wide Web. See *Web*.

X

X.25—International standard that defines how a connection between a DTE and DCE is maintained for remote terminal access and computer communications in packet-switched networks.

xDSL—Group term that refers to the different varieties of digital subscriber line, such as ADSL and HDSL. See *DSL*, *ADSL*, and *HDSL*.

X Window System—Distributed, network-transparent, device-independent, multitasking windowing and graphics system originally developed by MIT for communication between X terminals and UNIX workstations.

Z

ZIP—Zone Information Protocol. AppleTalk protocol that maps network numbers to zone names.

ZIP storm—Undesirable network event in which many ZIP queries are sent on numerous network segments.

zone—In AppleTalk, a logical group of network devices.

Zone Information Protocol—See *ZIP*.

Index